Microsoft® SQL Server™ 2005 Developer's Guide

Michael Otey
Denielle Otey

McGraw-Hill/Osborne

New York   Chicago   San Francisco
Lisbon   London   Madrid   Mexico City   Milan
New Delhi   San Juan   Seoul   Singapore   Sydney   Toronto

The *McGraw·Hill* Companies

McGraw-Hill/Osborne
2100 Powell Street, 10th Floor
Emeryville, California 94608
U.S.A.

To arrange bulk purchase discounts for sales promotions, premiums, or fund-raisers, please contact
McGraw-Hill/Osborne at the above address.

Microsoft® SQL Server™ 2005 Developer's Guide

1234567890 CUS CUS 0198765

ISBN 0-07-226099-8

Acquisitions Editor	Wendy Rinaldi
Project Editor	Carolyn Welch
Acquisitions Coordinator	Alexander McDonald
Technical Editor	Karl Hilsmann
Copy Editor	Bob Campbell
Proofreader	Susie Elkind
Indexer	Claire Splan
Composition	International Typesetting and Composition
Illustration	International Typesetting and Composition
Cover Series Design	Pattie Lee

This book was composed with Adobe® InDesign®.

To Mom and Dad, Ray and Dortha Marty,
For many years of dedication and encouragement,
and great bowling advice.

About the Authors

Michael Otey is Senior Technical Editor of *SQL Server Magazine* and co-author of *SQL Server 2000 Developer's Guide*, *SQL Server 7 Developer's Guide*, and *ADO.NET: The Complete Reference*. He is the president of TECA, Inc., a software development and consulting firm.

Denielle Otey is vice president of TECA, Inc. She has extensive experience developing commercial software products, and is the co-author of *ADO.NET: The Complete Reference*.

Contents

Acknowledgments

This book is the successor to the *SQL Server 2000 Developer's Guide*, which was extremely successful thanks to all of the supportive SQL Server developers who bought that edition of the book. Our first thanks go to all of the people who encouraged us to write another book about Microsoft's incredible new relational database server: SQL Server 2005.

Making a book is definitely a team effort, and this book is the epitome of that. We'd like to extend our deepest gratitude to the team at McGraw-Hill/Osborne, who helped to guide and shape this book as it progressed through its many stages. First, we'd like to thank Wendy Rinaldi, editorial director, for her encouragement in getting this project launched and her on-going support. We'd also like to thank acquisitions coordinator Alex McDonald for spearheading the effort to bring this project home. The book's content benefited immensely from the efforts of project editor Carolyn Welch, technical reviewer Karl Hilsmann, and copy editor Bob Campbell.

We'd also like to thank Tom Rizzo and Bill Baker from Microsoft for helping us to understand better where the product is headed and the emerging importance of BI and SQL Server 2005.

Introduction

SQL Server 2005 is a feature-rich release that provides a host of new tools and technologies for the database developer. This book is written to help database developers and DBAs become productive immediately with the new features and capabilities found in SQL Server 2005. This book covers the entire range of SQL Server 2005 development technologies from server side development using T-SQL to client side development using ADO, ADO.Net, and ADOMD.NET. In addition, it shows how to develop applications using the new SQL Server 2005 Notification Services, SQL Server Service Broker, Reporting Services, and SQL Server Integration Services subsystems.

The development management landscape for SQL Server 2005 has changed tremendously in SQL Server 2005, so Chapter 1 starts off by providing a guided tour of the new development and management tools in SQL Server 2005. Although SQL Server 2005 certainly embodies a huge number of significant changes, some things have stayed the same and one of those things is the fact that T-SQL is still the native development language for SQL Server 2005 and is the core for all SQL Server 2005 database development. Chapter 2 shows you how to use the new T-SQL development tools found in both SQL Server 2005 and Visual Studio 2005 as well as how to create both T-SQL DDL and DML solutions. Chapter 3 dives into the new SQL CLR integration capabilities of SQL Server 2005. The integration of the .NET CLR runtime with SQL Server 2005 is one of the biggest new changes in SQL Server 2005. This chapter shows you how to create and use all of the new SQL CLR database objects, including stored procedures, functions, triggers, user-defined types, and user-defined aggregates. Chapter 4 introduces the new SQL Server Service Broker subsystem that provides the basis for building asynchronous applications. Both the SQL Service Broker chapter and the Notification Services chapter (Chapter 5) provide an overview of the new subsystem and then go on to show how they are used in a sample application. ADO.NET is Microsoft's core data access technology, and Chapter 6 illustrates how to use all the primary ADO.NET objects to create robust data applications. The integration of XML with the relational database engine is another one of the big enhancements in SQL Server 2005. Chapter 7 shows how to use the new XML data type for both typed and untyped data as well as how to create Web Services that expose SQL Server stored procedures for heterogeneous platform integration. While most of this book concentrates on the newest .NET and XML-based technologies, the majority of SQL Server client applications are written in ADO and VB6. Chapter 8 illustrates all of the primary ADO techniques for building SQL Server database applications. Two of the hottest technologies in SQL Server 2005 are Reporting Services and the end-user oriented Report Builder report designer application. Chapter 9 dives into both of these new features, showing you how to build reports using Reporting Services as well as how to set up data models for use with Report Builder. Chapter 10 introduces the new SQL Server Integration Services subsystem. SQL Server Integration Services completely replaces the older DTS subsystem, and this chapter shows you how to build and deploy SSIS packages using the designer and the SSIS API. Chapter 11 illustrates building client Business Intelligence applications for Analysis Services using the new ADOMD.NET data access programming framework. SQL Server 2005 also introduces another completely new management framework called System Management Objects (SMO), which replaces the older Distributed Management Objects (DMO) object framework that was used in earlier versions of SQL Server. In Chapter 12 you can see how SMO can be used to build your own customized SQL Server management applications. SQL Server 2005 also provides an entirely new command line interface called sqlcmd that replaces the older isql and osql utilities. In Chapter 13 you can see how to develop management and data access scripts using the sqlcmd tool. Finally, this book concludes with an introduction to using SQL Profiler. SQL Profiler is key tool for both troubleshooting application performance as well as fine-tuning your data access queries.

All of the code presented in this book is available for download from McGraw-Hill/ Osborne's web site at www.osborne.com, and from our web site at www.teca.com.

SQL Server 2005's Design Goals

SQL Server 2005 faces a much different challenge today than it did in the eighties when SQL Server was first announced. Back then ease-of-use was a priority and having a database scaled to suit the needs of a small business or a department was adequate. Today SQL Server is no longer a departmental database. It's a full-fledged enterprise database capable of providing the data access functionality to the largest of organizations. To meet these enterprise demands, Microsoft has designed SQL Server 2005 to be highly scalable. In addition, it must also be secure; it must be able to be easily integrated with other platforms; it must be a productive development platform; and it must provide good return on investment.

Scalability

Scalability used to be an area where Microsoft SQL Server was criticized. With its roots as a departmental system and the limitations found in the Microsoft SQL Server 6.5 and earlier releases, many businesses didn't view SQL Server as a legitimate player in the enterprise database market. However, all that has changed. Beginning with the release of SQL Server 7, Microsoft made great strides in the scalability of the SQL Server platform. Using distributed partitioned views, SQL Server 7 jumped to the top of the TPC-C, and, in fact, its scores were so overwhelming that SQL Server 7 was a contributing factor to the TPC (Transaction Processing Councils) decision to break the transactional TPC-C test into clustered and nonclustered divisions. Although Microsoft and SQL Server 7 owned the clustered TPC-C score, demonstrating its ability to scale out across multiple systems, there was still some doubt about the platform's ability to scale up on a single platform. That too changed with the launch of Windows Server 2003 and the announcement of SQL Server 2000 Enterprise Edition 64-bit where Microsoft announced that for the first time Microsoft SQL Server reached the top of the nonclustered TPC-C scores. Today, with the predominance of web-based applications, scalability is more important than ever. Unlike traditional client/server and intranet applications, where you can easily predict the number of application users, web applications open up the door for very large numbers of users and rapid changes in resource requirements. SQL Server 2005 embodies the accumulation of Microsoft's scalability efforts, and builds on both the ability to scale out using distributed partitioned views as well as the ability to scale up using its 64-bit edition. Its TPC-C scores clearly demonstrate that SQL Server 2005 can deal with the very largest of database challenges—even up to the mainframe level. And the SQL Server 2005's self-tuning ability enables the database to quickly optimize its own resources to match usage requirements.

Security

While scalability is the stepping stone that starts the path toward enterprise-level adoption, security is the door that must be passed to really gain the trust of the enterprise. In the past, SQL Server, like many other Microsoft products, has been hit by a couple of different security issues. Both of these issues tended to be related to implementation problems rather than any real code defects. A study by one research firm showed that up to 5,000 SQL Server systems were deployed on the Internet with a blank sa password, allowing easy access to any intruders who wanted to compromise the information on those systems. Later, in 2002, the SQL Slammer virus exploited a SQL Server known vulnerability for which Microsoft had previously released a fix and even incorporated that fix into a general service pack.

In the first case, SQL Server essentially had the answer to this issue, supporting both standard security as well as Windows authentication; the users simply didn't take some very basic security steps. In the second case, Microsoft had generated a fix to a known problem but that fix wasn't widely applied. Plus, there was another basic security issue with this incident in which one of the ports on the firewall that should have been closed was left open by the businesses that were stricken by this virus.

To address these types of security challenges, SQL Sever 2005 has been designed following Microsoft's new security framework, sometimes called SD3 where the product is secure by design, secure by default, and secure by deployment. What this means for SQL Server 2005 is that the product is initially designed with an emphasis on security. Following up on their Trustworthy Computing initiative, Microsoft embarked on extensive security training for all of their developers and conducted code reviews and performed a comprehensive thread analysis for SQL Server 2005. In addition, all of the security fixes that were incorporated into the SP3 of SQL Server 2000 were rolled into SQL Server 2005. Next, secure by default means that when the product is installed Microsoft provides secure default values in the installation process whereby if you just follow the defaults you will end up with a secure implementation. For example, in the case of the sa password, the installation process prompts you to provide a strong password for the sa account. While you can select to continue the installation with a blank password, you have to explicitly select this path as well as respond to the Microsoft dialogs warning you about the dangers of using a blank password. Finally, SQL Server 2005 is secure by deployment, which means that Microsoft is providing tools and training for customers to help create secure deployments for SQL Server 2005. Here, Microsoft provides tools like the Microsoft Baseline Security Analysis, which can scan for known security vulnerabilities, in addition to a collection of white papers that are designed to educate customers on the best practices for creating secure implementations for a variety of different deployment scenarios.

Integration

In today's corporate computing environment it's rarely the case where only one vendor's products are installed in a homogenous setting. Instead, far more often, multiple dissimilar platforms simultaneously perform a variety of disparate tasks, and one of an organization's main challenges is exchanging information between these different platforms. SQL Server 2005 provides a number of different mechanisms to facilitate application and platform interoperability. For application interoperability, SQL Server 2005 supports the industry standard HTTP, XML, and SOAP protocols. It also allows stored procedures to be exposed as web services and provides a level 4

JDBC driver, allowing SQL Server to be used as a back-end database for Java applications. For platform interoperability, SQL Server 2005 sports an all-new redesigned Integration Services as well as heterogeneous database replication to Access, Oracle, and IBM DB2 UDB systems.

Productivity

Productivity is one of the other primary ingredients that enterprises require, and this is probably the area where SQL Server 2005 has made the biggest strides. The new release of SQL Server 2005 integrates the .NET Framework CLR into the SQL Server database engine. This new integration allows database objects like stored procedures, triggers, and user-defined functions to be created using any .NET compliant language including C#, VB.NET managed C++, and J#. Prior to this release SQL Server only supported the procedural T-SQL language for database programmability. The integration of the .NET Framework brings with it a fully object-oriented programming model that can be used to develop sophisticated data access and business logic routines. Being able to write database objects using the .NET languages also facilitates the ability to easily move those database objects between the database and the data access layer of an n-tiered web application.

Although the big news with this release is the .NET Framework, Microsoft has continued to enhance T-SQL, as well as bring several new capabilities to their procedural language and the reassurance to developers and DBAs that they have no plans for dropping support for T-SQL in the future. In addition, SQL Server 2005 answers the question of productivity from the DBA's perspective as well. The management console has been redesigned and integrated into a Visual Studio .NET integrated development environment. All of the dialogs are now fully modal, allowing the DBA to easily switch between multiple management tasks.

Return on Investment

One of the primary challenges for IT enterprises today is driving cost out of their businesses. That often means doing more with less, and SQL Server provides the tools that most businesses need to do more with the assets they already have. SQL Server 2005 is far more than just a relational database; its tightly integrated Business Intelligence (BI) toolset, including the built-in Analysis Services and Reporting Services, brings more value to the table than any other database platform. BI gives companies the ability to analyze data and make better business decisions—decisions that can make your company money as well as save your company money. Since the release of SQL Server 7, with its integrated OLAP Services (later renamed as Analysis Services), SQL Server has become the leading product in the BI market.

Overall, the new features in SQL Server 2005 give it a very high return on investment. Features like web services provide better connectivity to customers, paving the way to improved profitability. Likewise, XML integration enables better integration with business partners for improved profitability. Additionally, the inclusion of the .NET Framework, improved management tools, and Report Services empower employees, enabling them to be more productive.

A Brief History of Microsoft SQL Server

SQL Server 2005 is the latest version of a database server product that has been evolving since the late 1980s. Microsoft SQL Server originated as Sybase SQL Server in 1987. In 1988, Microsoft, Sybase, and Aston-Tate ported the product to OS/2. Later, Aston-Tate dropped out of the SQL Server development picture, and Microsoft and Sybase signed a co-development agreement to port SQL Server to Windows NT. The co-development effort cumulated in the release of SQL Server 4.0 for Windows NT. After the 4.0 release, Microsoft and Sybase split on the development of SQL Server; Microsoft continued forward with future releases targeted for the Windows NT platform while Sybase moved ahead with releases targeted for the UNIX platform, which they still market today. SQL Server 6.0 was the first release of SQL Server that was developed entirely by Microsoft. In 1996, Microsoft updated SQL Server with the 6.5 release. After a two-year development cycle, Microsoft released the vastly updated SQL Server 7.0 release in 1998. SQL Server 7.0 embodied many radical changes in the underlying storage and database engine technology used in SQL Server. SQL Server 2000, the accumulation of another two-year development effort, was released in September of 2000. The move from SQL Server 7.0 to SQL Server 2000 was more of an evolutionary move that didn't entail the same kinds of massive changes that were made in the move from 6.5 to 7.0. Instead, SQL Server 2000 built incrementally on the new code base that was established in the 7.0 release. Starting with SQL Server 2000, Microsoft began releasing updates to the basic release of SQL Server in the following year starting with XML for SQL Server Web Release 1, which added several XML features including the ability to receive a result set as an XML document. The next year they renamed the web release to the more succinctly titled SQLXML 2.0, which, among other things, added the ability to update the SQL Server database using XML updategrams. This was quickly followed by the SQLXML 3.0 web release, which included the ability to expose stored procedures as web services. Two years later, Microsoft SQL Server release history cumulates with the release of SQL Server 2005. SQL Server 2005 uses the same basic architecture that was established with SQL Server 7 and it adds to this all the features introduced with SQL Server 2000 and its web releases in conjunction with the integration of the .NET CLR and an array of powerful new BI functions. The following timeline summarizes the development history of SQL Server:

- ▶ **1987** Sybase releases SQL Server for UNIX.
- ▶ **1988** Microsoft, Sybase, and Aston-Tate port SQL Server to OS/2.
- ▶ **1989** Microsoft, Sybase, and Aston-Tate release SQL Server 1.0 for OS/2.
- ▶ **1990** SQL Server 1.1 is released with support for Windows 3.0 clients.
  - ▶ Aston-Tate drops out of SQL Server development.
- ▶ **1991** Microsoft and IBM end joint development of OS/2.
- ▶ **1992** Microsoft SQL Server 4.2 for 16-bit OS/2 1.3 is released.
- ▶ **1992** Microsoft and Sybase port SQL Server to Windows NT.
- ▶ **1993** Windows NT 3.1 is released.
- ▶ **1993** Microsoft and Sybase release version 4.2 of SQL Server for Windows NT.
- ▶ **1994** Microsoft and Sybase co-development of SQL Server officially ends.
  - ▶ Microsoft continues to develop the Windows version of SQL Server.
  - ▶ Sybase continues to develop the UNIX version of SQL Server.
- ▶ **1995** Microsoft releases version 6.0 of SQL Server.
- ▶ **1996** Microsoft releases version 6.5 of SQL Server.
- ▶ **1998** Microsoft releases version 7.0 of SQL Server.
- ▶ **2000** Microsoft releases SQL Server 2000.
- ▶ **2001** Microsoft releases XML for SQL Server Web Release 1 (download).
- ▶ **2002** Microsoft releases SQLXML 2.0 (renamed from XML for SQL Server).
- ▶ **2002** Microsoft releases SQLXML 3.0.
- ▶ **2005** Microsoft releases SQL Server 2005 on November 7th, 2005.

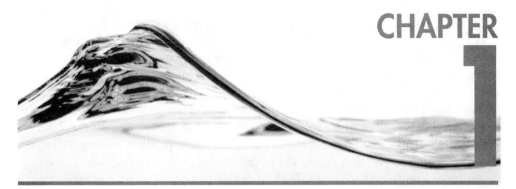

The Development Environment

IN THIS CHAPTER

SQL Server Management Studio

BI Development Studio

W hen it comes to server management, a lot has changed for the DBA in SQL Server 2005. The administrative tools that were used to manage the previous versions of SQL Server have been replaced, and new management tools have been added to help the DBA interact more efficiently with the database server. In this chapter, we'll first take a look at the new SQL Server Management Studio, which combines, into one integrated environment, the four previous tools: Enterprise Manager, Query Analyzer, Profiler, and Analysis Manager. While each of these tools allowed the DBA to perform their specific tasks, switching between the tools and remembering different interfaces and syntax could create unneeded headaches. By having one management environment, the DBA can focus on managing the server objects more efficiently. The second part of this chapter will explore the new Business Intelligence (BI) Development Studio. The BI Development Studio is an integrated development environment used to create Analysis Services databases, DTS packages, and Reporting Services reports. You can organize components into projects and solutions in the BI Development Studio in a disconnected mode, and then deploy the solutions at a later time.

SQL Server Management Studio

The SQL Server Enterprise Manager, which was the primary management tool for SQL Server versions 7 and 2000, has been replaced by the new SQL Server Management Studio, which also replaces the Query Analyzer tool, which was the core T-SQL development tool in SQL Server versions 7 and 2000. SQL Server 2005 also includes several other administrative tools, such as the new Administration Console, the Database Tuning Adviser, and the Profiler. The SQL Server Management Studio is accessed using the Start | Programs | Microsoft SQL Server | SQL Server Management Studio menu option. You can see the SQL Server Management Studio in Figure 1-1.

The SQL Server Management Studio can be used to manage SQL Server 2005 systems as well as SQL Server 2000 and SQL Server 7 systems; however, it cannot be used on SQL Server 6.5 or older systems. You can use the previous SQL Server 7/2000 Enterprise Manager to manage a new SQL Server 2005 system, but this isn't supported or recommended because of some architectural changes between the two releases. Likewise, the older management tools cannot access any of the new features that have been added to SQL Server 2005. The SQL Server Management Studio is the best choice for managing mixed SQL Server 2005 and SQL Server 7/2000 systems.

The SQL Server Management Studio has been completely rewritten and now uses the latest Microsoft technologies, like Winforms and the .NET Framework.

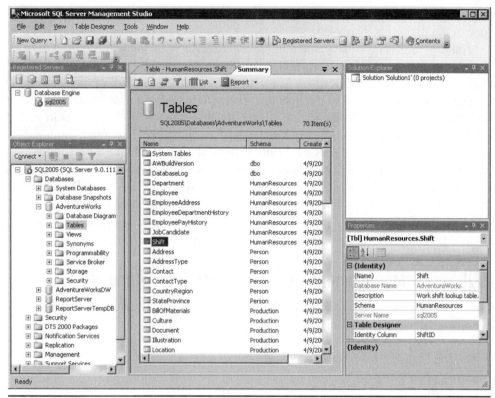

Figure 1-1   *SQL Server Management Studio*

This allows you to write, edit, run, and debug code, and it supports the creation of solution projects. It is also integrated with Visual SourceSafe for source code version control. It doesn't allow you to compile VB.NET, C#, J#, or VC++, like the Visual Studio 2005 development environment; instead, SQL Server Management Studio works with T-SQL, MDX, and DTS.

The SQL Server Management Studio User Interface

One of the important improvements the SQL Server Management Studio offers over the SQL Server Enterprise Manager lies in its use of dialog boxes. The displayed dialog boxes are now nonmodal, which means that you are not required to respond to the dialog before you can do anything else. In the older SQL Server Enterprise, if you opened a dialog, you couldn't do anything else until the dialog was closed. The new nonmodal dialogs used by the SQL Server Management Studio solve this problem and make it possible for the DBA to perform other management tasks while one of the dialogs is displayed.

Another important enhancement in the SQL Server Management Studio is how it deals with large numbers of database objects. In the previous versions of SQL Server, the SQL Server Enterprise Manager always enumerated all of the database objects when it connected to a registered server. This wasn't a problem for most small and medium-sized businesses, as their databases tended to be smaller in size. However, for companies with very large databases, which could contain thousands of database objects, the SQL Server Enterprise Manager could take a very long time listing all of the database objects and their properties. This basically left the SQL Server Enterprise Manager unusable until all of the objects were listed. With SQL Server 2005, the SQL Server Management Studio loads objects asynchronously, allowing the user to start to expand a database item that has many children, while at the same time performing other activities in the user interface.

SQL Server Management Studio User Interface Windows

This section gives you an overview of the SQL Server Management Studio user interface windows, including:

▶ The Registered Servers window

▶ The Object Explorer window

▶ The Solutions Explorer window

▶ The Properties window

▶ The Query Editor window

▶ The Results window

Registered Servers

As with the previous SQL Server Enterprise Manager, you must register servers in the SQL Server Management Studio before you can use it to manage them. To register new SQL Server systems, you use the SQL Server Management Studio's Registered Servers window (shown in the upper left-hand corner of Figure 1-1). You can also use the Registered Servers window to group common servers together into logical server groups. You can connect to and manage any SQL Server component using the SQL Server Management Studio, including instances of the Database Engine, Analysis Services, Reporting Services, Integration Services, and SQL Server Mobile Edition.

You register a new SQL Server system in the Registered Servers window by right-clicking the window and selecting the New | Server Registration option from the context menu. Likewise, you can create a new server group by right-clicking in the Registered Servers window and selecting the New | Server Group option from the context menu. The Registered Servers window also allows you to export or import registered servers information. This enables you to quickly populate the Registered Servers windows of other SQL Server Management Studios without having to manually reregister all of the managed servers.

Object Explorer

The Object Explorer window of SQL Server Management Studio allows you to connect to any of the SQL Server components. The Object Explorer window, shown in the lower left-hand corner of Figure 1-1, provides a tree-structured folder view of all the objects in the server and displays a user interface to manage the objects. The folders displayed under each server connection type are specific to the functions of the server. Table 1-1 describes the server types and their respective main folders.

The first thing you need to do in order to use Object Explorer is connect to a server type. You click the Connect button on the Object Explorer toolbar and choose the type of server from the drop-down list, which opens the Connect To Server dialog box as shown in Figure 1-2.

You must provide at least the name of the server and the correct authentication information to connect to the server. You can optionally specify additional connections in the Connect To Server dialog, and the dialog will retain the last used settings.

To work with the objects that are displayed in the Object Explorer, you right-click the desired object in the Object Explorer tree to display the object's context menu. The context menu provides a unique set of options for each of the different objects. For instance, the SQL Server | Databases folder displays a context menu that allows you to create, attach, back up, restore, copy, and generate scripts for a database; while the SQL Server | Databases | Tables | table context menu allows you to create, modify, open, rename, delete, or generate a script; to define a full-text index; and to view dependencies for a table.

Generating Scripts   A very useful enhancement in SQL Server Management Studio is the ability to generate scripts for database objects. You can create scripts using Object Explorer or by using the Generate SQL Server Scripts Wizard.

Object Explorer allows you to easily create scripts for an entire database, or for a single database object. You have the option of creating the script in a Query Editor window, to a file, or to the clipboard. The types of scripting options presented are dependent on the type of database object you choose to script. For example, if you

Server Type	Main Folder	Description
SQL Server	Databases	This folder contains the System Databases folder, the Database Snapshots folder, and any User Database folders. The objects that are contained in each database are in their own folders and include tables and views, synonyms, stored procedures, functions, triggers, assemblies, types, rules, defaults, users, roles, schemas, and symmetric keys.
	Security	This folder contains the Logins, Server Roles, Linked Servers, and Credential folders. The objects in these folders are available to the entire server, not just to a single database.
	DTS 2000 Packages	Folder for SQL Server 2000 DTS migration packages.
	Notification Services	You can start an instance of Notification Services that allows you to perform maintenance tasks and update notification applications in your environment, including: managing and monitoring security and permissions; starting and stopping instances and applications; backing up of application databases and definitions; updating application features; and moving, upgrading, or deleting instances of Notification Services.
	Replication	This folder contains information about Replication publications and subscriptions.
	Management	This folder contains the SQL Server Logs, Backup Devices, Server Triggers, and Maintenance Plans folders. It also has the Activity Monitor, SQL Mail, and Database Mail nodes.
	Support Services	This folder contains a tool for monitoring the Distributed Transaction Coordinator and Full-Text Search.
	SQL Server Agent	This folder contains the Jobs, Alerts, Operators, Proxies, and SQL Agent Error Logs folders. The SQL Server Agent is displayed only to members of the sysadmin role.
Analysis Server	Databases	This folder contains the SQL Server 2005 Analysis Services (SSAS) databases. You can manage existing databases; create new roles and database assemblies; and process cubes, dimensions, and mining structures.
	Assemblies	This folder contains the server assemblies information.
Integration Services	Running Packages	This folder contains the opened and running SQL Server 2005 Integration Services (SSIS) packages.
	Stored Packages	This folder contains links to all the SSIS packages stored in the file system or in the msdb database.
Report Server		You can manage one or more report servers in a workspace. The report servers are denoted as a node in the object hierarchy structure.
SQL Server Mobile		This folder contains a limited set of SQL Server nodes that includes: Tables, Views, Programmability, and Replication.

Table 1-1 *Server Types*

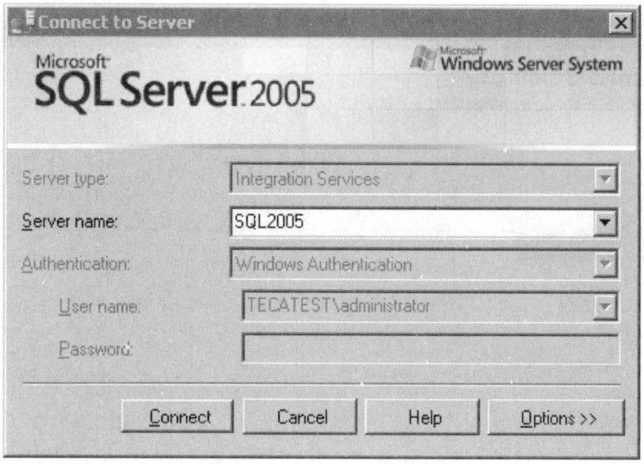

Figure 1-2   *The Connect To Server dialog box*

choose to script an entire database, the CREATE and DROP scripting options are available. However, if you choose to script a view, the CREATE and DROP scripting options are available, as well as ALTER, SELECT, INSERT, UPDATE, and DELETE. To script an object using Object Explorer, right-click the object and then select Script <object type> as an option from the context menu.

The Generate Scripts Wizard can be used and will walk you through the process of creating scripts. The wizard allows you to select a variety of objects to be scripted at once instead of selecting each object individually. It contains a variety of options for generating scripts, including permissions, collation, and constraints. The wizard is useful when you need to create scripts for a large number of objects. There are two ways to launch the Generate Scripts Wizard. The first way to open the Generate Scripts Wizard is by right-clicking an instance of a SQL Server Database Engine and selecting the Launch Wizard option. Then select the Generate Scripts option from the next context menu displayed. The second way is to expand the Databases folder in Object Explorer and right-click a database. Select the Tasks option from the context menu, and then select Generate Scripts. The Summary screen of the Generate Scripts Wizard is shown in Figure 1-3.

Summary Pages   When you select an item in Object Explorer, information about that object is presented in a document window called the Summary Page. You can configure the SQL Server Management Studio to display the Summary Page automatically, or you can disable the display of the Summary Page. To configure the display option for the Summary Page, click the Tools | Options option from the Management Studio menu. On the Environment/General page, select Open Object Explorer from the At Startup drop-down box to display the Summary Page when

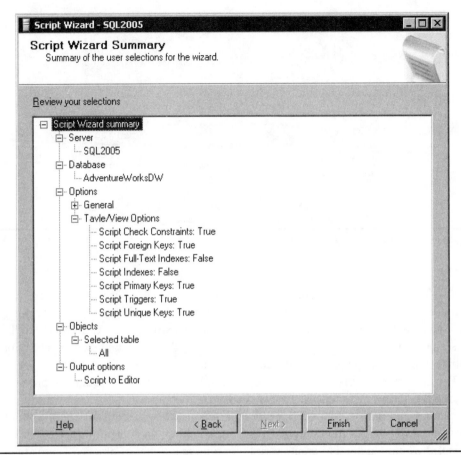

Figure 1-3   *Generate Scripts Wizard*

SQL Server Management Studio opens. Any other choice from the drop-down box will set the Summary Page to not be displayed automatically. The Summary Page displays information about the currently selected object of the Object Explorer window. The Summary Page for the columns of a table in a database can be seen in Figure 1-4.

Solution Explorer

The Solution Explorer is an important management tool that is provided as a part of the SQL Server Management Studio. You can see the Solution Explorer in the upper right-hand corner of Figure 1-1. The Solution Explorer is used to provide a hierarchical tree view of the different projects and files in a solution. A solution can

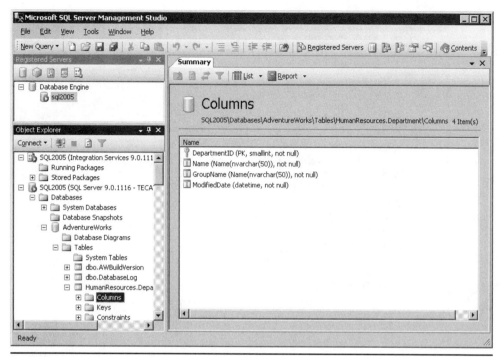

Figure 1-4   *Summary Page*

include one or more projects, in addition to files and metadata that help define the solution as a whole. A project is a set of files that contain connection information, query files, or other miscellaneous and related metadata files. Figure 1-5 shows the Solutions Explorer window.

The types of projects you can have in your solution include: SQL Server Scripts, SQL Mobile Scripts, and Analysis Services Scripts.

SQL Server Scripts   The SQL Server Scripts projects are used to group together related SQL Server connections and T-SQL scripts. A common use for this type of project is to group together Data Definition Language (DDL) queries that define the objects in your database.

Analysis Server Scripts   Analysis Server Scripts projects are intended to contain Analysis Server connections as well as MDX, DMX, and XMLA scripts. One way you can use this type of project is to have one project contain the scripts that create your data warehouse and another project contain the scripts to load your data warehouse.

Figure 1-5   *Solution Explorer*

SQL Mobile Scripts   SQL Mobile Scripts projects are used to group together the connections and queries for a SQL Server CE database. For a SQL Server CE project, a connection object represents the connection to the CE database.

The top item listed in the Solution Explorer is the name of the SQL Server Management Studio solution. By default this name is Solution 1, but you can change this to whatever name you want by right-clicking the solution and selecting Rename from the context menu. The files that are listed in the Solution Explorer can be associated with a project, or else they can be associated with the SQL Server Management Studio solution itself without an intermediate project.

Properties Window

The Properties window allows you to view the properties of files, projects, or solutions in SQL Server Management Studio. You can see the Properties window in the lower right-hand corner of Figure 1-1. If the Properties window is not already displayed, you can show it by selecting the View | Properties Window option from the Management Studio menu. The Properties window displays different types of editing fields, depending on the type of object selected. Properties shown in gray are read-only.

A Properties dialog is also available that permits you to view the properties of database objects. To display the Properties dialog, right-click a database object and select Properties from the context menu. An example of a Properties dialog is shown in Figure 1-6.

Query Editor

The Query Editor is the replacement for Query Analyzer found in previous versions of SQL Server. It allows you to write and run T-SQL scripts, MDX, DMX, XMLA queries, or mobile queries. You can see the Query Editor in the upper-middle portion of Figure 1-7.

You start the Query Editor from the SQL Server Management Studio by selecting the New Query option on the Management Studio main page and choosing the query

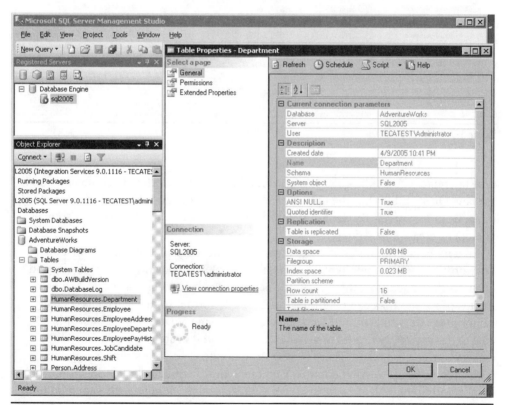

Figure 1-6   *Properties dialog box*

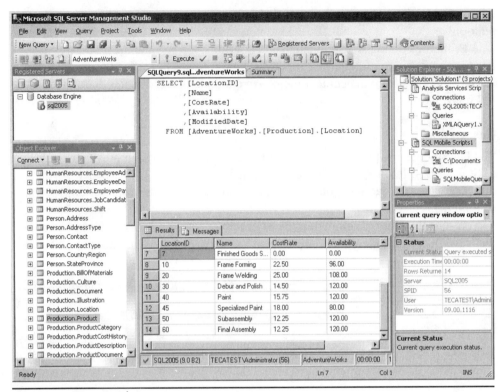

Figure 1-7   *Query Editor*

type to create. Unlike the Query Analyzer, which always worked in connected mode, the new Query Editor has the option of working in either connected or disconnected mode from the server. By default it automatically connects to the server as soon as you opt to create a new query.

Like its Visual Studio 2005 counterpart, the Query Editor supports color-coded keywords, visually shows syntax errors, and enables the developer to both run and debug code. In addition, the Query Editor supports the concept of projects, where groups of related files can be grouped together to form a solution. The new Query Editor also offers full support for source control using Visual SourceSafe. It is able to display query results in a grid or as text, and it is able to graphically show a query's execution plans. There is also an option to save your scripts using the built-in SourceSafe version control. Version control facilitates group development by preventing multiple developers from simultaneously changing the same module. Source code must be checked out of the code repository before it can be modified and then checked back in, giving you a central location to store your database code. Using version control with your database creation scripts provides a valuable method for isolating the source code associated with each release of your database schema. This can also act as a basis for comparing the schema of a deployed database to the expected schema that's been saved using version control.

Query Editor also has the capability to graphically represent a query's execution plan. The Execution Plan option graphically displays the data retrieval methods chosen by the Query Optimizer. Figure 1-8 shows the execution plan for the query shown in Figure 1-7.

Results Window

The results of the queries that are executed in the Query Editor are displayed in the SQL Server Management Studio's Results window. You can see the Results window in the lower-middle portion of Figure 1-7. You can set the Results window to display query results either in text format or in a grid.

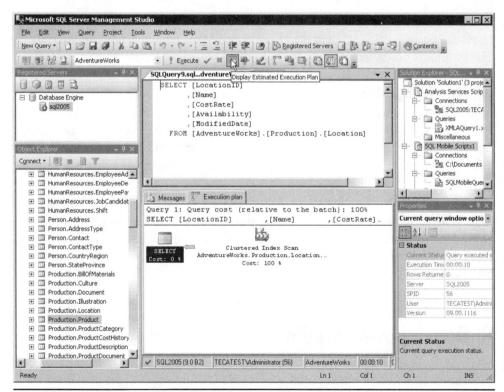

Figure 1-8   *Execution plan*

SQL Server 2005 Administrative Tools

This section gives you an overview of the SQL Server 2005 administrative tools, including:

- ► Profiler enhancements
- ► Database Tuning Advisor
- ► Assisted editors

Profiler Enhancements

With SQL Server 2005, Profiler gets an overhaul as well. The new Profiler now supports the ability to trace both SSIS and Analysis Services commands. SQL Server 2000 was limited to tracing relational database calls only. By having these capabilities, you can use these traces to debug any problems you have in these additional components of SQL Server. Also, Performance Monitor correlation works with these new trace types.

Profiler allows you to save the trace file as XML. Furthermore, a traced ShowPlan result can be saved as XML and then loaded into Management Studio for analysis. The Profiler is described in detail in Appendix A.

Database Tuning Advisor

Profiler also integrates with the new Database Tuning Advisor, which replaces the Index Tuning Wizard. The DTA has a rich, new interface and works with the newer features in SQL Server 2005; for instance, it will recommend partitioning your tables using the new table partitioning features in the database engine.

Assisted Editors

Management Studio contains new capabilities, called *assisted editors*, to make writing stored procedures, views, and functions easier. Instead of having to manually create the header information for these types of objects, you can use the assisted editors to quickly point and click to set information.

BI Development Studio

While SQL Server Management Studio is used to develop relational database projects and administer and configure existing objects in SQL Server 2005, the new Business Intelligence (BI) Development Studio is used to create Business Intelligence solutions.

Unlike the SQL Server Management Studio, the BI Development Studio is not really designed to be an administrative tool. You use the BI Development Studio to work with Analysis Services projects, to develop and deploy Reporting Services reports, and to design Integration Services (SSIS) packages.

The BI Development Studio is accessed using the Start | Programs | Microsoft SQL Server | Business Intelligence Development Studio menu option. You can see the BI Development Studio in Figure 1-9.

The BI Development Studio, like the SQL Server Management Studio, is built on the Visual Studio 2005 IDE. It provides a solution-oriented development environment and contains one or more projects in a solution. BI Development Studio enhances the development of business intelligence applications by allowing project development in a source-controlled, multiuser environment without requiring an active connection to a server. Each of the project types will contain the specific object definitions for those projects. For example, a Reporting Services project will contain Report definitions, while an SSIS project will contain SSIS package objects. Like the SQL Server

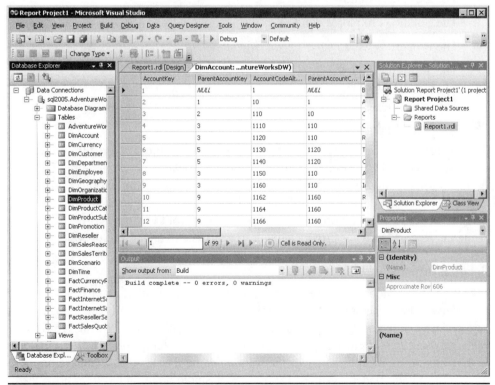

Figure 1-9   *Business Intelligence Development Studio*

Management Studio, the BI Development Studio doesn't allow you to compile VB.NET, C#, J#, or VC++. Instead, the BI Development Studio is designed expressly for working with BI projects like SSIS and Reporting Services. The BI Development Studio is also integrated with Visual SourceSafe for source code version control.

The Business Intelligence Development Studio User Interface

The Business Intelligence Development Studio user interface is an excellent environment for developing business intelligence solutions, including cubes, data sources, data views, reports, and data transformation packages.

BI Development Studio User Interface Windows

This section gives you an overview of the BI Development Studio user interface main windows, including:

▶ The Designer window

▶ The Solutions Explorer window

▶ The Properties window

▶ The Toolbox window

▶ The Output window

The Designer Window

The Designer window provides a graphical view of an object and is the central window in the BI Development Studio. A different designer type inhabits the designer window in response to the current BI Development Studio object type. For example, if you are developing an SSIS package, the Designer window provides the design surface to drag and drop objects from the Control Flow toolbox to the project, while the Report Designer provides the design surface to create and preview reports.

Solution Explorer

Like the SQL Server Development Studio, the BI Development Studio has a Solution Explorer window. The Solution Explorer is shown in the upper right-hand corner of the screen shown in Figure 1-9. The Solution Explorer provides a hierarchical tree view of the projects and files that compose a BI Development Studio solution. The top item in the Solution Explorer hierarchy is the solution name. The solution can have one or more project items under it. The BI Development Studio Solution Explorer provides project templates, including: Analysis Services Project, Integration Services Project,

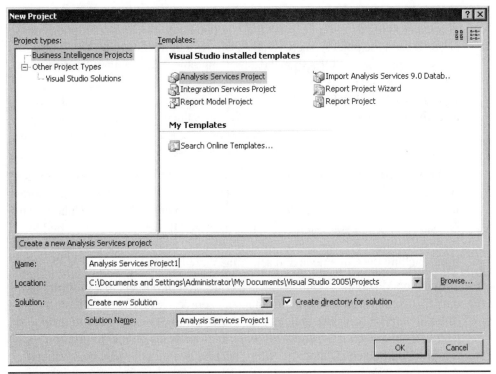

Figure 1-10   *Business Intelligence Development Studio—New Project*

Import Analysis Services 9.0 Database, Report Project, Report Project Wizard, and Report Model Project. As in the SQL Server Management Studio, BI Development Studio solutions are not restricted to one project. You can create solutions that are made up of any of the supported project types. You can see the Business Intelligence Development Studio's New Project dialog in Figure 1-10.

Analysis Services Project   Analysis Services projects contain the definitions for the objects in an Analysis Services database. These include designing and creating Analysis Services databases, data source views, cubes, and dimensions, as well as working with the data mining features.

▶ **Analysis Services database**   An Analysis Services database created using BI Development Studio includes the XML definitions for the database and its objects for later deployment to a specific instance of Analysis Services. To create an Analysis Services database, you select the File | New | Project option from the main BI Development Studio menu. Then from the dialog displayed, select the Analysis Services Project template from the Business Intelligence project type.

▶ **Data source views**   A data source view is a document that describes the schema of an underlying data source. Such a view contains names and descriptions of selected database objects, such as tables, views, and relationships, that online analytical processing (OLAP) and data mining objects in Analysis Services reference. These objects can be organized and configured to provide a complete schema. You can develop an Analysis Services project without having to have an active connection to the data source, because the data source view caches the metadata from the data source it is built upon. Using a data source view, you can define a subset of data from a larger data warehouse.

▶ **Cube Wizard**   A cube is a multidimensional structure that contains dimensions and measures; where dimensions define the structure of the cube, and measures provide the numerical values that the end user is interested in. The Cube Wizard is a visual tool that you can use to quickly create OLAP cubes. It is started by double-clicking the Cube node shown under an Analysis Services project or by right-clicking the Cube node and selecting View Designer.

▶ **Dimension Wizard**   A dimension is a collection of objects that describe the data that is provided by the tables in a data source view. You can organize these dimensions into hierarchies that allow you to navigate paths to the data in a cube. Typically, users will base their analyses on the description attributes contained in the dimensions, such as time, customers, or products. A Dimension Wizard is provided in the BI Development Studio to guide you through the steps for specifying the structure of a dimension.

▶ **Data Mining Designer**   A Data Mining Designer is provided as a primary environment, which allows you to work with mining models in Analysis Services. You can access the Data Mining Designer by selecting an existing item in a mining structure project, or you can use the Data Mining Wizard to create a new item. Using the Data Mining Designer, you can modify a mining structure, create new mining models, compare models, or create prediction queries.

Integration Services Project   Integration Services projects contain folders and files that allow you to manage the object definitions of data sources, data source views, and packages for SSIS solutions. *Data sources* are defined as project-level, which means you can have multiple projects in your solution that reference a single data source object. *Data source views* can be referenced by sources, transformations, and destinations in your project, and *packages* contain a collection of connections, control flow elements, data flow elements, event handlers, variables, and configurations.

SSIS Designer   The BI Development Studio contains an SSIS Designer, which is a graphical tool for creating packages. It has four tabs, one each for building the four elements of the SSIS project, including: the package control flow, the data flows, the event handlers, and one tab for viewing the contents of a package. A fifth tab that appears at run time allows you to view the execution progress of a package. After the package completes its run, the execution results can be viewed. The SSIS Designer is shown in Figure 1-11.

Separate design surfaces exist for building the control flow, data flows, and event handler elements in packages. Dialog boxes and windows, such as the variable window and the breakpoint window, are also included to help you add and configure variables and to troubleshoot your project. Wizards are included to add functionality and advanced features.

Import Analysis Services 9.0 Database   The Import Analysis Service 9.0 Database project enables you to create a new SQL Server 2005 Analysis Services project by importing the definitions for an existing SQL Server 2000 Analysis Services or SQL Server 7 OLAP Server database.

Report Project, Report Project Wizard, and Report Model Project   The BI Development Studio contains the Report Project template, the Report Project Wizard template,

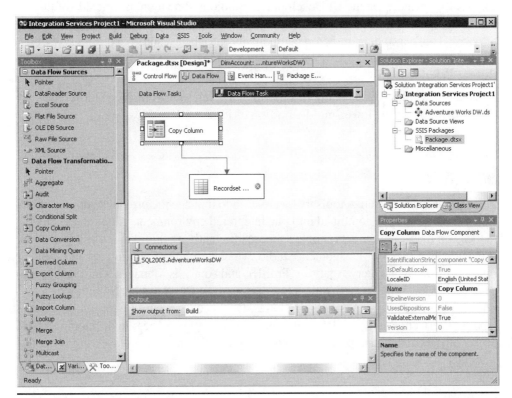

Figure 1-11   *SSIS Designer*

and the Report Model Project template to create Reporting Services projects. These reporting templates are used to design reports and control their deployment. Reporting Services project templates start the Reporting Services Designer, where you can select data sources and visually lay out reports. Reporting Services projects, the Report Designer, and the Report Project Wizard are covered in more detail in Chapter 9.

Properties

Like the Properties window in SQL Server Management Studio, the BI Development Studio Properties window allows you to view the properties of files, projects, or solutions. The Properties window shown in the bottom-right corner of Figure 1-9 is used at design time to set the properties of the objects selected in the Solution Explorer. If the Properties window is not already displayed, you can show it by selecting the View | Properties Window option from the BI Development Studio menu. The Properties window displays different types of editing fields, depending on the type of object selected.

Toolbox

The Toolbox window in the BI Development Studio is shown on the left side of the screen in Figure 1-11. The Toolbox is used by the SSIS Designer and the Reporting Services Designer to drag and drop components onto their respective design surfaces.

Output Window

The Output window displays the results when a solution is built. You can see the Output window in the lower-middle portion of Figure 1-9.

Summary

The separate administrative tools that were used to manage the previous versions of SQL Server have been combined into one integrated environment, allowing the DBA to focus on managing the server objects more efficiently. In this chapter, you got a look at the new SQL Server Management Studio, which combines the four previous tools: Enterprise Manager, Query Analyzer, Profiler, and Analysis Manager. This chapter also gave you a view of the new Business Intelligence (BI) Development Studio, which is used to create Analysis Services databases, DTS packages, and Reporting Services reports. These environments definitely improve your effectiveness in developing SQL Server objects and managing SQL Server administration tasks.

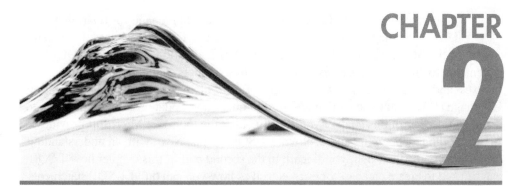

Developing with T-SQL

IN THIS CHAPTER

T-SQL Development Tools

Creating Database Objects Using T-SQL DDL

Querying and Updating with T-SQL DML

QL (Structured Query Language) is the standard language for relational database management systems (RDBMSs), and T-SQL is Microsoft's version of the SQL language. T-SQL includes Data Definition Language (DDL) statements to create databases as well as database objects such as tables, views, indexes, and stored procedures. In addition, T-SQL also includes Data Manipulation Language (DML) statements that are used to query and update relational data stored.

In the first part of this chapter you'll learn about the tools that Microsoft provides for developing, debugging, and deploying T-SQL scripts. Next, with an understanding of the tools under your belt, you'll learn in the second part of this chapter how T-SQL can be used to create database objects as well as how you can build T-SQL statements to query and update data.

T-SQL Development Tools

Microsoft provides two primary tools for developing T-SQL scripts. First, as a part of SQL Server 2005's SQL Server Management Studio (SSMS), there's the Query Editor, which provides a basic T-SQL development environment and is primarily intended to develop T-SQL DDL statements, perform performance tuning with graphical showplans, and run ad hoc queries. Next, to create more sophisticated T-SQL projects such as stored procedures and functions, Microsoft provides the new Database Project that's part of Visual Studio 2005 Professional Edition and higher. The Database Project takes up where the Query Editor leaves off. In addition to the ability to create and execute T-SQL, the Database Project also offers the ability to debug T-SQL, where you can single-step through the code in your T-SQL projects. In the next section of this chapter you'll see how to develop T-SQL management scripts using the SSMS Query Editor and then Visual Studio 2005's Database Project to develop and debug a T-SQL stored procedure.

NOTE

In addition to these two tools, you can also develop T-SQL scripts using a text editor like Notepad and then execute the scripts using the command-line SqlCmd or osql utilities. However, this basic level of development doesn't offer any of the more advanced development features, such as project management, color-coded syntax, or source control, that are available in the Query Editor or Visual Studio.

SQL Server Management Studio

The primary T-SQL development tool that's supplied with SQL Server 2005 is the Query Editor, which is a part of the SQL Server Management Studio (SSMS). You start

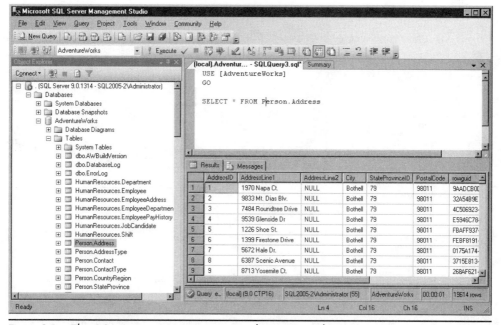

Figure 2-1   *The SQL Server Management Studio Query Editor*

the Query Editor by selecting the New Query option from the SSMS toolbar to display an editing window like the one shown in Figure 2-1.

SSMS and the Query Editor are built on the Visual Studio 2005 IDE and have a similar look and feel. The editor is very capable, providing color-coded syntax and cut-and-paste capabilities. It provides support for source control via SourceSafe as well as organizing your projects into solutions. However, it does not support IntelliSense or code snippets.

To use the Query Editor, you enter your T-SQL code into the Query Editor and then press F5 or click the green arrow in the toolbar. For query operation the results will be displayed in the Results window that you can see in the lower half of Figure 2-1. By default the Results window displays the results in a grid format, but you can also choose to display the results as text output or write the results to a file. The output options are set using the Query | Options menu option.

TIP

SSMS is quite different from the Enterprise Manager or Query Analyzer that were provided in the previous releases of SQL Server. You might not notice it at first, but the SSMS menus dynamically change depending on the window that has focus. For instance, if the focus is on the Object Explorer, the menu options will show the basic management options. If the focus moves to the Query Editor, then the Query And Community menu option will appear.

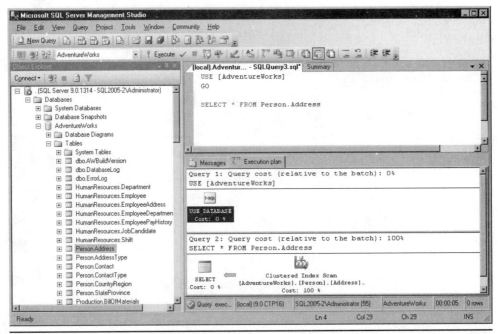

Figure 2-2   *Displaying a query's execution plan*

In addition to outputting the result data, the Query Editor can also display the execution plan that the SQL Server engine uses for a given query. By examining a query's execution plan, you can see how long the query is taking to execute, as well as if the query is using the appropriate indexes. To display the execution plan for a query, select the Query | Include Actual Execution Plan and then run the query. This will display a window like the one shown in Figure 2-2.

A graphical representation of the query's execution plan is shown in the Results window. In this example, you can see that the simple select * query is satisfied using the clustered index built over the Person.Address table. You can also output the showplan data in XML format.

Using the Query Builder

In addition to the standard Query Editor, which allows you to write and execute T-SQL queries that you build, SSMS also provides a Query Builder that enables you to visually design a query for which Query Builder will output the T-SQL source code. To run Query Builder, put your focus in the Query Editor window to display the Query menu on the SSMS toolbar and then select the Design Query In Editor option. This will display a Query Builder window like the one shown in Figure 2-3.

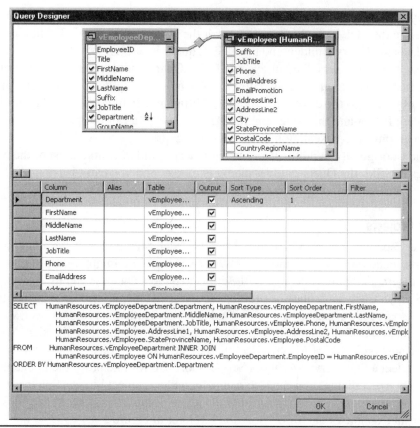

Figure 2-3   *Query Builder*

When the Query Builder first starts, it displays an Add Table dialog that enables you to select the tables that you want to query. Multiple tabs enable you to include views, functions, and synonyms. You add objects by selecting them and clicking Add. After you've selected the database objects that you want to include in the query, click Close.

Clicking the check box in front of each column name includes that column in the query. You indicate the desired join conditions by dragging and dropping column names from one table or view onto like columns from another table or view. The included tables and joins are used as a basis for building a T-SQL Select statement. Sort conditions are indicated by right-clicking the column names in the Table pane and then selecting the Sort Ascending or Sort Descending options from the pop-up menu.

Using the Columns pane, you can apply filters to the row selection criteria by putting a value in the filter column. Filters are translated into a T-SQL Where clause. You can also reorder the result set columns by dragging them up or down to a new location in the Columns pane.

As you graphically build the query, the generated T-SQL statement is continually updated in the SQL pane that you can see at the bottom of Figure 2-3. Clicking OK completes the Query Builder, and the T-SQL query is written into the Query Editor, where it can be further edited or executed. The Query Builder is a two-way tool in that it enables you to graphically build a query by selecting database objects, plus it allows you to go the other way. By highlighting an existing text-based query in the Query Editor and then selecting the Design Query In Editor option, you can view a graphical representation of the text-based query in Query Builder—even if you didn't originally build the query using Query Builder. Unlike most of the other dialogs in SSM, the Query Builder dialog is modal, and you can't leave it until you've finished designing your query.

Using Projects

Another capability that SSMS derives from its Visual Studio roots is the ability to organize related source files into projects. For instance, you might use a project to group together all of the related T-SQL scripts to build a database and its objects. SSMS projects are particularly useful for grouping together related code from different sorts of source files, such as you might find in a Notification Services project, where a combination of T-SQL and XML files combine to form a single application. You can create a new project in SSMS by selecting the File | New | Project option, which allows you to select a SQL Server, Analysis Services, or SQL Mobile project template from the New Project dialog. You can also manually build a project by selecting the View | Solution Explorer option and then right-clicking in Solution Explorer to add files. You can see an example of the SSMS Solution Explorer in Figure 2-4.

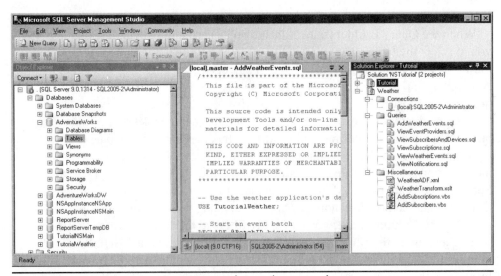

Figure 2-4   *SQL Server Management Studio's Solution Explorer*

SSMS projects are organized into Connections, Queries, and Miscellaneous. Connections defines the database connection properties, Queries generally contain T-SQL scripts, and Miscellaneous contains other types of source files, including XML and XSD files. SSMS projects are saved using the extension of .ssmssln (SQL Server Management Studio Solution).

Source Control

SSMS is also fully integrated with Microsoft's Visual SourceSafe version control system. Using version control enables you to ensure that multiple developers are not working on the same piece of source code at the same time—thus eliminating the possibility of overwriting one another's changes. Using source control also enables you to create and track database release versions, clearly separating all of the code that's used to create each given version of the database.

In order to use Visual SourceSafe with SSMS and SQL Server, a Visual SourceSafe server system must be installed and configured. In addition, the SourceSafe client code must be installed on the computer that's running SSMS. You install the Visual SourceSafe client code by running the netsetup program, which will display an installation wizard to step you through the client installation process. After the client code has been installed, a Visual SourceSafe snap-in will be available to SSMS. You can view the source control snap-in using the Tools | Options | Source Control Plug-in Selection option.

Visual Studio 2005

The SSMS Query Editor is most useful for developing administrative scripts and running ad hoc queries. However, its lack of debugging capabilities limits its use for developing more complex T-SQL functions and stored procedures. Fortunately, Visual Studio 2005 extends its support for database development by including a new Database Project type that fully supports T-SQL development and debugging. The Database project stores database references; can develop, run, and debug T-SQL scripts; and can be used to create batch files to run multiple scripts. Like SSMS, Visual Studio 2005 provides integrated source control via Visual SourceSafe and is able to organize multiple related files into projects that you can manage using the Solution Explorer. To create a new Database project, open Visual Studio 2005 and select the File | New | Project option, which will display a New Project dialog like the one shown in Figure 2-5.

To create a new Database Project, expand the Other Project Types node in Project Types pane and then open up the Database node. Under the Templates pane, select the Database Project template. Give your project a name and click OK. In Figure 2-5 you can see the project is named MyStoredProcedure. Clicking OK displays the Add Database Reference dialog that is shown in Figure 2-6.

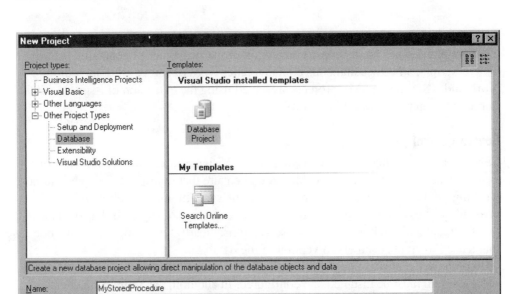

Figure 2-5 New Database Project

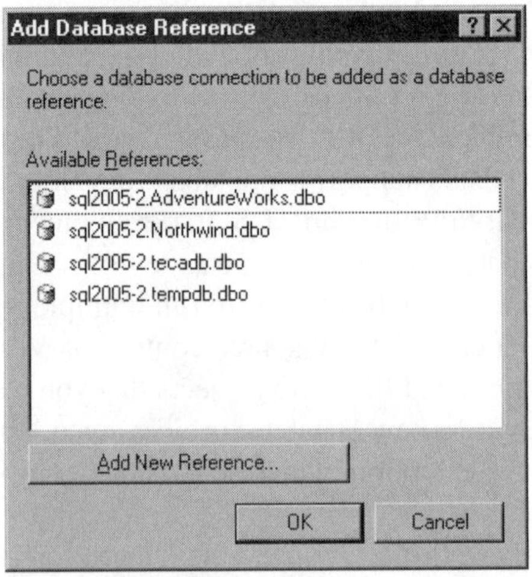

Figure 2-6 Add Database Reference

If you have created previous database projects or SQLCLR solutions that connect to SQL Server, you'll have existing connections as shown in Figure 2-6. You can either choose an existing connection or click Add New Reference to create a new database reference. In the example shown in Figure 2-6 you can see that an existing connection to the AdventureWorks database on a SQL Server system named SQL2005-2 has been selected. Clicking OK creates a new Visual Studio solution. The Visual Studio 2005 Solution Explorer will be shown on the right side of the screen; it provides an overview of the connections, projects, and files inside a solution. To get an SSMS-like view of the SQL Server databases and their objects, you can open the Server Explorer by selecting the View | Server Explorer option from Visual Studio 2005's IDE. A Visual Studio project will appear like the one shown in Figure 2-7.

The Solution Explorer shown on the right-hand portion of Figure 2-7 is divided into four sections: Change Scripts, Create Scripts, Queries, and Database References. When a project is first created, all of these items will be empty, except for Database References, where you can see the database connection that you selected earlier.

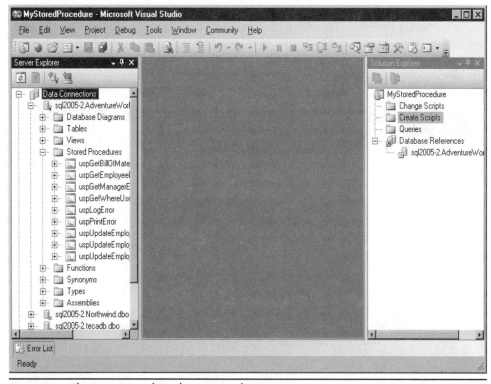

Figure 2-7   *The New Visual Studio 2005 solution*

The Server Explorer window enables you to browse through the objects in the SQL Server database. In addition, you can right-click the different objects shown in the Server Explorer to display a context menu that allows you to work with the objects. For instance, right-clicking a stored procedure will display a context menu that enables you to work with stored procedures. The available options are: Add New Stored Procedure, Open, Execute, Step Into Stored Procedure, Generate Create Script to Project, Copy, Delete, Refresh, and Properties.

To create a new stored procedure, click Add New Item from the Project menu or right-click a stored procedure in the Server Explorer and select the Add New Stored Procedure option to display the Add New Item dialog you can see in Figure 2-8.

Visual Studio 2005 has a number of different database project templates that you can see in Figure 2-8. These templates essentially supply you with the starter code for your project. The existing templates can be customized, or you can also add your own custom templates if you've developed your own set of starter code. To create a stored procedure, select the Stored Procedure Script template, name the script, and click OK. In Figure 2-8 you can see that the example stored procedure script will be named MyStoredProcedure.sql.

After you click OK, Visual Studio 2005 will generate the stub code to drop and create a stored procedure. However, the generated code is just a shell. It is up to you to name the stored procedure and fill in the required logic. You can see the complete example stored procedure in Figure 2-9.

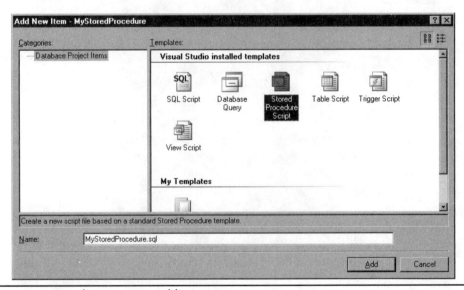

Figure 2-8   *Database Project: Add Item*

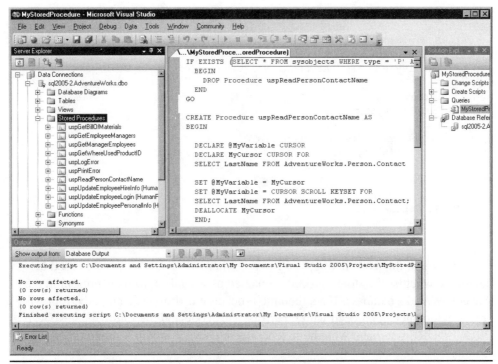

Figure 2-9   *Editing a stored procedure in Visual Studio 2005*

NOTE

Visual Studio supports the same Query Builder that was presented earlier in this chapter in the section "SQL Server Management Studio." To open the Query Builder in Visual Studio 2005, right-click in the editing window and select the Insert SQL option from the context menu.

In Figure 2-9 you can see that the stored procedure has been named uspRead PersonContactName. This example stored procedure reads through the Person .Contacts table on the AdventureWorks database. The complete code to create the uspReadPersonContactInfo stored procedure is shown in the following code listing:

```
IF EXISTS (SELECT * FROM sysobjects WHERE type = 'P' AND name =
'uspReadEmpMgrs')
  BEGIN
    DROP Procedure 'uspReadEmpMgrs'
  END
GO
```

```
CREATE Procedure 'uspReadEmpMgrs'AS
BEGIN
  DECLARE @ThisEmp int
  DECLARE EmpCursor CURSOR FOR
  SELECT EmployeeID FROM AdventureWorks.HumanResources.Employee

  OPEN EmpCursor
    WHILE @@FETCH_STATUS = 0
      BEGIN
        FETCH NEXT FROM EmpCursor INTO @ThisEmp
        PRINT 'EmployeeID:' + RTRIM(CAST(@ThisEmp AS VARCHAR(10)))
        EXEC uspGetEmployeeManagers @ThisEmp
      END

    CLOSE EmpCursor
    DEALLOCATE EmpCursor
END;
```

At the top of this code listing, you can see where an IF EXISTS test is used to determine whether the stored procedure named uspReadEmpMgrs is present in the AdventureWorks database. If so, then the procedure is dropped so that the following create statement can proceed with no errors. This code and the following CREATE PROCEDURE statement were both generated by Visual Studio's stored procedure template.

The code within the uspReadEmpMgrs stored procedure declares a variable to hold the information read from the HumanResources.Employee table, and a cursor is declared that enables the stored procedure to read through the HumanResources .Employee table one row at a time. For each row read, the uspGetEmployeeManagers stored procedure is called, passing the value of EmployeeID from the current row. At the end of the routine, the cursor is closed and then released.

NOTE

More information on creating stored procedures and other T-SQL coding techniques is presented later in this chapter. In general, using cursors limits application scalability, and therefore, they should normally be avoided. However, in this case a cursor was used to make it easier to illustrate the debugging and code-stepping techniques in Visual Studio 2005's T-SQL debugger.

To create the stored procedure, save your script and then select the Run option from Visual Studio 2005's Project menu. This will delete and re-create the stored procedure name uspReadEmpMgrs in the AdventureWorks database. Visual Studio 2005's Output window will show the result of the DROP and CREATE PROCEDURE statements.

To see the new stored procedure, go to the Server Explorer window and expand the Data Connections node. Then expand the connection you are using, right-click the Stored Procedure node, and select Refresh. The stored procedure you have created should now be visible in the list of procedures.

Executing and Debugging T-SQL with Visual Studio 2005

To execute a stored procedure using Visual Studio 2005, first open up Server Explorer and expand the Data Connections node for the desired database connection. The example that this chapter has used is sql2005-2.AdventureWorks. Next open the Stored Procedures node, right-click the stored procedure that you want to run, and select Execute from the pop-up menu. Visual Studio 2005 will execute the selected stored procedure, and the results will be shown in the Output pane at the bottom of the Visual Studio IDE.

Debugging a stored procedure from Visual Studio is very similar. You can debug a stored procedure from the Server Explorer. To debug a T-SQL stored procedure using the Server Explorer, first open the Server Explorer, expand the desired Data Connections node, expand the Stored Procedures node, and right-click the stored procedure that you want to debug. This will display the context menu. From the context menu, select the Step Into Stored Procedure option. If the stored procedure uses input parameters, Visual Studio 2005 will display a Run Stored Procedure dialog that allows you to pass in the required parameter values. In the case of the uspReadEmpMgrs stored procedure, no input parameters are required and Visual Studio 2005 opens up into the stored procedure debugger that you can see in Figure 2-10.

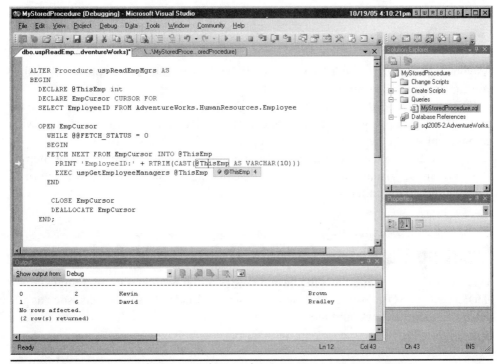

Figure 2-10   *Debugging T-SQL stored procedures*

Visual Studio loads the stored procedure source code into the IDE, and execution of the stored procedure stops at the first line of code. You can step through the T-SQL source code by clicking the Step Into, Step Over, or Step Out icon on the toolbar or by pressing F10. You can inspect the contents of a variable using Visual Studio 2005's DataTips feature by moving the mouse over the variable, causing the DataTips windows to automatically display. This is shown in Figure 2-10, where the contents of the @ThisEmp variable are displayed in the DataTips window. You can also use one of the Visual Studio debugging windows to see the contents of a T-SQL variable. The Visual Studio 2005 debugging windows are displayed using the Debug | Windows option, and the following windows are available:

▶ **Immediate**   Allows you to enter commands and change variables.

▶ **Locals**   Displays variables within the current scope.

▶ **Breakpoints**   Displays the set breakpoints.

▶ **Output**   Displays the output of the executing code.

▶ **Autos**   Displays variables used in the current statement.

▶ **Call Stack**   Displays the code call stack.

▶ **Threads**   Displays the ID of the current thread.

▶ **Watch**   Displays a watch window for watch variables that you define.

As you step through the code, the output will be displayed in the Output window that you can see at the bottom of Figure 2-10.

If the stored procedure you are debugging calls another stored procedure, you can press F11 when stepping over the line of code that calls the other procedure. This will automatically load the called stored procedure into the debugger. You can then step through the code in that procedure by pressing F10 or clicking the Step Into or Step Over icon in the Visual Studio 2005 toolbar. Clicking the Step Out icon will return the debugger to the caller.

Creating Database Objects Using T-SQL DDL

This part of the chapter covers the basic features of the Data Definition Language (DDL) parts of SQL. You see how to create several kinds of SQL objects, such as databases, tables, views, and indexes.

Databases

A *database* is the main container for tables, views, indexes, stored procedures, and other database objects. Using the CREATE DATABASE statement, you can create a new database along with the files used to store the database, you can create a database snapshot, or you can attach a database using the detached files of a previously created database. You can create 32,767 databases on an instance of SQL Server. The following statement creates a database:

```
CREATE DATABASE MyNewDatabase
```

When a database is created, two files are also created: a primary file (an .mdf file) and a transaction log file (an .ldf file). It is recommended that you keep these files in different drives from each other to simplify recovering your database in case your database becomes corrupted. You can also specify multiple data and transaction log files. The next code listing shows designating the .mdf and .ldf file locations in the CREATE DATABASE statement:

```
CREATE DATABASE MyNewDatabase
ON PRIMARY
    (Name ='MyDB_Data',
     FileName= 'C:\DBData\MyDB_Data.Mdf',
     Size=100MB,
     MaxSize=200MB,
     FILEGROWTH=10%)
LOG ON
    (Name = 'MyDB_Log',
     FileName= 'D:\DBLogs\MyDB_Log.Ldf',
     Size=30MB,
     MaxSize=50MB,
     FILEGROWTH=10%)
```

You can also use the CREATE DATABASE statement to create a database snapshot. A database snapshot is a read-only, static view of an existing database at the time the snapshot was created and does not create a log file. Database snapshots are a good way to create backup copies of your database. The following code creates a database snapshot:

```
CREATE DATABASE MyDBSnapshot
ON
    (NAME = MyDatabase_data,
     FILENAME = 'C:\temp\MyDatabase_data.ss')
AS SNAPSHOT OF MyNewDatabase
```

Tables

In your database, *tables* are objects that actually contain the data. In SQL Server 2005, you can create up to two billion tables per database and 1024 columns per table. The total size of the table and the number of rows are restricted only by the available storage, and the maximum number of bytes per rows is 8060. However, the row restriction has been adapted for tables with column types of varchar, nvarchar, varbinary, or sql_variant, or CLR user-defined types where the total combined table width can possibly exceed 8060 bytes. Each of the individual columns must stay within the 8060 byte limit, but the database engine moves the record column with the largest width to another page in the ROW_OVERFLOW_DATA allocation unit and maintains a 24-byte pointer on the original page.

The CREATE TABLE statement creates a database table. In the CREATE TABLE statement you must specify the table name and the column names and column definitions for the table. You can optionally specify other table creation options, such as the database name, schema name, filegroup, and setup constraints. The following code listing shows a basic CREATE TABLE statement for a new Warehouse table:

```
CREATE TABLE Sales.Warehouse
    (HouseID INT PRIMARY KEY,
     HouseName Char(50))
```

When this statement executes, a Warehouse table is created in the current database, in the Sales schema. It contains two columns, a HouseID column that is defined as an integer type and a HouseName column that is defined as a character type with a length of 50. The HouseID column is also set as a primary key.

Constraints

Constraints let you define the rules regarding the values that go into columns in your tables and help enforce the integrity of your database. The following list shows the constraint options:

- ▶ NOT NULL specifies that the column cannot accept NULL values.
- ▶ CHECK constraints limit the values that can be put in a column by evaluating a search condition that is applied to the values that are entered for the column, and returning True, False, or unknown.
- ▶ UNIQUE constraints do not allow two rows in the table to have the same value for the columns.

▶ PRIMARY KEY constraints identify the column or set of columns that have values that uniquely identify a row in a table. The value of NULL cannot be entered into a primary key column.

▶ FOREIGN KEY constraints reference relationships between tables.

There are two types of constraints: column constraints and table constraints. A column constraint is defined as part of a column definition in the CREATE TABLE statement and applies to only that column. A table constraint is declared using the CONSTRAINT keyword in the CREATE TABLE statement and can apply to more than one column in a table.

Temporary Tables

You can create two types of temporary tables: local and global. *Local* temporary tables are only visible in the current session, but *global* temporary tables are visible to all sessions. Temporary tables are useful when you need to create a specific index on them in your session, and they are automatically dropped when they go out of scope.

Local temporary table names are designated with single number sign (#*table_name*) prefix, and global temporary table names are designated with a double number sign (##*table_name*) prefix. Temporary table names have a limit of 116 characters.

The next listing shows how to create a temporary table:

```
CREATE TABLE #tempWarehouse
    (HouseCode Char(5) PRIMARY KEY,
     HouseID INT)
```

Data Types

With SQL Server 2005, not only will the CREATE TYPE statement allow you to create an alias data type that is based on a SQL Server native data type, but you can also create a user-defined data type (UDT) that is implemented through a class of an assembly in the Microsoft .NET Framework common language runtime (CLR).

Creating aliases of native SQL Server data types gives more meaningful names to data types that have specific characteristics for your users. This example shows creating an alias type based on the native varchar type:

```
CREATE TYPE EMAILADDRESS FROM varchar(128) NOT NULL
```

The following table shows the native SQL Server data types on which you can base your alias data type:

bigint	binary(n)	bit	char(n)
datetime	decimal	float	image
int	money	nchar(n)	ntext
numeric	nvarchar(n | max)	real	smalldatetime
smallint	smallmoney	sql_variant	text
tinyint	uniqueidentifier	varbinary(n | max)	varchar(n | max)

To create a UDT from a CLR assembly, you must first register the assembly in SQL Server using the CREATE ASSEMBLY statement. You can then use the CREATE TYPE statement to create the UDT. The following listing shows creating an assembly and then creating a UDT based on that assembly:

```
CREATE ASSEMBLY EmailAddress
    FROM 'C:\temp\EmailAddress.dll'

CREATE TYPE EMAILADDRESS
    EXTERNAL NAME EmailAddress.[EmailNameSpace.EmailClass]
```

A full description of creating an assembly for a UDT and deploying it to the server is covered in Chapter 3.

Indexes

Creating indexes on your database objects can effectively save on I/O operations and quicken processing time. Indexes can be created on tables, views, and temporary tables, or an XML index can be given on a table. An index can even be created before there is data in the table. The common types of indexes are NONCLUSTERED, CLUSTERED, and UNIQUE. The maximum size for an index key is 900 bytes.

Indexes provide an ordered lookup of information for your queries and are generally placed on key fields in your tables. However, a new feature of SQL Server 2005 allows you to include nonkey columns in your nonclustered indexes.

The following example shows a common CREATE INDEX statement. This statement creates a nonunique, nonclustered index on the TerritoryID column of the Sales.SalesPerson table:

```
CREATE INDEX IdxTerritoryID ON Sales.SalesPerson (TerritoryID)
```

NONCLUSTERED Indexes   A nonclustered index on a table or view is an index where the order of the index does not depend on the physical order of the data rows. In other words, the columns do not have to be next to each other to make up the index. You can create up to 249 nonclustered indexes for each table in your database. NONCLUSTERED is the default mode when no keyword is specified in the CREATE INDEX statement.

Included Columns in Indexes   In some cases, you may find that you are frequently querying a column in a table that is not a key column. In previous versions of SQL Server, you would generally create an indexed view to handle this situation. However, one of the restrictions to using an indexed view is that the index must be unique. SQL Server 2005 resolves this by allowing the inclusion of nonkey columns in a nonclustered index. This allows the query optimizer to locate all the required information from an index scan; the table or clustered index need not be accessed. SQL Server 2005 allows up to 1023 columns to be included as nonkey columns. The following shows an example of creating a nonclustered index, including nonkey columns:

```
CREATE NONCLUSTERED INDEX IdxTerritoryID_Date
    ON Sales.SalesPerson (TerritoryID)
    INCLUDE (ModifiedDate)
```

CLUSTERED Indexes   A clustered index has the index order the same as the physical order of the rows, and the table data is stored with the index. If you regularly access rows in your table in a particular order, a clustered index can significantly improve the speed of your queries. SQL Server allows you to create only one clustered index on each table. The following code shows creating a clustered index on the Sales .SalesPerson table:

```
CREATE CLUSTERED INDEX IdxPersonTerr
    ON Sales.SalesPerson (SalesPersonID, TerritoryID)
```

UNIQUE Indexes   You can create a unique index on a column to guarantee that the data in the column will not be duplicated on an Insert operation. The database engine checks for duplicate values each time data is added by an insert operation on a unique index column, and if a duplicate is found, the key values are rolled back and the database engine displays an error message.

Indexed Views   You can create a unique clustered index on a view to improve query performance. The view is stored in the database in the same way a table with a clustered index is stored. The query optimizer will automatically consider scanning the view index even though the view is not referenced in the query.

XML Indexes   XML data type columns can hold up to 2GB of data. You can query portions of the XML in these data types, so it's a good idea to create indexes for them. There are two types of indexes you can create for XML data: primary and secondary. A *primary* XML index covers all the elements in the column, and a *secondary* XML index covers the paths, values, and properties. The following code shows an example of how to create a primary index:

```
CREATE PRIMARY XML INDEX IdxXmlData ON Sales.SalesPerson(xml_Data)
```

Defaults

A *default* is bound to a column or alias data type and specifies a default value for the column or columns, when no value is supplied. The following example restricts the information that can be placed into the column to only the values in the rule list:

```
CREATE DEFAULT OrderQty AS '100'
```

NOTE

The CREATE RULE statement will be removed in later versions of SQL Server. It is recommended that you use the DEFAULT keyword for defining values when you create a table.

Rules

A *rule* is bound to a column or alias data type to specify the acceptable values that can be contained in that column. The following example restricts the information that can be placed into the column to only the values in the rule list.

```
CREATE RULE OrderQty
AS
@list IN ('100', '250', '500')
```

NOTE

The CREATE RULE statement will be removed in later versions of SQL Server. It is recommended that you create a CHECK constraint as part of the table definition when you create a table.

Views

Views are virtual tables that allow you to represent data in an alternate way. You can create a view only in the current database, and if you are creating a view in a batch query, the CREATE VIEW must be the first statement in the query. The following code creates a view called StorePersonnel based on the SalesPersonId and the name of the store from the Sales.Store table in the Adventureworks database:

```
CREATE VIEW StorePersonnel
AS SELECT SalesPersonID, Name FROM AdventureWorks.Sales.Store
WHERE SalesPersonID > 250
```

You can create a view with a maximum of 1024 columns. When a view is queried, the database engine checks for the existence of database objects and the validity of all objects referenced in the SELECT statement. If a table or view structure changes, the view dependent on that table or view needs to be dropped and re-created.

When you create a view, information about the view is stored in three catalog views: sys.view, sys.columns, and sys.sql_dependencies, and the text of the CREATE VIEW statement used to create the view is stored in the sys.sql_modules catalog view.

Synonyms

Synonyms are aliases you can create for your objects. They help you simplify the naming of remote objects or objects that are in another database or schema. Synonyms allow you to exchange underlying objects without affecting the code that references the objects. The following command creates a synonym called RetailLocation for the Sales.Store table in the AdventureWorks database:

```
CREATE SYNONYM RetailLocation FOR AdventureWorks.Sales.Store
```

The base object need not exist at the time the synonym is created, as SQL Server checks for the existence of the base object at runtime, instead of creation time. You can create synonyms for tables, temporary tables, views, procedures, and functions.

Stored Procedures

The CREATE PROCEDURE statement can be used to create a standard T-SQL *stored procedure*, which is a saved collection of T-SQL statements, or it can be used to create a stored procedure implemented through a class of an assembly in the Microsoft .NET Framework common language runtime (CLR). This example shows creating a simple stored procedure to return the SalesPersonID and Name from the Sales.Store table:

```
CREATE PROCEDURE Sales.usp_GetSalesPerson
AS
SELECT SalesPersonID, Name FROM Sales.Store
```

The following example shows calling the new stored procedure usp_GetSalesPerson and the returned results:

```
EXECUTE Sales.usp_GetSalesPerson

SalesPersonID     Name
------------------------------------------------
280               A Bike Store
283               Progressive Sports
277               Advanced Bike Components
277               Modular Cycle Systems
281               Metropolitan Sports Supply
276               Aerobic Exercise Company
```

In many cases, you will want to pass parameters to your stored procedures and return results. A parameter name begins with @ and can be any data type allowed for columns. A stored procedure can have as many as 2100 parameters. The OUTPUT keyword designates a parameter as an output parameter. The following code creates a stored procedure named usp_GetOneStore:

```
CREATE PROCEDURE Sales.usp_GetOneStore
(@InID int,
 @OutName nvarchar(50) OUTPUT)
AS
Set @OutName =
    (SELECT Name
     FROM Sales.Store
     WHERE CustomerID = @inID)
```

Notice that the procedure takes an input parameter named @InID and an output parameter named @OutName. The Set keyword sets the @OutName output parameter with the returned value of the SELECT statement.

The next listing shows calling the usp_GetOneStore stored procedure and its results:

```
DECLARE @StoreName nvarchar(50)
EXECUTE Sales.usp_GetOneStore 28, @StoreName Output
print @StoreName


----------------------
Commuter Bicycle Store
```

First you need to declare a variable for the output of the stored procedure. In this example, the @StoreName variable is declared as an nvarchar with a length of 50. Next the stored procedure is called with 28 as the input parameter and the

@StoreName variable as the output argument. The Output keyword must be used on the output argument on the EXECUTE statement.

To create a stored procedure from a CLR assembly, you must first register the assembly in SQL Server using the CREATE ASSEMBLY statement. You can then use the CREATE PROCEDURE statement to create the stored procedure. The following listing shows creating an assembly and then creating a stored procedure based on that assembly:

```
CREATE ASSEMBLY usp_GetSalesPerson
    FROM 'C:\temp\usp_GetSalesPerson.dll'

CREATE PROCEDURE usp_GetSalesPerson
    EXTERNAL NAME usp_GetSalesPerson.
        [usp_GetSalesPerson.StoredProcedures].usp_GetSalesPerson
```

A full description of creating an assembly for a stored procedure and deploying it to the server is covered in Chapter 3.

Functions

The CREATE FUNCTION statement can be used to create a standard T-SQL function, which is a saved collection of T-SQL statements, or it can be used to create a user-defined function (UDF) implemented through a class of an assembly in the Microsoft .NET Framework common language runtime (CLR). Two types of functions can be created: scalar-valued functions and table-valued functions. Functions that are scalar-valued return one of the scalar data types, whereas the RETURN clause of table-valued functions specifies TABLE.

When creating a function, you need to specify the function name and the RETURNS clause. Other options that can be included in the CREATE FUNCTION statement include a schema name and parameters. You can create a function with a maximum of 1024 parameters.

Scalar-Valued Functions

This example shows creating a simple scalar-valued function that returns the HouseName from the Sales.Warehouse table:

```
CREATE FUNCTION ufnGetHouseName
    ( @House int )
    RETURNS char(50)
    AS
    BEGIN
    RETURN
    (SELECT HouseName FROM Sales.Warehouse WHERE HouseID > @House)
    END
```

The following example shows calling the new function ufnGetHouseName and the return value:

```
SELECT dbo.ufnGetHouseName (1)

(No column name)
---------------------
Warehouse02
```

Table-Valued Functions

This next example shows creating a simple table-valued function that returns a table containing the SalesPersonID column of the Sales.Store table:

```
CREATE FUNCTION Sales.fn_PersonPerStore (@PersonID int)
RETURNS TABLE
AS
RETURN
(SELECT * FROM Sales.Store WHERE SalesPersonID = @PersonID)
```

Here you see calling the new function fn_PersonPerStore and the returned table results:

```
SELECT * FROM Sales.fn_PersonPerStore ('279')

CustomerID    Name                          SalesPersonID
------------------------------------------------------------
8             Exemplary Cycles              279
9             Tandem Bicycle Store          279
26            Stylish Department Stores     279
27            Sports Sales and Rental       279
45            Every Bike Shop               279
62            Manufacturers Inc             279
63            Metro Bike Mart               279
```

To create a UDF from a CLR assembly, you must first register the assembly in SQL Server using the CREATE ASSEMBLY statement. You can then use the CREATE FUNCTION statement to create the UDF. The following listing shows creating an assembly and then creating a UDF based on that assembly:

```
CREATE ASSEMBLY ufn_GetDataAsString
    FROM 'C:\temp\ufn_GetDataAsString.dll'

CREATE FUNCTION ufn_GetDateAsString()
RETURNS nvarchar(256)
EXTERNAL NAME
ufn_GetDateAsString.UserDefinedFunctions.ufn_GetDateAsString
```

A full description of creating an assembly for a UDF and deploying it to the server is covered in Chapter 3.

Triggers

A *trigger* is a kind of stored procedure that executes when an event occurs in the server. Data Manipulation Language (DML) triggers execute when a user tries to modify data. DML triggers are carried out on DML events such as INSERT, UPDATE, or DELETE statements. DML triggers are discussed in the next section of this chapter.

DDL Triggers

Earlier versions of SQL Server allowed triggers to be used only with DML events. SQL Server 2005 extends trigger usage by allowing triggers to be placed on Data Definition Language (DDL) events, including creating and dropping database objects such as tables, views, procedures, and logins. DDL triggers can be associated with CREATE, ALTER, and DROP statements. This enables the DBA to place restrictions on the type of DDL operations that can be performed in a given database, or you can use these triggers to send notification messages regarding important schema changes that take place in the database. The following example shows how to add a DDL trigger named NoTableUpdate to the DROP TABLE and ALTER TABLE DDL statements:

```
CREATE TRIGGER NoTableUpdate
ON DATABASE FOR DROP_TABLE, ALTER_TABLE
AS
PRINT 'DROP TABLE and ALTER TABLE statements are not allowed'
ROLLBACK
```

Here you can see how the new DDL trigger can be used to restrict the use of the DROP TABLE and ALTER TABLE statements. If an ALTER TABLE or DROP TABLE statement is issued, the NoTableUpdate trigger will print an error message and roll back the attempted DDL operation. An attempt to issue an ALTER TABLE statement in the database containing the NoTableUpdate trigger is shown here:

```
DROP TABLE and ALTER TABLE statements are not allowed
.Net SqlClient Data Provider: Msg 3609, Level 16, State 2, Line 1
Transaction ended in trigger. Batch has been aborted.
```

To make alterations to the tables in a database after this trigger is in place, you will first need to drop the DDL trigger.

Security

Securing a database from unwanted access is a must in any organization. With SQL Server 2005, the database server is in locked-down mode by default, which means each service and feature must be explicitly activated.

You can use the following T-SQL statements to set up authority and rights to your users for access to SQL Server 2005.

Logins

Logins are created to allow users admission to the server. For users to access the databases in the server, you need to create User objects, as described later in this chapter. There are four types of logins you can specify for gaining access to the server: SQL Server logins, Windows logins, certificate-mapped logins, and asymmetric key-mapped logins. Logins from certificates or asymmetric keys can be created only if the certificate or asymmetric key already exists in the master database. The following listing is an example of creating a login with a password:

```
CREATE LOGIN TecaGuest WITH PASSWORD = 'iMsoiLwR4E' MUST_CHANGE
```

In this example, the MUST_CHANGE option requires the user to change the password the first time they connect to the server.

Credentials

A *credential* is associated with a login, as it is a record that contains authentication information when SQL Server is used in Mixed authentication mode. The following listing creates a credential for AlternateGuest with a Windows user identity of Teca01Guest:

```
CREATE CREDENTIAL AlternateGuest WITH IDENTITY = 'Teca01Guest'
```

After you create a credential, you can map it to a SQL Server login by using CREATE LOGIN or ALTER LOGIN.

```
CREATE LOGIN Teca02Guest WITH PASSWORD = 'MBSim1tl',
    CREDENTIAL = AlternateGuest
```

Users

The User object is used to allow users access to the databases on the server. The CREATE USER statement maps a new database user to a login. The new user can also be restricted from mapping to a login. The following example uses the WITHOUT

LOGIN clause, which creates a user that is restricted to their own database. The user is not allowed to connect to other databases and cannot be mapped to any login:

```
CREATE USER TecaRestrictedUser WITHOUT LOGIN
```

Roles

Roles are database-level objects used for granting permissions to a group of role members. For example, you can create a role for the payroll department of your organization, configure the database-level permissions of the role, and then add only the payroll personnel to the role. The following code creates a Payroll role.

```
CREATE ROLE Payroll
```

Schemas

Schemas are objects that you can use to logically group together database objects like tables and views, and to set access rights to those objects. The CREATE SCHEMA statement can create a schema in the current database, as well as tables and views within the new schema. The following creates a schema named MonthSales:

```
CREATE SCHEMA MonthSales
```

Master Key

Each database can have a single master key that is a root encryption object for all keys, certificates, and data in the database. The following shows creating a master key:

```
CREATE MASTER KEY ENCRYPTION BY PASSWORD = '11y471%9dwvyb2ayup9#$Nn'
```

The created master key is encrypted with the triple DES algorithm and stored in two places. One storage location is the sys.symmetric_keys database table and encrypted by the supplied password; the second location is the sys.databases table in the master database and encrypted using the Service Master Key. You can use the master key to create three other types of keys: asymmetric keys, certificates, or symmetric keys.

Asymmetric keys are used for public key cryptography pairing a public and private key, certificates are basically wrappers for a public key, and symmetric keys are used for shared secrets where the same key both encrypts and decrypts data.

Asymmetric Keys   An asymmetric key is a security entity that uses the RSA algorithm with key sizes of 512, 1024, or 2048 bits. In its default form, the asymmetric key contains a public key and a private key, and the private key is managed and protected by the database master key. You can also specify a password-protected private key that you manage. The following shows the creation of an asymmetric key that is protected by the database master key:

```
CREATE ASYMMETRIC KEY AsymKeySales WITH ALGORITHM = RSA_2048
```

Certificates   A *certificate* is a security file or assembly that uses the X.509 standard encryption algorithm and supports X.509 V1 fields. The CREATE CERTIFICATE statement can load a certificate from either a file or an assembly. The following example creates a certificate from the master database:

```
CREATE CERTIFICATE TecaCert09
    WITH SUBJECT = 'TCert08 certificate in master database',
    EXPIRY_DATE = '01/31/2008'
```

You can then create a login mapped to the certificate.

```
CREATE LOGIN TCert08 FROM CERTIFICATE TecaCert08;
```

Symmetric Keys   The symmetric key security entity must be encrypted by using at least one certificate, password, symmetric key, or asymmetric key. It can be encrypted by using multiple certificates, passwords, symmetric keys, and asymmetric keys at the same time.

With symmetric keys, only one key is used for encryption and decryption, and both participants in the encrypting/decrypting action must know this key, but its performance is much faster than that of asymmetric keys. SQL Server supports the most widely used symmetric key algorithms, including DES, triple DES, RC2, RC4, DESX, AES_128, AES_192, and AES_256. The following listing shows creating a symmetric key:

```
CREATE SYMMETRIC KEY SymKeySales WITH ALGORITHM = AES_256
    ENCRYPTION BY PASSWORD 'cNIu284ry$bd%JDqT'
```

Storage for Searching

SQL Server contains full-text searching capabilities that allow you to search data that isn't necessarily an exact match to the full text of a column or a part of a column. For example, you can search for two words that are near each other, or you can perform a "fuzzy" search where SQL Server matches a word or phrase that is close to the search word or phrase.

Full-text searching is accomplished with the Microsoft Full-Text Engine for SQL Server (MSFTESQL) that runs as a service on the operating system. The MSFTESQL service is installed by default when you install SQL Server, but it runs only when full-text search is being used. MSFTESQL handles the actions of full-text searching, such as filtering and word breaking, as well as memory resources. Any indexes you build for full-text searching are kept in full-text catalogs and can be backed up and restored.

Full-Text Catalogs

Use the CREATE FULLTEXT CATALOG statement to create a full-text catalog for a database. Full-text catalog names are limited to 120 characters and cannot be created in the master, model, or tempdb databases.

```
CREATE FULLTEXT CATALOG StoreSearch
```

Once a catalog is created, you can define full-text indexing on a table in the database and associate it with the catalog. The following listing shows a full-text search on the Sales.Store table where the Name column contains the word "cycle":

```
SELECT Name
FROM Sales.Store
WHERE CONTAINS(Name, ' "*cycle*" ')
```

Querying and Updating with T-SQL DML

In the next section of this chapter you'll see how T-SQL can be used to query and update SQL Server databases. A full explanation of using T-SQL is beyond the scope of this chapter. Writing SQL queries is a topic that's big enough to warrant its own book, and in fact several books have been written on the topic. This chapter will present the core T-SQL concepts that you'll need to get started writing T-SQL queries and to better understand how they work.

Select and Joins

The SELECT statement is undoubtedly the key building block for using T-SQL as a basis for queries from your data access applications and T-SQL scripts, stored procedures, and functions. This is true even for client and *n*-tiered applications that connect to SQL Server using ODBC, OLE DB, and ADO.NET. These data access frameworks provide an object-oriented data access framework that makes it easy for applications to work with the data retrieved from a relational database, but at their core they all still submit T-SQL commands to retrieve and update data from the SQL Server database.

Building Queries Using the SELECT Statement

In its most basic form, the SELECT statement retrieves the rows and columns from a table. The following example illustrates using the SELECT statement to retrieve all of the rows and columns from the HumanResources.Department table in the sample AdventureWorks database:

```
use adventureworks
go
SELECT * FROM HumanResources.Department
```

The asterisk is a shorthand notation that indicates all of the columns will be retrieved. The FROM clause indicates that name of the table that will be accessed. This name can optionally be qualified with the full path to the database. For example, the query could have used the form AdventureWorks.HumanResources.Department. However, use of the AdventureWorks statement sets the current database to AdventureWorks, making it unnecessary to fully qualify the name.

NOTE

Using the SELECT * statement is fine for ad hoc queries. However, for most production applications, it is better to limit the data returned from the query by explicitly supplying just the desired columns in the SELECT statement as is shown in the following examples.

You can see the results of this basic SELECT statement in the following listing:

```
DepartmentID Name                          GroupName
------------ ----------------------------- -----------------------------------
1            Engineering                   Research and Development
2            Tool Design                   Research and Development
3            Sales                         Sales and Marketing
4            Marketing                     Sales and Marketing
5            Purchasing                    Inventory Management
6            Research and Development      Research and Development
7            Production                    Manufacturing
8            Production Control            Manufacturing
9            Human Resources               Executive General and Administration
10           Finance                       Executive General and Administration
11           Information Services          Executive General and Administration
12           Document Control              Quality Assurance
13           Quality Assurance             Quality Assurance
14           Facilities and Maintenance    Executive General and Administration
15           Shipping and Receiving        Inventory Management
16           Executive                     Executive General and Administration

(16 row(s) affected)
```

NOTE

The preceding is a partial listing of the complete result set. It was cut back to fit the publication page size.

Filtering Results Using the WHERE Clause

The WHERE clause is used to filter the rows that are returned by the SELECT statement. The following example illustrates using the WHERE clause to return a single row from the HumanResources.Department file:

```
SELECT DepartmentID, Name FROM HumanResources.Department
  Where DepartmentID = 7
```

Here the SELECT statement is retrieving only the values in the DepartmentID and Name columns. The WHERE clause will return a single row because only one row meets the equal condition. In other words, there's only one row in the HumanResources.Department table where the value of the DepartmentID column is equal to 7. The results are shown here:

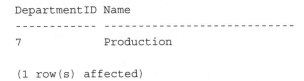

```
DepartmentID Name
------------ ----------------------------
7            Production

(1 row(s) affected)
```

While this example illustrates use of the equal expression, the WHERE clause is extremely flexible and supports a number of different expressions. The common expressions are listed in Table 2-1. A complete list can be found in Books On-Line.

Renaming Columns with AS

You can also use the AS keyword to rename the column headings that are returned by a SELECT statement. By default, the column headings from the source are used; however, AS lets you substitute new column headings as you can see here:

```
SELECT DepartmentID As ID, Name As Title FROM HumanResources.Department
  Where DepartmentID BETWEEN 5 AND 10
```

Here again this query retrieves the DepartmentID and Name columns from the HumanResources.Department table. However, in this example, the column heading of ID is substituted for DepartmentID, and the heading of Title is substituted for Name.

Condition	Description
=	Tests for an equal condition.
<>	Tests for a not-equal condition.
!=	Tests for a not-equal condition.
>	Tests for a greater-than condition.
>=	Tests for a greater-than or equal-to condition.
!>	Tests for a not-greater-than condition.
<	Tests for a less-than condition.
<=	Tests for a less-than or equal-to condition.
!<	Tests for a not-less-then condition.
[NOT] LIKE	Tests for a matching pattern.
ESCAPE 'escape_character'	Allows a wildcard character to be searched for.
[NOT] BETWEEN	Tests for a between condition. The AND keyword separates the starting and ending values.
IS [NOT] NULL	Tests for a null or optionally a not-null condition.
CONTAINS	Tests for fuzzy matching or words or phrases.
[NOT] IN	Tests if a value is included or excluded from a list. The list can be a set of constants enclosed in parentheses or a subquery.

Table 2-1   *Common Expressions for a WHERE Clause*

In addition, the WHERE clause restricts the rows returned to just those rows where the value of the DepartmentID column is between 5 and 10. The result set with the new column heading is shown here:

```
ID      Title
------  ----------------------------------------
5       Purchasing
6       Research and Development
7       Production
8       Production Control
9       Human Resources10       Finance

(6 row(s) affected)
```

Ordering Results with ORDER BY

In the preceding example the results were returned in the order of the DepartmentID column in the HumanResources.Department table. You can also use the SELECT statement's ORDER BY clause to order the results in alternate sequences. The following listing shows how to use the ORDER BY clause to order the results according to the Name column. The default order is ascending, but you can also specify descending results:

```
SELECT DepartmentID, Name
 FROM HumanResources.Department
 ORDER By Name
```

Here the DepartmentID column is selected from the HumanResources.Department table, and the ORDER BY clause is used to order the result by the values contained in the Name column. The results are shown here:

```
DepartmentID Name
------------ ------------------------------------
12           Document Control
1            Engineering
16           Executive
14           Facilities and Maintenance
10           Finance
9            Human Resources
11           Information Services
4            Marketing
7            Production
8            Production Control
5            Purchasing
13           Quality Assurance
6            Research and Development
3            Sales
15           Shipping and Receiving
2            Tool Design

(16 row(s) affected)
```

Grouping Results with GROUP BY

The GROUP BY clause enables you to group subgroups of the rows in a result set together. This is useful for applying aggregate functions to these groups. In the following listing the GROUP BY clause is used to group the results returned from the HumanResources.Department table according to the GroupName column.

In addition, the COUNT(*) operator is used to aggregate a count of all of the rows contained in each group:

```
SELECT GroupName, Count(*) As Departments
  FROM HumanResources.Department
  GROUP BY GroupName
```

Here the result set is created by selecting the GroupName column from the HumanResources.Department table, and the COUNT(*) operator is used to return the count of rows for each group. The GROUP BY clause specifies that the result set will be grouped according to the values in the GroupName column. You can see the results of using the GROUP BY clause in the following listing:

```
GroupName                            Departments
------------------------------------ -----------
Executive General and Administration 5
Inventory Management                 2
Manufacturing                        2
Quality Assurance                    2
Research and Development             3
Sales and Marketing                  2

(6 row(s) affected)
```

Eliminating Duplicate Rows with SELECT DISTINCT

For cases where you want to eliminate duplicate values in the result set, you can use the SELECT DISTINCT statement. For example, as you may have noticed in some of the previous listings, multiple occurrences of some of the values in the GroupName column exist for several of the rows in the HumanResources.Department table. You can use SELECT DINSTINCT as shown in the following listing to create a query that eliminates the duplicate results.

```
SELECT Distinct GroupName
  FROM HumanResources.Department
```

In the example, the SELECT DISTINCT statement retrieves all of the rows from the HumanResources.Department table, with the DISTINCT clause eliminating the duplicate values. You can see the results of the SELECT DISTINCT statement in the following listing:

```
GroupName
-------------------------------------------------
Executive General and Administration
Inventory Management
Manufacturing
Quality Assurance
Research and Development
Sales and Marketing

(6 row(s) affected)
```

Creating Tables Using SELECT INTO

Using SELECT INTO enables you to create tables using the results of a query. The data type of the columns used will all match the data type of the original columns. You can see an example of the SELECT INTO statement in the following listing:

```
SELECT * INTO #TempDepartment
 FROM HumanResources.Department
 Where GroupName LIKE '%Ex%'

SELECT * FROM #TempDepartment
```

In this listing you can see where a SELECT * statement is used to retrieve all of the columns from the HumanResources.Department table. The INTO clause directs the results of the SELECT statement into the temporary table named #TempDepartment. The WHERE clause filters the rows to only those rows where the value in the GroupName column contains the characters 'Ex'. After the #TempDepartment table is created, another SELECT statement is used to show the contents of the #TempDepartment table.

```
(5 row(s) affected)
DepartmentID Name                     GroupName
------------ ------------------------ ------------------------------------
9            Human Resources          Executive General and Administration
10           Finance                  Executive General and Administration
11           Information Services     Executive General and Administration
14           Facilities and Maintenance Executive General and Administration

16           Executive                Executive General and Administration
(5 row(s) affected)
```

Using the TOP Clause

The Top clause can be used to return a given percentage of the result set. In SQL Server 2000 you were forced to use a constant value in conjunction with the TOP clause. In other words, you could select the TOP 5 or TOP 10 rows, where the value of 5 or 10 was a constant. With SQL Server 2005 the TOP function now enables the use of an expression in conjunction with the TOP clause. An expression can be any allowed T-SQL expression, including a variable or a scalar subquery. The TOP clause is also supported in the INSERT, UPDATE, and DELETE statements. This gives the TOP clause a great deal more flexibility than ever before. An example of using the new TOP clause is shown here:

```
DECLARE @MyTop INT
SET @MyTop = 5
SELECT TOP (@MyTop) DepartmentID, Name FROM HumanResources.Department
```

The example returns the top 5 results from the HumanResources.Department table. The results of using the TOP clause are shown in the following listing:

```
DepartmentID Name
------------ ------------------------------------
12           Document Control
1            Engineering
16           Executive
14           Facilities and Maintenance
10           Finance

(5 row(s) affected)
```

Retrieving Related Data Using Joins

The previous examples illustrated the use of the basic SELECT statement that was working with a single table. The SELECT statement can also handle much more complex requirements by using the JOIN clause to join together rows from multiple tables, producing a single result set. Using joins is common in a relational database system like SQL Server, as the data composing the database tables is typically normalized to various degrees. Therefore related data is typically stored in several different tables that are intended to be joined together using columns from each table that contain common data. The following example illustrates using a three-table inner join to retrieve selected data from the HumanResources.Department table, the HumanResources.Employee table, and the HumanResources.Contact table:

```
SELECT e.EmployeeID, c.FirstName, c.LastName, e.Title,
    d.Name AS Department
FROM HumanResources.Employee e
    INNER JOIN Person.Contact c
    ON c.ContactID = e.ContactID
    INNER JOIN HumanResources.EmployeeDepartmentHistory h
    ON e.EmployeeID = h.EmployeeID
    INNER JOIN HumanResources.Department d
    ON h.DepartmentID = d.DepartmentID
Where h.EndDate IS NOT Null
```

In this example the SELECT statement specifies that the returned result set will consist of the EmployeeID and Title columns from the HumanResources.Employee table, the FirstName and LastName columns from the Person.Contacts table, and the Name column from the HumanResources.Department table. To make it easier to work with the column names, short name aliases are used for each of the tables. For example, the HumanResources.Employee table uses an alias of e, the HumanResources.Contacts table uses an alias of c, and the HumanResources.Department column uses an alias of d.

While the SELECT statement defines the result set that will be returned, the join conditions that tell SQL Server how to retrieve the data are specified in the FROM clause. In this example the HumanResources.Employee table is joined to the Person.Contact table on the Contact ID to retrieve the employee name information. Then the HumanResources.Employee table is joined to the HumanResources .EmployeeDepartmentHistory table on the EmployeeID column to retrieve the Department ID for the employee. Then the HumanResources.Employee table is joined to the HumanResources.Department table to retrieve the Department name. Finally, the Where clause indicates that only the rows where the EndDate in the EmployeeDepartmentHistory column are not null will be selected. In other words, the employee is still part of that department.

You can see the results of this three-table join in the following listing:

```
EmployeeID  FirstName  LastName  Title                      Department
----------- ---------- --------- -------------------------- -----------------
4           Rob        Walters   Senior Tool Designer       Engineering
6           David      Bradley   Marketing Manager          Purchasing
96          William    Vong      Scheduling Assistant       Production
140         Laura      Norman    Chief Financial Officer    Finance
274         Sheela     Word      Purchasing Manager         Marketing
274         Sheela     Word      Purchasing Manager         Quality Assurance

(6 row(s) affected)
```

Join Type	Description
INNER	All matching pairs of rows are returned. Unmatched rows from both tables are discarded. Inner is the default join type.
FULL [OUTER]	Rows from either the left or right table that do not meet the join condition are included in the result set. Any columns that correspond to the other table are set to NULL.
LEFT [OUTER]	Rows from the left table not meeting the join condition are included in the result set. Any columns from the other table are set to NULL.
RIGHT [OUTER]	Rows from the right table not meeting the join condition are included in the result set. Any columns that correspond to the other table are set to NULL.

Table 2-2   *Common Join Types*

While this example illustrates the use of the inner join, SQL Server supports a number of additional join conditions. The common join types are listed in Table 2-2. A complete list can be found in Books On-Line.

Combining Related Data Using UNIONs

The UNION statement combines the results of multiple queries into a single result set. In order to perform a UNION, the data being combined must meet two conditions. First, the number and the order of the columns must be the same. Next, the data types must be compatible.

```
SELECT *
INTO dbo.FirstHalfDept
FROM HumanResources.Department
WHERE DepartmentID <= 8
GO


SELECT *
INTO dbo.SecondHalfDept
FROM HumanResources.Department
WHERE DepartmentID > 8
GO


SELECT *
FROM dbo.FirstHalfDept
UNION
SELECT *
FROM dbo.SecondHalfDept
ORDER BY DepartmentID;
GO
```

The code block that you can see at the top of this listing essentially creates a new table named dbo.FirstHalfDept. This table is based on the rows in the HumanResources .Department table where the DepartmentID is less than or equal to 8. The next code block creates a second new table named dbo.SecondHalfDept using the rows in the HumanResources.Department table where the DepartmentID is greater than 8. The UNION statement will then take these two results sets and join them back together into a single result set.

The results of the union of the dbo.FirstHalfDept table and the dbo.SecondHalfDept table are shown in the following listing. As you can see, the UNION operation merged the two tables together back into a single table with the same contents as the original HumanResources.Department table that was used as a basis to create the other two tables:

```
(8 row(s) affected)

(8 row(s) affected)

DepartmentID Name                    GroupName
------------ ----------------------- ----------------------------------------
1            Engineering             Research and Development
2            Tool Design             Research and Development
3            Sales                   Sales and Marketing
4            Marketing               Sales and Marketing
5            Purchasing              Inventory Management
6            Research and Development Research and Development
7            Production              Manufacturing
8            Production Control      Manufacturing
9            Human Resources         Executive General and Administration
10           Finance                 Executive General and Administration
11           Information Services    Executive General and Administration
12           Document Control        Quality Assurance
13           Quality Assurance       Quality Assurance
14           Facilities and Maintenance Executive General and Administration
15           Shipping and Receiving  Inventory Management
16           Executive               Executive General and Administration

(16 row(s) affected)
```

Using Subqueries

A *subquery* is a query that's nested inside of another T-SQL query. Subqueries can be nested within SELECT, INSERT, UPDATE, or DELETE statements. More information about using INSERT, UPDATE, and DELETE statements is presented later in this chapter.

The following example illustrates using a subquery to retrieve all of the names of the employees in the AdventureWorks database who have the title of Tool Designer:

```
SELECT FirstName, LastName, e.Title
FROM Person.Contact c
Join HumanResources.Employee e
On e.ContactID = c.ContactID
WHERE EmployeeID IN
  (SELECT EmployeeID FROM
    HumanResources.Employee  WHERE Title = 'Tool Designer')
```

The SELECT statement specifies that the result set will contain three columns. The FirstName and LastName columns come from the Person.Contact table, while the Title column comes from the HumanResources.EmployeeID table. The Person.Contact table and the HumanResources.EmployeeID table are joined on the ContactID column. The subquery then further restricts the result set by specifying that only the rows from the HumanResources.EmployeeID table will be used where the value in the Title column is equal to 'Tool Designer'.

```
FirstName   LastName   Title
----------  ---------  --------------
Thierry     D'Hers     Tool Designer
Janice      Galvin     Tool Designer

(2 row(s) affected)
```

NOTE

In many cases, the same results that are produced using subqueries can also be produced using joins.

Row-at-a-Time Processing Using Cursors

T-SQL is a set-at-a-time language that is designed for dealing with sets of data at one time. However, there are circumstances where you may need to deal with the data contained in a table or result set on a row-by-row basis. *Cursors* are the T-SQL mechanism that enable single-row processing. Cursors limit scalability because they hold locks on the table while the cursor is open; however, they do provide a great deal of flexibility in dealing with individual results in a result set. The following example illustrates using a cursor to process a result set based on the HumanResources.Department table one row at a time.

```
DECLARE @ThisDept INT
DECLARE DeptCursor CURSOR FOR
   SELECT DepartmentID from HumanResources.Department
OPEN DeptCursor
WHILE @@FETCH_STATUS = 0
BEGIN
   PRINT 'Processing Department: ' + RTRIM(CAST(@ThisDept AS VARCHAR(10)))
    FETCH NEXT FROM DeptCursor INTO @ThisDept
END
CLOSE DeptCursor
DEALLOCATE DeptCursor
```

At the top of this listing you can see where two variables are declared. The first variable, named @ThisDept, will be used to store the value of the DepartmentID column that's returned by the cursor. The next variable is a handle for the cursor named DeptCursor. The rows this cursor will operate over are defined in the following SELECT statement, which returns just the DepartmentID column for all of the rows in the HumanResources.Department table. After the cursor has been defined, it's then opened using the OPEN statement, and then a WHILE loop is used to process all of the rows returned from the HumanResources.Department table. The WHILE loop will continue processing until the value of the @@FETCH_STATUS variable is not equal to zero, indicating that all of the rows have been read from the result set. BEGIN and END statements delimit the block of T-SQL statements that will perform the processing. In this example a simple PRINT statement is used to print the value of the DepartmentID column read, and then a FETCH NEXT operation is used to read the next row from the table. The output from this cursor processing example is listed here:

```
Processing Department: 1
Processing Department: 2
Processing Department: 3
Processing Department: 4
Processing Department: 5
Processing Department: 6
Processing Department: 7
Processing Department: 8
Processing Department: 9
Processing Department: 10
Processing Department: 11
Processing Department: 12
Processing Department: 13
Processing Department: 14
Processing Department: 15
Processing Department: 16
```

Cursor Type	Description
INSENSITIVE	Defines a cursor that makes a temporary copy of the data to be used by the cursor. All requests to the cursor are answered from this temporary table in tempdb. Modifications made to base tables are not reflected in the cursor.
SCROLL	Specifies that all fetch options (FIRST, LAST, PRIOR, NEXT, RELATIVE, ABSOLUTE) are available. SCROLL cannot be specified if FAST_FORWARD is also specified.
READ ONLY	Defines the cursor as read-only. The cursor cannot be referenced in a WHERE CURRENT OF clause in an UPDATE or DELETE statement.
UPDATE	Defines updatable columns that can be used with the cursor.
FORWARD_ONLY	Specifies that the cursor can only be scrolled from the first to the last row. FETCH NEXT is the only supported fetch option.
STATIC	Defines a cursor that makes a temporary copy of the data to be used by the cursor. All requests to the cursor are answered from this temporary table in tempdb. Modifications made to base tables are not reflected in the cursor.
KEYSET	Specifies that the membership of the rows in the cursor is fixed when the cursor is opened. The set of keys that uniquely identify the rows are built into a table in tempdb.
DYNAMIC	Defines a cursor that reflects all data changes made to the rows in its result set. The data values, order, and membership of the rows can change on each fetch.
FAST_FORWARD	Specifies a FORWARD_ONLY, READ_ONLY cursor with performance optimizations enabled. FAST_FORWARD cannot be specified if SCROLL or FOR_UPDATE is specified.
READ_ONLY	Defines the cursor as read-only. The cursor cannot be referenced in a WHERE CURRENT OF clause in an UPDATE or DELETE statement.
SCROLL_LOCKS	Specifies that positioned updates made through the cursor are guaranteed to succeed. SQL Server locks the rows as they are read into the cursor to ensure their availability for updating.
OPTIMISTIC	Specifies that positioned updates made through the cursor do not succeed if the row has been updated, since it was read into the cursor. SQL Server does not lock rows. Instead it uses timestamp column values or a checksum value to determine whether the row was modified. If the row was modified, the attempted update will fail.

Table 2-3   *Cursor Types*

SQL Server 2005 supports a number of different cursor types. The most common ones are presented in Table 2-3. For a complete listing, refer to Books On-Line.

Using Common Table Expressions (CTE)

Another new T-SQL feature is support for *common table expressions (CTEs)*. CTEs are a lot like views; however, they are embedded in a query. The main reason Microsoft introduced CTEs to SQL Server 2005 is to provide a mechanism for handling recursive queries. Recursion is achieved by the fact that a CTE is allowed to refer to itself. To avoid the possibility of overwhelming the system with a poorly constructed recursive query, SQL Server implements a server-wide limit on the maximum depth of recursion allowed, with a default maximum of 100 levels. A CTE is implemented as a part of the WITH keyword and can be used with SELECT, INSERT, UPDATE, and DELETE statements. To implement recursive queries using the new CTE, you must use a special syntax as shown in the simple code example that follows. This example performs a simple recursive query using the HumanResources.Employee table in the example AdventureWorks database:

```
USE AdventureWorks
WITH EmployeeChart(EmployeeID, ManagerID, Title)
AS
(SELECT EmployeeID, ManagerID, Title
 FROM HumanResources.Employee
 WHERE EmployeeID = 3
 UNION ALL
SELECT L2.EmployeeID, L2. ManagerID, L2.Title
 FROM HumanResources.Employee AS L2
 JOIN EmployeeChart
  ON L2.ManagerID = EmployeeChart.EmployeeID)
SELECT * FROM EmployeeChart
```

To use a CTE, you first write a WITH clause, which you use to name the CTE and specify the columns to bind to a SELECT statement. There must be a semicolon in front of the WITH keyword if it is not the first statement in a batch. The first SELECT statement is called the *anchor member*, and it must not refer to itself. In this case, it retrieves the EmployeeID, ManagerID, and Title columns from the AdventureWorks Employee table. The second SELECT statement references the CTE and is called the *recursive member*. In this case it retrieves the same columns and is joined to the anchor member on the ManagerID column. You can see the results of this CTE in the following listing:

```
EmployeeID  ManagerID   Title
----------- ----------- ----------------------------------------
3           12          Engineering Manager
4           3           Senior Tool Designer
9           3           Design Engineer
11          3           Design Engineer
158         3           Research and Development Manager
263         3           Senior Tool Designer
```

267	3	Senior Design Engineer
270	3	Design Engineer
5	263	Tool Designer
265	263	Tool Designer
79	158	Research and Development Engineer
114	158	Research and Development Engineer
217	158	Research and Development Manager

```
(13 row(s) affected)
```

Using PIVOT and UNPIVOT

The addition of the PIVOT and UNPIVOT relational operators is another new feature found in SQL Server 2005's T-SQL. The new PIVOT and UNPIVOT operators are most useful for OLAP scenarios where you're dealing with tabular data rather than relational data. The PIVOT operator transforms a set of rows into columns. As you might expect, the UNPIVOT operator reverses the PIVOT operator, transforming the pivoted columns back into rows. However, depending on the situation, the UNPIVOT operation may not exactly reverse the PIVOT operation. This situation occurs because the PIVOT operation is often set up such that it will omit certain values. If a value is omitted during the PIVOT operation, it obviously cannot be unpivoted. Therefore, the UNPIVOT operator doesn't always result in an exact mirror image of the original pivot condition.

Using SQL Server 2005's new PIVOT operator, you can transform this result set, which lists each year vertically, into a result set that lists the years horizontally for each customer and sums up the number of orders for each year. The sample PIVOT operation is shown in the following listing:

```
SELECT VendorID, [244] AS POCount1, [231] AS POCount2, [266] AS POCount3
FROM
(SELECT PurchaseOrderID, EmployeeID, VendorID
FROM Purchasing.PurchaseOrderHeader) p
PIVOT
(
COUNT (PurchaseOrderID)
FOR EmployeeID IN
( [244], [231], [266] )
) AS pvt
ORDER BY VendorID
```

Here the PIVOT operation is used with the SELECT statement to create a new result set. The first value of the pivot operator identifies the value that will be placed in the pivot column. In this example the COUNT(OrderID) aggregation sums up the number of orders for each pivot value. The FOR keyword identifies the column whose values will be pivoted. This example shows the pivot operation being performed on the OrderYear column. The values identified by the IN keyword list are the values from the pivoted column that will be used as column headings. You can see the pivoted result set in the following listing:

```
CustomerID  2000         2001         2002         2003         2004
----------- ----------- ----------- ----------- ----------- -----------
1           3           2           1           1           1
Warning: Null value is eliminated by an aggregate or other SET operation.

(1 row(s) affected)
```

Modifying Data

SQL's Data Manipulation Language (DML) provides data retrieval and update capabilities for a relational database system such as SQL Server. In this part of the chapter you will see how to use the Insert, Update, and Delete statements of DML. The Insert statement inserts new rows into tables or views. The Update statement is used to modify column values in existing rows. The Delete statement clears existing data from rows in a table or view. You'll also see how to use the BULK INSERT statement to load data from a data file into a table and how to commit or roll back database actions using transactions.

Insert

The INSERT statement is used to insert data into a table or a view. You can insert data into your tables several different ways. You can insert data into a table by simply specifying the table name, the columns into which you are inserting the data, and the actual value of the data to insert. You can insert data into a table by using a SELECT statement inside the INSERT statement to retrieve data from another table and store the results into your table. You can also use the EXECUTE statement inside the INSERT statement to execute a stored procedure and store the results in your table. For the examples in the following sections of this chapter, we will create a table called OrderSum. The code for creating our example table is listed here:

```
CREATE TABLE OrderSum
    (OrderID INT,
     CustomerID INT,
     OrderDate NCHAR(10))
```

The example table OrderSum has two integer columns, OrderID and CustomerID, and one character column, OrderDate.

INSERT ... VALUES   To simply insert data into a table, you can specify the table name, columns, and values in the INSERT statement. The following example inserts one row of data into the example OrderSum table:

```
INSERT INTO OrderSum
    (OrderID, CustomerID, OrderDate)
VALUES
    (100, 1, '01/28/2005')
```

The results from the insert are shown here:

```
SELECT * FROM OrderSum

OrderID     CustomerID  OrderDate
----------- ----------- ----------
100          1          01/28/2005
(1 row(s) affected)
```

When you insert a value into every column of the table, you can omit the list of column names from the INSERT statement, but for clarity and to reduce errors, it is recommended that you include the list of column names.

INSERT ... SELECT   Another way to insert data into your tables is to use a nested SELECT statement within the INSERT statement. Using the SELECT statement, you can retrieve data from another table and populate your table with the results. The code for using a nested SELECT statement is shown here:

```
INSERT OrderSum
    (OrderID, CustomerID, OrderDate)
    SELECT
        SalesOrderID,
        CustomerID,
        CONVERT(nchar(10), OrderDate, 101)
    FROM Sales.SalesOrderHeader
    WHERE SalesOrderID > 75120
```

As you can see, the SELECT statement is selecting three columns from the Sales .SalesOrderHeader table where the SalesOrderID value is greater than 75120, and the result of the select is inserted into the OrderSum table. The OrderSum table is shown here:

```
SELECT * FROM OrderSum

OrderID      CustomerID  OrderDate
-----------  ----------- ----------
100          1           01/28/2005
75121        15251       07/31/2004
75122        15868       07/31/2004
75123        18759       07/31/2004
(4 row(s) affected)
```

INSERT . . . TOP   Using the TOP keyword, you can specify a certain number or percent of rows to insert into your table. What follows is an example of using the TOP keyword to insert only the top five rows into the OrderSum table from the Sales.SalesOrderHeader table:

```
INSERT TOP (5) INTO OrderSum
    (OrderID, CustomerID, OrderDate)
    SELECT
        SalesOrderID,
        CustomerID,
        CONVERT(nchar(10), OrderDate, 101)
    FROM Sales.SalesOrderHeader
```

The results of the TOP keyword insert are shown here:

```
OrderID      CustomerID  OrderDate
-----------  ----------- ----------
100          1           01/28/2005
75121        15251       07/31/2004
75122        15868       07/31/2004
75123        18759       07/31/2004
43659        676         07/01/2001
43660        117         07/01/2001
43661        442         07/01/2001
43662        227         07/01/2001
43663        510         07/01/2001
(9 row(s) affected)
```

INSERT . . . EXECUTE   The next example shows how to use an EXECUTE expression in the INSERT statement to execute a stored procedure that returns rows to be inserted into the table. The stored procedure, usp_GetOneSalesOrder, takes one input parameter and retrieves a row from the Sales.SalesOrderHeader table. The code to create the stored procedure is shown here:

```
CREATE PROCEDURE usp_GetOneSalesOrder
    (@InID int)
AS
    (SELECT
        SalesOrderID,
        CustomerID,
        CONVERT(nchar(10), OrderDate, 101)
     FROM Sales.SalesOrderHeader
     WHERE SalesOrderID = @inID)
```

The next code listing shows how to call the stored procedure in the INSERT statement and the results of the insert:

```
INSERT OrderSum
    (OrderID, CustomerID, OrderDate)
EXECUTE usp_GetOneSalesOrder 43670

SELECT * FROM OrderSum

OrderID      CustomerID  OrderDate
-----------  ----------- ----------
100          1           01/28/2005
75121        15251       07/31/2004
75122        15868       07/31/2004
75123        18759       07/31/2004
43659        676         07/01/2001
43660        117         07/01/2001
43661        442         07/01/2001
43662        227         07/01/2001
43663        510         07/01/2001
43670        504         07/01/2001
(10 row(s) affected)
```

Bulk Insert

You can use a BULK INSERT statement to load an entire database table or view from a data file. In SQL Server 2005, BULK INSERT has been enhanced to enforce stricter data validation and data checks of data read from a file. Forms of invalid data, such as uneven byte length for Unicode data, that could be bulk-loaded in earlier versions of SQL Server might not load into the table now. In previous versions of SQL Server, the data would be loaded into the table, and an error would be returned to the user during the query if the data was invalid. By validating the data during the load, query failures on invalid data are kept to a minimum.

The BULK INSERT statement allows you to specify the database, schema, and table or view name to which the data is being loaded and the data file where the data is being loaded from. The data file is in a user-defined format, and you can specify to the BULK INSERT statement how the data is formatted. For example, you can specify a field terminator character, specify a row terminator character, set the first row and the last row of the data file to start and end the loading, specify the code page of the data in the data file, and set to check constraints on the table or view during the load process.

The following code listing shows the OrderSumFile.txt text file that contains data to load to the OrderSum table:

```
100,1,01/28/2005
75121,15251,07/31/2004
75122,15868,07/31/2004
75123,18759,07/31/2004
43659,676,07/01/2001
43660,117,07/01/2001
43661,442,07/01/2001
43662,227,07/01/2001
43663,510,07/01/2001
43670,504,07/01/2001
```

The next listing shows the BULK INSERT statement for the OrderSumFile.txt file. You can see that the location, including the full path for the file, is specified in the FROM clause and that the FIELDTERMINATOR character is set to a comma (,) and the ROWTERMINATOR character is set to the newline character (\n).

```
BULK INSERT OrderSum
    FROM 'C:\temp\OrderSumFile.txt'
    WITH
      (
          FIELDTERMINATOR =',',
          ROWTERMINATOR ='\n'
      )

(10 row(s) affected)
```

Update

The UPDATE statement is used to modify the data in one or more columns in a table or view. Updating data is typically straightforward, in that you state what object you want to update and then state what you want to update it with. A simple update is shown in the following listing:

```
UPDATE OrderSum
SET OrderID = 42530,
    CustomerID = 510,
    OrderDate = '09/22/2005'
```

You can see in this code listing that the OrderSum table is being updated and the SET clause is used to set the values of 42530, 510, and 09/22/2005 into *all* the rows of the table. In this case all of the rows are updated because no WHERE clause is used that would filter the rows. The result is shown here:

```
OrderID      CustomerID   OrderDate
-----------  -----------  ----------
42530        510          09/22/2005
42530        510          09/22/2005
42530        510          09/22/2005
42530        510          09/22/2005
42530        510          09/22/2005
42530        510          09/22/2005
42530        510          09/22/2005
42530        510          09/22/2005
42530        510          09/22/2005
42530        510          09/22/2005

(10 row(s) affected)
```

The WHERE clause is used in the UPDATE statement to specify only certain rows to be updated. In the next example, we will update the OrderDate field in the OrderSum table where the value of the OrderDate column is 07/01/2001, setting it to 07/01/2005.

```
UPDATE OrderSum
SET OrderDate = '07/01/2005'
WHERE OrderDate = '07/01/2001'

(6 row(s) affected)
```

Another way to modify data in your table or view is to update the data from another table. The following example shows updating the OrderDate field of the OrderSum table with the SalesOrderHeader.OrderDate information for rows that match OrderSum .OrderID to SalesOrderHeader.SalesOrderID and the OrderID/SalesOrderID value is between 43659 and 43670:

```
UPDATE OrderSum
SET OrderDate = CONVERT(nchar(10), soh.OrderDate, 101)
FROM Sales.SalesOrderHeader AS soh
JOIN OrderSum AS oSum
    ON soh.SalesOrderID = oSum.OrderID
    WHERE soh.SalesOrderID BETWEEN 43659 AND 43670


(6 row(s) affected)
```

The TOP clause allows you to specify a number of rows to modify or a percentage of random rows to modify. The following code adds one (1) to four of the rows from the OrderSum table:

```
UPDATE TOP (4) OrderSum
SET OrderID = OrderID + 1
```

Delete

You can use the DELETE statement to delete one or more rows from a table or view. Any table that has all rows removed remains in the database. The DELETE statement removes only rows from the table, not the table from the database. To remove the table from the database, you use the DROP TABLE statement.

An example of the simplest form of the DELETE statement deletes all the rows from a specified table as shown here:

```
DELETE FROM OrderSum
```

You can delete a set of rows from your table by using the WHERE clause and specifying the criteria by which the rows are selected for removal. This code listing shows deleting rows from the OrderSum table where the OrderID is less than 44000:

```
DELETE FROM OrderSum
WHERE OrderID < 44000


(4 row(s) affected)
```

You can also delete rows from your table according to a subquery that is run against another table. In the following example, rows from the OrderSum table will be deleted where the OrderID column value matches the returned results of the SELECT query on the Sales.SalesOrderHeader table:

```
DELETE FROM OrderSum
WHERE OrderID IN
     (SELECT SalesOrderID
      FROM Sales.SalesOrderHeader
      WHERE TaxAmt > 2000.00)
```

```
(2 row(s) affected)
```

Using the TOP keyword in the DELETE statement is another way to delete rows from your table. The TOP keyword allows you to specify a number of rows to delete or a percentage of random rows to delete. The following code deletes 2.5 percent of the rows from the OrderSum table.

```
DELETE TOP (2.5) PERCENT
FROM OrderSum
```

```
(2 row(s) affected)
```

INSTEAD OF Triggers

New to SQL Server 2005 is an INSTEAD OF trigger that you can define on an UPDATE or DELETE statement. Earlier versions of SQL Server supported only AFTER triggers defined on UPDATE and DELETE statements. If you define an INSTEAD OF trigger on an UPDATE or DELETE action, the trigger is executed instead of the action, allowing you to enforce business rules and data integrity.

The following example shows how to add a DML trigger named NoInsert to the INSERT DDL statements:

```
CREATE TRIGGER NoInsert
ON OrderSum
INSTEAD OF INSERT
AS
If @@rowcount >= 10 BEGIN
    PRINT 'Cannot insert any more rows in OrderSum table'
    RETURN
END
```

```
result:
Cannot insert any more rows or in OrderSum table
```

A message is printed out if a user tries to insert rows into the OrderSum table.

Using Transactions

Using transaction processing, you can maintain database integrity by ensuring that batches of SQL operations execute completely or not at all. You start a transaction by using the BEGIN TRANSACTION statement. You then process SQL statements until you commit the transaction to be written or roll back the transaction to its state before the transaction started.

The following shows an example of the BEGIN TRANSACTION statement and a COMMIT TRANSACTION statement:

```
BEGIN TRANSACTION
DELETE OrderSum WHERE OrderID = 24550
DELETE SalesOrderHeader WHERE SalesOrderID = 24550
COMMIT TRANSACTION
```

In this example, order number 24550 is deleted completely from the database. This involves updating two tables, the OrderSum table and the SalesOrderHeader table. A transaction block is used to ensure that the order is not partially deleted. The COMMIT statement writes the change to the tables only if no errors occur. In other words, if the first DELETE worked but the second DELETE did not work, the DELETE transactions would not be committed.

The ROLLBACK TRANSACTION statement undoes all data modifications made from the start of the transaction. Resources held by the transaction are also freed. The following example undoes a DELETE statement on the OrderSum table:

```
BEGIN TRANSACTION
DELETE OrderSum
ROLLBACK TRANSACTION
```

Using Output

Another new T-SQL feature found in SQL Server 2005 is the ability to produce output from T-SQL INSERT, UPDATE, and DELETE DML statements. The new OUTPUT clause returns the modified data. For instance, the following DELETE statement removes all of the rows from the OrderSum table:

```
DECLARE @MyOrderSumTVar TABLE(
    OrderID int,
    CustomerID int,
    OrderYear nchar(10));
DELETE FROM OrderSum

OUTPUT DELETED.* INTO @MyOrderSumTVar

SELECT * FROM @MyOrderSumTVar
```

Here the OUTPUT DELETED.* clause specifies that all deleted rows will be output. With earlier versions of SQL Server, you would just see the number of rows that were affected by the statement. You can see the results of the new T-SQL DML Output clause here:

```
OrderID      CustomerID  OrderDate
-----------  ----------- ----------
75121        15251       07/31/2004
75122        15868       07/31/2004
75123        18759       07/31/2004
(3 row(s) affected)
```

Error Handling

Another important advance embodied by T-SQL in SQL Server 2005 is improved transaction abort handling. With SQL Server 2005, a new Try-Catch model has been added to the transaction. The new Try-Catch structure enables transaction abort errors to be captured with no loss of the transaction context. With SQL Server 2000, although you can abort a transaction, there's no way to maintain the context of the transaction so that you can completely recover the aborted transaction. SQL Server 2005's new Try-Catch transaction abort handling enables you to maintain the complete context of the aborted transaction, giving you the option to re-create the transaction. The following code listing shows the basic T-SQL Try-Catch structure:

```
BEGIN TRY
    SELECT 1/0
END TRY
BEGIN CATCH
    SELECT
        ERROR_NUMBER() AS ErrorNumber,
        ERROR_SEVERITY() AS ErrorSeverity,
        ERROR_LINE() as ErrorLine,
        ERROR_MESSAGE() as ErrorMessage,
        ERROR_STATE() as ErrorState,
        ERROR_PROCEDURE() as ErrorProcedure
END CATCH
```

The SELECT statement in the Try block produces a simple divide by zero error. The error is caught in the Catch block, and the information about the error is shown in the results here:

```
(0 row(s) affected)

ErrorNumber ErrorSeverity ErrorLine   ErrorMessage
----------- ------------- ----------- --------------------------------
8134        16            2           Divide by zero error encountered.

(1 row(s) affected)
```

Summary

T-SQL is SQL Server 2005's core development language. T-SQL can be used to create custom management scripts capable of creating and managing all of the SQL Server operations. In addition, you can use T-SQL to create datacentric stored procedures, functions, and triggers that make up the core of most database applications. In this chapter you learned how to use SQL Server Management Studio and Visual Studio 2005 to develop and debug T-SQL scripts. You also saw how to use T-SQL DDL to create all of the core SQL Server database objects. Then you saw how to use the basic T-SQL DML statements to query and join data as well as perform updates, use transactions, and perform error handling.

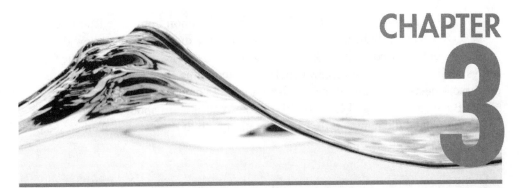

Developing CLR Database Objects

IN THIS CHAPTER

The integration of the .NET Framework's Common Language Runtime (CLR) with SQL Server 2005 is arguably the most significant new development featured in the SQL Server 2005 release. The integration of the CLR brings with it a whole host of new capabilities, including the capability to create database objects using any of the .NET-compatible languages, including C#, Visual Basic, and managed C++. In this chapter you'll learn about how Microsoft has implemented the new .NET CLR integration with SQL Server as well as see how to create CLR database objects.

Understanding CLR and SQL Server 2005 Database Engine

The integration of the CLR with SQL Server extends the capability of SQL Server in several important ways. While T-SQL, the existing data access and manipulation language, is well suited for set-oriented data access operations, it also has limitations. Designed more than a decade ago, T-SQL is a procedural language, not an object-oriented language. The integration of the CLR with SQL Server 2005 brings with it the ability to create database objects using modern object-oriented languages like VB.NET and C#. While these languages do not have the same strong set-oriented nature as T-SQL, they do support complex logic, have better computation capabilities, provide access to external resources, facilitate code reuse, and have a first-class development environment that provides much more power than the old Query Analyzer.

The integration of the .NET CLR with SQL Server 2005 enables the development of stored procedures, user-defined functions, triggers, aggregates, and user-defined types using any of the .NET languages. The integration of the .NET CLR with SQL Server 2005 is more than just skin deep. In fact, the SQL Server 2005 database engine hosts the CLR in-process. Using a set of APIs, the SQL Server engine performs all of the memory management for hosted CLR programs.

The managed code accesses the database using ADO.NET in conjunction with the new SQL Server .NET Data Provider. A new SQL Server object called an *assembly* is the unit of deployment for .NET objects with the database. To create CLR database objects, you must first create a DLL using Visual Studio 2005. Then you import that DLL into SQL Server as an assembly. Finally, you link that assembly to a database object such as a stored procedure or a trigger. In the next section you'll get a more detailed look at how you actually use the new CLR features found in SQL Server 2005.

CLR Architecture

The .NET Framework CLR is very tightly integrated with the SQL Server 2005 database engine. In fact, the SQL Server database engine hosts the CLR. This tight level of integration gives SQL Server 2005 several distinct advantages over the .NET integration that's provided by DB2 and Oracle. You can see an overview of the SQL Server 2005 database engine and CLR integration in Figure 3-1.

As you can see in Figure 3-1, the CLR is hosted within the SQL Server database engine. A SQL Server database uses a special API or hosting layer to communicate with the CLR and interface the CLR with the Windows operating system.

Hosting the CLR within the SQL Server database gives the SQL Server database engine the ability to control several important aspects of the CLR, including

- Memory management
- Threading
- Garbage collection

The DB2 and Oracle implementation both use the CLR as an external process, which means that the CLR and the database engine both compete for system resources. SQL Server 2005's in-process hosting of the CLR provides several important advantages over the external implementation used by Oracle or DB2. First, in-process hosting enables SQL Server to control the execution of the CLR, putting

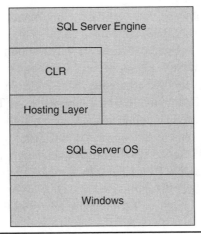

Figure 3-1   *The SQL Server CLR database architecture*

essential functions such as memory management, garbage collection, and threading under the control of the SQL Server database engine. In an external implementation the CLR will manage these things independently. The database engine has a better view of the system requirements as a whole and can manage memory and threads better than the CLR can do on its own. In the end, hosting the CLR in-process will provide better performance and scalability.

Enabling CLR Support

By default, the CLR support in the SQL Server database engine is turned off. This ensures that update installations of SQL Server do not unintentionally introduce new functionality without the explicit involvement of the administrator. To enable SQL Server's CLR support, you need to use the advanced options of SQL Server's sp_configure system stored procedure, as shown in the following listing:

```
sp_configure 'show advanced options', 1
GO
RECONFIGURE
GO
sp_configure 'clr enabled', 1
GO
RECONFIGURE
GO
```

CLR Database Object Components

To create .NET database objects, you start by writing managed code in any one of the .NET languages, such as VB, C#, or Managed C++, and compile it into a .NET DLL (dynamic link library). The most common way to do this would be to use Visual Studio 2005 to create a new SQL Server project and then build that project, which creates the DLL. Alternatively, you create the .NET code using your editor of choice and then compiling the code into a .NET DLL using the .NET Framework SDK. ADO.NET is the middleware that connects the CLR DLL to the SQL Server database. Once the .NET DLL has been created, you need to register that DLL with SQL Server, creating a new SQL Server database object called an assembly. The *assembly* essentially encapsulates the .NET DLL. You then create a new database object such as a stored procedure or a trigger that points to the SQL Server assembly. You can see an overview of the process to create a CLR database object in Figure 3-2.

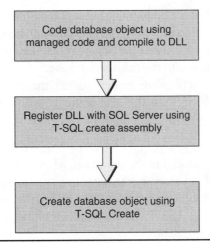

Figure 3-2 *Creating CLR database objects*

SQL Server .NET Data Provider

If you're familiar with ADO.NET, you may wonder exactly how CLR database objects connect to the database. After all, ADO.NET makes its database connection using client-based .NET data providers such as the .NET Framework Data Provider for SQL Server, which connects using networked libraries. While that's great for a client application, going through the system's networking support for a database call isn't the most efficient mode for code that's running directly on the server. To address this issue, Microsoft created the new SQL Server .NET Data Provider. The SQL Server .NET Data Provider establishes an in-memory connection to the SQL Server database.

Assemblies

After the coding for the CLR object has been completed, you can use that code to create a SQL Server assembly. If you're using Visual Studio 2005, then you can simply select the Deploy option, which will take care of both creating the SQL Server assembly as well as creating the target database object.

If you're not using Visual Studio 2005 or you want to perform the deployment process manually, then you need to copy the .NET DLL to a common storage location of your choice. Then, using SQL Server Management Studio, you can execute a T-SQL CREATE ASSEMBLY statement that references the location of the .NET DLL, as you can see in the following listing:

```
CREATE ASSEMBLY MyCLRDLL
FROM '\\SERVERNAME\CodeLibrary\MyCLRDLL.dll'
```

The CREATE ASSEMBLY command takes a parameter that contains the path to the DLL that will be loaded into SQL Server. This can be a local path, but more often it will be a path to a networked file share. When the CREATE ASSEMBLY is executed, the DLL is copied into the master database.

If an assembly is updated or becomes deprecated, then you can remove the assembly using the DROP ASSEMBLY command as follows:

```
DROP ASSEMBLY MyCLRDLL
```

Because assemblies are stored in the database, when the source code for that assembly is modified and the assembly is recompiled, the assembly must first be dropped from the database using the DROP ASSEMBLY command and then reloaded using the CREATE ASSEMBLY command before the updates will be reflected in the SQL Server database objects.

You can use the sys.assemblies view to view the assemblies that have been added to SQL Server 2005 as shown here:

```
SELECT * FROM sys.assemblies
```

Since assemblies are created using external files, you may also want to view the files that were used to create those assemblies. You can do that using the sys.assembly_files view as shown here:

```
SELECT * FROM sys.assembly_files
```

Creating CLR Database Objects

After the SQL Server assembly is created, you can then use SQL Server Management Studio to execute a T-SQL CREATE PROCEDURE, CREATE TRIGGER, CREATE FUNCTION, CREATE TYPE, or CREATE AGGREGATE statement that uses the EXTERNAL NAME clause to point to the assembly that you created earlier.

When the assembly is created, the DLL is copied into the target SQL Server database and the assembly is registered. The following code illustrates creating the MyCLRProc stored procedure that uses the MyCLRDLL assembly:

```
CREATE PROCEDURE MyCLRProc
AS EXTERNAL NAME
MyCLRDLL.StoredProcedures.MyCLRProc
```

The EXTERNAL NAME clause is new to SQL Server 2005. Here the EXTERNAL NAME clause specifies that the stored procedure MyCLRProc will be created using a .SQL Server assembly. The DLL that is encapsulated in the SQL Server assembly can contain multiple classes and methods; the EXTERNAL NAME statement uses the following syntax to identify the correct class and method to use from the assembly:

```
Assembly Name.ClassName.MethodName
```

In the case of the preceding example, the registered assembly is named MyCLRDLL. The class within the assembly is StoredProcedures, and the method within that class that will be executed is MyCLRProc.

Specific examples showing how you actually go about creating a new managed code project with Visual Studio 2005 are presented in the next section.

Creating CLR Database Objects

The preceding section presented an overview of the process along with some example manual CLR database object creation steps to help you better understand the creation and deployment process for CLR database objects. However, while it's possible to create CLR database objects manually, that's definitely not the most productive method. The Visual Studio 2005 Professional, Enterprise, and Team System Editions all have tools that help create CLR database objects as well as deploy and debug them. In the next part of this chapter you'll see how to create each of the new CLR database objects using Visual Studio 2005.

NOTE
The creation of SQL Server projects is supported in Visual Studio 2005 Professional Edition and higher. It is not present in Visual Studio Standard Edition or the earlier releases of Visual Studio.

CLR Stored Procedures

Stored procedures are one of the most common database objects that you'll want to create using one of the managed .NET languages. One of the best uses for CLR stored procedures is to replace existing extended stored procedures. T-SQL is only able to access database resources. In order to access external system resources, Microsoft has provided support in SQL Server for a feature known as extended stored procedures. *Extended stored procedures* are unmanaged DLLs that run in the SQL Server process space and can basically do anything a standard executable program can do, including accessing system resources that are external to the database, such as reading and writing to the file system, reading and writing to the Registry, and accessing the network. However, because extended stored procedures run in the same process space as the SQL Server database engine, bugs, memory violations, and memory leaks in the extended stored procedure could potentially affect the SQL Server database engine. CLR stored procedures solve this problem because they are implemented as managed code and run within the confines of the CLR. Another good candidate for CLR stored procedures is to replace existing T-SQL stored procedures that contain complex logic and embody business rules that are difficult to express in T-SQL. CLR stored procedures can take advantage of the built-in functionality provided by the classes in the .NET Framework, making it relatively easy to add functionality such as complex mathematical expressions or data encryption. Plus, since CLR stored procedure are compiled rather than interpreted like T-SQL, they can provide a significant performance advantage for code that's executed multiple times. However, CLR stored procedures are not intended to be used as a replacement for T-SQL stored procedures. T-SQL stored procedures are still best for data-centric procedures.

To create a CLR stored procedure in Visual Studio 2005, first select the New | Project option and then select the SQL Server Project template as is shown in Figure 3-3.

Give your project a name and click OK to create the project. In this example you can see that I've used the name usp_ImportFile for my stored procedure. This stored

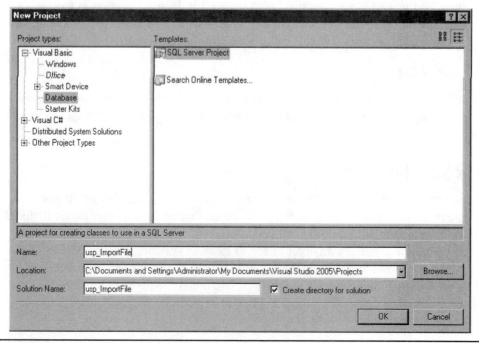

Figure 3-3   *Creating a new SQL Server stored procedure project*

procedure shows how you can replace an extended stored procedure with a CLR stored procedure. In this case the CLR stored procedure will read the contents of a file and store it in a SQL Server column. After naming the project, click OK. Before Visual Studio generates the project code, it displays the New Database Reference dialog that you can see in Figure 3-4.

Visual Studio 2005 uses the New Database Reference dialog to create a connection to your SQL Server 2005 system. That connection will be used to both debug and deploy the finished project. Drop down the Server Name box and select the name of the SQL Server that you want to use with this project. Then select the type of

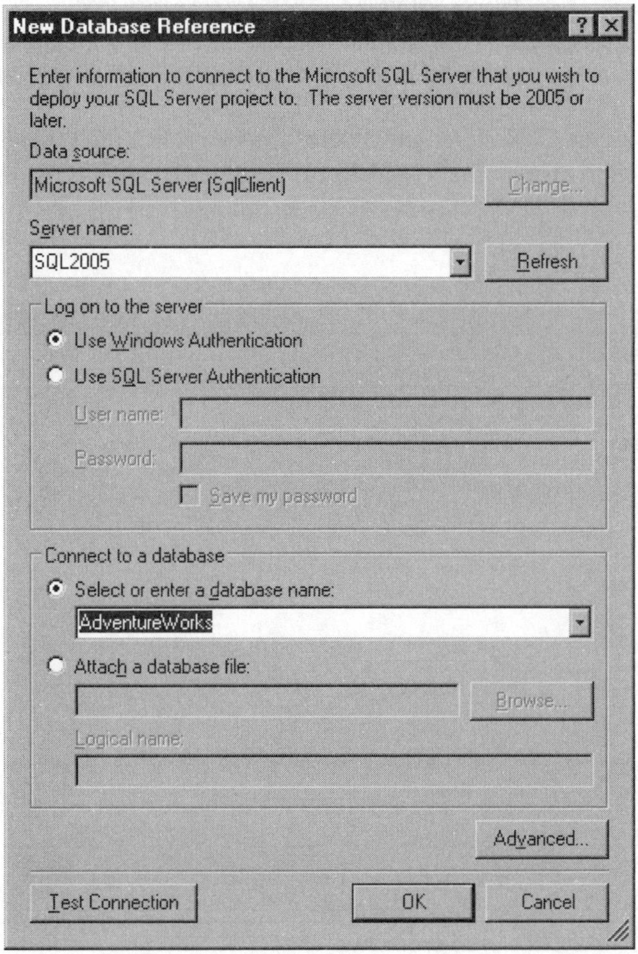

Figure 3-4   *The New Database Reference dialog*

authentication that you want to use and the database where the CLR stored procedure will be deployed. In Figure 3-4 you can see that I've selected the SQL Server system named SQL2005. The project will connect using Windows authentication, and the stored procedure will be deployed to the AdventureWorks database. You can verify the connection properties by clicking the Test Connection button. Once the connection properties are set up the way you want, click OK. All of the required references will automatically be added to your SQL Server project, and Visual Studio 2005 will generate a SQL Server starter project.

NOTE

While Visual Studio 2005 lets you group multiple stored procedures, triggers, and other CLR database objects in a single DLL, it's really better to create each CLR database object as a separate DLL. This gives you more granular control in managing and later updating the individual database objects.

Next, to create the CLR stored procedure, you can select the Project | Add Stored Procedure option to display the Visual Studio installed templates dialog that's shown in Figure 3-5.

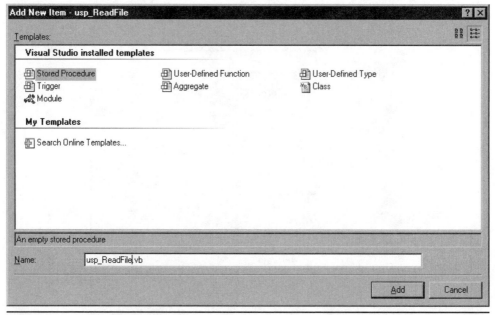

Figure 3-5 *Adding a CLR stored procedure*

From the Add New Item dialog, select the Stored Procedure option from the list of templates displayed in the Templates list and then provide the name of the stored procedure in the Name field that you can see at the bottom of the screen. Here you can see that the stored procedure will be created using the source file usp_ImportFile.vb. Visual Studio 2005 will add a new class to your project for the stored procedure. The generated class file is named after your stored procedure name and will include all of the required import directives as well as the starter code for the stored procedure. You can see the SQL Server CLR stored procedure template in Figure 3-6.

By default the SQL Server .NET Data Provider is added as a reference, along with an include statement for its System.Data.SqlServer namespace. Plus, you can see the System.Data reference, which provides support for ADO.NET and its data-oriented objects such as the DataSet and the System.Data.SqlTypes namespace that provides support for the SQL Server data types.

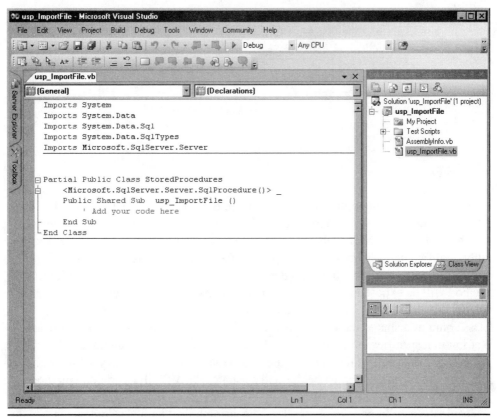

Figure 3-6   *The CLR stored procedure template*

It's up to you to fill in the rest of the code that makes the stored procedure work. The following example illustrates the source code required to create a simple CLR stored procedure that imports the contents of a file into a varchar or text column:

```
Imports System
Imports System.Data
Imports System.Data.Sql
Imports System.Data.SqlTypes
Imports Microsoft.SqlServer.Server
Imports System.IO

Partial Public Class StoredProcedures
    <Microsoft.SqlServer.Server.SqlProcedure()> _
    Public Shared Sub usp_ImportFile _
    (ByVal sInputFile As String, ByRef sColumn As String)
        Dim sContents As String
        Try
            Dim stmReader As New StreamReader(sInputFile)
            sContents = stmReader.ReadToEnd()
            stmReader.Close()
            sColumn = sContents
        Catch ex As Exception
            Dim sp As SqlPipe = SqlContext.Pipe()
            sp.Send(ex.Message)
        End Try
    End Sub
End Class
```

The first important point to note in this code is the directive that imports the Microsoft.SqlServer.Server namespace. This enables the usp_ImportFile project to use the SQL Server .NET Data Provider without always needing to reference the fully qualified name. The second thing to notice is the <Microsoft.SqlServer.Server. SqlProcedure()> attribute that precedes the method name; it tells the compiler this method will be exposed as a SQL Server stored procedure. Next, you can see that the default class name for this stored procedure is set to StoredProcedures. This class contains a shared method named usp_ImportFile that accepts two parameters: a string that specifies the name of the file that will be imported and a second input parameter that specifies the name of a column that will contain the contents of the file. For C#, the method must be defined as static. For VB.NET code, the method would need to be defined as Shared.

Inside the usp_ImportFile method, a new string object named sContents is declared that will contain the contents of the file. Next, a Try-Catch loop is used to capture any errors that may occur during the file import process. Within the Try-Catch loop a new StreamReader named stmReader is created that will be used to read the file from the operating system. The name of the file that will be read is passed into the StreamReader's instantiation call. Then the stmReader's ReadToEnd method is used to read the entire contents of the file into the sContent string variable. After the contents of the file have been read, the stmReader StreamReader is closed and the contents of the sContents variable are assigned to the SQL Server column.

If any errors occur while the input file is being read, then the code in the Catch portion of the Try-Catch structure is executed. Within the Catch block a SqlPipe object named sp is created and then used to send those errors back to the caller of the stored procedure. This code block uses the SqlPipe object, which represents a conduit that passes information between the CLR and the calling code. Here, the SqlPipe object enables the stored procedure to pass error information to the external caller.

Setting the Stored Procedure Security

At this point the code is finished for the stored procedure, but because of security concerns, it still can't execute. By default SQL Server CLR objects can only access database resources, and they cannot access external resources. In the case of the usp_ImportFile example, the stored procedure needs to access the file system, so the default security settings need to be changed. To enable external access, you need to open the project's properties and click the Database tab. Then in the Permissions Level drop-down you need to change the value from Safe to External. More information about the CLR security options is presented later in this chapter.

Deploying the Stored Procedure

After the CLR stored procedure source code has been compiled into an assembly, you can then add that assembly to the database and create the CLR stored procedure. You can do this in two ways. If you're using Visual Studio 2005 to create the SQL Server CLR database objects, then you can interactively deploy the CLR stored procedure directly from Visual Studio. To deploy the stored procedure to SQL Server, select the Build | Deploy Solution option from the Visual Studio menu.

You can perform the deployment manually as was shown in the earlier section "Creating CLR Database Objects". To do this, you essentially need to move the compiled DLL to a directory or file share where it can be accessed by SQL Server. Then run the CREATE ASSEMBLY statement to register the DLL and copy it into the database.

```
create assembly usp_ImportFile
from 'C:\temp\usp_ImportFile.dll'
WITH PERMISSION_SET = EXTERNAL
```

The CREATE ASSEMBLY statement copies the contents of the usp_ImportFile.dll file in the c:\temp directory into the SQL Server database. The WITH PERMISSION SET clause is used to specify that this assembly can access resources that are external to the SQL Server database. That's needed here because the stored procedure reads an external file.

```
CREATE PROCEDURE usp_ImportFile
 @filename nvarchar(1024),
 @columnname nvarchar(1024) OUT
AS
EXTERNAL NAME usp_ImportFile.[usp_ImportFile.StoredProcedures]
.usp_ImportFile
```

The CREATE PROCEDURE statement is used to create a new SQL Server stored procedure that uses the CLR assembly. This CLR stored procedure uses two parameters. The first is an input parameter, and the second is an output parameter. The EXTERNAL NAME clause uses a three-part name to identify the target method in the DLL. The first part of the name refers to the assembly name. The second part refers to the class. If the class is part of a namespace, as is the case here, then the namespace must preface the class name and both should be enclosed in brackets. Finally, the third part of the name identifies the method that will be executed.

Using the Stored Procedure

After the CLR stored procedure has been created, it can be called exactly like any T-SQL stored procedure, as the following example illustrates:

```
DECLARE @myColumn ntext
EXEC usp_ImportFile 'c:\temp\testfile.txt' @myColumn
```

User-Defined Functions

Creating .NET-based *user-defined functions (UDFs)* is another new feature that's enabled by the integration of the .NET CLR. User-defined functions that return scalar types must return a .NET data type that can be implicitly converted to a SQL Server data type. Scalar functions written with the .NET Framework can significantly outperform T-SQL in certain scenarios because unlike T-SQL functions, .NET functions are created using compiled code. User-defined functions can also return table types, in which case the function must return a result set.

To create a UDF using Visual Studio 2005, select the New | Project option and then select the SQL Server Project template as shown in Figure 3-7.

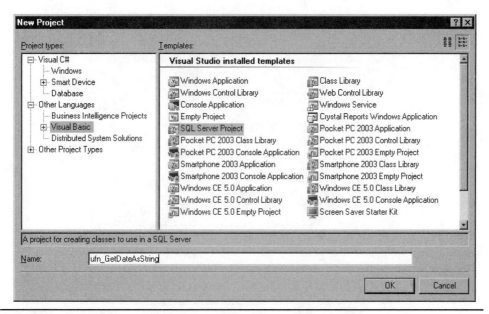

Figure 3-7   *Creating a new SQL Server UDF project*

As in the Stored Procedure example that was presented earlier, first give your project a name and click OK to create the project. In the example shown in Figure 3-7, you can see that I've used the name ufn_GetDateAsString for my user-defined function. This function returns a string value containing the system date and time. After naming the project, click OK to display the New Database Reference dialog for the CLR Function project, which will resemble the one shown in Figure 3-8.

> **NOTE**
>
> *The Add Database Reference dialog is shown instead of the New Database Reference dialog when a database reference has already been created. This would be the case if you created the ufn_GetDateAsString function immediately after the usp_ImportFile project.*

The New Database Reference dialog defines the connection between your Visual Studio project and SQL Server. The project will connect to the SQL Server system named sql2005, and the function will be deployed to the AdventureWorks database.

Once the Visual Studio project has been created and the connection has been defined, you use the Project | Add Function menu option to display the Add New Item dialog that you can see in Figure 3-9.

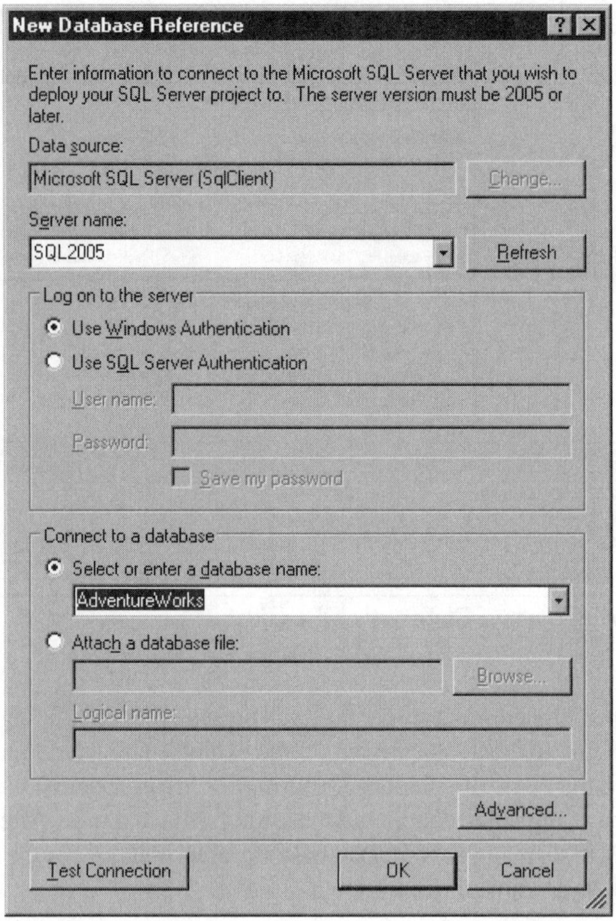

Figure 3-8 *The New Database Reference dialog*

Visual Studio uses the SQL Server Function project template to create a starter project that includes the reference to the SQL Server .NET Data Provider and a basic function wrapper for your source code. It's up to you to fill in the rest of the code. The following code listing shows the completed CLR function, ufn_ GetDateAsString, that performs a basic date-to-string conversion:

```
Imports System
Imports System.Data
Imports System.Data.Sql
```

```
Imports System.Data.SqlTypes
Imports Microsoft.SqlServer.Server

Partial Public Class UserDefinedFunctions
    <Microsoft.SqlServer.Server.SqlFunction()> _
    Public Shared Function ufn_GetDateAsString() As SqlString
        Dim dtDataTime As New DateTime
        Return dtDataTime.ToString()
    End Function
End Class
```

Here, the Microsoft.SqlServer.Server namespace is not needed, as this particular function does not perform any data access. Next, Visual Studio 2005 generated the UserDefinedFunctions class to contain all of the methods that this assembly will expose as UDFs. You can also see that the <Microsoft.SqlServer.Server. SqlFunction()> attribute is used to identify the ufn_GetDateAsString method as a UDF. The code in this simple example just converts the system date to a string data type that's returned to the caller.

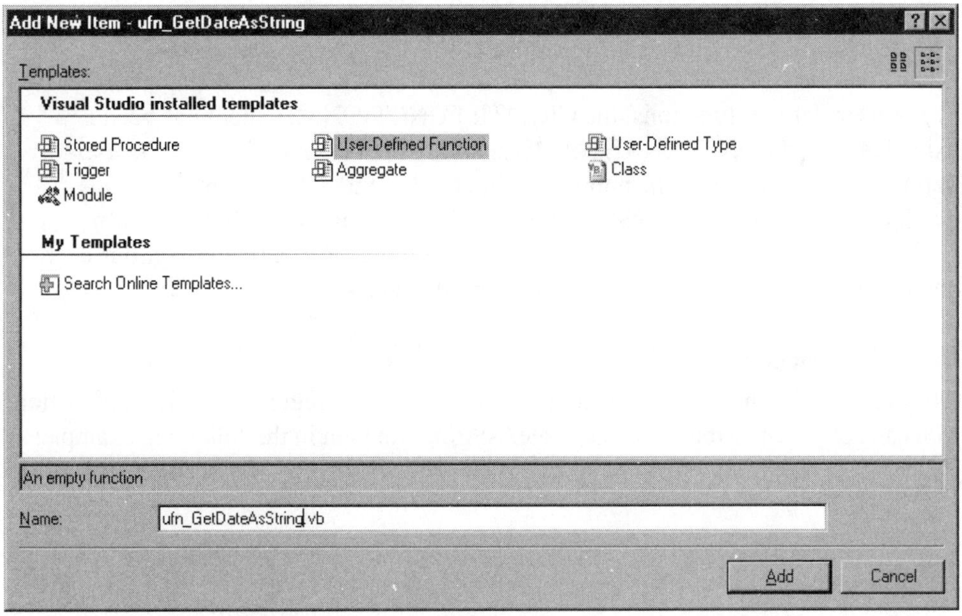

Figure 3-9   *Adding a CLR user-defined function*

Deploying the Function

To create the function in a SQL Server database, the assembly must first be created, as you saw in the stored procedure example. Then if you're using Visual Studio 2005, you can simply select the Build | Deploy Solution option and you're done.

If you're doing this manually, you'll need to copy the ufn_GetDataAsString. dll file to a location that's accessible by the SQL Server system and then create the assembly, followed by the function. The following CREATE ASSEMBLY statement can be used to copy the contents of ufn_GetDataAsString.dll into the SQL Server database:

```
CREATE ASSEMBLY ufn_GetDataAsString
FROM '\\MyFileShare\Code Library\ufn_GetDataAsString.dll'
```

The CREATE FUNCTION statement is then used to create a new SQL Server function that executes the appropriate method in the assembly. The following listing illustrates how the CREATE FUNCTION statement can create a .CLR user-defined function:

```
CREATE FUNCTION ufn_GetDateAsString()
RETURNS nvarchar(256)
EXTERNAL NAME
ufn_GetDateAsString.UserDefinedFunctions.ufn_GetDateAsString
```

For user-defined functions, the CREATE FUNCTION statement has been extended with the EXTERNAL NAME clause, which essentially links the user-defined function name to the appropriate method in the .NET assembly. In this example, the ufn_GetDateAsString function is using the assembly named ufn_GetDateAsString. Within that assembly, it's using the UserDefinedFunctions class and the ufn_GetDateAsString method within that class.

Using the Function

After the function has been created, it can be called like a regular SQL Server function. You can see how to execute the GetDateAsString function in the following example:

```
SELECT dbo.GetDateAsString()
```

Triggers

In addition to stored procedures and user-defined functions, the new .NET integration capabilities found in SQL Server 2005 also provide the ability to create CLR triggers. To create a trigger using Visual Studio 2005, you start your project as you saw in the

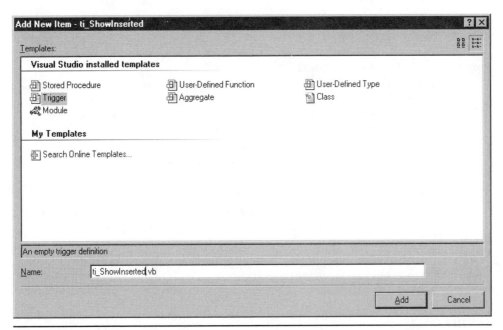

Figure 3-10   *Adding a CLR trigger*

earlier examples. To create a trigger using Visual Studio 2005, select the New | Project option, give your project a name, and click OK to create the project. For this project, I used the name ti_ShowInserted for my trigger. This trigger essentially retrieves the values of the row being inserted in a table and displays them. After naming the project and clicking OK, I filled out the New Database Reference dialog using the same values that were shown in the previous examples. Next, I used the Project | Add Trigger menu option that you can see in Figure 3-10 to create a starter project for the CLR trigger.

As you saw in the earlier example of CLR database objects, you select the Trigger option from the list of templates and then provide the name of the trigger in the name prompt. Visual Studio 2005 will generate a starter project file that you can add your code to. The starter project includes the appropriate import directives as well as generating a class, in this case appropriately named Triggers, and a method named ti_ShowInserted with its appropriate method attribute. The following code listing shows the completed code for the CLR trigger named ti_ShowInserted:

```
Imports System
Imports System.Data
Imports System.Data.Sql
Imports System.Data.SqlTypes
```

```
Imports Microsoft.SqlServer.Server
Imports System.Data.SqlClient

Partial Public Class Triggers
    ' Enter existing table or view for the target and uncomment
      the attribute line
    <Microsoft.SqlServer.Server.SqlTrigger(Name:="ti_ShowInserted", _
        Target:="Person.ContactType", Event:="FOR INSERT")> _
    Public Shared Sub ti_ShowInserted()
        Dim oTriggerContext As SqlTriggerContext = _
          SqlContext.TriggerContext
        Dim sPipe As SqlPipe = SqlContext.Pipe
        If oTriggerContext.TriggerAction = TriggerAction.Insert Then
            Dim oConn As New SqlConnection("context connection=true")
            oConn.Open()
            Dim oCmd As New SqlCommand("Select * from inserted", oConn)
            sPipe.ExecuteAndSend(oCmd)
        End If
    End Sub
End Class
```

The example CLR trigger displays the contents of the data that is used for an insert action that's performed on the Person.ContactTypes table in the Adventureworks database. The first thing to notice in this code listing is the Attribute for the ti_ShowInserted subroutine (the code enclosed within the < > markers). The Attribute is used to name the trigger and identify the table the trigger will be applied to as well as the event that will cause the trigger to fire. When the Visual Studio 2005 trigger template initially generates this Attribute, it is prefaced by a comment symbol— essentially making the line a comment. This is because the trigger template doesn't know how or where you want the trigger to be used. In order for Visual Studio 2005 to deploy the trigger, you need to uncomment the Attribute line and then fill in the appropriate properties. The following table lists the properties used by the Visual Studio 2005 trigger template:

Property Name	Description
Name	The name the trigger will use on the target SQL Server system.
Target	The name of the table that the trigger will be applied to.
Event	The action that will fire the trigger. The following trigger events are supported: FOR INSERT, FOR UPDATE, FOR DELETE, AFTER INSERT, AFTER UPDATE, AFTER DELETE, INSTEAD OF INSERT, INSTEAD OF UPDATE, INSTEAD OF DELETE

In this example, the resulting trigger will be named ti_ShowInserted. It will be applied to the table named Person.ContactType, which is in the AdventureWorks database, and the trigger will only be fired for an insert operation.

The primary code for the trigger is found within the ti_ShowInserted subroutine. This code example makes use of another new ADO.NET object: SqlTriggerContext. The SqlTriggerContext object provides information about the trigger action that's fired and the columns that are affected. The SqlTriggerContext object is always instantiated by the SqlContext object. Generally, the SqlContext object provides information about the caller's context. Specifically, in this case, the SqlContext object enables the code to access the virtual table that's created during the execution of the trigger. This virtual table stores the data that caused the trigger to fire.

Next, a SqlPipe object is created. The SqlPipe object enables the trigger to communicate with the external caller, in this case to pass the inserted data values to the caller. The TriggerAction property of the SqlContext object is used to determine if the trigger action was an insert operation. Using the TriggerAction property is quite straightforward. It supports the following values:

TriggerAction Value	Description
TriggerAction.Insert	An insert operation was performed.
TriggerAction.Update	An update action was performed.
TriggerAction.Delete	A delete action was performed.

If the TriggerAction property equals TriggerAction.Insert, then an insert was performed and the contents of the virtual trigger table are retrieved and sent to the caller using the SqlPipe object's Execute method. In order to retrieve the contents of the virtual table, a SqlConnection object and a SqlCommand object are needed. These objects come from the System.Data.SqlClient namespace. You should note that when used with server-side programming, the Connection String used by the SqlConnection object must be set to the value of "context Connection=true". Then a SqlCommand object named oCmd is instantiated that uses the statement "Select * from inserted" to retrieve all of the rows and columns from the virtual table that contains the inserted values. Finally, the ExecuteAndSend method of SqlPipe object is used to execute the command and send the results back to the caller.

Deploying the Trigger

Once the code has been created, you can either deploy it to the database using the Visual Studio 2005 Build | Deploy solution option or manually drop and re-create the assembly and any dependent objects you saw in UDF examples earlier in this chapter.

To manually deploy the code, you'd need to copy ti_ShowInserted.dll to the SQL Server system or to a share that's accessible to the SQL Server system and then execute the following T-SQL Server commands:

```
Use AdventureWorks

create assembly ti_showinserted
from 'C:\temp\ti_ShowInserted.dll'
go

CREATE TRIGGER ti_ShowInserted
ON Person.ContactType
FOR INSERT
AS EXTERNAL NAME ti_ShowInserted.[ti_ShowInserted.Triggers].ti_ShowInserted
go
```

This example assumes that ti_ShowInsert.dll was copied into the c:\temp directory on the SQL Server system. First, the Create Assembly statement is used to copy the DLL into the SQL Server database and then the Create Trigger statement is used with the As External Name clause to create a trigger named ti_ShowInserted and attach it to the Person.ContactTypes table. As in the earlier examples, the As External Name clause identifies the assembly using a three-part name: *asssembly.class.method.* Pay particular attention to the class portion of this name. For triggers you must bracket the class name and include the namespace just before the class name. In this example, the assembly is named ti_ShowInserted. The Namespace is ti_ShowInserted. The class is named Triggers, and the method is named ti_ShowInserted.

Using the Trigger

After the CLR trigger has been deployed, it will be fired for every insert operation that's performed on the base table. For example, the following INSERT statement will add a row to the Person.ContactType table, which will cause the CLR trigger to fire:

```
INSERT INTO Person.ContactType VALUES(102, 'The Big Boss',
  '2005-05-17 00:00:00.000')
```

The example trigger, ti_ShowInserted, performs a select statement on the inserted row value. Then it uses the SqlPipe object to send the results back to the caller. In this example the trigger will send the contents of the inserted row values back to the caller:

```
ContactTypeID Name                                               ModifiedDate
------------- -------------------------------------------------- --------------
21            The Big Boss                                       2005-05-17
00:00:00.000
(1 row(s) affected)
(1 row(s) affected)
```

User-Defined Types

Another important new feature in SQL Server 2005 that is enabled by the integration of the .NET CLR is the ability to create true *user-defined types (UDTs)*. Using UDTs, you can extend the raw types provided by SQL Server and add data types that are specialized to your application or environment.

In the following example you'll see how to create a UDT that represents a gender code: either M for male or F for female. While you could store this data in a standard one-byte character field, using a UDT ensures that the field will accept only these two values with no additional need for triggers, constraints, or other data validation techniques.

To create a UDT using Visual Studio 2005, select the New | Project option, give your project a name, and click OK to create the project. For this project I used the name of Gender for the new UDT. After naming the project and clicking OK, I filled out the New Database Reference dialog using the required connection values to deploy the project to the appropriate SQL Server system and database. Next, I used the Project | Add User-Defined Type option to display the Add New Item dialog that you can see in Figure 3-11.

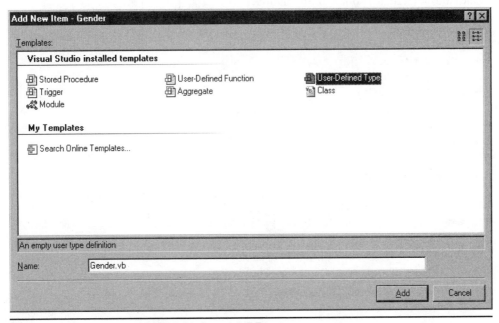

Figure 3-11   *Creating a .NET SQL Server UDT*

Method	Description
IsNull	This required method is used to indicate if the object is nullable. SQL Server 2005 requires all UDTs to implement nullability, so this method must always return true.
Parse	This required method accepts a string parameter and stores it as a UDT.
ToString	This required method converts the contents of the UDT to a string.
Default constructor	This required method creates a new instance of the UDT.

Table 3-1   *Required UDT Methods*

Select User-Defined Type from the list of SQL Server templates. Enter the name that you want to assign to the class and then click Open to have Visual Studio generate a starter project file for the UDT. The starter project file implements the four methods that SQL Server 2005 requires for all UDTs. These methods are needed to fulfill the SQL Server UDT contract requirements—it's up to you to add the code to make the UDT perform meaningful actions. The four required UDT methods are listed in Table 3-1.

You can see the completed Gender class that is used to implement a UDT for M (male) and F (female) codes in this listing:

```
Imports System
Imports System.Data
Imports System.Data.Sql
Imports System.Data.SqlTypes
Imports Microsoft.SqlServer.Server
Imports System.IO


<Serializable()> _
<Microsoft.SqlServer.Server.SqlUserDefinedType _
 (Format.UserDefined, _
  IsFixedLength:=True, MaxByteSize:=2)> _
Public Structure Gender
    Implements INullable, IBinarySerialize

    Public Sub Read(ByVal r As BinaryReader) _
        Implements IBinarySerialize.Read
        m_value = r.ReadString.ToString()
    End Sub
```

```vb
Public Sub Write(ByVal w As BinaryWriter) _
    Implements IBinarySerialize.Write
    w.Write(m_value.ToString())
End Sub

Public Overrides Function ToString() As String
    If m_value.IsNull = False Then
        Return m_value.Value
    Else
        Return Nothing
    End If
End Function

Public ReadOnly Property IsNull() As Boolean _
    Implements INullable.IsNull
    Get
        If m_value.IsNull = True Then
            Return True
        Else
            Return False
        End If
    End Get
End Property

Public Shared ReadOnly Property Null() As Gender
    Get
        Dim h As Gender = New Gender
        h.m_Null = True
        Return h
    End Get
End Property

Public Shared Function Parse(ByVal s As SqlString) As Gender
    If s.IsNull Then
        Return Null
    End If

    Dim u As Gender = New Gender
    u.Value = s
    Return u
End Function
```

```
' Create a Value Property
Public Property Value() As SqlString
    Get
         Return m_value
    End Get

    Set(ByVal value As SqlString)
         If (value = "M" Or value = "F") Then
             m_value = value
         Else
             Throw New ArgumentException _
                ("Gender data type must be M or F")
         End If
    End Set
End Property

' Private members
Private m_Null As Boolean
Private m_value As SqlString

End Structure
```

To create a UDT, the code must adhere to certain conventions. The class's attributes must be serializable, the class must implement the INullable interface, and the class name must be set to the name of the UDT. You can optionally add the IComparable interface. In this example, Gender is the class name. Near the bottom of the listing you can see where a private string variable named m_value is declared to hold the value of the data type.

Like the other CLR database objects, the Attribute plays an important part in the construction of the CLR UDT. The SQL Server UDT Attribute accepts the property values shown in Table 3-2.

The first thing to notice in the code is the use of the INullable and IBinarySerialize interfaces. The INullable interface is required for all UDTs. The IBinarySerialize interface is required for UDTs that use the Format.UserDefined attribute. Because this example uses a String data type, the Format.UserDefined attribute is required, which means that this UDT also needs code to handle the serialization of the UDT. In practical terms, this means that the class must implement the IBinarySerialize Read and Write methods, which you can see in the following section of code.

At first it may seem a bit intimidating to use the IBinarySerialize interfaces, but as you can see in the Read and Write subroutines, it's actually pretty simple. The Read subroutine simply uses the ReadString method to assign a value to the UDT's

Property	Description
Format.Native	SQL Server automatically handles the serialization of the UDT. The Format.Native value can only be used for UDTs that contain fixed-sized data types. The following data types are supported: bool, byte, sbyte, short, ushort, int, uint, long, ulong, float, double, SqlByte, SqlInt16, SqlInt32, SqlInt64, SqlDateTime, SqlSingle, SqlDouble, SqlMoney. If this property is used, the MaxByteSize property cannot be used.
Format.UserDefined	The UDT class is responsible for serializing the UDT. The format. UserDefined value must be used for variable-length data types like String and SQLString. If this value is used, the UDT must implement the IBinarySerialize interface and the Read and Write routines. If this property is used, the MaxByteSize property must also be specified.
MaxByteSize	Specifies the maximum size of the UDT in bytes.
IsFixedLength	A Boolean value that determines if all instances of this type are the same length.
IsByteOrdered	A Boolean value that determines how SQL Server performs binary comparisons on the UDT.
ValidationMethodName	The name of the method used to validate instances of this type.
Name	The name of the UDT.

Table 3-2   *UDT Attribute Properties*

m_value variable (which contains the UDT's value). Likewise, the Write subroutine uses the Write method to serialize the contents of the m_value variable.

The ToString method checks to see if the contents of the m_value variable are null. If so, then the string "null" is returned. Otherwise, the m_value's ToString method returns the string value of the contents.

The next section of code defines the IsNull property. This property's get method checks the contents of the m_value variable and returns the value of true if m_value is null. Otherwise, the get method returns the value of false. Next, you can see the Null method, which was generated by the template to fulfill the UDT's requirement for nullability.

The Parse method accepts a string argument, which it stores in the object's Value property. You can see the definition for the Value property a bit lower down in the code. The Parse method must be declared as static, or if you're using VB.NET, it must be a Shared property.

The Value property is specific to this implementation. In this example, the Value property is used to store and retrieve the value of the UDT. It's also responsible for editing the allowable values. In the set method, you can see that only the values of M or F are permitted. Attempting to use any other values causes an exception to be thrown that informs the caller that the "Gender data type must be M or F".

Deploying the UDT

Very much like a CLR stored procedure or function, the UDT is compiled into a DLL after the code is completed. That DLL is then imported as a SQL Server assembly using the CREATE ASSEMBLY and CREATE TYPE statements or by simply using the Visual Studio 2005 Deploy option. You can see the T-SQL code to manually create the CLR UDT in the following listing:

```
create assembly Gender
from 'C:\temp\Gender.dll'
go


CREATE TYPE Gender
EXTERNAL NAME Gender.[Gender.Gender]
go
```

This listing assumes that gender.dll has been copied into the c:\temp that's on the SQL Server system. One thing to notice in the CREATE TYPE statement is the class parameter. As in the earlier CLR examples, the first part of the External Name clause specifies the assembly that will be used. In the case of a UDT, the second part of the name identifies the namespace and class. In the Gender example, the Namespace was Gender and the UDT's class was also named Gender.

Using the UDT

Once the UDT is created, you can use it in T-SQL much like SQL Server's native data types. However, since UDTs contain methods and properties, there are differences. The following example shows how the Gender UDT can be used as a variable and how its Value property can be accessed:

```
DECLARE @mf Gender
SET @mf='N'
PRINT @mf.Value
```

In this listing the UDT variable is declared using the standard T-SQL DECLARE statement, and the SET statement is used to attempt to assign the value of N to the UDT's Value property. Because N isn't a valid value, the following error is generated:

```
.Net SqlClient Data Provider: Msg 6522, Level 16, State 1, Line 2
A CLR error occurred during execution of 'Gender':
System.ArgumentException: Gender data type must be M or F
at Gender.set_Value(SqlString value)
```

Just as UDTs can be used as variables, they can also be used to create columns. The following listing illustrates creating a table that uses the Gender UDT:

```
CREATE TABLE MyContacts
(ContactID int,
FirstName varchar(25),
LastName varchar(25),
MaleFemale Gender)
```

While creating columns with the UDT type is the same as when using a native data type, assigning values to the UDT is a bit different than the standard column assignment. Complex UDTs can contain multiple values. In that case you need to assign the values to the UDT's members. You can access the UDT's members by prefixing them with the (.) symbol. In this case, since the UDT uses a simple value, you can assign values to it exactly as you can any of the built-in data types. This example shows how to insert a row into the example MyContacts table that contains the Gender UDT:

```
INSERT INTO MyContacts VALUES(1, 'Michael', 'Otey', 'M')
```

To retrieve the contents of the UDT using the SELECT statement, you need to use the UDT.Member notation as shown here when referencing a UDT column:

```
SELECT ContactID, LastName, MaleFemale.Value FROM MyContacts
```

To see the UDTs that have been created for a database, you can query the sys.Types view as shown here:

```
SELECT * FROM sys.Types
```

Aggregates

The CLR aggregate is another new type of .NET database object that was introduced in SQL Server 2005. Essentially, a *user-defined aggregate* is an extensibility function that enables you to aggregate values over a group during the processing of a query. SQL Server has always provided a basic set of aggregation functions like MIN, MAX, and SUM that you can use over a query. User-defined aggregates enable you to extend this group of aggregate functions with your own custom aggregations. One really handy use for CLR aggregates is to enable the creation of aggregate functions for CLR UDTs. Like native aggregation functions, user-defined aggregates allow you to execute calculations on a set of values and return a single value. When you create a CLR aggregate, you supply the logic that will perform the aggregation. In this section you'll see how to create a simple aggregate that calculates the maximum variance for a set of numbers.

To create an aggregate using Visual Studio 2005, select the New | Project option, give your project a name, and click OK to create the project. This example uses the name of MaxVariance. After naming the project and clicking OK, complete the New Database Reference dialog using the required connection values for your SQL Server system and database. Next, to create the aggregate I used the Project | Add Aggregate option to display the Add New Item dialog that you can see in Figure 3-12.

Select Aggregate from the list of SQL Server templates and then enter the name for the class and click OK. As you can see in Figure 3-12, I used the name MaxVariance. Visual Studio will generate a starter project for the aggregate class. Much as with a UDT, the template for a SQL Server CLR aggregate implements four methods that SQL Server 2005 requires for all CLR aggregates. The four required methods are listed in Table 3-3.

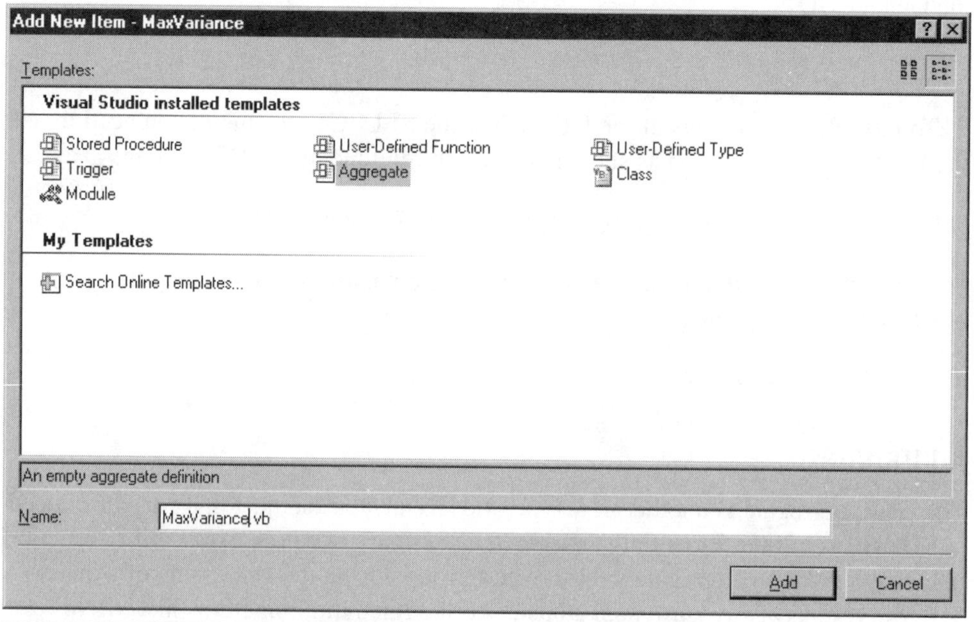

Figure 3-12   *Creating a CLR aggregate*

Method	Description
Init	This required method initializes the object. It is invoked once for each aggregation.
Accumulate	This required method is invoked once for each item in the set being aggregated.
Merge	This required method is invoked when the server executes a query using parallelism. This method is used to merge the data from the different parallel instances together.
Terminate	This required method returns the results of the aggregation. It is invoked once after all of the items have been processed.

Table 3-3   *Required Aggregate Methods*

You can see the code to implement the MaxVariance aggregate in the following listing:

```
Imports System
Imports System.Data
Imports System.Data.Sql
Imports System.Data.SqlTypes
Imports Microsoft.SqlServer.Server


<Serializable()> _
<SqlUserDefinedAggregate(Format.Native)> _
Public Structure MaxVariance

    Public Sub Init()
        m_LowValue = 999999999
        m_HighValue = -999999999
    End Sub

    Public Sub Accumulate(ByVal value As Integer)
        If (value > m_HighValue)
            m_HighValue = value
        End If
        If (value < m_LowValue)
            m_LowValue = value
        End If
    End Sub

    Public Sub Merge(ByVal Group as MaxVariance)
        If (Group.GetHighValue() > m_HighValue)
            m_HighValue = Group.GetHighValue()
        End If
```

```
        If (Group.GetLowValue() < m_LowValue)
            m_LowValue = Group.GetLowValue()
        End If
    End Sub

    Public Function Terminate() As Integer
        return m_HighValue - m_LowValue
    End Function

    ' Helper methods
    Private Function GetLowValue() As Integer
        return m_LowValue
    End Function

    Private Function GetHighValue() As Integer
        return m_HighValue
    End Function

    ' This is a place-holder field member
    Private m_LowValue As Integer
    Private m_HighValue As Integer

End Structure
```

At the top of this listing you can see the standard set of Imports statements used by CLR objects, followed by the serialization attribute that's required by CLR aggregate objects. After that, in the Init method the two variables, m_LowValue and m_HighValue, are assigned high and low values, ensuring that they will be assigned values from the list. These two variables are declared near the bottom of the listing, and they serve to hold the minimum and maximum values that are encountered by the aggregate routine. The Init method is called one time only—when the object is first initialized.

While the Init method is called just once, the Accumulate method is called once for each row in the result set. In this example, the Accumulate method compares the incoming value with the values stored in the m_HighValue and m_LowValue variables. If the incoming value is higher than the current high value, it is stored in the m_HighValue variable. If the value is lower than the value of m_LowValue, it is stored in m_LowValue. Otherwise, no action is performed by the Accumulate method.

NOTE

Because aggregates are serialized, you need to be aware of the total storage requirements for some uses. The aggregate's value is serialized following each invocation of the Accumulate method, and it cannot exceed the maximum column size of 8000 bytes.

The Merge method is used when the aggregate is processed in parallel, which typically won't be the case for most queries. If the Merge is called, its job is to import the current aggregation values from the parallel instance. You can see here that it does that using two helper methods that essentially export the values in the m_HighValue and m_LowValue variables. These values are compared to the existing values, and if they are higher or lower, they will replace the current values in m_HighValue and m_LowValue.

The Terminate method is called once after all of the results have been processed. For this example, the Terminate method simply subtracts the lowest value found from the highest value found and returns the difference to the caller.

Deploying the Aggregate

After compiling the class into a DLL, you can import the DLL as a SQL Server assembly using either the Visual Studio 2005 Deploy option or manually using the CREATE ASSEMBLY statement and CREATE AGGREGATE statement as is shown in the following listing:

```
create assembly MaxVariance
from 'C:\temp\MaxVariance.dll'
go

CREATE AGGREGATE MaxVariance (@maXVar int)
RETURNS Int
EXTERNAL NAME MaxVariance.[MaxVariance.MaxVariance]
go
```

Like the earlier examples, this listing assumes that maxvariance.dll has been copied into the c:\temp directory on the local SQL Server system. In the CREATE AGGREGATE statement and the EXTERNAL NAME clause the first part of the name specifies the assembly that will be used, and the second part of the name identifies the namespace and class. Here all of these values are named MaxVariance.

Using the Aggregate

You can use the aggregate just like SQL Server's built-in aggregate functions. One small difference is that the UDAGG needs to be prefixed with the schema name to allow the system to locate it. The following line illustrates using the MaxVariance Aggregate:

```
SELECT dbo.MaxVariance(MinQty) FROM Sales.SpecialOffer
```

The result of this statement will show the difference between the high and low values found in the Sales.SpecialOffer column as is shown here:

```
-----------
61

(1 row(s) affected)
```

Debugging CLR Database Objects

One of the coolest features found in the integration of the .NET Framework, Visual Studio 2005, and SQL Server 2005 is the ability to debug the CLR database objects that you create. This tight level of integration sets SQL Server way ahead of competing database products like Oracle and DB2 that offer the ability to create stored procedures and functions using .NET code. While the other database products provide for the creation of these objects, they do not support the ability to provide integrated debugging. Visual Studio 2005 enables you to set breakpoints in your CLR database objects and then seamlessly step through your code and perform all of the debugging tasks that you would expects for a standard Windows or Web application, including the ability to set breakpoints, single-step through the code, inspect and change variables, and create watches—even between T-SQL and CLR code. Visual Studio 2005 automatically generates test scripts that are added to your projects. You can customize and use these test scripts to execute the CLR database objects that you create.

NOTE

You must compile and deploy the CLR database object before you can debug it.

To debug a SQL Server project using Visual Studio 2005, first open the project that you want to debug and then go to the Servers window and right-click the database connection. From the pop-up menu select the option Allow SQL/CLR Debugging as is shown in Figure 3-13.

Next, set up the script that you want to use to run the database object. Using the Solution window, open the Test Scripts folder and then the Test.sql file. You can set up multiple test scripts, but the Test.sql script is provided by default. If you want to change the script that Visual Studio 2005 uses to run the CLR database object, you simply right-click the desired script listed under the Test Scripts folder and select the Set As Default Debug Script option as is shown in Figure 3-14.

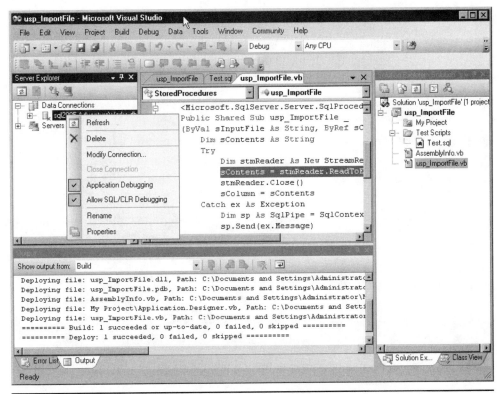

Figure 3-13   *Setting the Allow SQL/CLR Debugging option*

To use the default Test.sql script, open the file using the Visual Studio editor. Here you can see T-SQL boilerplate code for testing each of the different CLR database object types. Go to the section that you want and edit the code to execute the database object. You can see the test code for the usp_ImportFile stored procedure in the following listing:

```
-- Examples for queries that exercise different SQL objects
 -- implemented by this assembly
----------------------------------------------------------------------
-- Stored procedure
----------------------------------------------------------------------
declare @MyColumn varchar(30)
exec usp_ImportFile 'c:\temp\testfile.txt',@MyColumn
Select @MyColumn
```

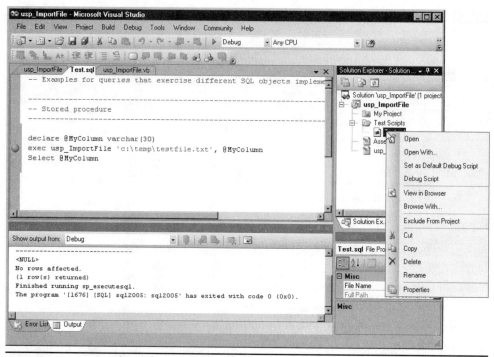

Figure 3-14 *Setting the default debug script*

When the test script is ready to go, use Visual Studio's Debug | Start option or simply press F5 to launch the Test.sql that will execute your CLR database object. You can see an example of using the Visual Studio 2005 debugger to step through a SQL Server project in Figure 3-15.

At this point you can step through the code, set new breakpoints, and change and inspect variables.

NOTE

Debugging should be performed on a development system, not on a production system. Using the SQLCRL debugger from Visual Studio causes all SQLCLR threads to stop, which prevents other CLR objects from running.

.NET Database Object Security

No discussion of the new CLR features would be complete without a description of the security issues associated with using .NET assemblies and the SQL Server CLR.

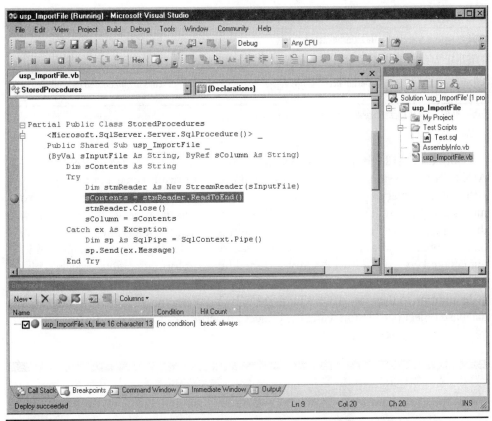

Figure 3-15 *Debugging Visual Studio 2005 SQL Server projects*

Unlike T-SQL, which doesn't have any native facilities for referencing resources outside the database, .NET assemblies are fully capable of accessing both system and network resources. Therefore, securing them is an important aspect of their development. With SQL Server 2005, Microsoft has integrated the user-based SQL Server security model with the permissions-based CLR security model. Following the SQL Server security model, users are able to access only database objects—including those created from .NET assemblies—to which they have user rights. The CLR security model extends this by providing control over the types of system resources that can be accessed by .NET code running on the server. CLR security permissions are specified at the time the assembly is created by using the WITH PERMISSION_SET clause of the CREATE ASSEMBLY statement. Table 3-4 summarizes the options for CLR database security permissions that can be applied to SQL Server database objects.

CRL Security	External Access Allowed	Calls to Unmanaged Code
SAFE	No external access	No calls to unmanaged code
EXTERNAL_ACCESS	External access permitted via management APIs	No calls to unmanaged code
UNSAFE	External access allowed	Calls to unmanaged code allowed

Table 3-4   *CLR Database Object Security Options*

Using the SAFE permission restricts all external access. The EXTERNAL_ ACCESS permission enables some external access of resources using managed APIs. SQL Server impersonates the caller in order to access external resources. You must have the new EXTERNAL_ACCESS permission in order to create objects with this permission set. The UNSAFE permission is basically an anything-goes type of permission. All system resources can be accessed, and calls to both managed and unmanaged code are allowed. Only system administrators can create objects with UNSAFE permissions.

In addition to using the CREATE ASSEMBLY statement, you can also set the CLR database object permission using the project properties as is shown in Figure 3-16.

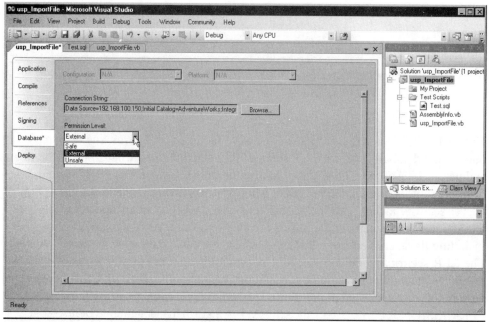

Figure 3-16   *Setting the CLR permission*

System View	Description
sys.objects	Contains all database objects. CLR database objects are identified in the typ_desc column.
sys.assemblies	Contains all of the assemblies in a database.
sys.assembly_files	Contains all of the filenames that were used to create the assemblies in a database.
sys.assembly_types	Contains all of the user-defined types that were added to a database.
sys.assembly_references	Contains all of the assembly references in a database.

Table 3-5   *System Views to Manage CLR Database Objects*

To interactively set the CLR permission level, open the project properties by selecting the Project | Properties option from the Visual Studio 2005 menu. Then open the Database tab and click the Permission Level drop-down. The project must be redeployed before the changes will take place.

Managing CLR Database Objects

As shown in Table 3-5, SQL Server 2005 provides system views that enable you to see the different CLR objects that are being used in the database.

Summary

Database objects created using the CLR are best suited for objects that replace extended stored procedures, require complex logic, or are potentially transportable between the database and the data tier of an application. They are not as well suited to raw data access and update functions as T-SQL. By taking advantage of CLR database objects, you can add a lot of power and flexibility to your database applications.

CHAPTER

4

SQL Server Service Broker

The SQL Server Service Broker is a new subsystem that provides a framework for building asynchronous applications using SQL Server 2005. The ability to support asynchronous queuing expands the scalability of SQL Server 2005 applications. Asynchronous queuing is an important factor for scalability because it allows an application to respond to more requests than the platform may be able to physically handle. Asynchronous queuing is found in many other highly scalable applications, such as the operating system's I/O subsystems, Web servers, and even the internal operations of the SQL Server database engine itself. For instance, in the case of a Web server, if ten thousand users simultaneously requested resources from the server, without asynchronous queuing the Web server would be overwhelmed as it attempted to synchronously handle all of the incoming requests one at a time. Asynchronous queuing enables all of the requests to be captured in a queue. Then instead of being overwhelmed, the Web server can process entries from the queue at its maximum levels of efficiency. The addition of the SQL Server Service Broker to SQL Server 2005 enables you to build this same type of scalability into your database applications.

In this chapter you'll learn how to develop asynchronous applications using the new SQL Server Service Broker. First you'll get an overview of the new subsystem and learn about its core components. Next, you'll learn about the new T-SQL Data Definition Language (DDL) and Data Manipulation Language (DML) commands that Microsoft has added to SQL Server 2005 that enable you to create and use SQL Server Service Broker. Then you'll see how to you create a basic SQL Server Service Broker application. First, you'll see how to activate the SQL Service Broker subsystem and create all of the objects required by a SQL Server Service Broker application. Then you'll see how to use the new T-SQL commands to send and receive data using those SQL Server Service Broker objects.

SQL Server Service Broker Architecture

It's important to keep in mind that the SQL Server Service Broker is an application framework. Its goal is to take on the hard work of building asynchronous applications, and it does that by handling all of the heavy lifting for the asynchronous application. SQL Server Service Broker takes care of all of the hard-to-code details like guaranteed-in-order message routing and delivery. In other words, SQL Server Service Broker provides the plumbing for an asynchronous application but doesn't provide the application itself. It is still up to you to build the application that uses the framework supplied by the SQL Server Service broker subsystem. Microsoft has made use of the SQL Server Service Broker subsystem to enable functionality in several other areas of SQL Server 2005, including Notification Services, Reporting Services, and asynchronous query notifications.

The SQL Server Service Broker is completely integrated with the SQL Server 2005 engine and is fully transactional. Transactions can incorporate queued events and can be both committed and rolled back. In addition, the new SQL Server Service Broker also supports reliable delivery of messages to remote queues. This means that information sent via SQL Server Service Broker can span multiple SQL Server systems and still provide guaranteed in-order, one-time-only message delivery— even to remote queues that must be reached across multiple routing steps. The SQL Server Service Broker will take care of the mechanics required to break the large messages into smaller chunks that are sent across the network and then reassemble them at the other end. You can see an overview of the SQL Server Service Broker architecture in Figure 4-1.

Messages

Messages are the core bits of information that are sent by a SQL Server Service Broker application. These messages can be text messages or consist of binary data or XML. For XML messages, SQL Server can validate that the messages are well formed and that they comply with a predefined schema. You create a SQL Server Service Broker message by running the CREATE MESSAGE TYPE command, which is where you specify the type of content that the message will have. The messages that are sent across the queues can be very large—up to 2GB.

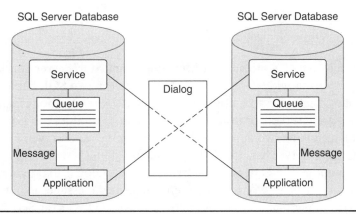

Figure 4-1   *SQL Service Broker Architecture*

Queues

SQL Server Service Broker *queues* contain a collection of related messages. Each queue is associated with a service. When a SQL Server Service Broker application sends a message, that message must first be placed in a queue. Likewise, when that message is received by the target system, it is received into a queue. Messages are validated when they are received by the target queue. If a message is not valid, then the service returns an error to the sender. Then the application can read the queue and process the message. You create a SQL Server Service Broker queue by running the CREATE QUEUE command.

Contracts

Contracts essentially define which messages can be used by a given queue. In order to be processed, a contract must first be created between a SQL Server Service Broker message and a queue or, more specifically, the queue's service. The contract provides information to the service about the type of messages it will process. The contract also prevents errant messages from being sent to and used by an unintended target application. You create a SQL Server Service Broker message by running the CREATE CONTRACT command.

Services

A SQL Server Service Broker *service* is a specific Service Broker task or set of tasks. Each queue has an associated service. Conversations occur between services. The contracts associated with the service define the specific messages that will be processed by the service.

Dialogs

Dialogs are an essential component of Microsoft's new SQL Server Service Broker. Essentially, dialogs provide two-way messaging between two SQL Server Service Broker services. Dialogs can be used for interserver communications for services running on different servers or instances, or they can be used for intraserver communications linking two applications running on the same server. Figure 4-2 illustrates the SQL Server Services Broker's dialog.

The main purpose of a SQL Server Service Broker dialog is to provide an ordered message delivery. In other words, dialogs enable queued messages to always be read in the same order that they are put into the queue. SQL Server Service Broker

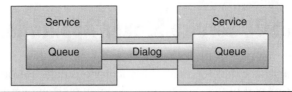

Figure 4-2   *SQL Service Broker dialog*

dialogs maintain reliable event ordering across servers even if network, application, or other failures temporarily disrupt the communications between dialog endpoints. When the communications are restored, the events will continue to be processed in order from the point of the last processed queued entry. Dialogs can be set up to process messages in either full-duplex mode or half-duplex mode.

Message Transport

The SQL Server Service Broker message transport protocol enables messages to be sent across the network. It is based on TCP/IP, and the overall architecture of the SQL Server Service Broker message transport is a bit like the architecture used by TCP/IP and FTP. By default the SQL Service Broker uses TCP/IP port 4022. The SQL Server Service Broker message transport is composed of two protocols: the Adjacent Broker Protocol, which is a lower-level protocol like TCP, and the Dialog Protocol, which is a higher-level protocol like FTP that rides on top of the lower-level Adjacent Broker Protocol.

Adjacent Broker Protocol   The Adjacent Broker Protocol is a highly efficient low-level TCP/IP protocol that provides the basic message transport. It is a bidirectional and multiplexed protocol and so can handle the message transport for multiple SQL Server Service Broker dialogs. It doesn't worry about message order or confirming message delivery. That's all handled by the Dialog Protocol. Instead, the Adjacent Broker Protocol simply sends messages across the network as quickly as it can.

Dialog Protocol   The Dialog Protocol is a higher-level protocol that utilizes the services of the Adjacent Broker Protocol to handle end-to-end communications for a SQL Server Service Broker dialog. It is designed to provide one-time-only, in-order delivery of messages, handling the sending and acknowledgment of messages. It also provides symmetric failure handling where both end nodes are notified of any message delivery failures. In addition, the Dialog Protocol is responsible for authentication and encryption of messages.

Developing SQL Service Broker Applications

As you saw in the first part of this chapter, the SQL Server Service Broker is a subsystem that enables the development of asynchronous database-oriented messaging applications. The first part of this chapter provided you with an overview of the primary components of the SQL Service Broker subsystem and gave you an idea of the functions and interactions of those components. This section will present the new T-SQL commands that you can employ to create and use SQL Server Service Broker objects; it will then present a sample SQL Server Service Broker application.

SQL Server Service Broker DDL and DML

SQL Server 2005 utilizes a new set of T-SQL commands to describe the database objects used in a Service Broker application as well as new commands that enable you to access those objects in your applications.

T-SQL DDL

T-SQL has been enhanced with several new statements that enable the native integration of SQL Server Service Broker messaging with traditional database procedures. Table 4-1 summarizes the new T-SQL DDL statements that are used to create SQL Server Service Broker objects.

T-SQL DML

In addition to the new T-SQL DDL statements that are used to create the new SQL Server Service Broker objects, there are also a group of new T-SQL statements that enable your applications to set up conversations and work with the messages in a SQL Server Service Broker application. Table 4-2 lists the new SQL Server Service Broker–related T-SQL DML statements.

Enabling SQL Server Broker

Before you can begin to build SQL Server Service Broker applications, you must first enable the SQL Server Service Broker subsystem. Like the new SQL Server 2005 CLR support, to enhance out-of-the-box security, SQL Server 2005 ships with

T-SQL DDL	Description
CREATE MESSAGE TYPE	Creates a new message type. Message types can be text, binary, or XML.
CREATE CONTRACT	Creates a new contract associating a message type and service.
CREATE QUEUE	Creates a new queue in a database.
CREATE ROUTE	Creates a new route in a database.
CREATE SERVICE	Creates a new service in a database.
ALTER MESSAGE TYPE	Changes a message type.
ALTER CONTRACT	Changes a contract.
ALTER QUEUE	Changes a queue.
ALTER ROUTE	Changes a route.
ALTER SERVICE	Changes a service.
DROP MESSAGE TYPE	Deletes a message type from a database.
DROP CONTRACT	Deletes a contract from a database.
DROP QUEUE	Deletes a queue from a database.
DROP ROUTE	Deletes a route from a database.
DROP SERVICE	Deletes a service from a database.

Table 4-1   *The New T-SQL DDL Statements Used to Create SQL Server Service Broker Objects*

T-SQL DML	Description
BEGIN DIALOG CONVERSATION	Opens a new dialog between two endpoints.
END CONVERSATION	Ends a conversation used by a dialog.
MOVE CONVERSATION	Moves a conversation to a new dialog.
GET CONVERSATION GROUP	Retrieves a conversation group identifier for the next message to be received.
RECEIVE	Receives a message from a queue.
SEND	Sends a message to a queue.
BEGIN DIALOG TIMER	Opens a timed dialog. A message is placed on the dialog when the timer expires.

Table 4-2   *The New SQL Server Service Broker–Related T-SQL DML Statements*

the SQL Server Service Broker disabled. The following code illustrates how to enable the SQL Server Service Broker for the AdventureWorks database:

```
IF NOT EXISTS
  (SELECT * FROM sys.databases
   WHERE name = 'AdventureWorks'
   AND is_broker_enabled = 1)
BEGIN
  ALTER DATABASE AdventureWorks SET ENABLE_BROKER ;
END ;
```

This checks the is_broker_enabled property of the AdventureWorks database. If the is_broker_enabled value is not 1—if, in other words, Service Broker is not enabled—then the ALTER DATABASE SET ENABLE BROKER command is used to enable the Service Broker. This command sets the is_broker_enabled value to 1. As you might have noticed, the SQL Server Service Broker is enabled on a per-database basis.

Using Queues

While the idea of queuing in applications may be a bit foreign to most relational database designers, queues are common in highly scalable applications. Among the most well known of these types of applications are the airline reservation systems used by all major airlines like United, Delta, and American, as well as online travel brokers like Expedia and CheapTickets.com. To get an idea of how queuing is used in one of these applications, you can refer to Figure 4-3, where you can see the design of a sample queued application.

Figure 4-3 presents a high-level overview of an example airline reservation system. Here you can see that the application's presentation layer is delivered to the end user's browser by an application running on a web farm. That application could be written using ASP.NET or some other web development language. The front-end application will then interact with the actual reservation system, which is normally running on another computer system. Because applications like these must support thousands of simultaneous users, they can't afford to lock rows while a given user waits to decide on the final details of a flight or even starts a reservation and then goes to lunch, planning to finish later. Row locking in this type of scenario would seriously inhibit the application's scalability and even the application's usability. Queuing solves this problem by enabling the application to make an asynchronous request for a reservation, sending the request to the back-end reservation system

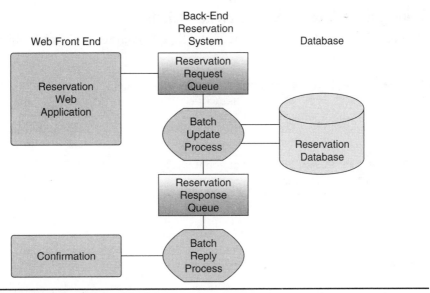

Figure 4-3   *Queued Application Design*

and immediately freeing the front-end application for other work. At no point in the process of placing the reservation have any locks been placed on the database tables. The back-end reservation system, which is essentially operating in batch mode, will take the reservation request off the queue and then perform the update to the database. Since the update is being done in a batch-style mode, it happens very quickly with no user interaction, and minimal time is needed to lock rows while the update is performed. If the request is successful, the end user's reservation is confirmed. Otherwise, if the request is denied because all seats were booked or for some other reason, then the reservation will not be accepted and the user will be contacted with the status.

Sample SQL Server Service Broker Application

This section will now dive into the code and show you how to create a sample SQL Server Service Broker application. First you'll see how to create the required SQL Server Service Broker objects, and then you'll see how to use those objects. The sample application is a simple messaging system that places a simple XML message on an input queue and then reads that message off the queue.

Creating the SQL Server Service Broker Objects

The code that's used to create the required SQL Server Service Broker objects is shown in the following listing:

```
-- Create the XML SBSampleMessage message type
CREATE MESSAGE TYPE SBSampleMessage
    VALIDATION = WELL_FORMED_XML ;
GO


-- Create the SBSampleContract contract
CREATE CONTRACT SBSampleContract
    ( SBSampleMessage SENT BY INITIATOR);
GO


-- Create the queue
CREATE QUEUE [dbo].[ReceiverQueue];
GO


-- Create the queue for the Sender service
CREATE QUEUE [dbo].[SenderQueue];
GO


-- Create the service
CREATE SERVICE SenderService
    ON QUEUE [dbo].[SenderQueue];
GO


-- Create the target service
CREATE SERVICE ReceiverService
    ON QUEUE [dbo].[ReceiverQueue]
    (SBSampleContract);
GO
```

The first step to creating a SQL Server Service Broker application is the creation of the required message types, which describe the messages that will be sent. The first statement shows the creation of the message type named SBSampleMessage. The VALIDATION keyword indicates that this message will be an XML message, and SQL Server will check to make sure the XML is well formed.

Next, a contract is created. The contract describes all of the messages that can be received using a particular service. The first argument is used to name the contract. Here the contract is named SBSampleContract. The SENT BY clause specifies which endpoint can send a message of the indicated message type. INITIATOR indicates that only the initiator of the conversation can send messages of the SBSampleMessage type.

Then the queues must be created. This example shows the creation of two queues: the ReceiverQueue and the SenderQueue. As their names suggest, the SenderQueue will be used to send messages and ReceiverQueue will be used to receive messages of the SBSampleMessage type.

After the queues are created, you can display the contents of the queues by using the SELECT statement exactly as if the queue were a standard database table. The following line of code shows how you can display the contents of the Request queue:

```
SELECT * FROM ReceiverQueue
```

At this point, however, since there are no messages in the queues, the result set will be empty. However, running SELECT statements on the queue is a great way to check out functionality of the SQL Server Service Broker applications you are developing.

After the queues have been created, the next step is to create the services for the queues using the CREATE SERVICE statement. The first parameter names the service. The ON QUEUE clause identifies the queue associated with the service, and then the contracts that are associated with the service are listed. In the preceding listing, you can see two services being created: the SenderService and the ReceiverService. The SenderService handles messages in the SenderQueue, while the ReceiverService handles messages in the ReceiverQueue.

If one of the services were located on a remote system, you would also need to create a route. The CREATE ROUTE statement supplies the SQL Server Service Broker with the system address where the remote service is found. In this case, since both services reside on the same system, no route is needed.

Sending Messages to a Queue

After the necessary SQL Service Broker objects have been created, you're ready to use them in your queuing applications. The following code listing shows how you can add a message to the ResRequestQueue queue:

```
USE AdventureWorks ;
GO

-- Begin a transaction
BEGIN TRANSACTION ;
GO
```

```
-- Declare a variable for the message
DECLARE @SBmessage XML ;
SET @SBmessage = N'<message>Service Broker is Cool</message>' ;

-- Declare a variable for the conversation ID
DECLARE @conversationID UNIQUEIDENTIFIER ;

-- Begin a dialog between the services
BEGIN DIALOG CONVERSATION @conversationID
    FROM SERVICE SenderService
    TO SERVICE 'ReceiverService'
    ON CONTRACT SBSampleContract ;

-- Put the message on the queue
SEND ON CONVERSATION @conversationID
  MESSAGE TYPE SBSampleMessage
  (@SBmessage) ;

-- End the conversation
END CONVERSATION @conversationID ;
GO

-- Commit the transaction to send the message
COMMIT TRANSACTION ;
GO
```

At the start of this listing you can see where a transaction is started. Using transactions enables all of the actions that are performed by the SQL Server Service Broker to commit and, optionally, to roll back any changes that are made within the context of the transaction. Next, a variable named SBMessage is declared that contains the message that will be sent by SQL Service Broker. Then the conversationID variable is created that contains a unique identifier that will be used by a SQL Server Service Broker dialog. Then the BEGIN DIALOG COVERSATION statement is used to open up a new conversation. When you declare a dialog, you always need to specify two endpoints. The FROM SERVICE identifies the sender of the messages, while the TO SERVICE keyword identifies the target endpoint. Here, the sender is named SenderService and the target is named ReceiverService. While this example uses simple names, Microsoft BOL recommends that you use a URL name to uniquely identify the SQL Server Service Broker objects. For example, to ensure uniqueness in the network, they recommend using names like [///AdventureWorks.com/MySample/SenderService]. The ON CONTRACT keyword specifies the contract that's used for the dialog. The Contract specifies the contract that will be used.

Then a SEND operation is executed to send a message on the conservation that was started. Finally, the transaction is committed. The target service will receive the message and add it to the queue that is associated with that service.

At this point you can see the message on the ReceiverQueue by running the following SELECT command:

```
USE AdventureWorks ;
GO
SELECT * FROM ReceiverQueue
```

This shows two entries in the ReceiverQueue. The first entry on the queue is for the message that was placed on the queue by the sample application, and the second entry was created by the END CONVERSATION command. A partial view of the result set showing the contents of the ReceiverQueue is shown here:

```
status priority queuing_order          conversation_group_id
1        0        0                     82C5F460-3305-DA11-8D17-005056C00008
1        0        1                     82C5F460-3305-DA11-8D17-005056C00008

(2 row(s) affected)
```

In order to see the contents of the message, you need to cast the contents of the message_body column in the results set to a varchar, as is shown in the following listing:

```
USE AdventureWorks ;
GO
SELECT CAST(message_body as nvarchar(MAX)) from ReceiverQueue
```

The result set showing the contents of the message is listed here:

```
<message>Service Broker is Cool</message>
NULL

(2 row(s) affected)
```

Retrieving Messages from a Queue

Now that you've seen how to add a message to a queue, the next example will illustrate how to retrieve the messages off the queue. You can see the T-SQL code in the following listing:

```
use Adventureworks
GO

DECLARE @conversationID UNIQUEIDENTIFIER
DECLARE @message_type_id int
DECLARE @message_body NVARCHAR(1000)
DECLARE @message NVARCHAR(1000)

while(1=1)
BEGIN

    BEGIN TRANSACTION

        WAITFOR        (RECEIVE top(1)
        @message_type_id = message_type_id,
        @message_body = message_body,
        @conversationID = conversation_handle
        FROM ReceiverQueue), TIMEOUT 200;

        IF @@ROWCOUNT = 0 OR @@ERROR <> 0 BREAK;

                IF @message_type_id =2
                BEGIN
                    Print 'Conversation Ended'
                    END CONVERSATION @conversationID ;
                END ;

                SELECT @message = 'Received: ' + @message_body;
                PRINT CONVERT(nvarchar(100), @message)
                COMMIT TRANSACTION
            END
    COMMIT TRANSACTION
```

A variable that will contain the receiver dialog identification is declared at the top of this listing, followed by three variables that will be used to pull back information from the queue that's being read. Then a loop is initiated to read all of the entries from the queue. Within the loop a transaction is started and the RECEIVE statement is used to receive a message. In this example, the TOP(1) clause is used to limit the procedure to receiving only a single message at a time. If the TOP clause were omitted, you could receive all of the messages that were present on the queue. The RECEIVE statement populates the three variables. The message_type_id identifies the type of message, which is typically either a user-defined message or an EndDialog message. The @message_body variable contains the contents of the actual message, while the @ReceiverQueue variable contains a handle that identifies the sending dialog.

Then the result set is checked to ensure that a message was actually received. If no rows were received or an error is encountered, then the procedure is ended. Otherwise, the contents will be processed. If the message_type_id is a 2 (meaning the message was an EndDialog message), then the dialog conversation is stopped. Otherwise, the Select statement is used to access the message contents. The received message is concatenated with the string "Received:", the message is printed, and the transaction is committed. You can see the sample text results in the following listing:

```
(1 row(s) affected)
Received: <message>Service Broker is Cool</message>

(1 row(s) affected)
Conversation Ended

(0 row(s) affected)
```

SQL Server Service Broker Activation

SQL Server Service Broker activation is another unique feature of the SQL Server Service Broker subsystem. Activation enables you to create a stored procedure that is associated with a given input queue. The purpose of the stored procedure is to automatically process messages from that queue. As each new message comes in, the associated stored procedure is automatically executed to handle the incoming messages. If the stored procedure encounters an error, it can throw an exception and be automatically recycled.

Periodically, the SQL Server Service Broker checks the status of the input queue to find out if the stored procedure is keeping up with the incoming messages on the input queue. If the SQL Server Service Broker determines that there are waiting messages on the queue, then it will automatically start up another instance of the queue reader to process the additional messages. This process of automatically starting additional queue readers can continue until the preset MAX_QUEUE_READERS value is reached. Likewise, when the SQL Server Service Broker determines that there are no remaining messages on the queue, it will begin to automatically reduce the number of active queue readers.

SQL Server Service Broker queues don't necessarily need to be associated with just stored procedures. Messages that require more complex processing can also be associated with external middle-tier procedures. Since these middle-tier processes are external to the database, they need to be activated differently. To enable the automatic activation of external processes, the SQL Server Service Broker also supports firing a SQL Server event. These events can be subscribed to using WMI (Windows Management Instrumentation).

Dialog Security

When dialogs are created, they can optionally be secured using the WITH ENCRYPTION clause. When a dialog is created using the WITH ENCRYPTION clause, a session key is created that's used to encrypt the messages sent using the dialog. One important point about dialog security is the fact that it is an end-to-end security. In other words, the message is encrypted when it is first sent from a dialog, and it is not decrypted until the message reaches its endpoint. The message contents remain encrypted as the message is forwarded across any intermediate hops. To implement dialog security, the SQL Service Broker uses certificate-based authentication, where the certificate of the sending user is sent along with the message. Because of the asynchronous nature of SQL Service Broker, the security information is stored in the message headers and retrieved by the receiving service when the message is retrieved. This enables SQL Service Broker applications to avoid the need to establish a connection to authenticate messages.

System Views

SQL Server 2005 supplies several new system views that enable you to retrieve information about SQL Service Broker objects and its current status. Table 4-3 lists the new system views.

System View	Description
sys.service_message_types	Lists all the message types that have been created. System message types are listed at the top, while user-defined message types are listed at the end of the display.
sys.service_contracts	Lists all of the contracts that have been created.
sys.service_contract_message_usages	Lists the relationships between contracts and message types. Relationships can be one-to-one or one-to-many.
sys.services	Lists the created services.
sys.service_contract_usages	Lists the relationships between contracts and services. Relationships can be one-to-one or one-to-many.
sys.service_instances	Lists the services that are active at the current time.
sys.conversation_endpoints	Lists the conversation endpoints that are currently active.
sys.routes	Lists the created routes.
sys.remote_service_bindings	Lists the relationship of the services and the users that will execute them.
sys.transmission_queue	Lists all of the messages that are queued to be sent.
sys.service_queues	Lists the queues that have been created.

Table 4-3 *SQL Server 2005 New System Views*

Summary

SQL Server Service Broker is an all new subsystem that enables you to create highly scalable asynchronous applications. In this chapter you learned about the new SQL Server Service Broker architecture and you saw how to create and use the objects that make up a SQL Server Service Broker application.

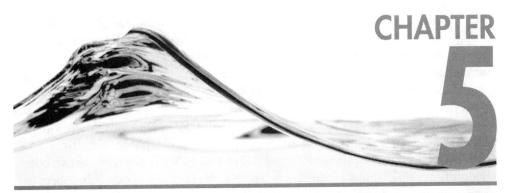

Developing with Notification Services

Notification Services is a new subsystem that Microsoft has added to SQL Server 2005. First introduced as a Web download for SQL Server 2000, Notification Services provides a framework that enables you to develop custom notification applications that monitor for specific data events and then push customized notification information concerning those events to multiple subscribers and devices.

Notification Services is used in a number of well-known scenarios. Microsoft's MSN Messenger uses Notification Services to alert your cell phone of traffic. NASDAQ's Nasdaq.com site and *The New York Times'* NYTimes.com are two other high-profile Notification Services users. The Nasdaq.com site allows subscribers to receive personalized notifications about changes in financial data. Here subscribers can ask to be alerted about specific changes in market prices. The NYTimes.com site uses Notification Services to push new real estate listings in the East Coast market to subscribers. In this scenario, renters or buyers specify the property characteristics that they are interested in, and they receive notifications whenever a property matching their criteria is listed in *The New York Times* real estate classified section.

In this chapter you'll learn how to create a Notification Services application. In the first part of this chapter you'll get an overview showing you how the new subsystem works. In the second part of the chapter you'll see how to build a Notification Services application. Later in the chapter you'll learn how to update a Notification Services application, as well as how to build a .NET subscription/event application.

Notification Services Overview

A Notification Services application is a software layer that sits between an information source and the intended recipient of that information. The Notification Services application monitors certain predefined events and can intelligently filter and route the information about those events to a variety of different target devices using a personalized delivery schedule. Notification Services applications consist of three basic components: events, subscriptions, and notifications. Figure 5-1 provides a very high-level overview of a Notification Services application.

Events

In a Notification Services application, *events* are just what they sound like—things happening that you want to be informed about. In the case of the NASDAQ, an event might be a given stock price rising to a certain level. In a typical database application

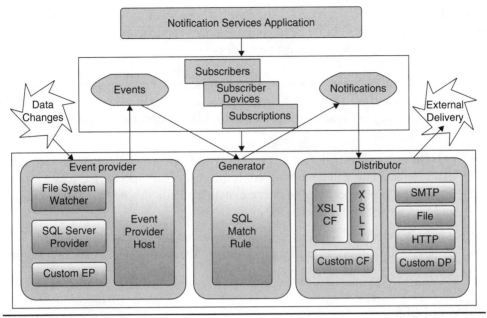

Figure 5-1   *Notification Services overview*

an event could be associated with the value of a given column. Here the event would be fired if the column's value passed a certain predefined threshold.

Event Providers

A Notification Services application monitors for events using an *event provider.* There are three types of Notification Services event providers: hosted, non-hosted, and standard event providers.

Hosted Providers   *Hosted* event providers are directly executed by Notification Services. When Notification Services starts, it automatically initializes and runs enabled hosted event providers.

Non-Hosted Providers   *Non-hosted* event providers are external applications that do not run within the Notification Services process. Non-hosted event providers post event data to a Notification Services application using the EventCollector class; the EventLoader class; or the NseventBeginBatch, NSEventWrite, or NSEventFlushBatch stored procedures.

Standard Providers   SQL Server 2005 ships with a base set of standard event providers that you can readily use to build Notification Services applications. Notification Services provides the following event providers:

▶ **File System Watcher**   The File System Watcher event provider monitors the file system and is triggered when a file is added to the monitored directory. It reads the directory contents into memory and then writes event information to the event table.

▶ **SQL Server**   The SQL Server event provider uses a T-SQL query to specify database data that will be monitored. It then uses Notification Services–provided stored procedures to create events based on this new or updated data and then write these events to the event table.

▶ **Analysis Services**   The Analysis Services event provider uses a static or dynamic MDX query to gather data from an Analysis Services cube and submit the data as events to an application.

Subscriptions

Subscriptions correlate users and the types of events that they are interested in. For example, with the NASDAQ example, a user might create a subscription to get a notification when a given stock price drops below $50 per share. SQL Server 2005's Notification Services stores subscriptions, like events, as rows in a table.

Notifications

The *notification* is essentially a message that will be sent to the end user that contains the information regarding the event that the user subscribed to. Notifications can be delivered in various formats to a variety of different target devices, including XML, HTML, e-mail, WAP, and other formats.

Notification Engine

The Notification Services engine receives external events from the event provider and looks for matches between events and registered subscriptions. When an event matches a subscription, the Notification Services engine sends a notification to the end user.

   The scalability of a Notification Services application depends in a large part on how well the Notification Services engine matches events to subscriptions. Microsoft has designed the underlying Notification Services framework to be scalable at an Internet level, meaning that with the appropriate platform, SQL Server 2005's Notification Services can scale upward to handle millions of events, subscriptions, and notifications. To do that, Notification Services takes advantage of SQL Server

2005's efficient relational database engine to join the rows from the events table with the rows in the subscriptions table in order to match events to subscriptions.

Developing Notification Services Applications

In the first part of this chapter you got an overview of the new SQL Server 2005 Notification Services. In this next section, you learn about the actual steps required to develop SQL Server 2005 Notification Services applications. First, you'll see a quick overview of the development process, and next we'll dive in and build a sample Notification Services application.

The process for developing Notification Services applications begins with defining the rules that govern how the application works. Next, you must compile the application. Then you need to construct an interface that allows the user to add subscriptions to the application. Finally, you'll need to add any custom components that may be needed by the application. Let's look at each of these steps in more detail.

Defining the Application

The Notification Services developer uses a combination of XML and T-SQL to define the application's schema and rules. When you define the schema and the rules for a Notification Services application, you are essentially describing the events that the application will monitor as well as the application's subscriptions, its notifications, and the logic that will be used to match the events to the subscriptions. The Notification Services application's rules are primarily defined in two files—an application definition file and an instance configuration file. Although you can also define them using the Notification Management Objects (NMO) API interface, the application definition file and the instance configuration file are typically created using a standard text editor or an XML-aware editor such as Visual Studio 2005 or XMLSpy. More detailed information about the specific contents of the application definition file and the instance configuration file is presented later in this chapter.

Compiling the Application

After the schema and the rules have been created, the next step in building a Notification Services application is to compile all of the code and register a service that will run the Notification Services applications. To compile the application, you can use the Notification Services node in the SQL Server Management Studio or the nscontrol command-line utility. These tools create the Notification Services instance and database, if required.

Building the Notification Subscription Management Application

The first two steps build the core engine of the Notification Services application. However, users still need a way of adding their own subscription information to the application. To enable users to enter their subscription information, the Notification Services application needs a subscription management interface, which is typically a Web or Windows application built using ASP.NET, VB.NET, or C# technologies. This application updates entries to the Notification Services subscription database.

Adding Custom Components

Finally, the last step in building your Notification Services application is to optionally add any custom components that might be needed by the application. Custom components would include any required custom event providers, content formats, or notification delivery protocols that are not included in the base SQL Server 2005 Notification Services product.

Notification Services Application Sample

The sample Notification Services application that is presented in the next part of this section represents a simple shipping notification application. In this example, events consist of shipment information, which identifies a store ID that will receive the shipment as well as the date, the product ID, the product name, and the number of units that are being shipped. Subscribers will select a store ID where they want to be notified about the incoming shipments.

To make all of this work, an event will be created that is fired if the value of the store ID for a shipment matches a store ID that has been registered by a subscriber. The user must enter a subscription for that event, and a rule must be added to allow the Notification Services engine to match the events to the subscriptions. When an event matches the event rule, the distribution provider will create a file-based notification. Now that you've got an overview of the sample Notification Services application, let's see how it's built.

Creating the ICF File

Notification Services applications consist of two primary files: an *application definition file (ADF)* and an *instance configuration file (ICF)*—both XML files that must be built in accordance with their XSD schemas. The XSD schemas serve to make sure that both documents possess the required elements and attributes. The ICF and

ADF files are essentially the source code for a Notification Services application. The ADF file is the core file for the Notification Services; the different sections of the ADF describe the event, subscription, rules, and notification structure that will be employed by the Notification Services application. The ICF file defines the name of the Notification Services application as well as its instance name and the application's directory path. The instance name is essentially the name of a Windows service that runs the Notification Services application.

Fortunately you're not required to build these files from scratch. SQL Server 2005 Notification Services provides two templates that can be used as a starting point for creating your own ADF and ICF files. The Minimal template includes only the absolutely essential elements required by the ADF file. The Complete ADF template includes all of the possible elements in the ADF template. However, if you're tempted to use the Complete template, be aware that some of the entries are actually conflicting and cannot be present in the same file. In most cases it's better to start with the Minimal template and add in just those elements that your application requires. Both templates can be found in the SQL Server BOL by searching for ADF Template.

To create the ADF and ICF files using Visual Studio 2005's XML editor, open Visual Studio 2005 and then select the File | New | File option to display the New File dialog shown in Figure 5-2.

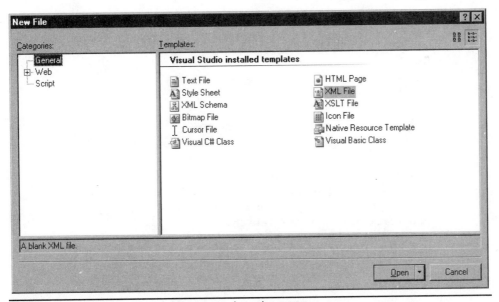

Figure 5-2   *Creating an ADF file in Visual Studio 2005*

The default filename is created as XMLFile1.xml. Select the File | Save XMLfile1
.xml As option and save the file into the desired target directory using the name of
icf.xml. Repeat the process for adf.xml, except that when you select the Save As
option, you'll name the file adf.xml.

The following listing shows the ICF file, icf.xml, that's used for this Notification
Services sample application:

```xml
<?xml version="1.0" encoding="utf-8"?>
<NotificationServicesInstance
xmlns:xsd="http://www.w3.org/2001/XMLSchema"
xmlns:xsi="http://www.w3.org/2001/XMLSchema-instance"
xmlns="http://www.microsoft.com/MicrosoftNotificationServices/
ConfigurationFileSchema">

  <ParameterDefaults>
    <Parameter>
      <Name>_NSEngineInstance_</Name>
      <Value>%COMPUTERNAME%</Value>
    </Parameter>
    <Parameter>
      <Name>_ServerName_</Name>
      <Value>%COMPUTERNAME%</Value>
    </Parameter>
    <Parameter>
      <Name>_InstancePath_</Name>
      <Value>c:\temp\</Value>
    </Parameter>
  </ParameterDefaults>

    <InstanceName>NSAppInstance</InstanceName>
    <SqlServerSystem>%_NSEngineInstance_%</SqlServerSystem>
    <Applications>
      <Application>
        <ApplicationName>NSApp</ApplicationName>
        <BaseDirectoryPath>%_InstancePath_%</BaseDirectoryPath>
        <ApplicationDefinitionFilePath>
          %_InstancePath_%\ADF.xml
        </ApplicationDefinitionFilePath>
          <Parameters>
            <Parameter>
              <Name>_ServerName_</Name>
              <Value>%_ServerName_%</Value>
```

```
          </Parameter>
            <Parameter>
              <Name>_InstancePath_</Name>
              <Value>%_InstancePath_%</Value>
            </Parameter>
          </Parameters>
    </Application>
      </Applications>
      <DeliveryChannels>
        <DeliveryChannel>
          <DeliveryChannelName>FileChannel</DeliveryChannelName>
          <ProtocolName>File</ProtocolName>
          <Arguments>
            <Argument>
              <Name>FileName</Name>
              <Value>%_InstancePath_%\NSAppNotification.htm</Value>
            </Argument>
          </Arguments>
        </DeliveryChannel>
      </DeliveryChannels>
</NotificationServicesInstance>
```

You can see that the ICF is a relatively simple document. This file can be created
using any text or XML-aware editor. The first section to notice is the Parameters
section, which enables you to more easily deploy the Notification Services application
to other systems by passing in environment variables to the creation scripts. In this
example the _NSEngineInstance_ and _ServerName_ variables are assigned the value
of the local computer name. The _InstancePath_ variable is assigned the value of
c:\temp. This designates where the ICF and ADF files will be located. The next section
contains the elements that define the Notification Services instance.

The most important points to notice are the SqlServerSystem, InstanceName,
ApplicationName, BaseDirectoryPath, and ApplicationDefinitionFilePath tags.
As you might guess, the SqlServerSystem name tag contains the name of the SQL
Server system that will host the Notification Services databases, the InstanceName
tag defines the instance name for the application, and the ApplicationName tag
defines the name of the Notification Services application. In both cases, the values
for these come from the parameter variables that were defined in the Parameters
section. You should note that when the parameter variables are used in the ICF or
ADF file, they are enclosed using % % symbols. The BaseDirectoryPath tells the
compiler where to find the ADF file, and the ApplicationDefinitionFilePath tag

supplies the name of the XML document that contains the ADF code. One point to notice here is that the Application section also contains a Parameters section that defines the parameters that are passed to the ADF file. In order to use parameters in the ADF file, they must be defined in the Application section of the ICF file. Here you can see that the parameters are basically chained together. The Application section defines a _ServerName_ variable that in turn gets its value from the %_ServerName _% variable in the ICF file. Likewise an _InstancePath_ variable is defined that gets its value from the %_ InstancePath _% variable.

In addition to these basic items, the ACF also uses the DeliveryChannel tag to define how notifications will be delivered. In this example, the DeliveryChannel tag uses the File protocol to deliver notifications to the file system, and notifications will be output to the file named NSAppNotifications.htm in the directory c:\temp, which was defined by the %_InstancePath_% variable.

Defining the ADF File

While the ACF file describes the server and the locations where the application definition files are found, the core definitions that control how a Notification Services application works are described in the ADF.

Defining the Events

The first thing that needs to be done to build the example application is to build the schema for the events. The event defines the data that can be submitted to your Notification Services application and is used to generate notifications. In the ADF file the EventClasses element contains the XML code that's used to define the Notification Services events. The EventClasses element can contain multiple event definitions. Each event definition is described in a separate EventClass subelement. The following code section from the first part of the adf.xml file illustrates the XML code used to define the schema and events for the NSApp sample application:

```
<?xml version="1.0" encoding="utf-8" ?>
<Application xmlns:xsd="http://www.w3.org/2001/XMLSchema"
xmlns:xsi="http://www.w3.org/2001/XMLSchema-instance"
xmlns="http://www.microsoft.com/MicrosoftNotificationServices/
ApplicationDefinitionFileSchema">

<!-- Describe the Events  -->
<EventClasses>
  <EventClass>
```

```
      <EventClassName>ShipData</EventClassName>
      <Schema>
        <Field>
          <FieldName>StoreID</FieldName>
          <FieldType>int</FieldType>
            <FieldTypeMods>not null</FieldTypeMods>
        </Field>
        <Field>
          <FieldName>Date</FieldName>
          <FieldType>datetime</FieldType>
          <FieldTypeMods>not null</FieldTypeMods>
        </Field>
        <Field>
          <FieldName>ProductID</FieldName>
          <FieldType>int</FieldType>
          <FieldTypeMods>not null</FieldTypeMods>
        </Field>
        <Field>
          <FieldName>ProductName</FieldName
          <FieldType>nvarchar(40)</FieldType>
          <FieldTypeMods>not null</FieldTypeMods>
        </Field>
        <Field>
          <FieldName>Units</FieldName>
          <FieldType>int</FieldType>
          <FieldTypeMods>not null</FieldTypeMods>
        </Field>
      </Schema>
      <IndexSqlSchema>
        <SqlStatement>
          CREATE INDEX ShipDataIndex ON ShipData ( StoreID )
        </SqlStatement>
      </IndexSqlSchema>
    </EventClass>
</EventClasses>
```

All ADF files must begin with the application elements, which, as you might guess, represent the Notification Services application. This code snippet shows the beginning tag. (The ending tag is shown in a later code snippet.) The primary elements within the application element that define the application are the EventClasses, SubscriptionClasses, and NotificationClasses elements.

NOTE

This is not the entire adf.xml file. The adf.xml file is continued in the following listings.

The definition of the event is shown in the EventClasses section of the ADF. Because this sample application uses only a single event, the EventClasses element contains only one EventClass element, named ShipData. The Schema section within the EventClass element defines the event schema that the Notification Services application will monitor. In this case, five columns are defined: the StoreID column, which identifies a store ID to receive a shipment, a Date representing the shipment date, ProductID and ProductName fields to contain the product identification, and a Units field that shows the number of units in the shipment. Notification Services uses these definitions to create a table in the Notification Services database. The IndexSqlSchema tag is use to create an index over the StoreID column.

Defining the ADF Providers

After defining the events that the application will monitor, the next step in defining the ADF application is to specify the provider that will deliver those events to the application. What follows is the next section of the adf.xml file. Here you can see the definition for the SQL Server event provider that is used to connect the Notification Services application to SQL Server:

```
<Providers>
  <HostedProvider>
    <ProviderName>SQLData</ProviderName>
    <ClassName>SQLProvider</ClassName>
    <SystemName>%_ServerName_%</SystemName>
    <Schedule>
      <Interval>P0DT00H00M60S</Interval>
    </Schedule>
    <Arguments>
      <Argument>
        <Name>EventsQuery</Name>
        <Value>SELECT StoreID, Date, ProductID, ProductName, Units
          FROM ShipData</Value>
      </Argument>
      <Argument>
        <Name>EventClassName</Name>
        <Value>ShipData</Value>
      </Argument>
    </Arguments>
  </HostedProvider>
</Providers>
```

The Providers section of the ADF describes the event providers used by the Notification Services application. In this example, the HostedProvider element defines the SQL Server event provider. In other words, a SQL Server table will be the source of the events that the application is monitoring. The ProviderName element is used to assign a name to the provider, and the SystemName element supplies the name of the SQL Server system that the provider will connect to. Here you can see that the actual value is supplied by the %_ServerName_% variable that was passed in from the ICF file.

The Schedule element defines how often the provider will connect to the system; this interval is governed by the value defined in the Interval element. The value in the Interval element uses the XML duration data type. The 0DT portion of this value represents a date interval with a value of 0. The 00HR portion represents an hourly interval with a value of 0. The 00M segment represents a minute interval with a value of 0. The 60S portion represents a second's interval with a value of 60. The value of P0DT00H00M60S thus sets the polling interval to 60 seconds.

The Arguments element supplies the query that will be used to extract data from the event source. In this example, the contents of the ShipData table will be retrieved every 60 seconds for the event class named ShipData that was defined in the preceding EventClass element.

Defining the ADF Subscription

Once the events have been described, the next step in creating the ADF file is defining the subscriptions. When you define a subscription class, you are defining the schema that will be used to store subscriptions. To create the subscription class, you define fields for the subscription data you collect. As you saw earlier with the event class, Notification Services uses the subscription class definitions to create database objects like tables, views, indexes, and stored procedures for the subscription class.

The following code listing shows the next portion of the adf.xml file, which describes the subscriptions used by the sample Notification Services application:

```xml
<!-- Describe the Subscription -->
<SubscriptionClasses>
  <SubscriptionClass>
    <SubscriptionClassName>ShipStore</SubscriptionClassName>
    <Schema>
      <Field>
        <FieldName>DeviceName</FieldName>
        <FieldType>nvarchar(255)</FieldType>
        <FieldTypeMods>not null</FieldTypeMods>
      </Field>
```

```
      <Field>
        <FieldName>SubscriberLocale</FieldName>
        <FieldType>nvarchar(10)</FieldType>
        <FieldTypeMods>not null</FieldTypeMods>
      </Field>
      <Field>
        <FieldName>StoreID</FieldName>
        <FieldType>int</FieldType>
        <FieldTypeMods>not null</FieldTypeMods>
      </Field>
    </Schema>
    <IndexSqlSchema>
      <SqlStatement>
      CREATE INDEX ShipStoreIndex ON ShipStore( StoreID )
      </SqlStatement>
    </IndexSqlSchema>
      <EventRules>
      <EventRule>
        <RuleName>ShipEventRule</RuleName>
        <EventClassName>ShipData</EventClassName>
        <Action>
          INSERT INTO ShipNotifications(SubscriberId,
            DeviceName, SubscriberLocale, StoreId, Date,
            ProductID, ProductName, Units)
          SELECT s.SubscriberId, s.DeviceName, s.SubscriberLocale,
            e.StoreID, e.Date, e.ProductID, e.ProductName, e.Units
          FROM ShipData e,ShipStore s WHERE e.StoreId = s.StoreId;
        </Action>
      </EventRule>
    </EventRules>
  </SubscriptionClass>
</SubscriptionClasses>
```

Like EventClasses, the SubscriptionClasses section of the ADF document can describe multiple subscriptions, where each subscription is described in a separate SubscriptionClass element. This example uses a single SubscriptionClass named ShipStore. The Schema section describes the data used by the subscription. The DeviceName field identifies that target device type. The SubLocale is used to optionally change the language that the subscriber will use to receive the notification.

The StoreID field identifies the store for which events will be subscribed to. The IndexSqlSchema element is used to create an index on the StoreID column. As you saw with the event class, Notification Services uses the subscription class descriptions to create database objects when the Notification Services application is generated.

After the subscriptions have been set up, the next section of code in the EventRules element defines the logic that the Notification Services application will use to match events to subscriptions. While the Event and Subscription information is defined using XML, the event rules are created using T-SQL code that's stored in the EventRules Action element. In this example, the most important thing to notice is that when the join condition is met, a row for the subscriber will be created. In other words, when an event record is added where the StoreID matches the StoreID from a subscription record, then a new row will be written to the ShipNotifications table creating a notification. That notification will contain the information from the subscription, including the SubscriberID, the DeviceName, and the SubscriberLocale, as well as information from the event, including the StoreID, the Date, the ProductID, the ProductName, and the number of Units.

Defining the ADF Notification Schema

The final part of the ADF file defines the notification as described in the NotificationClasses section. The NotificationClasses describe how the notification information will be delivered. The NotificationClasses element could describe multiple notification types, where each type is described in its own NotificationClass element. Because this sample application uses only one type of notification, the NotificationClasses section contains a single NotificationClass element.

```
<!-- Describes the Notifications -->
<NotificationClasses>
  <NotificationClass>
    <NotificationClassName>ShipNotifications</NotificationClassName>
      <Schema>
        <Fields>
          <Field>
            <FieldName>StoreID</FieldName>
            <FieldType>int</FieldType>
          </Field>
          <Field>
            <FieldName>Date</FieldName>
            <FieldType>datetime</FieldType>
          </Field>
```

```
        <Field>
          <FieldName>ProductID</FieldName>
          <FieldType>int</FieldType>
        </Field>
        <Field>
          <FieldName>ProductName</FieldName>
          <FieldType>nvarchar(40)</FieldType>
        </Field>
        <Field>
          <FieldName>Units</FieldName>
          <FieldType>int</FieldType>
        </Field>
      </Fields>
    </Schema>

    <!-- Specify the Content Format XSLT -->
    <ContentFormatter>
      <ClassName>XsltFormatter</ClassName>
        <Arguments>
          <Argument>
            <Name>XsltBaseDirectoryPath</Name>
            <Value>%_InstancePath_%</Value>
          </Argument>
          <Argument>
            <Name>XsltFileName</Name>
            <Value>NSApp.xslt</Value>
          </Argument>
        </Arguments>
    </ContentFormatter>
    <Protocols>
      <Protocol>
        <ProtocolName>File</ProtocolName>
      </Protocol>
    </Protocols>
  </NotificationClass>
</NotificationClasses>

<Generator>
  <SystemName>%_ServerName_%</SystemName>
</Generator>
<Distributors>
```

```
    <Distributor>
      <SystemName>%_ServerName_%</SystemName>
    </Distributor>
  </Distributors>

  <!-- ApplicationExecutionSettings -->
  <ApplicationExecutionSettings>
    <QuantumDuration>PT15S</QuantumDuration>
    <DistributorLogging>
      <LogBeforeDeliveryAttempts>false</LogBeforeDeliveryAttempts>
      <LogStatusInfo>false</LogStatusInfo>
      <LogNotificationText>false</LogNotificationText>
    </DistributorLogging>
    <Vacuum>
      <RetentionAge>P1D</RetentionAge>
      <VacuumSchedule>
        <Schedule>
          <StartTime>3:00:00</StartTime>
          <Duration>P0DT02H00M00S</Duration>
        </Schedule>
      </VacuumSchedule>
    </Vacuum>
  </ApplicationExecutionSettings>
</Application>
```

In this listing you can see that the notification class is named ShipNotifications. The ShipNotifications class' Schema element defines the information that will be sent to the subscriber. Here you can see that the values of the StoreID, Date, ProductID, ProductName, and Units will be sent as part of the notification.

The ContentFormatter element defines how the notification will be formatted when it is sent to the subscriber. This example illustrates using the built-in XSLTFormatter. The Arguments element describes the directory where the XSLT file is found as well as the name of the file. In this listing you can see that the XSLT file is found in the %_InstancePath_% directory (which, as you saw in the ICF file, points to C:\temp) and is named NSApp.xslt. The value of File in the Protocols section indicates that the notification will be generated in the file system.

The Generator, Distributor, and ApplicationExecutionSettings elements specify the SQL Server system that will be used to generate notifications, the system that will be used to distribute notifications, the interval at which system performance counters will be updated, and the interval at which the notification tables will be cleaned up of undelivered notifications, respectively.

Formatting the Notification Output

In the preceding listing you saw that the notification was formatted using the NSApp.xslt style sheet. You can see what that example style sheet looks like in the following listing:

```
<?xml version="1.0" encoding="UTF-8" ?>
<xsl:stylesheet version="1.0"
xmlns:xsl="http://www.w3.org/1999/XSL/Transform">
<xsl:template match="notifications">
<HTML>
  <BODY>
    <xsl:apply-templates />
    <I>
        This message was generated using
        <BR/>Microsoft SQL Server Notification Services
    </I><BR/><BR/>
  </BODY>
</HTML>
</xsl:template>
  <xsl:template match="notification">
    <P>
        There is a shipment for: <B><xsl:value-of select="StoreID"/></B>
        <BR/>Date: <B><xsl:value-of select="Date"/></B>
        <BR/>Product ID: <B><xsl:value-of select="ProductID"/></B>
        <BR/>Product Name: <B><xsl:value-of select="ProductName"/></B>
        <BR/>Units: <B><xsl:value-of select="Units"/></B>
    </P>
  </xsl:template>
</xsl:stylesheet>
```

The style sheet used to format the Notification Services application's output is a standard XSLT style sheet. In the template section you can see where the StoreID, Date, ProductID, ProductName, and Units fields from the NotificationClass are displayed in the notification.

Building the Notification Services Application

After the required XML and T-SQL application code has been created, you're ready to build the Notification Services application. Notification Services applications can be created interactively using the SQL Server Management Studio, or they can be created using the nscontrol utility. First, you'll see how to create them using the SQL Server Management Studio, and then you'll see how you can create Notification Services applications using the nscontrol commands in the batch file.

Building Notification Services Applications Using SQL Server Management Studio

After the icf.xml and adf.xml files that define the Notification Services have been created, you can use them to build your Notification Services application from the SQL Server Management Studio by first opening the Object Browser and right-clicking the Notification Services node. Then you can select the New Notification Services Instance option from the context menu to display a screen like the one in Figure 5-3.

To create a new Notification Services application using the New Notification Services Instance dialog, you click Browse and navigate to the directory that contains your application's instance configuration file. For this example that file is named icf.xml, so next you select the icf.xml file and click OK. If you want the application

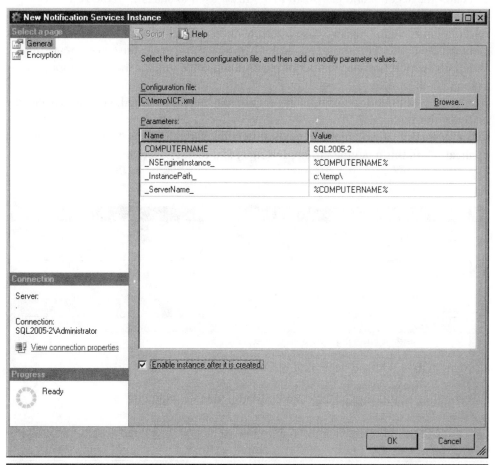

Figure 5-3   *The New Notification Services Instance dialog*

to be immediately enabled after it is created, you need to check the Enable Instance After It Is Created check box. Clicking OK generates the Notification Services application and displays the summary dialog that you can see in Figure 5-4.

At this point, although the application has been created and enabled, it's still not ready to be used. Before it can be used, the application must be registered and then started. Registering the application creates a Windows service, and starting the application starts that service. To register the newly created Notification Services application, open the SQL Server Management Studio and then, in Object Explorer, expand the Notification Services node. Right-click the name of your Notification Services application; in this example, the name is NSAppInstance. Select the Tasks option and then select Register. Then select the Create Windows Service check box and enter the account and password that will be used to start the Windows service. If you use SQL Server Authentication, you'll need to enter the SQL Server login information as well. Otherwise, just use the default value of Windows Authentication and then click OK. This will register the Notification Services instance, create the Windows service, and create a set of performance counters for the application. Figure 5-5 illustrates registering the Notification Services application.

After the Notification Services application has been registered, you can go ahead and start the application. To do so, go to SQL Server Management Studio, open Object Explorer, and navigate to the Notification Services node. Right-click your application, in this example NSAppInstance, and then choose Start.

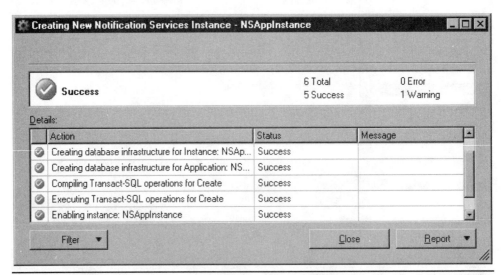

Figure 5-4 *The Notification Services Creation Status dialog*

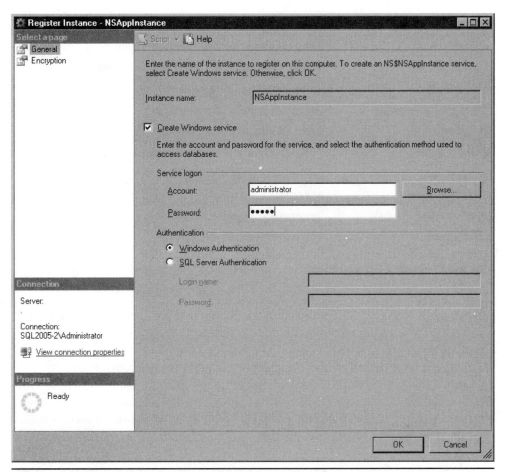

Figure 5-5   *Registering the Notification Services application*

NOTE

If the Notification Services application doesn't start, the most likely problem is the account used by the Notification Services Windows service. Check to make sure you are using a valid account and it has permissions to access the Notification Services databases. Otherwise, you will need to recheck the values used in your ADF.

Building Notification Services Applications Using nscontrol

As an alternative to using the SQL Server Management Studio to create Notification Services applications, you can use the nscontrol commands. A command-line tool that's used to create and administer Notification Services applications, nscontrol

nscontrol Command	Description
nscontrol create	Creates a Notification Services application and its databases.
nscontrol delete	Deletes a Notification Services application and its databases.
nscontrol disable	Disables a Notification Services application.
nscontrol displayargumentkey	Displays the key used to encrypt event data.
nscontrol enable	Enables a Notification Services application.
nscontrol listversions	Displays the version of Notification Services and any registered applications.
nscontrol register	Registers a Notification Services application.
nscontrol status	Displays the status of a Notification Services application.
nscontrol unregister	Unregisters a Notification Services application.
nscontrol update	Updates a Notification Services application.

Table 5-1 *Nscontrol Commands*

understands a number of different action commands that you can use to work with Notification Services applications. Table 5-1 lists the available nscontrol action commands.

Creating a Notification Services application is a multistep process. First, the application needs to be created using the nscontrol create command. This creates the database used by the Notification Services application. Then the application needs to be registered using the nscontrol register command. This creates the service that is used to run the application. Finally, the application needs to be enabled using the nscontrol enable command. The following batch file illustrates the command sequence needed to create the example NSSample Notification Services application:

```
echo off
cls
set NSdir="C:\Program Files\Microsoft SQL Server\90\NotificationServices\9.0.242\bin"
echo =======================================
echo Beginning NSAppInstance Creation
echo =======================================
echo .
echo Create the application databases
%NSdir%\nscontrol create -in ICF.xml

echo Register the application
%NSdir%\nscontrol register -name NSAppInstance -service
```

```
echo Enable the application
%NSdir%\nscontrol enable -name NSAppInstance

echo start the NS app as a service
net start NS$NSAppInstance

echo Display the status of the app
%NSdir%\nscontrol status -name NSAppInstance
```

The nscontrol create command's –in argument specifies the name of the Notification Services ICF. In this example, the ICF is named icf.xml. Running the nscontrol create command creates two databases on the server, NSSampleInstanceMain and NSSamp leInstanceNSSample, which store the Notification Services application definition and data events.

The nscontrol register command uses the –name argument to identify the instance name of the Notification Services application to register. The –service switch directs it to register a service named NS$NSSampleInstance.

The nscontrol enable command uses the –name parameter to identify the instance name of the application that will be enabled.

Once the application is enabled, its service can be started using the net start command. For testing, you can also execute the NS$NSSampleInstance application from the command prompt or the Run dialog.

Updating Notification Services Applications

Like all other applications, Notification Services applications need to be updated and changed from time to time. To re-create the Notification Services application, you could delete the entire application instance and then re-create, enable, and register the application. However, in most cases there's no need for that many steps. Instead, to update a Notification Services application, you can make changes to your application definition file and then save those changes. Next, open up SQL Server Management Studio and then use Object Explorer to navigate to your Notification Services application listed under the Notification Services node. First, disable the application by right-clicking it and then selecting Disable. Next, right-click the application again and then select Tasks | Update.

As you may have guessed, you can also update a Notification Services application using the nscontrol commands.

Building a .NET Subscription/Event Application

While the core logic of a Notification Services application is defined using the ICF and the ADF files, subscribers, devices, and subscriptions are typically created by client applications that use the Notification Services API. You can see an example Notification Services client application in Figure 5-6.

The sample application shown in Figure 5-6 adds subscribers, devices, and subscriptions to the Notification Services application using the Subscribers tab. The Event tab is used to generate event data, and the Notification tab is used to display the resulting notification.

Client applications connect to Notification Services using the managed code APIs that Microsoft provides with SQL Server 2005 Notification Services. Microsoft's .NET Framework APIs enable you to add, update, and delete subscribers, as well as subscriber devices and subscriptions. While the Notification Services API is provided via managed code classes, you can also access the API from unmanaged code by using Win32-based COM applications.

The Notification Services API is located in Microsoft.SqlServer.NotificationServices .dll, which must be added to your .NET project as a reference. Then you can use the Notification Services classes to manage subscriptions to your Notification Services applications. To add a reference to the Notification Services API, select the Project | Add Reference menu option to display the Add Reference dialog. Scroll through the list until you see Microsoft.SqlServer.NotificationService, and then select the object, as shown in Figure 5-7. Clicking OK adds the reference to your project.

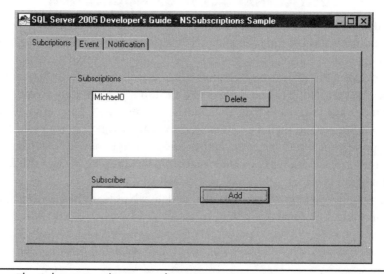

Figure 5-6   *The Subscription/Event application*

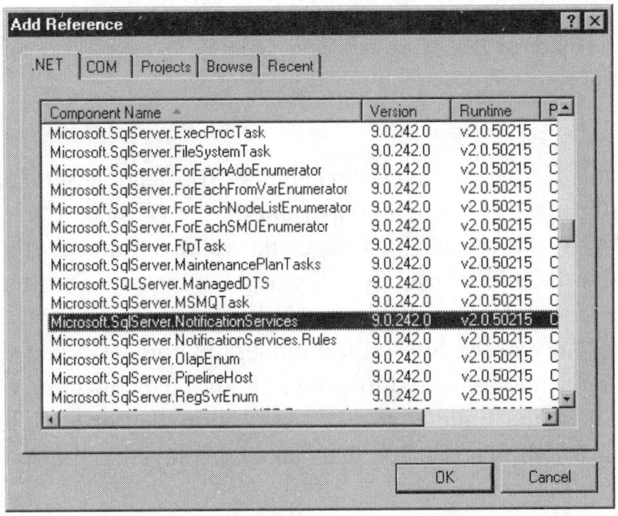

Figure 5-7 *Adding a reference to the Notification Services library*

Next, add an import directive for the NotificationServices namespace to the Declarations section of your project. Using the import directive enables you to use the classes in the NotificationServices namespace without requiring you to fully qualify the names. The import directive appears as follows:

```
Imports Microsoft.SqlServer.NotificationServices
```

After adding the reference to your project and its associated namespace, you can create the code to add a subscriber to your Notification Services application.

Listing Subscriptions

To list the subscriptions that have been created on a Notification Services instance, you can use the SubscriberEnumeration object as is shown in the following listing:

```
' Create the Instance object
Dim myNSInstance As New NSInstance("NSAppInstance")

'Populate the list box
Dim oSubscribers As SubscriberEnumeration = New _
    SubscriberEnumeration(myNSInstance)


ListBox1.Items.Clear()
' Iterate through a collection
```

```
For Each oSub As Subscriber In oSubscribers
    ' Add each Subscriber Name to the List
    ListBox1.Items.Add(oSub.SubscriberId)
Next
```

At the top of this listing you can see where the Notification Services instance called MyNSInstance is created. The important thing to notice in this line is the fact that the value "MSAppInstance" must match the value defined in your ICF file. This value can also been found by using SQL Server Management Studio to open the Notification Services node that lists the active instances.

Next, a new instance of the SubscriberEnumeration object called oSubscribers is created and a For-Each loop is used to iterate through the collection of subscribers exposed by the SubscriberEnumeration object. Within the For-Each loop the name of each subscriber is added to a ListBox that can be displayed to the end user.

Adding Subscriptions

Of course, before you can list subscribers you must first add them. The following code sample shows how you can add a subscription using the Notification Services managed code API:

```
' Create the Instance object
Dim myNSInstance As New NSInstance("NSAppInstance")
' Create the Application object
Dim myNSApp As New NSApplication(myNSInstance, "NSApp")
' Create the Subscriber
Dim oSubscriber As New Subscriber(myNSInstance)
oSubscriber.SubscriberId
= TextSub.Text
oSubscriber.Add()

' Add a device for the subscriber
' DeviceName must match subscription
Dim oDevice As New SubscriberDevice(myNSInstance)
oDevice.DeviceName = "myDevice"
oDevice.SubscriberId = TextSub.Text
oDevice.DeviceTypeName = "File"
oDevice.DeviceAddress = TextSub.Text & "@teca.com"
oDevice.DeliveryChannelName = "FileChannel"
oDevice.Add()

' Create the subscription
Dim oSubscription As New Subscription(myNSApp, "ShipStore")
oSubscription("DeviceName") = "myDevice"
```

```
oSubscription("SubscriberLocale") = "en-US"
oSubscription.SubscriberId = TextSub.Text
' Hard code  the store ID for the example
oSubscription("StoreID") = 1
'Dim sSubId As String = oSubscription.Add()
oSubscription.Add()

'Display the new Subscriber ID
ListBox1.Items.Add(TextSub.Text)
TextSub.Text = ""
```

First a Notification Services instance object named myNSInstance is created,
followed by an Application object named myNSApp. These must correspond to the
definitions that were previously defined in the XML-based Notification Services
configuration file. For this example, the NSInstance object must be created using the
value of "NSAppInstance," which must match the name of the Notifications Services
Instance as defined in the <InstanceName> element of the ICF file. Likewise, the
Application object, NSApplication, must use the value of "NSApp" to match the value
used in the <ApplicationName> element of the ICF file. You can also see these values
beneath the Notification Services node in the SQL Server Management Studio.

Next, a Subscriber must be created and notification delivery devices must be
added to the subscriber. A new subscriber is created by passing the Notification
Services Instance name to the Subscriber object's constructor. Once the Subscriber
object has been instantiated, the SubscriberID property is set with a string value that
identifies the subscriber. Here that value comes from a Textbox named TextSub.
Then the Add method is called to create the subscriber. As you might expect, the
Delete and Update methods must be used if you subsequently want to modify or
delete the subscriber information.

NOTE

*Adding a subscriber updates the NSDataSubSubscriptions table along with a couple of other tables
in the NSAppInstanceNSApp database. However, you should not directly update these tables.
Instead, you should only add, update, and delete subscribers using the NotificationServices API or
the stored procedure generated with the Notification Services application.*

Once the subscriber has been added, at least one device must be added to the
subscriber using the SubscriberDevice object. The SubscriberId in combination with
the DeviceName property uniquely identifies the device in the system. The value used
for the DeliveryChannel property specifies the method by which the notification will

be generated. In this example, the notification will be created in the file system. The actual output file was defined in the ICF file and will be named NSAppNotification .htm. You might notice that the device and the subscriber are defined separately. This enables a subscriber to have multiple notification delivery mechanisms. The Add method is then used to add the device. Once the subscriber has been created and a device has been added for the subscriber, you can then create a subscription. The subscription links the subscriber to a specific event. When you create a new subscription object, you pass in the Application object followed by the name of the subscription class that was defined in your ADF file. In this case, the subscription class was named "ShipStore." Next, the Subscription object's properties are assigned values. You should note that the StoreID is assigned a hard-coded value of 1. This essentially creates a subscription for the subscriber to shipment data for StoreID 1. Then, the Add method is called to actually add the subscription to the database. At the end of this code, the subscriber's name is also added to a ListBox that will be displayed to the end user.

NOTE

If you get an ArgumentOutOfRangeException while attempting to create a subscription, it typically means that the values you've passed to the subscription object do not match the values that were created in the subscribers section of the acf.xml file.

You can view the subscribers and the devices that have been added by querying the NSSubscriberDeviceView, as shown in the following listing. For this sample application, the view is found in the NSAppInstanceNSMain database. As mentioned earlier, the name of this database is based in the name of the Notification Services application.

```
-- View subscribers and devices
USE NSAppInstanceNSMain
SELECT * FROM NSSubscriberDeviceView
```

The NSShipStore view in the NSAppInstanceNSApp database enables you to view the subscriptions that have been created. In this case, the name of the view is based on the name of the event class that was created in the application definition file. You can see the query to view the subscribers for the example application in the following listing:

```
-- View Subscriptions
USE NSAppInstanceNSApp
SELECT * FROM NSShipStoreView ORDER BY SubscriberId;
```

Deleting Subscriptions

The following code shows how you can delete subscriptions that have been previously displayed in a ListBox. Like the previous example, the Notification Services Subscriber object provides the required method to work with the subscriber data.

```
If ListBox1.SelectedIndex < 0 Then
    MsgBox("No subscriber has been selected.")
Else
    ' Create the Instance object
    Dim myNSInstance As New NSInstance("NSAppInstance")
    ' Delete the Subscriber

    Dim oSubscriber As New Subscriber(myNSInstance)
    oSubscriber.SubscriberId = ListBox1.SelectedItem
    oSubscriber.Delete()

    ' Remove the entry from the list
    ListBox1.Items.Remove(ListBox1.SelectedItem)
End If
```

Firing the Data Event Using .NET

Events are data that your notification application uses to generate notifications. The notification generation queries you write join event data and subscription data to produce notifications. The queries that generate notifications are fired during each generator quantum that has data to process. Event rules run in any quantum in which one or more event batches arrived. Scheduled rules run in any quantum that has scheduled subscriptions expected to be processed.

You can see the screen that the example Notification Services client application uses to create Notification Services events in Figure 5-8.

On the Event tab, the user can enter the store ID, the product ID, the product name, and the number of units shipped. In the earlier listing that created a subscription, you saw that a subscription was created for store ID 1. Therefore, if the user enters a value for store ID 1, then a Notification Services event will be created. Any other store ID values will not cause an event to fire. In the case of the sample application, no data validation is performed, so you need to enter data values for all of the fields.

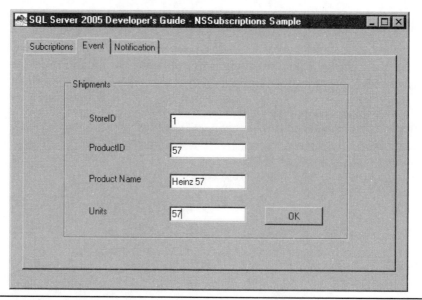

Figure 5-8   *The subscription application*

Once all of the data has been entered, clicking the OK button will execute the code
that you can see in the following listing:

```
' Create the Instance object
Dim myNSInstance As New NSInstance("NSAppInstance")
' Create the Application object
Dim myNSApp As New NSApplication(myNSInstance, "NSApp")
Dim oEvent As New _
Microsoft.SqlServer.NotificationServices.Event( _
myNSApp, "ShipData")
Dim oEventCollector As New EventCollector(myNSApp, "SQLData")

' Supply the event data
oEvent("StoreId") = TextStore.Text
oEvent("Date") = Now
oEvent("ProductId") = TextProdID.Text
oEvent("ProductName") = TextProdName.Text
oEvent("Units") = TextUnits.Text
oEventCollector.Write(oEvent)
Dim iCountOfCommittedEvents As Integer = oEventCollector.Commit()
```

At the top of this listing, you can see where the NSInstance and NSApplication objects are created. Next, a new Notification Services Event object named oEvent is created by passing an instance of the NSApp NSApplication object along with the value of "ShipData", the name of the Notification Services event class, to the Event object's constructor.

The next section of code supplies the required event data. The values used for these field names must match the field values that compose the event class that was created in the application definition file. The ShipData event class used five fields. The StoreId is assigned the value that codes from the TextStore TextBox. The Date field is assigned the current date and time. The ProductID, ProductName, and Units fields are all assigned values from the TextBoxes that you saw earlier in Figure 5-6. After all of the field values have been assigned, the EventCollector Write method is used to write the events and the Commit method is used to send the events to the Notification Services application.

Figure 5-9 shows the notification that was generated using the values you saw on Figure 5-8. The sample application used the WebBrowser object with the URL property pointed to the NSApplication.htm file to display the notification.

It should be noted that for this sample application, the notification does not appear immediately. Instead, it is generated according to the schedule that was defined in the notification class section of the application definition file. The example uses a value of 60 seconds.

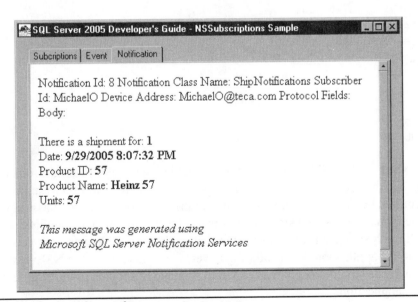

Figure 5-9   *Viewing the notification*

If no notifications are generated, you can use the NSDiagnosticFailedNotifications stored procedure to begin troubleshooting the problem. You can see an example of running the NSDiagnosticFailedNotifications stored procedure in the following listing:

```
-- View diagnostics
USE NSAppInstanceNSMain
EXEC NSDiagnosticFailedNotifications
```

Firing the Data Event Using T-SQL

The preceding example illustrated firing a Notification Services event using the NotificationServices API from a client application. However, you can also use T-SQL to generate events for your Notification Services application. The following listing illustrates calling the NSEventWriteShipData stored procedure to fire an event. The NSEventWriteShipData stored procedure is automatically created with your Notification Services application. Its actual name is based on the Event Class Name used in the ADF file.

```
USE NSAppInstanceNSApp;
-- Start an event batch
DECLARE @BatchID bigint;
EXEC dbo.NSEventBeginBatchShipData N'SQLData', @BatchID OUTPUT;
EXEC dbo.NSEventWriteShipData
  @EventBatchId=@BatchID,
  @StoreID = 1,
  @Date='October 1, 2005',
  @ProductID = 31,
  @ProductName = "Item ThirtyOne",
  @Units=31

-- Flush event batch
EXEC dbo.NSEventFlushBatchShipData @BatchID;
```

The NSEventWriteShipData stored procedure is intended to be used for batch loading and requires a batch ID as its first parameter. Next, you need to supply the data required by the event that you defined in the application's event class. In this example, you can see that a store ID of 1 is used to ensure that the event gets fired. You call the NSEventWriteShipData stored procedure for each event that you want to sent to the application. When all of the events have been sent, the NSEventFlush BatchShipData stored procedure is called to send the event data to the Notification Services application.

Summary

Notification Services is a powerful new subsystem you can use as a basis for building your own notification applications. In this chapter you learned how to define a sample Notification Services application by creating the instance configuration file and application definition file as well as how to use the Notification Services API to add subscribers, subscriptions, and fire notification events.

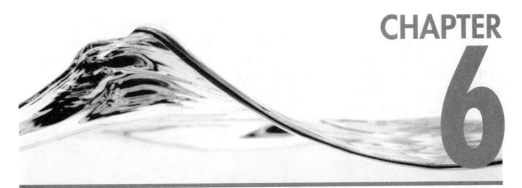

CHAPTER

6

Developing Database Applications with ADO.NET

I n this chapter, you will see how to develop SQL Server database applications using Visual Basic and ADO.NET. The first part of the chapter provides you with an overview of the ADO.NET data access technology. The second part of this chapter introduces you to the different ADO.NET namespaces and gives you an overall understanding of the functions of the different classes that compose the ADO.NET architecture. Finally, the last section of this chapter covers the classes that are used by the ADO.NET DataSet object. In this part of the chapter, you'll get an understanding of DataTable, DataColumn, DataRow, and other classes used by the new ADO.NET DataSets.

The ADO.NET Architecture

At its essence, ADO.NET is data access middleware that enables the development of database applications. ADO.NET builds on the platform provided by the .NET Framework. ADO.NET is built using managed code from the Microsoft .NET Framework, which means that it enjoys the benefits of the robust .NET execution time environment. Designed primarily to address the issues of Web and distributed applications, ADO.NET consists of a set of classes or namespaces within the .NET Framework that provide data access and management capabilities to .NET applications.

As a data access framework, ADO.NET has been primarily designed to allow it to work in the disconnected data access model that is required by *n*-tiered Web-based applications. ADO, the direct predecessor of ADO.NET, was primarily designed to accommodate a two-tiered client/server style of applications, which typically open a database connection when the application first starts and then hold that connection open until the application ends. This technique works fine for most intranet-style applications where the total number of client connections is a known quantity, and where the state of the application is typically controlled by the application and therefore is also a known quantity. Although this approach worked well for single-tier desktop applications and two-tiered client/server-style applications, it ran into serious limitations for *n*-tiered Web-style applications. Because the Web is a public environment, the total number of open connections required by Web applications isn't a known quantity. It could vary greatly and quickly: At one minute, an application may need only a handful of connections, but the need can jump to thousands of connections just a few minutes later. Keeping open connections in this type of environment hurts scalability because each connection must go through the overhead of initializing the connection with the back-end database, plus each open connection requires system resources to be held open—reducing the resources available for other database operations. As ADO evolved, Microsoft added mechanisms such as disconnected recordsets to help deal with Web-style applications, but these were never part of ADO's original design.

Microsoft designed ADO.NET to be able to handle the disconnected computing scenario required by Web-based applications. This disconnected design enables ADO.NET to be readily scalable for enterprise applications because an open connection isn't maintained between each client system and the database. Instead, when a client connection is initiated, a connection to the database is briefly opened, the requested data is retrieved from the database server, and the connection is closed. The client application then uses the data completely independently from the data store maintained by the database server. The client application can navigate through its subset of the data, as well as make changes to the data, and the data remains cached at the client until the application indicates that it needs to post any changes back to the database server. At that point, a new connection is briefly opened to the server and all of the changes made by the client application are posted to the database in an update batch and the connection is closed.

The core ADO.NET component that enables this disconnected scenario is the DataSet. The DataSet is essentially a miniature in-memory database that is maintained independently of the back-end database. Connections to the data source are opened only to populate the DataSet or to post changes made to the data in the DataSet back to the database. This disconnected computing scenario minimizes the system overhead and improves application throughput and scalability. The in-memory database provided by the ADO.NET DataSet provides many of the functions that you'll find in a full-blown database, including support for data relations, the capability to create views, and support for data constraints, as well as support for foreign key constraints. However, being an in-memory structure, it doesn't provide support for many of the more advanced database features that you would find in enterprise-level database products like SQL Server. For example, the DataSet doesn't support triggers, stored procedures, or user-defined functions.

Support for disconnected Web-based applications was one of Microsoft's priorities in the design of ADO.NET; however, that isn't all that ADO.NET is capable of. The disconnected model may be appropriate for Web applications, but it really isn't the best model for client/server and desktop applications. These types of applications can perform better and more efficiently when they run in a connected fashion. To support this connected style of computing, ADO.NET also provides a DataReader object. The DataReader essentially provides fast forward–only cursor style of data access that operates in a connected fashion. While the DataSet provides the basis for disconnected Web applications, the DataReader enables the fast connected style of data access needed by desktop and client/server applications.

In this section, you got a high-level overview of the ADO.NET data access middleware. Here you saw that ADO.NET provides the tools to build applications that support both disconnected Web applications as well as connected client/server style applications. In the next section, you'll get a close look at the different namespaces that make up the ADO.NET architecture.

ADO.NET Namespaces

ADO.NET is implemented as a set of classes that exist within the .NET Framework. These ADO.NET classes are grouped together beneath the .NET Framework's System.Data namespace. Several important namespaces make up the ADO.NET data access technology. First, the .NET Data Providers are implemented in the System.Data.SqlClient, System.Data.OracleClient, System.Data.OleDbClient, and System.Data.Odbc namespaces. The classes in these four namespaces provide the underlying database connectivity that's required by all of the other ADO.NET objects. The System.Data.SqlClient namespace provides connectivity to SQL Server 7, SQL Server 2000, and SQL Server 2005 databases. The System.Data. OracleClient namespace provides connectivity to Oracle 8 and 9 databases. The System.Data.OleDbClient namespace provides connectivity to SQL Server 6.5 and earlier databases, as well as Access and Oracle databases. And the System.Data. Odbc namespace provides connectivity to legacy databases using ODBC drivers. These classes also provide support for executing commands, retrieving data in a fast forward-only style of access, and loading ADO.NET DataSets. Next, there are the classes contained in the System.Data namespace itself. These classes can be considered the core of the ADO.NET technology, and they provide support for the new ADO.NET DataSet class and its supporting classes. As you learned earlier in this chapter, the DataSet is an in-memory database cache that's designed to be used in a disconnected fashion. The DataSet consists of a complete collection of tables, columns, constraints, rows, and relationships, plus appropriately named DataTables, DataColumns, DataConstraints, DataRows, and DataRelations. You can see an illustration of the overall ADO.NET architecture in Figure 6-1.

.NET Data Providers

The .NET Data Providers are responsible for connecting your .NET application to a data source. The .NET Framework comes with four built-in .NET Data Providers. Each of the .NET Data Providers is maintained in its own namespace within the .NET Framework.

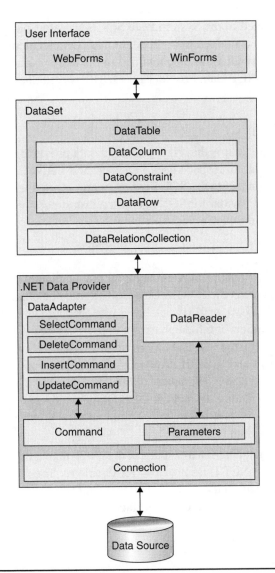

Figure 6-1   *Overall ADO.NET architecture*

Namespaces for the .NET Data Providers

Four .NET Data Providers are delivered with the .NET Framework: the .NET Data Provider for SQL Server, the .NET Data Provider for Oracle, the .NET Data Provider for OLE DB, and the .NET Data Provider for ODBC. The .NET Data Provider for

SQL Server is contained in the System.Data.SqlClient namespace. The .NET Data Provider for Oracle is contained in the System.Data.OracleClient namespace. The .NET Data Provider for OLE DB is contained in the System.Data.OleDbClient namespace. And the .NET Data Provider for ODBC is contained in the System.Data.Odbc namespace.

System.Data.SqlClient

The System.Data.SqlClient is the .NET managed data provider for SQL Server. The System.Data.SqlClient namespace uses SQL Server's native TDS (Tabular Data Stream) protocol to connect to the SQL Server system. Using the native TDS protocol makes the .NET Data Provider for SQL Server the fastest possible connection between a client application and SQL Server.

System.Data.OleDb

The System.Data.OleDb namespace is the .NET managed data provider for OLE DB data sources. Whereas the System.Data.SqlClient namespace can be used to access SQL Server 7, 2000, or 2005 databases, the System.Data.OleDb namespace is used to access SQL Server 6.5 databases or earlier, as well as Oracle and Access databases. Theoretically, the .NET Data Provider for OLE DB can access any database where there's an OLE DB Provider—with the exception of the Microsoft OLE DB Provider for ODBC. Microsoft purposely restricted the capability to access ODBC from the .NET Data Provider for OLE DB.

System.Data.OracleClient

The System.Data.OracleClient namespace is the .NET managed data provider for Oracle databases. The .NET Data Provider for Oracle requires that the Oracle 8 or higher client be installed on the system. The System.Data.OracleClient namespace uses Oracle's native OCI (Oracle Call Interface) to connect to Oracle 8 and higher databases.

System.Data.Odbc

The System.Data.Odbc namespace is the .NET managed data provider for ODBC data sources. Microsoft designed the .NET Data Provider for ODBC to be able to access any ODBC-compliant database. However, Microsoft officially supports only connections using the Microsoft SQL Server ODBC driver, the Microsoft ODBC driver for Oracle, and the Microsoft Jet ODBC driver. However, we have successfully used this provider to connect to DB2 databases as well.

Core Classes for the .NET Data Providers

All of the.NET Data Providers included in the .NET Framework are essentially architected the same. In other words, the classes contained in each namespace have nearly identical methods, properties, and events. However, the classes each use a slightly different naming convention. For instance, all of the classes in the .NET Data Provider for SQL Server, found in the System.Data.SqlClient namespace, begin with a prefix of "Sql"; the classes that are part of the .NET Provider for OLE DB, found in the System.Data.OleDb namespace, all begin with the prefix of "OleDb". Both namespaces contain classes that are used to initiate a connection to a target data source. For the System.Data.SqlClient namespace, this class is named SqlConnection. For the System.Data.OleDb namespace, this class is named OleDbConnection. In each case, the methods that are provided and their parameters are basically the same. Because the function and usage of these classes are basically the same, they are grouped together in the following section under their generic function names. The following section presents an overview of the primary classes contained in the .NET Data Provider namespaces.

Connection

The Connection class is used to open a connection to a target data source. A Connection object is required in order to populate either the DataReader object or the DataSet object with data from the target data source. Likewise, an active Connection object is required in order to execute any commands or stored procedures that exist on the database from the client .NET applications. Unlike most other .NET objects, Connection objects are not automatically destroyed when they go out of scope. This means that you must explicitly close any open ADO.NET Connection objects in your applications. If multiple Connection objects are opened that use the same connection string, they will be automatically added to the same connection pool.

NOTE

The actual functionality provided by the OleDbConnection class and the OdbcConnection class is dependent on the capabilities of the underlying OLE DB Provider and ODBC driver. Not all providers and drivers will necessarily support the same functionality.

Command

The Command class is used to execute either a stored procedure or a SQL statement on the data source that's associated with the active Connection object. Three types of commands are supported: ExecuteReader, ExecuteNonQuery, and ExecuteScalar. ExecuteReader commands return a result set. ExecuteNonQuery commands are used to execute SQL action queries like Insert, Update, and Delete statements that do not return any rows. ExecuteScalar commands are used to execute stored procedures or SQL queries that return a single value.

Parameter

The Parameter class is used to represent a parameter that's passed to a Command object. Parameter objects have properties that define their attributes. For instance, the different properties of a Parameter object specify the parameter's name, its direction, its data type, its size, and its value. Parameter names are not case-sensitive, but when naming Parameter objects that represent stored procedure parameters, naming the parameter the same as the stored procedure parameter is typically a good idea. For instance, if the Parameter object represents a stored procedure parameter named @CustomerID, using that same name when instantiating the Parameter object is a good practice. A Parameter object can also be mapped to a DataColumn in the DataSet.

DataReader

The DataReader class returns a forward-only stream of data from the target data source that's associated with the active connection object. Unlike objects in most other ADO.NET classes that are instantiated by calling the constructor, objects created from the DataReader class are instantiated by calling the ExecuteReader method.

DataAdapter

The basic task of the DataAdapter class is to serve as a link between a DataSet object and the data source represented by the active Connection object. The DataAdapter class includes properties that allow you to specify the actual SQL statements that will be used to interact between the DataSet and the target database. In other words, the DataAdapter is responsible for both filling up the DataSet as well as sending changes made in the DataSet back to the data source. For example, the DataAdapter class provides the SelectCommand property, which controls the data that will be retrieved; the InsertCommand property, which indicates how new data in the DataSet will be added to the database; the UpdateCommand property, which controls how changed rows in the DataSet will be posted to the database; and the DeleteCommand property, which controls how rows deleted in the DataSet will be deleted from the database.

CommandBuilder

The CommandBuilder class provides a mechanism for automatically generating the SQL commands that will be used to update the target database with changes in an attached DataSet. The CommandBuilder uses the metadata returned by the SQL statement in the DataAdapter's SelectCommand property to generate any required Insert, Update, and Delete statements. Changes made in the DataSet are not automatically posted to the database unless SQL commands are assigned to the DataAdapter InsertCommand, UpdateCommand, and DeleteCommand properties or unless a CommandBuilder object is created and attached to the active DataAdapter object. Only one CommandBuilder object can be associated with a given DataAdapter at one time.

Transaction

The Transaction class represents a SQL transaction. SQL transactions basically allow multiple database transactions to be treated as a unit where an entire group of database updates can either be posted to the database or all be undone as a unit. The Transaction object uses the BeginTransaction method to specify the start of a transaction and then either the Commit method to post the changes to the database or the Rollback method to undo the pending transaction. A Transaction object is attached to the active Connection object.

Error

The Error class contains error information that is generated by the target data source. The active Connection object is automatically closed when an error with a severity of greater than 20 is generated by the target database. However, the connection can be subsequently reopened.

Exception

The Exception class is created whenever the .NET Data Provider encounters an error generated by one of its members. An Exception object always contains at least one instance of the Error object. You trap exceptions in your code by using the .NET Frameworks Try-Catch structure error handling.

Core Classes in the ADO.NET System.Data Namespace

The core classes that make up the ADO.NET technology are found in the .NET Framework's System.Data namespace. The following section presents an overview of the functionality of the most important classes found in the System.Data namespace.

DataSet

At the heart of the new ADO.NET architecture is the DataSet. The DataSet class is located in the .NET Framework at System.Data.DataSet. The DataSet is essentially a cache of records that have been retrieved from the database. You can think of the DataSet as a miniature database. It contains tables, columns, constraints, rows, and relations. These DataSet objects are called DataTables, DataColumns, DataRows, Constraints, and Relations. The DataSet essentially allows a disconnected application to function as if it were actively connected to a database. Applications typically need to access multiple pieces of related database information in order to present useful information to the end user. For example, to work with an order an application would typically need to access a number of different database tables, including product tables, customer tables, inventory tables, and shipping tables. All of the related information from this set of tables can be grouped together in the DataSet, providing the disconnected application with the capability to work with all of the related order information that it needs.

In the disconnected model, going back to the data source to get each different piece of related information would be inefficient, so the DataSet is typically populated all at once via the active Connection object and DataAdapter from the appropriate .NET Data Provider. A database connection is briefly opened to fill the DataSet and then closed. Afterward the DataSet operates independently of the back-end database. The client application then accesses the Table, DataRow, Data Column, and DataView objects that are contained within the DataSet. Any changes made to the data contained in the DataSet can be posted back to the database via the DataAdapter object. In a multitier environment, a clone of the DataSet containing any changed data is created using the GetChanges method. Then the cloned DataSet is used as an argument of the DataAdapter's Update method to post the changes to the target database. If any changes were made to the data in the cloned DataSet, these changes can be posted to the original DataSet using the DataSet's Merge method. Figure 6-2 provides an overview of the ADO.NET DataSet architecture.

DataTable

The DataTable class is located in the .NET Framework at System.Data.DataTable. The DataTable class represents a table of in-memory data that is contained with a DataSet object. The DataTable object can be created automatically by returning result sets from the DataAdapter to the DataSet object. DataTable objects can also be created programmatically by adding DataColumns objects to the DataTable's DataColumns collection. Each DataTable object in a DataSet is bindable to data-aware user interface objects found in the .NET Framework's WinForm and WebForm classes.

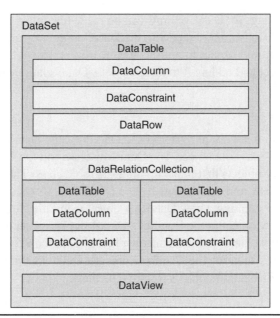

Figure 6-2   *The DataSet architecture*

When changes are made to the data contained in a DataTable object, the ColumnChanging, ColumnChanged, RowChanging, and RowChanged events are fired. When data is deleted from a DataTable object, the RowDeleting and RowDeleted events are fired. New rows are added to a DataTable by calling the DataTable's NewRow method and passing it a DataRow object. The maximum number of rows that can be stored in a DataTable is 16,777,216. The DataTable is also used as a basis to create DataView objects.

DataColumn

The DataColumn class is located in the .NET Framework at System.Data.DataColumn. The DataColumn class represents the schema of a column in a DataTable object. The DataColumn class contains several properties that are used to define the type of data contained in the DataColumn object. For example, the DataType property controls the type of data that can be stored in the DataColumn object, the DataValue property contains the DataColumn's value, the AllowDBNull property specifies whether the DataColumn can contain NULL values, the MaxLength property sets the maximum length of a Text DataType, and the Table property specifies the DataTable object that the DataColumn belongs to. DataColumns can be made to contain unique values by associating a UniqueConstraint object with the DataColumn object. In addition, you can relate a DataColumn object to another DataColumn object by creating a DataRelation object and adding it to the DataSet's DataRelationCollection.

DataRow

Found in the .NET Framework at System.Data.DataRow, the DataRow class represents a row of data in the DataTable object. The DataRow class and the DataColumn class represent the primary objects that make up the DataTable class. The DataRow object is used to insert, update, and delete rows from a DataTable. Rows can be added to a DataTable by either creating a new DataRow object using the NewRow method or by Adding a DataRow object to the DataSet's DataRowCollection. DataRow objects are updated by simply changing the DataRow object's DataValue property. You delete a DataRow object by executing the DataRow object's Delete method or by calling the DataSet's DataRowCollection object's Remove method.

DataView

Found in the .NET Framework at System.Data.DataView, the DataView class offers a customized view of a subset of rows in a DataTable object. Like the DataTable object, DataView objects can be bound to both WinForm and WebForm controls. The DataView classes's RowFilter and Sort properties can allow the data presented by the DataView to be displayed in a different order than the data presented by the base DataTable object. Like the DataTable object, the data contained in a DataView object is updatable. You can add new rows by using the AddNew method, and you can delete rows by using the Delete method.

DataViewManager

The DataViewManager class is located in the .NET Framework at SystemData.DataViewManager. The DataViewManager class is a bit different than the other classes in the System.Data namespace. Essentially, the DataViewManager class tracks the DataViewSetting objects for each DataTable in the DataSet in its DataViewSettingsCollection. The DataViewSettingsCollection is a group of DataViewSetting objects where each DataViewSetting object contains properties like the RowFilter, RowStateFilter, and Sort that define each DataView object.

DataRelation

The DataRelation class is located in the .NET Framework at System.Data.
DataRelation. The DataRelation class is used to represent parent-child relationships
between two DataTable objects contained in a DataSet. For example, you could
create a DataRelation object between an OrderID DataColumn in an Order Header
table to the corresponding OrderID DataColumn in an Order Detail table. The basic
function of the DataRelation object is to facilitate navigation and data retrieval
from related DataTables. In order to create a relationship between two DataTable
objects, the two DataTables must contain DataColumn objects that have matching
attributes. When a DataRelation is first created, the .NET Framework checks to
make sure that the relationship is valid and then adds the DataRelation object to the
DataRelationCollection, which tracks all of the data relations for the DataSet. The
DataRelation class supports cascading changes from the parent table to the child
table, and this is controlled through the ForeignKeyConstraint class.

Constraint

Found in the .NET Framework at System.Data.Constraint, the Constraint class
represents a set of data integrity rules that can be applied to a DataColumn object.
There is no base constructor for the Constraint class. Instead, constraint objects are
created using either the ForeignKeyConstraint constructor or the UniqueConstraint
constructor.

ForeignKeyConstraint

The ForeignKeyConstraint class is located in the .NET Framework at SystemData.
ForeignKeyConstraint. The ForeignKeyConstraint class governs how changes in
a parent table affect rows in the child table when a DataRelation exists between the
two tables. For example, when you delete a value that is used in one or more related
tables, a ForeignKeyConstraint class's DeleteRule property determines whether the
values in the related tables are also deleted. Deleting a value from the parent table
can delete the child rows; set the values in the child table's rows to null values; set
the values in the child table's rows to default values; or throw an exception.

UniqueConstraint

The UniqueConstraint class is located in the .NET Framework at SystemData.
UniqueConstraint. The UniqueConstraint class ensures that all values entered into
a DataColumn object have a unique value.

DataException

Found in the .NET Framework at System.Data.DataException, the DataException class represents an error that is thrown by one of the System.Data classes. For example, code that violates a UniqueConstraint on a DataColumn by attempting to add a duplicate value to the DataColumn will cause a DataException object to be created and added to the DataExceptionCollection. You can use the DataException objects to report error conditions in your ADO.NET applications.

Using the .NET Framework Data Provider for SQL Server

The .NET Framework Data Provider for SQL Server will give you a significant performance boost if your application only needs to connect to SQL Server and it doesn't need to connect to any other database systems. When accessing SQL Server databases, the .NET Framework Data Provider for SQL Server is more efficient than the .NET Framework Data Provider for OLE DB or ODBC because it communicates between the client application and the SQL Server system using SQL Server's native TDS (Tabular Data Stream) protocol. The System.Data.SqlClient namespace also includes a new signaling solution called Query Notifications. Query Notifications can be implemented using the SqlDependency object discussed later in this section.

Adding the System.Data.SqlClient Namespace

While using the visual connection components that are provided by the Visual Studio.NET design environment makes it pretty easy to create an initial connection to a SQL Server system, they also tend to clutter up the design environment. After your first couple of connections using them, you'll probably be ready to forgo the visual components in the Data Toolbox and establish your database connection exclusively using code. Using the ADO.NET objects in code requires only a couple of extra steps. In return you get more screen real estate for the Designer window and more control over exactly when and how the SqlConnection objects get created.

Before you can use the .NET Framework Data Provider for SQL Server in your code, you must first specify an import directive for the System.Data.SqlClient namespace in your project. This step isn't required when using the visual data components, but it is required in order to use the objects contained in the System. Data.SqlClient namespace with code. The System.Data.SqlClient namespace contains all of the related SQL Server connection and data access classes. To add an import directive for the System.Data.SQLClient to a VB.NET project, you would add the following code to the declaration section of your source file:

```
Imports System.Data.SqlClient
```

Using the SqlConnection Object

After adding an import directive to your code, you're ready to begin using the different classes contained in the System.Data.SqlClient namespace. The most essential of those classes is the SqlConnection class. As its name implies, the System.Data.SqlClient SqlConnection class is used to connect to a SQL Server database. You can use several different techniques to connect the System.Data.SqlClient namespace to SQL Server. The technique that's probably most familiar to developers with previous ADO experience is setting the ConnectionString property with a valid connection string and then invoking the Open method. The following example illustrates how to make a SQL Server connection by setting the System.Data.SqlClient namespace's ConnectionString Property:

```
Private Sub SQLConnectString(ByVal sServer, ByVal sUser, ByVal sPassword)
    Dim cn As New SqlConnection()
    ' Set the connection string
    cn.ConnectionString = "SERVER=" & sServer & _
        ";UID=" & sUser & ";PWD=" & sPassword
    Try
        ' Open the connection
        cn.Open()
    Catch ex As Exception
        ' Display any error messages
        MessageBox.Show("Connection error: :" & ex.ToString())
    End Try
    ' Close the connection
    cn.Close()
End Sub
```

In this case string variables containing the name of the SQL Server system to connect to along with the user ID and password are passed into the top of the routine. Next, a new instance of the System.Data.SqlClient Connection object named cn is created. Then the ConnectionString property of the System.Data. SqlClient Connection object is assigned the .NET Framework Data Provider for SQL Server connection string. This connection string uses the SERVER keyword to identify the SQL Server system that it will be connected to. The UID and PWD keywords provide the authentication values required to log in to SQL Server if you are connecting using mixed security. A UID and a PWD are not required in the connection string if you are connecting using a trusted connection, as discussed later in this chapter. A complete list of the valid the .NET Framework Data Provider for SQL Server connection string keywords is presented in the next section, "The .NET Framework Data Provider for SQL Server Connection String Keywords." After the ConnectionString property has been assigned the appropriate connection string, a Try-Catch block is used to execute the cn Connection object's Open method. After the Open method completes, a connection to the SQL Server system identified in the connection string is initiated. If there was an error with the connection string or the specified SQL Server system is not available, the code in the Catch block will be executed and a message box will be displayed showing the error information. After a successful connection has been established, the Connection object is closed using the Close method.

NOTE

Explicitly using the Close method is very important in ADO.NET to ensure that the resources allocated by the Connection object are released when they are no longer needed. In .NET applications the Connection object is not necessarily destroyed when it goes out of scope. Executing either the Close or Dispose method is required to make sure that the connection resources are released. The Close method closes the current connection, but the underlying .NET managed resources used for connection pooling will remain available. Close can be called multiple times — even when the connection is already closed — without raising an error. The Dispose method can release all managed and unmanaged resources used by a connection, and it can only be called for an active connection.

The .NET Framework Data Provider for SQL Server Connection String Keywords

The SQL Server .Net Data Provider connection string is much like the OLE DB connection string that was used by ADO. However, unlike in the OLE DB connection string, the login values contained in the connection string are not returned to the application unless you explicitly tell the provider to do so via the Persist Security Info connection string keyword. In addition, the SQL Server .NET Data Provider also supports a few new keywords. Table 6-1 lists all the SQL Server .NET Data Provider–specific keywords supported by the SQLConnection object's ConnectionString property.

Keyword	Description
Application Name	Identifies the current application.
AttachDBFilename -or- Extended properties -or- Initial File Name	Identifies the full path and name of a file that will be attached as a SQL Server database. This keyword must be used in conjunction with the Database keyword.
Connect Timeout -or- Connection Timeout	Specifies the length of time in seconds to wait before terminating a connection attempt. The default is 15.
Connection Lifetime	Specifies the length of time in seconds to wait before destroying a connection returned to the connection pool. This keyword is used for load balancing in a cluster. The default is 0.
Connection Reset	Specifies that a connection will be reset when it is returned from the connection pool. The default is 'true'.
Current Language	Specifies the SQL Server language name to be used for this connection.
Data Source -or- Server -or- Address -or- Addr -or- Network Address	Identifies the name or network address of a SQL Server instance to connect to.
Enlist	Determines whether the current thread will be enlisted as part of the current transaction context. The default value is 'true'.
Encrypt	Determines whether SSL will be used to encrypt the data stream sent between the application and SQL Server. The default value is 'false'.
Initial Catalog -or- Database	The SQL Server target database name.
Integrated Security -or- Trusted_Connection	Uses a value of 'true' or 'SSPI' to indicate where Windows authentication is to be used to connect to the database and a value of 'false' to indicate that mixed or SQL Server authentication should be used.
Max Pool Size	The default value is 100.
Min Pool Size	The default value is 0.
Network Library -or- Net	Specifies the network library DLL to be used. Supported values include 'dbnmpntw' (Named Pipes), 'dbmsrpcn' (Multiprotocol), 'dbmsadsn' (AppleTalk), 'dbmsgnet' (VIA), 'dbmsipcn' (Shared Memory), 'dbmsspxn' (IPX/SPX), and 'dbmssocn' (TCP/IP). The default value is 'dbmssocn'. The value used by this keyword should not include the path of the .dll file extension.
Packet Size	Used to alter the network packet size. The default packet size is 8192.
Password -or- Pwd	The password associated with the login ID (used for SQL Server authentication).

Table 6-1 *SQL Server .NET Data Provider Connection String Keywords*

Keyword	Description
Persist Security Info	Specifies whether security-sensitive information such as login information is returned to the application after a successful connection. The default value is 'false'.
Pooling	The default value is 'true'.
User ID -or- UID	The login ID for the data source (used for SQL Server authentication).
Workstation ID	Identifies the client workstation.

Table 6-1 *SQL Server .NET Data Provider Connection String Keywords* (Continued)

NOTE

Some of the keywords displayed contain spaces. If so, those spaces are required. In addition, for those items that have multiple keywords designated by the -or-, you can use any of the keywords. The .NET Framework Data Provider for SQL Server connection string keywords are not case-sensitive. However, it's good programming practice to be consistent in your usage of keyword case in all of your applications.

Opening a Trusted Connection

The previous example illustrated how to establish a SQL Server connection using a connection string that specified the UID and PWD keywords along with an associated SQL Server login. (This is also known as using Mixed Security.) However, because this incorporates the actual user ID and password into your code, this certainly isn't the most secure way to authenticate your connection to the SQL Server system.

Using Windows Security, also known as Integrated Security, provides for a more secure connection because the same values used for the client's Windows NT/2000/ NET login are also used for SQL Server authentication—there's no need to specify the user ID or the password from the application. In addition, Integrated Security can make administration easier by eliminating the need to create a set of SQL Server login IDs that are separate and must be maintained independently from the Windows NT/2000/NET login information. The following example illustrates how to use VB.NET to make a trusted connection to SQL Server using the .NET Framework Data Provider for SQL Server:

```
Private Sub SQLConnectSSPI(ByVal sServer As String)
    ' Create the connection object
    Dim cn As New SqlConnection("SERVER=" & sServer & _
        ";INTEGRATED SECURITY=True")
    Try
        ' Open the connection
        cn.Open()
    Catch ex As Exception
        ' Display any error messages
        MessageBox.Show("Connection error: :" & ex.ToString())
    End Try
    ' Close the connection
    cn.Close()
End Sub
```

In the beginning of this subroutine, you can see where the server name is passed in as a string value. Next, an instance of the SqlConnection object is created and the ConnectionString property is assigned as one of the arguments of the constructor. Like the previous example, the connection string uses the SERVER keyword to specify the SQL Server instance to connect to, and the INTEGRATED SECURITY keyword is set to true, indicating that the SQL Server authentication will be performed using Integrated Security rather than by passing in a login ID and password as part of the connection string.

After an instance of the SqlConnection object named cn has been instantiated, a Try-Catch block is used to execute the Open method. Again, if the Open method fails, then the code in the Catch block will be executed and a message box will be displayed showing the specific error message. After the connection has been established, it is immediately closed using the Connection object's Close method.

Using Connection Pooling

Connection pooling is an important scalability feature that's particularly significant to *n*-tier-style web applications, which may need to quickly support hundreds of simultaneous connections. Each open connection to SQL Server requires system overhead and management. And initially establishing the connection is the highest-overhead activity associated with each connection. Connection pooling makes the overall connection process more efficient by sharing a group or pool of connections between incoming users. Rather than immediately opening individual connections for each user, with connection pooling all connections that share exactly the same connection characteristics share the same connection, reducing the total number of new connections that must be established and maintained by SQL Server. To further improve efficiency, open connections are not immediately closed when a given client disconnects from the server. Rather, the connection is left open for a short period of time (determined by the Connection Lifetime keyword that's used in the SqlConnection object's ConnectionString property). This makes it possible for the connection to be immediately available for any new clients that can share the same connection characteristics, thereby avoiding the overhead associated with establishing a new connection.

Better still, the .NET Framework Data Provider for SQL Server automatically performs connection pooling without requiring any special setup. When a connection is opened, a connection pool is created based on the values used in the ConnectionString property of the SqlConnection object. Each connection pool is associated with a unique connection string. When a new connection is opened, the SqlConnection object checks to see if the value in the ConnectionString property matches the connection string used for an existing pool. If the string matches, the new connection is added to the existing pool. Otherwise, a new pool is created. The SqlConnection object will not destroy a connection pool until the application ends. The following VB.NET example illustrates creating two different connections that are both added to the same connection pool:

```
Private Sub SQLConnectPool(ByVal sServer As String)
    ' Create the first connection object
    Dim cn As New SqlConnection("SERVER=" & sServer & _
        ";INTEGRATED SECURITY=True")
    ' Create the second identical connection object
    Dim cn2 As New SqlConnection("SERVER=" & sServer & _
        ";INTEGRATED SECURITY=True")
    Try
        ' Open the connections
        cn.Open()
        cn2.Open()
    Catch ex As Exception
        ' Display any error messages
        MessageBox.Show("Connection error: :" & ex.ToString())
    End Try
    ' Close the connections
    cn.Close()
    cn2.Close()
End Sub
```

A string variable containing the server name is passed in to the beginning of this subroutine, and then two SqlConnection objects, cn and cn2, are created that have identical connection strings. In both cases, the ConnectionString property uses the SERVER keyword to identify the SQL Server instance to connect to and the INTEGRATED SECURITY keyword to specify that Windows integrated security will be used.

After the two SqlConnection objects have been created, a Try-Catch loop is used to open the connection to SQL Server and capture any run-time errors. Since the values of these connection strings are identical, they will both be part of the same connection pool. If the connection strings were different in any way, then two separate connection pools would have been created. After the connections have been established, the Close method is used to close each connection.

Pooling Related Connection String Keywords

While the .NET Framework Data Provider for SQL Server automatically handles connection pooling for you, there are still several connection string keywords that you can use to alter the SQLConnection object's connection pooling behavior. Table 6-2 presents the ConnectionString values you can use to customize the SQL Server .NET Data Provider's connection pooling behavior.

Name	Description
Connection Lifetime	After a connection is closed, it's returned to the pool. Then its creation time is compared with the current time and the connection is destroyed if the difference exceeds the value specified by Connection Lifetime. A value of 0 specifies that pooled connections will have the maximum lifespan.
Connection Reset	When 'True', this specifies that the connection is reset when it's removed from the pool. For Microsoft SQL Server version 7.0, you can set this value to 'False' to avoid an additional server round trip after opening a connection. However, the previous connection state and database context will not be reset.
Enlist	When this value is 'True', the connection is automatically created in the current transaction context of the creation thread if a transaction context exists.
Max Pool Size	Specifies the maximum number of connections allowed in the pool.
Min Pool Size	Specifies the minimum number of connections maintained in the pool.
Pooling	When this value is 'True', connection pooling is automatically enabled. 'False' allows you to turn off connection pooling.

Table 6-2   *Pooling-Related Connection String Keywords*

NOTE

For those connection string keywords that contain spaces, the spaces are a required part of the keyword.

Using the SqlCommand Object

Executing dynamic SQL statements and stored procedures are two of the most common database actions that are required by an application. Dynamic SQL statements are SQL statements that are read by the database server and executed when they are sent to the database server from the client application. When the database receives these SQL statements, they are first parsed to ensure that their syntax is correct, and then the database engine creates an access plan—essentially determining the best way to process the SQL statement—and then executes the statements. Unlike dynamic SQL statements, which are often used for executing SQL DML operations like creating tables or for data access operations like performing ad hoc queries, stored procedures are typically used to perform predefined queries and database update operations. Stored procedures form the backbone of most database applications. The primary difference between dynamic SQL statements and stored procedures is that stored procedures are typically created before the application is executed and reside in the database itself. This gives stored procedures a significant performance advantage over dynamic SQL statements because the jobs of parsing the SQL statement and creating the data access plan have already been completed. It's worth noting that changes made to data contained in an ADO.NET DataSet can be posted back to the database using dynamic SQL statements created by the SqlCommandBuilder class, or else they can be written back to the database using stored procedures. However, you don't need to use the DataSet and DataAdapter in order to update the database. In cases where you don't need the data binding and navigation functions provided by the DataSet, the Command objects can provide a much lighter-weight and more efficient method of updating the database. In the next sections, you'll see how to use the SqlCommand object to execute an ad hoc query, then to execute a SQL DDL statement to build a table on the target database, followed by two examples using the stored procedure. The first stored procedure example illustrates passing parameters to a stored procedure, and the second example illustrates executing a stored procedure that supplies a return value.

Table 6-3 lists all of the different SQL command execution methods supported by both the SqlCommand object and the OleDbCommand object.

Method	Description
ExecuteNonQuery	The ExecuteNonQuery method is used to execute a SQL statement on the connected data source. It is used for DDL statements; action queries like Insert, Update, and Delete operations; as well as ad hoc queries. The number of rows affected is returned, but no output parameters or result sets are returned.
ExecuteReader	The ExecuteReader method is used to execute a SQL Select statement on the data source. A fast forward–only result is returned.
ExecuteScalar	The ExecuteScalar method is used to execute a stored procedure or a SQL statement that returns a single scalar value. The first row of the first column of the result set is returned to the calling application. Any other returned values are ignored.
ExecuteXMLReader	The ExecuteXMLReader method is used to execute a FOR XML SELECT statement that returns an XML data stream from the data source. The ExecuteXMLReader command is compatible only with SQL Server 2000 and later.

Table 6-3   *SqlCommand SQL Statement Execution Methods*

Executing Dynamic SQL Statements

Dynamic SQL provide an extremely flexible mechanism for working with the database. Dynamic SQL allows you to execute ad hoc queries and return the results from action queries, as well as executing SQL DDL statements to create database objects. The following SQLCommandNonQuery subroutine provides an example illustrating how you can use dynamic SQL with the ADO.NET SqlCommand object to check for the existence of a table and conditionally create it if it doesn't exist:

```
Private Sub SQLCommandNonQuery(cn As SqlConnection)
    Dim sSQL As String = ""
    Dim cmd As New SqlCommand(sSQL, cn)
    Try
        ' First drop the table
        sSQL = "IF EXISTS " _
            & "(SELECT * FROM dbo.sysobjects WHERE id = " _
            & "object_id(N'[Department]') " _
            & "AND OBJECTPROPERTY(id, N'IsUserTable') = 1) " _
            & "DROP TABLE [department]"
        cmd.CommandText = sSQL
```

```
        cmd.ExecuteNonQuery()
        ' Then create the table
        sSQL = "CREATE TABLE Department " _
            & "(DepartmentID Int NOT NULL, " _
            & "DepartmentName Char(25), PRIMARY KEY(DepartmentID))"
        cmd.CommandText = sSQL
        cmd.ExecuteNonQuery()
    Catch e As Exception
        MsgBox(e.Message)
    End Try
End Sub
```

In the first part of the SQLCommandNonQuery subroutine, you can see where the SQL Server connection object is passed as a parameter. The sSQL variable that will be used to contain the dynamic SQL statements and an instance of the SqlCommand object named cmd are instantiated. In this example, the constructor of the cmd SqlCommand object uses two parameters—the first being a string containing the SQL statement that will be executed and the second being the SqlConnection object that will provide the connection to the target database server. Here the sSQL string is initially empty. Next, a Try-Catch structure is set up to execute the SQL commands. The first action that you can see within the Try-Catch block assigns a SQL statement to the sSQL variable that checks for the existence of the department table. In this SQL statement, you can see that a SELECT statement queries the SQL Server sysobjects table to determine if a User Table named Department exists. If the Department table is found, a DROP TABLE statement will be executed to remove the table from the target database. Otherwise, if the Department table isn't found, no further action will be taken. In order to actually execute the SQL statement, that value in the sSQL variable is then assigned to the CommandText property of the cmd object, and then the ExcuteNonQuery method of the cmd SqlCommand object is used to send the command to the SQL Server system. The ExecuteNonQuery method is used to execute a SQL statement that doesn't return a result set or a specific return value.

After the first DROP TABLE SQL command has been issued, the same sequence is followed to execute a Create Table command. First the sSQL variable is assigned a SQL CREATE TABLE statement that creates a table named Department that consists of two columns. The first column is an integer data type named DepartmentID, which is also the primary key, and the second column is a 25-character data type named DepartmentName. Then the value in the sSQL variable is copied to the cmd object's CommandText property, and the ExecuteNonQuery method is called to execute the CREATE TABLE SQL statement. Following the successful completion of the ExecuteNonQuery method, the Department Table will exist in the database that was earlier identified in the sDB variable.

If an error occurs during any of the operations contained in the Try block, the code in the Catch block will be executed, and a message box will be displayed showing the text of the exception condition.

Executing Parameterized SQL Statements

In addition to executing dynamic SQL statements, the SqlCommand object can also be used to execute stored procedures and parameterized SQL statements. The primary difference between dynamic SQL and prepared SQL is that dynamic SQL statements must be parsed and an access plan must be created before each run. (Technically, some database systems like SQL Server are very smart about the way this is handled, and they will actually store dynamic statements for a period of time. Then when the statement is subsequently executed, the existing access plan will be used. Even so, this depends on the database activity, and with dynamic SQL there's no guarantee that the plan will be immediately available.) You can think of prepared SQL statements as sort of a cross between stored procedures and dynamic SQL. Like stored procedures, they can accept different parameter values at run time. Like dynamic SQL, they are not persistent in the database. The SQL statement is parsed, and the access plan is created when the application executes the SQL statements. However, unlike dynamic SQL, the prepared SQL is parsed and the access plan is created only once, when the statement is first prepared. Subsequent statement execution takes advantage of the existing access plan. The access plan will typically remain in the procedure cache until the connection is terminated. The following example shows how to create and execute a prepared SQL statement using the ADO. NET SqlCommand object:

```
Private Sub SQLCommandPreparedSQL(cn As SqlConnection)
    ' Set up the Command object's parameter types
    Dim cmd As New SqlCommand("INSERT INTO department VALUES" & _
        "(@DepartmentID, @DepartmentName)", cn)
    Dim parmDepartmentID = _
        New SqlParameter("@DepartmentID", SqlDbType.Int)
    parmDepartmentID.Direction = ParameterDirection.Input
    Dim parmDepartmentName = _
        New SqlParameter("@DepartmentName", SqlDbType.Char, 25)
    parmDepartmentName.Direction = ParameterDirection.Input
    ' Add the parameter objects to the cmd Parameter's collection
    cmd.Parameters.Add(parmDepartmentID)
    cmd.Parameters.Add(parmDepartmentName)
```

```
Try
    cmd.Prepare()
    ' Execute the prepared SQL statement to insert 10 rows
    Dim i As Integer
    For i = 0 To 10
        parmDepartmentID.Value = i
        parmDepartmentName.Value = "New Department " & CStr(i)
        cmd.ExecuteNonQuery()
    Next
Catch e As Exception
    MsgBox(e.Message)
End Try
End Sub
```

At the top of the CommandPrepareSQL subroutine, you can see where the SqlConnection object named cn is passed in, followed by the creation of a new SqlCommand object named cmd. In this example, the constructor takes two arguments. The first argument is used to assign a SQL statement to the cmd object. This can either be a SQL statement or the name of a stored procedure. Here, the SQL statement is an INSERT statement that adds the values of two columns to the Department table.

NOTE

The Department table was created in the earlier section of this chapter.

The important point to note in this example is the format of the parameter markers that are used in the SQL statement. Parameter markers are used to indicate the replaceable characters in a prepared SQL statement. At run time, these parameters will be replaced with the actual values that are supplied by the SqlCommand object's Parameters collection. Unlike ADO, which uses the question mark character (?) to indicate replaceable parameters, the SqlCommand object requires that all parameter markers begin with the @ symbol. This example shows two parameter markers: @DepartmentID and @DepartmentName. The second argument of the SqlCommand constructor associates the cmd SqlCommand object with the cn SqlConnection object that was passed in earlier.

Next, you can see where two SqlParameter objects are created. The first parameter object, named parmDepartmentID, will be used to supply values to the first parameter marker (@DepartmentID). Likewise, the second parameter object, named parmDepartmentName, will supply the values used by the second replaceable parameter (@DepartmentName). The code example used in this subroutine shows three parameters being passed to the SqlParameter's constructor. The first parameter supplies the parameter name. Here you need to make sure that the name supplied to the SqlParameter object's constructor matches the name that was used in the parameter marker of the prepared SQL statement. The second parameter that's passed to this overloaded version of the SqlParameter constructor specifies the parameter's data type.

Here the Direction property is set to input using the ParameterDirection.Input enumeration. Table 6-4 lists the valid enumerations for the SqlParameter Direction property.

After the SqlParameter objects have been created, the next step is to add them to the SqlCommand object's Parameters collection. In the previous listings, you can see that you use the Add method of the SqlCommand object's Parameters collection to add both the parmDepartmentID and parmDepartmentName SqlParameter objects to the cmd SqlCommand object. The order in which you add the SqlParameter objects isn't important. Next, within the Try-Catch block the Prepare statement is used to prepare the statement. Note that the Prepare method is executed after all of the parameter attributes have been described.

NOTE

Using the Prepare operation provides an important performance benefit for parameterized queries because it instructs SQL Server to issue an sp_prepare statement, thereby ensuring that the statement will be in the Procedure cache until the statement handle is closed.

Next a For-Next loop is used to add ten rows to the newly created Department table. Within the For-Next loop, the Value property of each parameter object is assigned a new data value. For simplicity, the parmDepartmentID parameter is assigned the value of the loop counter contained in the variable i, while the parmDepartmentName parameter is assigned a string containing the literal "New Department" along with the current value of the loop counter. Finally, the SqlCommand object's ExecuteNonQuery method is used to execute the SQL statement. In this case, ExecuteNonQuery was

Enumeration	Description
ParameterDirection.Input	The parameter is an input parameter.
ParameterDirection.InputOutput	The parameter is capable of both input and output.
ParameterDirection.Output	The parameter is an output parameter.
ParameterDirection.ReturnValue	The parameter represents a return value.

Table 6-4 *SqlParameterDirection Enumeration*

used because this example is using a SQL action query that doesn't return any values. From the SQL Server perspective, running the ExecuteNonQuery method results in the server issuing an sp_execute command to actually perform the insert.

NOTE

If you need to pass a null value as a parameter, you need to set the parameter to the value DBNull.Value.

If an error occurs during any of these operations, the code in the Catch block will be executed and a message box will be displayed showing the text of the exception condition.

Executing Stored Procedures with Return Values

Stored procedures are the core of most database applications—and for good reason. In addition to their performance benefits, stored procedures can also be a mechanism for restricting data access to the predefined interfaces that are exposed by the stored procedures. Similar to prepared SQL statements, stored procedures get significant performance benefits from the fact that they are compiled before they are used. This allows the database to forgo the typical parsing steps that are required as well as skipping the need to create an access plan. Stored procedures are the true workhorse of most database applications, and they are almost always used for database insert, update, and delete operations, as well as for retrieving single values and results sets. In the following examples, you see how to execute SQL Server stored procedures using the SqlCommand object. In the first example that follows, you'll see how to execute a stored procedure that accepts a single input parameter and returns a scalar value.

The following listing presents the T-SQL source code required to create the CostDiff stored procedure that will be added to the sample AdventureWorks database. You can create this stored procedure by executing this code using SQL Server Management Studio.

```
CREATE PROCEDURE CostDiff
    @ProductID int
AS

DECLARE @CostDiff money

SELECT CostDiff = (ListPrice - StandardCost)
FROM Production.Product WHERE ProductID = @ProductID

RETURN @CostDiff
```

In this listing, you can see that the CostDiff stored procedure accepts a single input parameter. That parameter is an Integer value that's used to identify the ProductID. The CostDiff stored procedure returns the cost difference of that ProductID from the Production.Product table in the AdventureWorks database. The cost difference is calculated by retrieving the ListPrice number and subtracting it from the value in the StandardCost column. The results are then assigned to the @CostDiff variable, which is returned as a scalar value by the stored procedure. After the sample stored procedure has been created in the AdventureWorks database, it can be called by your ADO.NET applications. The following example shows how to use the SqlCommand class from VB.NET to execute the CostDiff stored procedure and retrieve the scalar value that it returns:

```
Private Sub SQLCommandSPScalar(cn As SqlConnection)
    ' Create the command object and set the SQL statement
    Dim cmd As New SqlCommand("CostDiff", cn)
    cmd.CommandType = CommandType.StoredProcedure
    ' Create the parameter
    cmd.Parameters.Add("@ProductID", SqlDbType.Int)
    cmd.Parameters("@ProductID").Direction = _
        ParameterDirection.Input
    cmd.Parameters("@ProductID").Value = 1
    Try
        Dim nCostDiff As Decimal
        nCostDiff = cmd.ExecuteScalar()
        ' Put to textbox on displayed form
        txtMid.Text = nCostDiff
    Catch e As Exception
        MsgBox(e.Message)
    End Try
End Sub
```

In the beginning of this routine you can see where the cn SqlConnection object is passed in, followed by the creation of the SqlCommand object named cmd. In this example, the constructor for the SqlCommand object uses two parameters. The first parameter is a string that accepts the command that will be executed. This can be either a SQL statement or the name of the stored procedure. In this example, you can see that the name of the CostDiff stored procedure is used. The second parameter is used for the name of the SqlConnection object that will be used to connect to the target database. After the cmd SqlCommand object has been created, its CommandType property is set to CommandType.StoredProcedure, indicating that a stored procedure will be executed. The CommandType property can accept any of the values shown in Table 6-5.

CommandType Values	Description
CommandType.StoredProcedure	The command is a stored procedure.
CommandType.TableDirect	The command is the name of a database table.
CommandType.Text	The command is a SQL statement.

Table 6-5   *CommandType Values*

After the SqlCommand object's CommandType property is set to CommandType. StoredProcedure, the SqlParameter object used to supply the input value to the CostDiff stored procedure is created. SqlParameter objects can be created either by using the SqlParameter class constructor or by executing the SqlCommand object's Parameters collection Add method. In this example, the parameter is created using the Add method of the SqlCommand object's Parameters collection. The first parameter supplied to the Add method is a string containing the name of the parameter, in this case "@ProductID". Again, note that replaceable parameters used by the SqlParameter object must begin with the ampersand symbol (@). The second parameter uses the SqlDbType.Int enumeration to indicate that the parameter will contain an Integer value. The next line sets the Direction property to the value ParameterDirection.Input to indicate that this is an input parameter. Finally, the SqlParameter object's Value property is set to 1—storing a value of 1 to pass to the CostDiff stored procedure.

The next section of code sets up a Try-Catch block to execute the CostDiff stored procedure. The important point to note in the Try-Catch block is that the cmd SqlCommand object's ExecuteScalar method is used to execute the CostDiff stored procedure and the return value is assigned to the nCostDiff variable. The contents of the nCostDiff variable are then assigned to a text box named txtMid that is defined on the Windows form for this project. As in earlier examples, if the stored procedure fails, a message box showing the error text will be displayed to the end user.

Executing Transactions

Transactions enable you to group together multiple operations that can be performed as a single unit of work, which helps to ensure database integrity. For instance, transferring funds from your saving account to your checking account involves multiple database operations, and the transfer cannot be considered complete unless all of the operations are successfully completed. A typical transfer from your savings account to your checking account requires two separate but related operations: a withdrawal from your savings account and a deposit to your checking account. If either operation fails, the transfer is not completed. Therefore both of these functions would be considered part of the same logical transaction. From the database standpoint, to ensure database integrity, both the withdrawal and the deposit would be grouped together as a single transaction. If the withdrawal operation succeeded, but the deposit failed, the entire transaction could be rolled back, which would restore the database to the condition it had before the withdrawal operation was attempted. Using transactions is an essential part of most production-level database applications.

ADO.NET supports transactions using the Transaction classes. In order to incorporate transactions into your ADO.NET applications, you first need to create an instance of the SqlTransaction object and then execute the BeginTransaction method to mark the beginning of a transaction. Under the covers this will cause the database server to begin a transaction. For instance, using the SqlTransaction object to issue a BeginTransaction statement will send a T-SQL BEGIN TRANSACTION command to SQL Server. After the transaction has started, the database update operations are performed and then the Commit method is used to actually write the updates to the target database. If an error occurs during the process, then the RollBack operation is used to undo the changes. The following SQLCommandTransaction subroutine shows how to start a transaction and then either commit the results of the transaction to the database or roll back the transaction in the event of an error:

```
Private Sub SQLCommandTransaction(cn As SqlConnection)
    Dim cmd As New SqlCommand()
    Dim trans As SqlTransaction
    ' Start a local transaction
    trans = cn.BeginTransaction()
    cmd.Connection = cn
    cmd.Transaction = trans
    Try
        ' Insert a row  transaction
        cmd.CommandText = _
            "INSERT INTO Department VALUES(100, 'Transaction 100')"
        cmd.ExecuteNonQuery()
        ' This next insert will result in an error
        cmd.CommandText = _
            "INSERT INTO Department VALUES(100, 'Transaction 101')"
        cmd.ExecuteNonQuery()
        trans.Commit()
    Catch e As Exception
        MsgBox(e.Message)
        trans.Rollback()
    End Try
End Sub
```

In the beginning of this subroutine, you can see where the SqlConnection object is passed in and a new instance of the SqlCommand object is created, followed by the definition of a SqlTransaction object named trans. Next, a local transaction is started by using the cn SqlConnection object's BeginTransaction method to create a new instance of a SqlTransaction object. Note that the connection must be open before you execute the BeginTransaction method. Next, the cmd SqlCommand Connection property is assigned with the cn SqlConnection and the Transaction property is assigned with the trans SqlTransaction object.

Within the Try-Catch block, two commands are issued that are within the local transaction scope. The first command is an INSERT statement that inserts two columns into the Department table that was created previously in this chapter. The first insert statement adds the DepartmentID of 100 along with a DepartmentName value of "Transaction 100." The SqlCommand ExecuteNonQuery method is then used to execute the SQL statement. Next, the cmd object's CommandText property is set to another SQL INSERT statement. However, this statement will cause an error because it is attempting to insert a duplicate primary key value. In this second case, the DepartmentID of 100 is attempted to be inserted along with the DepartmentName value of "Transaction 101." This causes an error because the DepartmentID of 100 was just inserted by the previous INSERT statement. When the ExecuteNonQuery method is executed, the duplicate primary key error will be issued and the code in the Catch portion of the Try-Catch block will be executed.

Displaying the exception message in a message box is the first action that happens within the Catch block. You can see an example of this message in Figure 6-3.

After the message box is displayed, the trans SqlTransaction object's RollBack method is used to roll back the attempted transaction. Note that because both insert statements were within the same transaction scope, both insert operations will be rolled back. The resulting department table will not contain either DepartmentName "Transaction 100" or DepartmentName "Transaction 101."

Figure 6-3   *A duplicate primary key error prevents the Commit operation.*

Using the SqlDependency Object

SQL Server 2005 and ADO.NET 2.0 now contain a signaling solution in the data provider and the database called Query Notifications. Query Notifications allows your application to request a notification from SQL Server when the results of a query change. You can design applications that query the database only when there is a change to information that the application has previously retrieved.

Query Notifications are implemented through the SQL Server 2005 Query Engine, the SQL Server Service Broker, a system stored procedure (sp_DispatcherProc), the ADO.NET System.Data.Sql.SqlNotificationRequest class, the System.Data. SqlClient.SqlDependency class, and the ASP.NET System.Web.Caching.Cache class. The basic process is as follows:

1. The SqlCommand object contains a Notification property that is a request for notification. When the SqlCommand is executed and the Notification property is not null, a request of notification is appended to the command request.

2. SQL Server registers a subscription regarding the request for notification with Query Notifications and then executes the command.

3. SQL Server monitors the SQL statements for anything that would change the originally returned rowset. If the rowset is changed, a message is sent to the Service Broker Service. The message can either send a notification back to the registered client, or wait on the Service Broker's Queue for retrieval by an advanced client's custom processing routine.

The following example demonstrates the System.Data.SqlClient.SqlDependency object. Note that the application creates a System.Data.SqlClient.SqlDependency object and registers to receive notifications via the System.Data.SqlClient. SqlDependency.OnChange event handler.

```
Imports System
Imports System.Data
Imports System.Data.SqlClient
Imports System.ComponentModel
Public Class Form1
    Dim cn As New SqlConnection()
    Dim cmd As New SqlCommand
    Private Sub StartNotification_Click( & _
      ByVal sender As System.Object, ByVal e As System.EventArgs) & _
      Handles StartNotification.Click
        ' Set the connection string
```

```vb
        cn.ConnectionString = "SERVER=" & txt_Server.Text & _
            ";database=AdventureWorks" & _
            ";UID=" & txt_UserID.Text & ";PWD=" & txt_Password.Text
        cmd.CommandText = "SELECT Category, Description, " & _
            "DiscountPct FROM Sales.SpecialOffer"
        cmd.Connection = cn
        StartNotify()
End Sub
Private Sub StartNotify()
    ' Command Notification property starts as nothing
    cmd.Notification = Nothing
    ' a SqlDependency object is attached to the Command object
    Dim dep As New SqlDependency
    dep.AddCommandDependency(cmd)
    AddHandler dep.OnChange, New OnChangeEventHandler( & _
        AddressOf MyOnChange)

    Try
        ' Open the connection
        cn.Open()

        Dim rdr As SqlDataReader
        ' Create the reader
        rdr = cmd.ExecuteReader()
        ' Read results and add to a listbox on displayed form
        list_Results.Items.Clear()
        Do While rdr.Read()
            list_Results.Items.Add(rdr("Category") & vbTab & _
            rdr.Item("Description") & vbTab & _
            rdr.Item("DiscountPct"))
        Loop
        rdr.Close()

        cn.Close()
        list_Results.Update()
    Catch e As Exception
        MsgBox(e.Message)
    End Try
End Sub
Private Sub MyOnChange(ByVal sender As Object, & _
    ByVal args As SqlNotificationEventArgs)
    ' Check for safe UI update.
    Dim i As ISynchronizeInvoke = CType(Me, ISynchronizeInvoke)
```

```
      ' If InvokeRequired True, code executing on a worker thread.
      If i.InvokeRequired Then
          ' Create a delegate to perform the thread switch.
          Dim tempDelegate As New OnChangeEventHandler( & _
            AddressOf MyOnChange)
          Dim argues() As Object = {sender, args}
          ' Marshal the data from worker thread to UI thread.
          i.BeginInvoke(tempDelegate, argues)
          Return
      End If
      ' Remove the handler.
      Dim dep As SqlDependency = CType(sender, SqlDependency)
      RemoveHandler dep.OnChange, AddressOf MyOnChange
      StartNotify()
    End Sub
End Class
```

In the beginning of the code listing, the Import statements are placed in the declarations section of the project file and a Form1 class is started. A SqlConnection object named cn is created and a new SqlCommand object named cmd is created. The next statement is the StartNotification_Click subroutine, which refers to the click event of a button on a sample windows form. Inside the subroutine, the SqlConnection's ConnectionString property is set using three textboxes on the form that provide the server name, userid, password. The database of Adventureworks is also used, but in this case is hardcoded. The SqlCommand's CommandText property is set to select the Category, Description, and DiscountPct field from the Sales.SpecialOffer table in the AdventureWorks database. Next, the cmd object's Connection property is set to the previously created cn object. A subroutine called StartNotify is then called. The StartNotify subroutine is shown next in the code listing. The cmd object's Notification property is first set to Nothing, then the SqlDependency object is created and added to the cmd object using the AddCommandDependency method. This will set the cmd object's Notification property to the SqlDependency object, which will append a notification request to the command request when the command is executed. An OnChangeEventHandler is then created to process any change notifications that are sent back to the application. In the Try/Catch block, you can see that the connection is then opened, a SqlDataReader is created, and the ExecuteReader function is called. The ExecuteReader command will retrieve the records from the Sales.SpecialOffer table, as the SQL SELECT statement requested. The SqlDataReader then reads through the retrieved data and outputs it to a listbox on the windows form. The reader and connection are then closed and the listbox is refreshed to show the data.

The next subroutine, MyOnChange, is the event handler that will execute when any of the originally retrieved data is changed at the server. Here we do a little fancy footwork to move the incoming data from the notification from the worker thread it came in on to the UI thread, so it can be displayed on the windows form. The BeginInvoke method of the ISynchronizeInvoke object is used to set the receive notification process to asynchronous, which allows switching of communication threads. A temporary event handler is created to handle the marshaled data and the original handler is removed. While a discussion on the ISynchronizeInvoke object is beyond the scope of this chapter, this subroutine gives you a brief sample of how to marshal data between threads. The StartNotify subroutine is then called to reset the handler and process the newly changed data and display it to the user in the listbox.

Using the SqlDataReader Object

The DataReader is a unique entity in the ADO.NET framework. While the rest of the ADO.NET framework was explicitly designed to work in a disconnected model, the DataReader has been designed to work in a more traditional connected fashion. The DataReader essentially provides a fast forward–only stream of data that's sent from the database server to the application. Thanks to these attributes, this is also known as a fire hose cursor. Unlike the much more feature-laden DataSet, the DataReader is a very lightweight, high-performance object. Also unlike the DataSet, the DataReader is one-way. In other words, it doesn't allow you to directly update the data that's retrieved. That doesn't mean that the data retrieved by the DataReader can't be changed—it can, but the DataReader doesn't have any built-in mechanisms that allow updating. To update the data retrieved by the DataReader, you would need to execute either SQL statements or stored procedures, or else move the data into a DataSet. The DataReader is also created a bit differently than the other ADO.NET objects. While most of the other ADO.NET objects, such as the Connection and Command objects, can be instantiated using a constructor (for instance, when you use the New keyword), to create a DataReader, you must call the ExecuteReader method of the Command object. One important consideration to keep in mind with the DataReader is that while the DataReader is in use, it will monopolize the associated Connection object. No other operations can be performed using the Connection (other than closing it) until the Close method of the DataReader is executed.

Retrieving a Fast Forward—Only Result Set

Retrieving a fast read-only stream of results from a SQL Server database is the SqlDataReader's primary purpose. Retrieving quick read-only subsets of data is one of the most common operations for a SQL Server database application, and the SqlDataReader is the best ADO.NET object for this task in that it provides the best data read performance of any ADO.NET object and has minimal overhead. The SqlDataReader maintains a constant connection state to the database from the time the query is started until the database has returned the result stream, which means that the SqlConnection object can't be used for anything else while the SqlDataReader is active. The following example illustrates the basic usage of the SqDataReader. In this example you'll see how to retrieve a basic read-only result set from the SQL Server AdventureWorks database and then process the individual data elements that compose the result stream.

```
Private Sub SQLReaderForward(cn As SqlConnection)
    ' Setup the command
    Dim cmd As New SqlCommand _
        ("SELECT CustomerID, CustomerType FROM Sales.Customer " _
        & "WHERE TerritoryID = 4", cn)
    cmd.CommandType = CommandType.Text
    Dim rdr As SqlDataReader
    Try
        ' Create the reader
        rdr = cmd.ExecuteReader(CommandBehavior.CloseConnection)
        ' Read the results and add them to a listbox on displayed form
        lstResults.Items.Clear()
        Do While rdr.Read()
            lstResults.Items.Add(rdr("CustomerID") & vbTab & _
            rdr.Item("CustomerType"))
        Loop
        rdr.Close()
    Catch e As Exception
        MsgBox(e.Message)
    End Try
End Sub
```

In the beginning of the SQLReaderForward subroutine, a SqlConnection object named cn is passed in and a new SqlCommand object named cmd is created. The constructor sets the Command Property to a SQL SELECT statement that retrieves the value of the CustomerID and CustomerType columns from the Sales.Customer

Table in the AdventureWorks database for all rows where the TerritoryID column is equal to 4. Since this is a SQL command, the CommandType is set to CommandText and then a new SqlDataReader named rdr is declared.

NOTE

At this point you can't use the SqlDataReader because, although the SqlDataReader object is declared, it has not been instantiated. The SqlDataReader is only instantiated after the SqlCommand object's ExecuteReader method has been called.

Inside the Try block the cmd SqlCommand object's ExecuteReader is used to instantiate the SqlDataReader. At this point the SqlDataReader is opened and ready to use. You might notice that the ExecuteReader method uses CommandBehavior. CloseConnection enumeration, which automatically closes the connection when the SqlDataReader is closed. The CommandBehavior member provides the Command object a description of the results of the query and also influences the effects of the query on the database. Table 6-6 describes the available CommandBehavior options.

Option	Description
CloseConnection	The associated Connection object is closed when the DataReader object is closed.
Default	No options are set. This is equivalent to calling ExecuteReader().
KeyInfo	The query returns column and primary key information. This flag causes the SQL Server .NET Data Provider to append a FOR BROWSE clause to the statement being executed.
SchemaOnly	The query only returns column metadata and does not return a result set.
SequentialAccess	This flag is used to handle access to BLOB (Binary Large Objects). When this option is used, the DataReaders loads data as a stream rather than loading the entire row. The GetBytes or GetChars methods can then be used to read the data buffer that's returned.
SingleResult	The query is restricted to returning a single result set.
SingleRow	The query is expected to return a single row. Using the SingleRow flag with the ExecuteReader method of the OleDbCommand object causes the object to perform single-row binding using the OLE DB IRow interface. Otherwise, the OLE DB .NET Provider will perform binding using the IRowset interface.

Table 6-6   *ExecuteReader CommandBehavior Enumeration*

Next, a While loop is used to read the forward-only data stream returned by the SqlDataReader. Within the While loop the two different data elements in the data stream are added to a list box named lstResults that is defined on the Windows form for this project. In this example, each column in the result set is accessed using a string that identifies the column name. In other words, rdr("CustomerID") is used to access the CustomerID column and rdr("CustomerType") is used to access the CustomerType column. Alternatively, you could also access the column returned by the DataReader in a couple of other ways. First you could use each column's ordinal position rather than the column name. In this case you could use rdr(0) and rdr(1). Using ordinals may execute a tiny bit faster, but the price you pay in code readability isn't worth the minuscule performance difference. Next, each of the columns in the result set returned by the SqlDataReader could also have been accessed using the rdr.GetInt32(0) and rdr.GetString(1) methods. The main difference between these options is the fact that when you reference the DataReader columns directly using the named columns, you get back the native .NET Data Provider data type types. Using the GetInt32, GetString, or other similar data access methods returns the .NET Framework data type, and an error will be thrown if the data doesn't match the data type expected by the method. In addition, the GetString, GetInt32, and other data access methods accept only ordinal values and can't be used with string identified. You should note that in all of these cases each column must be accessed in the order it appears in the result set. You cannot access the columns out of order. This is because the DataReader provides one-way streams of results to the client application. After all of the results have been retrieved, the rdr.Read method will return the value of False and the while loop will be terminated; then the rdr. Close method is used to close the SqlDataReader. Since the CommandBehavior. CloseConnection flag was used earlier by the ExecuteReader method, the connection to the SQL Server database will also be closed.

NOTE

Explicitly closing all of the ADO.NET objects is especially important because unlike in ADO, the objects aren't destroyed when they go out of scope. Instead, if left to their own devices they are destroyed when the .NET garbage collector decides to remove them. However, explicitly closing the DataReader is particularly important because the connection can't be used for anything else until the DataReader is closed.

The code in the Catch block will be executed if an error occurs while using the SqlDataReader. In this case, the exception message will be captured and displayed in a message box.

Reading Schema-Only Information

The previous examples illustrated how to retrieve the data and basic column headings using the SqlDataReader. However, the SqlDataReader can also retrieve more detailed table schema information. The metadata returned can help you determine how to process the columns that are returned by the DataReader. The column schema information returned includes the column name and its data type, as well as other information such as whether the column can accept null values. The following SQLReaderSchema subroutine illustrates using the SqlDataReader's GetTableSchema method to return the schema information for a given query:

```
Private Sub SQLReaderSchema(cn As SqlConnection)
    ' Setup the command
    Dim cmd As New SqlCommand("SELECT * FROM Sales.Customer", cn)
    cmd.CommandType = CommandType.Text
    Dim rdr As SqlDataReader
    Try
        ' Create the reader
        rdr = cmd.ExecuteReader(CommandBehavior.SchemaOnly)
        ' bind the returned DataTable to the grid & close
        grdResults.SetDataBinding(rdr.GetSchemaTable(), "")
        rdr.Close()
    Catch e As Exception
        MsgBox(e.Message)
    End Try
End Sub
```

Like the previous examples, the SQLReaderSchema subroutine begins by creating a new SqlCommand object named cmd. In this case, the SqlCommand object contains a SQL SELECT statement that retrieves all of the columns from the Sales.Customer table. You might note that since this example doesn't actually retrieve any data, it's okay to use an unqualified query like this. However, if this were a production query, you would have to make sure to specify the exact columns and rows that your application needed. Next the CommandText property is set to CommandType.Text and a SqlDataReader object named rdr is declared.

Next a Try block is used to execute the SqlDataReader. If an error occurs inside the Try block, the code in the Catch block will be executed and message box will be displayed. There are two important points to notice about this example. First, the cmd SqlCommand object's ExcuteReader method uses the CommandBehavior. SchemaOnly enumeration to specify that only schema metadata should be returned by the SqlDataReader and that no data will be returned to the calling application.

The next point to notice is the use of the rdr SqlDataReader's GetSchemaTable method to actually retrieve the metadata for the query. The GetTableSchema method returns a DataTable object, which is then bound to the DataGrid named grdResults using the grid's SetDataBinding method.

NOTE

While this example illustrates retrieving the column metadata information from a single table, the DataReader's GetTableSchema method works just as well with the results of multiple tables.

Asynchronous Support

Asynchronous query support is a feature that was present in ADO but was missing in the earlier releases of ADO.NET. *Asynchronous queries* provide client applications the ability to submit queries without blocking the user interference. The new ADO. NET asynchronous support provides the ability for server applications to issue multiple database requests on different threads without blocking the threads. With SQL Server 2005, ADO.NET provides asynchronous support for both opening a connection and executing commands. The asynchronous operation is started using the object's BEGIN*xxx* method and is ended using the END*xxx* method. The IAsyncResult object is used to check the completion status of the command. The following VB.NET code shows an asynchronous query to return all the rows of the Production.Product table from the AdventureWorks database:

```
Private Sub SQLAsync(ByVal sServer As String)
    ' Create the connection object
    Dim cn As New SqlConnection("SERVER=" & sServer & _
        ";INTEGRATED SECURITY=True;DATABASE=AdventureWorks" & _
        ";ASYNC=True")
    Dim cmd As New SqlCommand("SELECT * FROM Production.Product", cn)
    cmd.CommandType = CommandType.Text
    Dim rdr As SqlDataReader
    Try
        ' Open the connection
        cn.Open()
        Dim myResult As IAsyncResult = cmd.BeginExecuteReader()
        Do While (myResult.IsCompleted <> True)
            ' Perform other actions
        Loop
        ' Process the contents of the reader
        rdr = cmd.EndExecuteReader(myResult)
        ' Open the reader
```

```
            rdr.Close()
    Catch ex As Exception
        ' Display any error messages
        MessageBox.Show("Error: :" & ex.ToString())
    End Try
    ' Close the connection
    cn.Close()
End Sub
```

The first significant feature in this example is the connection string. In order to implement asynchronous support, the connection string must contain the async=true keywords. Next, note the IAsynchResult object within the Try block. The SqlCommand object's BeginExecuteReader method is used to start an asynchronous query that returns all of the rows in the Production.Product table. Control is returned to the application immediately after the statement is executed; the application doesn't need to wait for the query to finish. Next, a While loop is used to check the status of the IAsyncResult object. When the asynchronous command completes, the IsCompleted property is set to true. At this point, the While loop completes and the EndExecuteReader command is used to assign the asynchronous query to a SqlDataReader for processing.

Multiple Active Result Sets (MARS)

The ability to take advantage of SQL Server 2005's new multiple active result sets (MARS) feature is another enhancement found in the new ADO.NET version. In prior versions of ADO.NET and SQL Server, you were limited to one active result set per connection. And while COM-based ADO and OLE DB had a feature that allowed the application to process multiple result sets, under the covers that feature was actually spawning new connections on your behalf in order to process the additional commands. The new MARS feature in ADO.NET takes advantage of SQL Server 2005's capability to have multiple active commands on a single connection. In this model you can open a connection to the database, then open the first command and process some results, then open the second command and process results, and then go back to the first command and process more results. You can freely switch back and forth between the different active commands. There's no blocking between the commands, and both commands share a single connection to the database. The feature provides a big performance and scalability gain for ADO.NET 2.0 applications. Since this feature relies on a SQL Server 2005 database, it can be used only with SQL Server 2005 databases and doesn't work with prior versions of SQL Server. The following example illustrates using MARS:

```vb
Private Sub SQLMARS(ByVal sServer As String)
    ' Create the connection object
    Dim cn As New SqlConnection("SERVER=" & sServer & _
      ";INTEGRATED SECURITY=True;DATABASE=AdventureWorks")
    Dim cmd1 As New SqlCommand("SELECT * FROM " & _
      "HumanResources.Department", cn)
    cmd1.CommandType = CommandType.Text
    Dim cmd2 As New SqlCommand("SELECT * FROM " & _
      "HumanResources.Employee", cn)
    cmd2.CommandType = CommandType.Text

    Dim rdr1 As SqlDataReader
    Dim rdr2 As SqlDataReader
    Try
        cn.Open()
        rdr1 = cmd1.ExecuteReader()
        While (rdr1.Read())
            If (rdr1("Name") = "Production") Then
                rdr2 = cmd2.ExecuteReader()
                While (rdr2.Read())
                    ' Process results
                    rdr2.Close()
                End While
            End If
        End While
        rdr1.Close()
    Catch ex As Exception
        ' Display any error messages
        MessageBox.Show("Error: :" & ex.ToString())
    Finally
        ' Close the connection
        cn.Close()
    End Try
End Sub
```

In this example you can see that both cmd1 and cmd2 share the same SqlConnection object, named cn. The cmd1 object is used to open a SqlDataReader that reads all of the rows from the HumanResources.Department table. When the Department named Production is found, the second SqlCommand object, named cmd2, is used to read the contents of the HumanResources.Employee table. The important point to note is that the SqlCommand named cmd2 is able to execute using the active SqlConnection object that is also servicing the cmd1 object.

Retrieving BLOB Data

The previous examples illustrated retrieving result sets that consisted of standard character and numeric data. However, it's common for modern databases to also contain large binary objects, more commonly referred to as BLOBs (Binary Large Objects). BLOBs are typically graphical images such as product and employee photos contained in .BMP, .JPG, or .TIF files. They can also be small sound bytes like .WAV files or MP3s. Although these are some of the common types of data files that are stored as BLOBs in the database, the BLOB storage provided by most modern database such as SQL Server, Oracle, and UDB can accommodate all binary objects, including Word documents, PowerPoint presentations, standard executable files (.EXEs), and even XML documents. While the database is fully capable of storing BLOB data, the potential size of these objects means that they must be accessed and managed differently than standard text and numeric data types. Previous SQL Server versions use three different data types for BLOB storage: Text, nText, and Image. The Text and nText data types can be used to store variable-length text data. The Text data type can accommodate up to 2GB of non-Unicode text data, while the nText data can accommodate up to 1GB of Unicode text data. The Image data type is undoubtedly the most versatile of the SQL Server BLOB storage types. The Image data type can store up to 2GB of binary data, which also enables it to store standard text data as well. These data types do, however, require some special programming to import and export them from the database, making them a bit cumbersome.

SQL Server 2005 introduces a new MAX specifier for variable-length data types, such as varchar, nvarchar, and varbinary. This specifier allows storage of up to 2^{31} bytes of data, and for Unicode, it is 2^{30} bytes. Data values in the varchar(max) and nvarchar(max) data types are stored as character strings, whereas data in the varbinary(max) data type is stored as bytes. Database tables and Transact-SQL variables now have the ability to specify varchar(max), nvarchar(max), or varbinary(max) data types, allowing for a more consistent programming model. In ADO.NET, the new max data types can be retrieved by a DataReader, and can also be declared as both input and output parameters without any special handling. In this section you'll see how to retrieve BLOB data from a SQL Server database using the SqlDataReader.

Before jumping directly into the code, it's worth briefly exploring the advantages and disadvantages of integrating BLOB data within the database. Storing these types of objects in the database along with the more common text and numeric data enables you to keep all of the related information for a given database entity together. This enables easy searching and retrieval of the BLOB data by querying its related text information. The common alternative to this is storing the binary files outside of the database and then including a file path or URL to the object within the database. This separate storage method has a couple of advantages. It is somewhat easier to program for, and it does allow your databases to be smaller because they don't include the binary objects, which can be quite large. However, you have to manually create and maintain some type of link between the database and external file system files, which can easily become out of sync. Next, some type of unique naming scheme for the OS files is usually required to keep the potentially hundreds or even thousands of files separate. Storing the BLOB data within the database eliminates these problems.

The following example illustrates using the SqlDataReader to retrieve the photo images stored in the AdventureWorks Production.ProductPhoto table. As you'll see in the following code listing, using the SqlDataReader to retrieve BLOB data is similar to retrieving character and number data, but there are some important differences. The main difference is the use of the CommandBehavior.SequentialAccess access flag on the Command object ExecuteReader method. As you saw in the earlier example, the DataReader is always instantiated by calling the ExecuteReader method, and the CommandBehavior flag influences how the database will send information to the DataReader. When you specify SequentialAccess, it changes the default behavior of the DataReader in a couple of ways. First, you are not required to read from the columns in the order they are returned. In other words, you can jump ahead to an offset in the data stream. However, once your application has read past a location in the returned stream of data, it can no longer read anything prior to its current location. Next, the CommandBehavior.SequentialAccess flag turns off the DataReader's normal buffering mode, where the DataReader always returns one row at a time; instead, results are streamed back to the application. Because this subroutine writes data to the file system, you need to import the .NET System.IO namespace into your application to enable access to the file system. To import the System.IO namespace, you need to add the following code to your projects:

```
Imports System.IO
```

The following SQLReaderBLOB subroutine illustrates retrieving BLOB data from the SQL Server database:

```
Private Sub SQLReaderBLOB(cn As SqlConnection)
    Dim cmd As SqlCommand = New SqlCommand _
        ("SELECT LargePhoto FROM Production.ProductPhoto " _
        & "WHERE ProductPhotoID = 70", cn)
    Dim fs As FileStream
    Dim bw As BinaryWriter
    Dim bufferSize As Integer = 32678
    Dim outbyte(bufferSize - 1) As Byte
```

```
    Dim sOutputFileName As String
    sOutputFileName = TextBox1.Text

    fs = New FileStream(sOutputFileName, FileMode.OpenOrCreate, _
       FileAccess.Write)
    bw = New BinaryWriter(fs)
    ' Open the connection and read data into the DataReader.
    cn.Open()
    Dim rdr As SqlDataReader = cmd.ExecuteReader( _
       CommandBehavior.SequentialAccess)
    Do While rdr.Read()
        Dim bBLOBStorage() As Byte = rdr("LargePhoto")
        bw.Write(bBLOBStorage)
        bw.Flush()
    Loop
    ' Close the reader and the connection.
    rdr.Close()
    cn.Close()
    bw.Close()
    bw = Nothing
    fs = Nothing
    PictureBox1.SizeMode = PictureBoxSizeMode.StretchImage
    PictureBox1.Image = Image.FromFile(TextBox1.Text)
End Sub
```

The SQLReaderBLOB subroutine begins by creating a new SqlCommand object named cmd. Here the SqlCommand object contains a SQL SELECT statement that retrieves the LargePhoto column from the Production.ProductPhoto table in the AdventureWorks database where the value of ProductPhotoID is equal to 70.

Since the purpose of this subroutine is to export the contents of a BLOB column to the file system, this subroutine will need a mechanism capable of writing binary files, and that is precisely what the fs FileStream and bw BinaryWriter objects do. The fs FileStream object is created by passing three parameters to the FileStream's constructor. The first parameter specifies the filename. The second parameter uses the FileMode enumerator of FileMode.OpenOrCreate to specify that if the file already exists, it will be opened; otherwise, a new file will be created. The third parameter uses the FileAccess.Write enumerator to indicate that the file will be opened for writing, thereby allowing the subroutine to write binary data to the file. Next, a BinaryWriter object named bw is created and attached to the fs FileStream object.

Next, a new SqlDataReader named rdr is declared. In this example, the most important point to notice is that the ExecuteReader's CommandBehavior. SequentialAccess option is used to enable streaming access to BLOB data. Then a While loop is used to read the data that's returned by the query associated with the SQLCommand object, which in this case will be the contents of the LargePhoto column. While this example just retrieved a single varbinary(max) column for the sake of simplicity, there's no restriction about mixing varbinary(max) columns and character and numeric data in the same result set. Inside the While loop the code basically reads the binary data from the LargePhoto column and writes it to the bw BinaryWriter object. The While loop continues writing the binary data from the rdr SqlDataReader to the bBLOBStorage array until all of the data from the SqlDataReader has been read. The Flush method is called to ensure that all of the data will be cleared from the bw BinaryWriter's internal buffer and written out to disk. Then the bw BinaryWriter and the associated fs FileStream objects are closed.

After all of the data has been returned from the SqlDataReader, the DataReader is closed using the Close method. The temporary file that was created is then read in from disk using the Image classes' FromFile method and assigned to the Image property of a PictureBox control that is defined on the Windows form of the project.

Using the SqlDataAdapter Object

The SqlDataAdapter is used in combination with the SqlConnection object and the SqlCommand object to fill a DataSet with data and then resolve the information back to a Microsoft SQL Server database.

Populating the DataSet

After adding an import directive to your code, you're ready to begin using the different classes contained in the System.Data.SqlClient namespace. The SqlDataAdapter uses the SqlConnection object of the .NET Framework Data Provider for SQL Server to connect to a SQL Server data source, and a SqlCommand object that specifies the SQL statements to execute to retrieve and resolve changes from the DataSet back to the SQL Server database. Once a SqlConnection object to the SQL Server database has been created, a SqlCommand object is created and set with a SELECT statement to retrieve records from the data source. The SqlDataAdapter is then created and its SelectCommand property is set to the SqlCommand object. Next, you create a new DataSet and use the Fill method of the SqlDataAdapter to retrieve the records from the SQL Server database and populate the DataSet. The following example illustrates how to make a SQL Server connection, create a SqlCommand object, and populate a new DataSet with the SqlDataAdapter. The contents of the DataSet will then be displayed to the user in a grid:

```
Private Sub FillDataSetSql(cn As SqlConnection, ByVal sTable As String)
    Dim cmdSelect = New SqlCommand("SELECT * FROM " & sTable, cn)
    Dim sqlDA = New SqlDataAdapter()
    sqlDA.SelectCommand = cmdSelect
    Dim ds = New DataSet()
    Try
        sqlDA.Fill(ds, sTable)
    Catch e As Exception
        MsgBox(e.Message)
    End Try
    grdResults.DataSource = ds
    grdResults.DataMember = sTable
End Sub
```

An instance of a SqlConnection object is passed in at the top of the subroutine, along with a string variable containing a table name. The next statement creates a SqlCommand object and sets its CommandText property to a SQL SELECT statement and its Connection property to the previously passed in SqlConnection object. Next, an instance of a SqlDataAdapter is created and its SelectCommand property is set to the SqlCommand object. An empty DataSet is then created, which will be populated with the results of the SELECT query command. The DataSet is then filled using the SqlDataAdapter's Fill method, which is executed inside a Try-Catch block. If the Fill method fails, the code in the Catch block is executed and a message box appears showing the error message. Finally, a DataGrid's DataSource property is set to the DataSet and the DataGrid's DataMember property is set to the table and displayed to the user. Notice here that the SqlConnection object was not explicitly opened or closed. When the Fill method of the SqlDataAdapter is executed, it opens the connection it is associated with, provided the connection is not already open. Then, if the Fill method opened the connection, it also closes the connection after the DataSet has been populated. This helps to keep connections to the data source open for the shortest amount of time possible, freeing resources for other user applications.

Using the CommandBuilder Class

Using the visual SqlDataAdapter component that is provided by the Visual Studio. NET design environment allows you to easily create update commands for updating the database, but you may also use the CommandBuilder class in code to automatically create update commands. The CommandBuilder is useful when a SELECT command is specified at run time instead of at design time. For example, a user may dynamically create a textual SELECT command in an application. You may then create a CommandBuilder object to automatically create the appropriate Insert, Update, and Delete commands for the specified SELECT command. To do this, you create a DataAdapter object and set its SelectCommand property with a SQL SELECT statement. Then you create a CommandBuilder object, specifying as an argument the DataAdapter for which you want to create the update commands. The CommandBuilder is used when the DataTable in the DataSet is mapped to a single table in the data source.

The following example uses the SqlDataAdapter and CommandBuilder objects to automatically generate insert, update, and delete commands to change the data in the Sales.SpecialOffer table of the AdventureWorks database.

Insert Using the CommandBuilder

The first bit of code shows inserting a new record into the Sales.SpecialOffer table.

```
Private Sub DataSetInsertSql(cn As SqlConnection)
    Dim sqlDA As SqlDataAdapter = New SqlDataAdapter( _
      "SELECT * FROM Sales.SpecialOffer", cn)
    Dim ds = New DataSet()
    Dim sqlCB = New SqlCommandBuilder(sqlDA)
    Try
        ' Populate the dataset
        sqlDA.Fill(ds, "SpecialOffer")
        ' Add a new record to the datatable
        Dim sqlDR = ds.Tables("SpecialOffer").NewRow()
        sqlDR("Description") = "For a limited time"
        ds.Tables("SpecialOffer").Rows.Add(sqlDR)
        ' Insert the record into the database table
        sqlDA.Update(ds, "SpecialOffer")
    Catch e As Exception
        MsgBox(e.Message)
    End Try
End Sub
```

The first statement creates a SqlDataAdapter, passing to the constructor a SQL SELECT statement and the cn SqlConnection object. This automatically sets the SqlDataAdapter's SelectCommand property to the SQL SELECT statement. An empty DataSet is then created that will be populated with the results of the SELECT query command. The next statement creates a CommandBuilder object and takes as an argument the SqlDataAdapter. At this point the CommandBuilder executes the SELECT SQL statement contained in the SelectCommand property of the SqlDataAdapter and automatically creates the InsertCommand, UpdateCommand, and DeleteCommand according to the contents of the SQL SELECT statement. The automatically created commands are set to the SqlDataAdapter's InsertCommand, UpdateCommand, and DeleteCommand properties, respectively. If a command already exists for one of these properties, then the existing property will be used. The DataSet is then filled using the SqlDataAdapter's Fill method, which is executed inside a Try-Catch block. Next, the table's NewRow method is called to create an empty record in the SpecialOffer DataTable in the DataSet, and a DataRow object is returned. The Description column of the DataRow is set with text. Now that the DataRow object contains the data that you want to insert, you need to add the DataRow to the DataTable's Rows collection as shown in the next statement. Finally, the SqlDataAdapter's Update method is called. The Update method will evaluate the changes that have been made to the DataTable in the DataSet and determine which of the commands to execute. In this case, the Table.Rows.RowState property shows Added for the new row, so the InsertCommand is executed and the new record is added to the Sales.SpecialOffer table in the database.

Update Using the CommandBuilder

The next example shows changing existing data in a DataSet and then sending those changes to the database.

```
Private Sub DataSetUpdateSql(cn As SqlConnection)
    ' Create the dataadapter and commandbuilder
    Dim sqlDA As SqlDataAdapter = New SqlDataAdapter( _
      "SELECT * FROM Sales.SpecialOffer", cn)
    Dim ds = New DataSet()
    Dim sqlCB = New SqlCommandBuilder(sqlDA)
    Try
        ' Populate the dataset
        sqlDA.Fill(ds, "SpecialOffer")
        ' Update a record in the datatable
        Dim sqlDR = ds.Tables("SpecialOffer").Rows( _
          ds.Tables("SpecialOffer").Rows.Count - 1)
        sqlDR("Description") = "indefinite discount"
        ' Update the record in the database table
        sqlDA.Update(ds, "SpecialOffer")
    Catch e As Exception
        MsgBox(e.Message)
    End Try
End Sub
```

Here you can see again how the connection object has been passed in at the top of the routine. DataAdapter, DataSet, and CommandBuilder objects are then created. The DataSet is then filled inside the Try-Catch loop. The next statement shows retrieving the last row in the SpecialOffer table into a DataRow object. The Description field of the DataRow is then set with a new value, which changes the Table.Rows.RowState property for this row to reflect Modified. The next statement calls the DataAdapter's Update method. The Update method determines the appropriate command to execute from the value of the RowState property; in this case, it will call the UpdateCommand of the DataAdapter to resolve the changed row back to the data source.

Delete Using the CommandBuilder

The next example shows deleting a record from the database.

```
Private Sub DataSetDeleteSql(cn As SqlConnection)
    ' Create the dataadapter, and commandbuilder
    Dim sqlDA As SqlDataAdapter = New SqlDataAdapter( _
      "SELECT * FROM Sales.SpecialOffer", cn)
    Dim ds = New DataSet()
    Dim sqlCB = New SqlCommandBuilder(sqlDA)
    Try
        ' Populate the dataset
        sqlDA.Fill(ds, "SpecialOffer")
        ' Mark the record in the datatable for deletion
        Dim sqlDR = ds.Tables("SpecialOffer").Rows( _
          ds.Tables("SpecialOffer").Rows.Count - 1)
        sqlDR.Delete()
        ' Delete the record from the database table
        sqlDA.Update(ds, "SpecialOffer")
    Catch e As Exception
        MsgBox(e.Message)
    End Try
End Sub
```

Again you can see the connection object passed into the routine, and the DataAdapter, DataSet, and CommandBuilder objects being created. Then the DataSet is filled in the Try-Catch loop. The next statement retrieves the last row from the SpecialOffer DataTable into a DataRow object. Then the DataRow's Delete method is called to delete the row from the DataTable SpecialOffer. In reality, this does not physically delete the row from the DataTable but instead sets the Table.Rows.RowState property to Deleted. Next, when the DataAdapter's

Update method is called, the DeleteCommand of the DataAdapter will execute
and delete the record from the database. In contrast, if you call the DataTable's
Remove or RemoveAt method, the row will be physically removed from the
DataTable in the DataSet. If you use the Remove or RemoveAt method and then
call the Update method, the row in the data source will not be deleted, because
the DataAdapter's Update method determines what action to take from the Table.
Rows.RowState property and all of the remaining rows in the DataTable have
a RowState of Unmodified; therefore, no action will take place at the data source.

Summary

In this chapter, you got a view of how to develop SQL Server database applications
using Visual Basic and ADO.NET. You were introduced to the different ADO.NET
namespaces and given an overall understanding of the functions of the different
classes that compose the ADO.NET architecture.

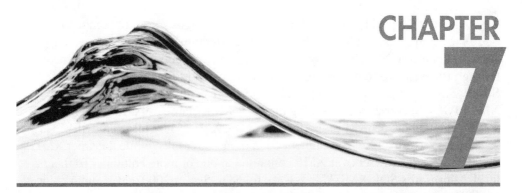

CHAPTER 7

Developing with XML

XML (Extensible Markup Language) is the lingua franca of computer languages. XML's flexible text-based structure enables it to be used for an incredibly wide array of network tasks, including for data/document transfer, for Web page rendering, and even as a transport for Web services via SOAP (Simple Object Access Protocol). Microsoft first added basic support for XML to SQL Server 2000, by adding the FOR XML clause as part of the SELECT statement and the OpenXML function. The FOR XML clause allowed a SELECT statement to return an XML document containing the results, while the OpenXML function created a rowset over XML contained in one or more columns. To this basic level, Microsoft's SQL XML Web release for SQL Server 2000 added support for UpdateGrams, Templates, and BulkLoad to XML Views, as well as stored procedure access via Web services and SOAP. However, SQL Server 2000's support for XML had some limitations. The XML data needed to be stored in a SQL Server database using either the Text or Image data type. Once it was stored, there was little that SQL Server could do with it. SQL Server 2000 was unable to natively query the stored XML. SQL Server had no checks on the validity of the data, and in order to query the XML documents, you essentially needed to extract and parse each document on a one-at-a-time, per-row basis.

SQL Server 2005 builds on this starting point by adding support for many new XML features. First, SQL Server 2005 provides a new level of unified storage for XML and relational data by adding a new XML data type. SQL Server 2005's native XML data type provides support for both native XML queries using XQuery as well as strong data typing by associating the XML data type to an XSD (Extensible Schema Definition). The XML support is tightly integrated with the SQL Server 2005 relational database engine. SQL Server 2005 provides support for triggers on XML, replication of XML data, and bulk load of XML data, as well as enhanced support for data access via SOAP. In this chapter you'll see how to develop applications that make use of SQL Server 2005's native XML support.

The XML Data Type

The XML data type can be used as a column in a table or a variable or parameter in a stored procedure. It can be used to store both typed and untyped data. If the data stored in an XML column has no XSD schema, then it is considered untyped. If there is an associated XSD schema, then SQL Server 2005 will check all data inserted into the data type against the schema to make sure that the data store complies with the schema definition. In all cases, SQL Server 2005 checks the data that is stored in the XML data type to ensure that it is well formed, although partial documents are allowed. If you attempt to insert invalid data into the XML data type, SQL Server 2005 will raise an error and the data will not be stored. The XML data type can accept a maximum of 2GB of data, and its on-disk storage structure is like the varbinary(max) data type.

The following listing illustrates creating a simple table that uses the new XML data type:

```
CREATE TABLE MyXMLDocs
  (DocID INT PRIMARY KEY,
   MyXmlDoc XML)
```

Here the MyXmlDoc column uses the XML data type to specify that the column will store XML data. You can populate an XML column in the same way that you do other data types, using either T-SQL or ADO.NET client applications. The following example shows how you can store a value in an XML column using a T-SQL INSERT statement:

```
INSERT INTO MyXmlDocs Values
(1,'<MyXMLDoc>
    <DocumentID>1</DocumentID>
    <DocumentText>Text</DocumentText>
</MyXMLDoc>')
```

Data Validation Using an XSD Schema

The native XML data type checks to ensure that any data that's stored in an XML variable or column is a valid XML document. On its own, it doesn't check any more than that. However, Microsoft designed the XML data type to be able to support more sophisticated document validation using an XSD schema. When an XSD schema is defined for an XML data type column, the SQL Server engine will check to make sure that all of the data stored in the XML column complies with the definition that's supplied by the XSD schema.

Creating the XSD Schema

The following listing shows a sample XSD schema for the simple XML document that was used in the preceding example:

```
<xs:schema xmlns:xs="http://www.w3.org/2001/XMLSchema"
elementFormDefault="qualified" targetNamespace="MyXMLDocSchema"
xmlns="MyXMLDocSchema">
  <xs:element name="MyXMLDoc">
    <xs:complexType>
```

```
    <xs:sequence>
      <xs:element name="DocumentID" type="xs:int" />
      <xs:element name="DocumentBody" type="xs:string" />
    </xs:sequence>
  </xs:complexType>
 </xs:element>
</xs:schema>
```

This XSD schema uses the namespace of MyXMLDocSchema and defines an XML document that has a complex element named MyXMLDoc. The MyXMLDoc complex element contains two simple elements. The first simple element must be named DocumentID, and a second simple element is named DocumentBody. The DocumentID element must contain an integer, while the DocumentBody element must contain XML string-type data.

To create a strongly typed XML column or variable, you first need to register the XSD schema with SQL Server using the CREATE XML SCHEMA COLLECTION statement. This registers the schema in the SQL Server database. After the XSD schema is registered, it can be used by an XML data type. You can see an example of using the CREATE XML SCHEMA COLLECTION statement in the following listing:

```
CREATE XML SCHEMA COLLECTION MyXMLDocSchema AS
N'<?xml version="1.0"?>
<xs:schema xmlns:xs="http://www.w3.org/2001/XMLSchema"
 elementFormDefault="qualified" targetNamespace="http://MyXMLDocSchema">
  <xs:element name="MyXMLDoc">
    <xs:complexType>
      <xs:sequence>
        <xs:element name="DocumentID" type="xs:int" />
        <xs:element name="DocumentBody" type="xs:string" />
      </xs:sequence>
    </xs:complexType>
  </xs:element>
</xs:schema>'
```

The CREATE XML SCHEMA COLLECTION statement takes a single argument that names the collection. Next, after the AS clause it expects a valid XSD schema enclosed in single quotes. If the schema is not valid, an error will be issued when the statement is executed. The CREATE XML SCHEMA COLLECTION statement is database specific, and the schema that is registered can be accessed only in the database for which the schema is registered.

NOTE

The CREATE XML SCHEMA COLLECTION statement requires that the XSD schema be passed as a variable. It cannot read the schema in from a disk file.

Once you've registered the XML schema with a SQL Server 2005 database, you can go ahead and associate XML variables and columns with that schema. You associate the XML data type with the schema when it is first created. Providing the XML data type with a schema allows SQL Server to check that any XML data that is placed in that data type will adhere to the definition provided by the associated schema. The following example illustrates how you can create a table that uses the MyXMLDocSchema that was created earlier:

```
CREATE TABLE MyXMLDocs
   (DocID INT PRIMARY KEY,
    MyXmlDoc XML(MyXMLDocSchema))
```

NOTE

If you previously created the MyXMLDocs table in your example database, you would need to drop the table before running this code.

As in the earlier example, the MyXMLDocs table is created using the CREATE TABLE statement. However, in this example the MyXMLDoc column is created using an argument that specifies that name of the registered XSD schema definition named MyXMLDocSchema.

There's no change to the basic way that you insert data into the typed XML column. However, once the DocumentBody column has been typed, all of the data that's stored there must comply with XSD schema definition. The following listing shows how you can use an INSERT statement to add data to the MyXMLDoc column:

```
INSERT INTO MyXMLDocs (DocID, MyXMLDoc)Values
   (1,'<MyXMLDoc xmlns="http://MyXMLDocSchema">
       <DocumentID>1</DocumentID>
       <DocumentBody>"My text"</DocumentBody>
</MyXMLDoc>')
```

The value for the DocID column is a standard integer data type of 1. The XML data that's inserted into the MyXMLDoc column must comply with the MyXMLDoc Schema. The XML document must reference the associated XML namespace http://MyXMLDocSchema. It must also possess a complex element named MyXMLDoc, which in turn contains the DocumentID and DocumentBody elements. The SQL Server engine will raise an error if you attempt to insert any other XML document into the MyXMLDocs column. For example, the code in the following listing attempts to insert a row that contains XML data that doesn't comply with the MyXMLDocSchema:

```
INSERT INTO MyXmlDocs (DocID, MyXMLDoc) Values
(3,'<root>empty</root>')
```

Because the data does not conform to the associated XSD schema, SQL Server will return an error message like the one shown in the following listing:

```
Msg 6913, Level 16, State 1, Line 1
XML Validation: Declaration not found for element 'root'.
Location: /*:root[1]
```

NOTE

As you might expect from their dependent relationship, if you assign a schema to a column in a table, that table must be altered or dropped before that schema definition can be updated.

Retrieving a Registered XML Schema

Once you import a schema using CREATE XML SCHEMA COLLECTION, the schema components are stored by SQL Server. The stored schema can be listed by querying the sys.xml_schema_collections system view, as you can see in the following example:

```
SELECT * FROM sys.xml_schema_collections
```

The sys.xml_schema_collections view is database specific. This statement will return a result set showing all of the registered schemas in a database like the one that follows:

```
xml_collection_id schema_id   principal_id name
----------------- ----------- ------------ --------------------------
---
1                 4           NULL         sys
65537             1           NULL         MyXMLDocSchema

(2 row(s) affected)
```

You can also use the new XML_SCHEMA_NAMESPACE function to retrieve the XML schema. The following listing illustrates retrieving the MyXMLDocSchema schema.

```
SELECT XML_SCHEMA_NAMESPACE(N'dbo',N'MyXMLDocSchema')
```

This statement will return a result set showing the registered schema, as you can see here:

```
<xsd:schema xmlns:xsd=http://www.w3.org/2001/XMLSchema
xmlns:t="http://MyXMLDocSchema" targetNamespace="http://MyXMLDocSchema"
elementFormDefault="qualified">
  <xsd:element name="MyXMLDoc">
    <xsd:complexType>
      <xsd:complexContent>
        <xsd:restriction base="xsd:anyType">
          <xsd:sequence>
            <xsd:element name="DocumentID" type="xsd:int" />
            <xsd:element name="DocumentBody" type="xsd:string" />
          </xsd:sequence>
        </xsd:restriction>
      </xsd:complexContent>
    </xsd:complexType>
  </xsd:element>
</xsd:schema>
```

NOTE

Executing this script with SQL Server Management Studio's Query Editor returns a grid with a single column containing a hyperlink. Clicking the hyperlink displays the XSD in the XML Editor, which displays the result that you can see in the preceding listing.

XQuery Support

In the preceding section you saw how XQuery is used in the new XML data type's methods. XQuery is based on the XPath language created by the W3C (www.w3c.org) for querying XML data. XQuery extends the XPath language by adding the ability to update data as well as support for better iteration and sorting of results. T-SQL supports a subset of the XQuery language that is used for querying the XML data type. One of the coolest things about SQL Server's XQuery support is the tight integration it has with the relational engine. XQuery is closely integrated with T-SQL, and the XML queries are not restricted to the contents of a single XML row but instead can cross multiple rows exactly like relational queries, without the need to extract and parse the XML for each row.

A description of the XQuery language is beyond the scope of this book, but this section will show you some of the basics for getting started using XQuery to query SQL Server's XML data type.

Querying Element Data

XQuery is a flexible query language that's well suited to querying XML documents that have a hierarchical structure. In this section you'll learn about the basics of using XQuery in conjunction with T-SQL to query the data store in SQL Server 2005's XML data type.

Querying Multiple Elements

XQuery can return the result from one XML node or multiple nodes. The following example illustrates returning all of the subelements and their values:

```
DECLARE @x xml
SET @x = '<Myroot><Element1>One</Element1><Element2>Two</Element2></Myroot>'
SELECT @x.query('/Myroot')
```

Here the new variable @x of the XML data type is populated using the SET statement and has the following structure:

```
<Myroot>
    <Element1>One</Element1>
    <Element2>Two</Element2>
</Myroot>
```

The XQuery is executed using the XML data type's Query method. (More information about the XML data type methods is presented in the following section.) The XQuery itself basically requests all of the nodes that are children of the /Myroot node. You can see the results in the following listing:

```
----------------------------------------------------------------
<Myroot><Element1>One</Element1><Element2>Two</Element2></Myroot>

(1 row(s) affected)
```

Querying a Single Element

The preceding example showed how to query all of the nodes from a parent node. This example illustrates querying a single node:

```
DECLARE @x xml
SET @x = '<Myroot><Element1>One</Element1><Element2>Two</Element2></Myroot>'
SELECT @x.query('/Myroot/Element1')
```

Each level in the XML document hierarchy is closed by the / symbol. Here the XQuery returns the value of just the Element1 node, as is shown in the following listing:

```
-----------------------
<Element1>One</Element1>

(1 row(s) affected)
```

Querying Single Element Values

Unlike T-SQL, XQuery also has the capability to query for single sets of node values according to their predicate or position in the set. The following listing shows how to retrieve the first value from the Element2 node:

```
DECLARE @x xml
SET @x = '<Myroot><Element1>One</Element1><Element2>Two</Element2></Myroot>'
SELECT @x.query('(/Myroot/Element2)[1]')
```

In this example the hierarchy of nodes is placed within parenthesis. The desired node number follows enclosed in brackets. You can see the results in the following listing:

```
-----------------------
<Element2>Two</Element2>

(1 row(s) affected)
```

Querying Typed XML

Typed XML (i.e., XML that has an associated schema) requires that you declare the appropriate namespace in order to retrieve the nodes from the XML document. The following listing illustrates an XQuery that queries the sample MyXMLDocs table that was used in the earlier examples. The MyXMLDoc column in this table contains typed XML.

```
SELECT MyXMLDoc.query('declare namespace tns="http://MyXMLDocSchema";
/tns:MyXMLDoc/..') As MyXMLBody
FROM MyXMLDocs
```

The declare namespace directive creates a namespace named tns and assigns that namespace the value of http://MyXMLDocSchema. This value must match the namespace from the schema. The XQuery needs to preface the node names with the namespace. You can see the results in the following listing:

```
------------------------------------------------------------------
<MyXMLDoc xmlns="http://MyXMLDocSchema"><DocumentID>1</DocumentID>
       <DocumentBody>Modified Body</DocumentBody></MyXMLDoc>
<MyXMLDoc xmlns="http://MyXMLDocSchema"><DocumentID>2</DocumentID>
       <DocumentBody>"My text2"</DocumentBody></MyXMLDoc>

(2 row(s) affected)
```

FLWR (For-Let-Where-Return)

The XPath-style queries work well for standard queries. However, they aren't as flexible as T-SQL. The FLWR (For-Let-Where-Return) statement adds a level of flexibility to SQL Server's XQuery implementation. In SQL Server 2005, the Let clause is not supported but the For, Order By, Where, and Return clauses are supported. In addition, the FLWR syntax looks more like T-SQL and is probably more readily usable for experienced T-SQL coders. You can see an example of using the FLWR query in the following listing:

```
SELECT MyXMLDoc.query
('declare namespace tns="http://MyXMLDocSchema";
for $db in /tns:MyXMLDoc
where /tns:MyXMLDoc/tns:DocumentID = 1
return $db')
FROM MyXMLDocs
```

This code uses the example MyXMLDocs table that was created earlier in this chapter. Because the MyXMLDoc column has an attached schema, a namespace must be declared at the top of the XQuery. Like the SQL SELECT clause the FOR clause is used to tell the query where to look for data. The WHERE clause restricts the result set. The RETURN clause specifies the data that will be returned. Here, the XQuery looks in the document MyXMLDoc for elements where the DocumentID element is equal to the value of 1. You can see the results in the following listing:

```
----------------------------------------------------------------
<MyXMLDoc xmlns="http://MyXMLDocSchema"><DocumentID>1</DocumentID>
   <DocumentBody>Modified Body</DocumentBody></MyXMLDoc>

(3 row(s) affected)
```

This section presented some of the basics about XQuery; the topic is definitively large enough to be covered in its own book. For more details about the W3C XQuery standard, you can refer to http://www.w3.org/XML/Query and http://www.w3.org/TR/2004/WD-xquery-20040723/. The SQL Server 2005 Books Online also has an introduction to the XQuery language.

XML Data Type Methods

SQL Server 2005 provides several new built-in methods for working with the XML data type. Unlike standard relational data, XML data is usually hierarchical, complete with structures and metadata, and in order to provide true XML integration, SQL Server needed a way to seamlessly access the data stored in an XML document. The XML data type's built-in methods enable you to drill down into the content of XML documents that are stored using the XML data type. This section will show you how to use the XML data type's methods.

Exist(XQuery)

The XML data type's Exists method enables you to check the contents of an XML document for the existence of elements or attributes using an XQuery expression. The Exists method takes one parameter that consists of a XQuery statement and returns the following values:

Return Value	Description
0	The node was not found (FALSE).
1	The node exists (TRUE).
Null	The XML data type was null.

The following listing shows how to use the XML data type's Exist method:

```
SELECT * FROM MyXMLDocs
  WHERE MyXmlDoc.exist('declare namespace tns="http://MyXMLDocSchema";
   /tns:MyXMLDoc/tns:DocumentID=1') = 1
```

The first parameter of the XML Exist method is required and takes an XQuery expression. Here the XQuery tests for a DocumentID element equal to a value of 1. A namespace is declared because the MyXMLDoc column is typed—meaning it has an associated schema. The Exist method can return the value of TRUE (1) if the XQuery expression returns an XML node, FALSE (0) if the expression doesn't return a node, or NULL if the XML data type instance is null. Using the XML data from the previous examples, you can see the results of the XML Exist method here:

```
DocID      MyXmlDoc
---------- -------------------------------------------------------------
1          <MyXMLDoc xmlns="http://MyXMLDocSchema">
           <DocumentID>1</DocumentID>
           <DocumentBody>"My text"</DocumentBody></MyXMLDoc>
(1 row(s) affected)
```

NOTE

The preceding listing was reformatted to make it more readable in the published page width.

Modify(XML DML)

While the previous examples illustrated how to use XQuery to retrieve information from an XML document, XQuery can also be used for deleting, inserting, and updating part of an XML document. The Modify method enables you to modify a stored XML document. You can use the Modify method either to update the entire XML document or to update just a selected part of the document. You can see an example of using the Modify method in the following listing:

```
UPDATE MyXMLDocs
SET MyXMLDoc.modify('declare namespace tns="http://MyXMLDocSchema";
  replace value of  (/tns:MyXMLDoc/tns:DocumentBody)[1] with
  "Modified Body"') WHERE DocID = 1
```

The XML data type's Modify method uses an XML Data Modification Language (XML DML) statement as its parameter. XML DML is a Microsoft extension to the XQuery language that enables modification of XML documents. The Modify method supports the Insert, Delete, and Replace values of XML DML statements. In addition, the Modify method can be used only in the SET clause of an UPDATE statement. In this example, since the MyXMLDoc XML column is typed, the XML DML statement must specify the namespace for the schema. Next, you can see where the Replace value of the XML DML command is used to replace the value of the DocumentBody element with the new value of "Modified Body" for the row where the DocID column is equal to 1. The [1] notation indicates that the operation is for a single value.

NOTE

While this example illustrates performing a replace operation, the Modify method also supports insert and delete operations, allowing the addition of new elements and the deletion of existing elements.

Once the previous Modify method has been executed, you can run the following SELECT statement to see the updated values:

```
Select MyXMLDoc from MyXM#LDocs
```

Given the earlier insert example, this statement would produce the following result, where you can see the updated value in the DocumentBody element:

```
MyXMLDoc
-----------------------------------------------------------------<MyXMLDoc
xmlns="http://MyXMLDocSchema"><DocumentID>1</DocumentID>
<DocumentBody>Modified Body</DocumentBody></MyXMLDoc>

(1 row(s) affected)
```

Query(XQuery)

The XML data type's Query method can retrieve either the entire contents of an XML document or selected sections of the XML document. The Query method accepts an XQuery statement as a parameter. You can see an example of using the Query method in the following listing:

```
SELECT DocID, MyXMLDoc.query('declare namespace tns="http://MyXMLDocSchema";
  /tns:MyXMLDoc/tns:DocumentBody') AS Body
FROM MyXMLDocs
```

This XQuery expression returns the values from the XML document's DocumentBody element. Again, the namespace is specified because the MyXMLDoc XML data type has an associated schema, named MyXMLDocSchema. In this example, you can see how SQL Server 2005 easily integrates relational column data with XML data. Here, DocID comes from a relational column, while the DocumentBody element is queried out of the XML column. The following listing shows the results of the XQuery:

```
DocID       Body
----------- -----------------------------------------------------------
1           <tns:DocumentBody xmlns:tns="http://MyXMLDocSchema">
             Modified Body</tns:DocumentBody>
2           <tns:DocumentBody xmlns:tns="http://MyXMLDocSchema">
            "My text2"</tns:DocumentBody>
(2 row(s) affected)
```

NOTE

The preceding listing was reformatted to make it more readable in the published page width.

Value(XQuery, [node ref])

The Value method enables the extraction of scalar values from an XML data type. You can see an example of how the XML data type's Value method is used in the following listing:

```
SELECT MyXMLDoc.value('declare namespace xd="http://MyXMLDocSchema";
    (/xd:MyXMLDoc/xd:DocumentID)[1]', 'int') AS ID
FROM MyXMLDocs
```

Unlike the other XML data type methods, the XML Value method requires two parameters. The first parameter is an XQuery expression, and the second parameter specifies the SQL data type that will hold the scalar value returned by the Value method. This example returns all of the values contained in the DocumentID element and converts them to the int data type, as shown in the following results:

```
ID
-----------
1
2

(2 row(s) affected)
```

XML Indexes

The XML data type supports a maximum of 2GB of storage, which is quite large. The size of the XML data and its usage can have a big impact on the performance the system can achieve when querying XML data. To improve the performance of XML queries, SQL Server 2005 provides the ability to create indexes over the columns that have the XML data type.

Primary XML Indexes

In order to create an XML index on an XML data type column, a clustered primary key must exist for the table. In addition, if you need to change the primary key for the table, you must first delete the XML index. An XML index covers all the elements in the XML column, and you can have only one XML index per column. An XML index cannot have the same name as an existing index. XML indexes can be created only on XML data types in a table. They cannot be created on columns in views or on XML data type variables. A primary XML index consists of a persistent shredded representation of the data in the XML column. The following shows an example of how to create a primary XML index on the MyXMLDocs table that was used in the earlier examples:

```
CREATE PRIMARY XML INDEX MyXMLDocsIdx ON MyXMLDocs(MyXMLDoc)
```

This example shows the creation of a primary XML index named MyXMLDocsIdx. This index is created on the MyXMLDoc XML data type column in the MyXMLDocs table. Just like regular SQL Server indexes, XML indexes can be viewed by querying the sys.indexes view.

Secondary XML Indexes

In addition to the primary index, you can also build secondary XML indexes. SQL Server 2005 supports the following secondary XML indexes:

Secondary index type	Description
Path	The document path is used to build the index.
Value	The document values are used to build the index.
Property	The document's properties are used to build the index.

Secondary indexes are always partitioned in the same way as the primary XML index. The following listing shows the creation of a secondary-path XML index:

```
CREATE XML INDEX My2ndXMLDocsIdx ON MyXMLDocs(MyXMLDoc)
 USING XML INDEX MyXMLDocsIdx FOR PATH
```

Using the For XML Clause

The FOR XML clause was first added to the T-SQL SELECT clause with SQL Server 2000. The For XML clause enables SQL Server to return XML results from a query. In this section you first learn about the preexisting FOR XML Raw, Auto, and Explicit support. Next you'll see how to use some of the new capabilities that are found in SQL Server 2005, including support for the XML data type via a new Type mode, added support for result shaping using the PATH mode, nested FOR XML queries, and inline XSD schema generation.

For XML Raw

The For XML Raw mode returns a result set where each result row is returned in an element named using a generic identifier for the row. The value of each column is returned using attribute pairs. This form typically is used where some other applications will provide additional processing of the data. However, an external, B2B-type transfer will typically require the use of more descriptive tags and a more flexible structure. The For XML Raw results are essentially the XML equivalent of CSV (Command Separated Value) files. The following listing presents an example of using the For XML Raw mode:

```
SELECT Top 3 title, FirstName, LastName from Person.Contact FOR XML RAW

XML_F52E2B61-18A1-11d1-B105-00805F49916B
-------------------------------------------------------
<row title="Mr." FirstName="Gustavo" LastName="Achong"/>
<row title="Ms." FirstName="Catherine" LastName="Abel"/>
<row title="Ms." FirstName="Kim" LastName="Abercrombie"/>

(5 row(s) affected)
```

NOTE

The T-SQL code in the preceding listing is designed to work with Person.Contact table in the AdventureWorks sample database.

For XML Auto

The For XML Auto mode provides more flexibility in terms of the tags that are returned by a SQL statement. However, it is still limited in the structure of the XML results that are generated. By default, the SQL Server Table or View name is used as the element name, and column names are used as the attributes for each element. You can use the Elements directive to specify that each column is made into a child element.

Nesting of elements is controlled by the order of the columns used in the Select statement. While the results of Auto mode won't produce XML documents that conform to industry standards, they do support loosely coupled systems and can be used for simple B2B transfers. The following listing presents an example of using the For XML Auto mode:

```
SELECT Top 3 title, FirstName, LastName from Person.Contact FOR XML AUTO

XML_F52E2B61-18A1-11d1-B105-00805F49916B
------------------------------------------------------------------
<Person.Contact title="Mr." FirstName="Gustavo" LastName="Achong"/>
<Person.Contact title="Ms." FirstName="Catherine" LastName="Abel"/>
<Person.Contact title="Ms." FirstName="Kim" LastName="Abercrombie"/>


(3 row(s) affected)
```

For XML Explicit

The For XML Explicit mode produces the most flexible results and can be used to meet complex requirements. Explicit mode affords you complete control over the names of the tags and the hierarchy and nesting of the elements produced. Columns can be individually mapped to various elements or attributes. However, the For Explicit mode requires the use of complex SQL queries that must specify the structure of a universal table that describes the desired XML document. The syntax required by Explicit mode is demanding, and it's up to you to make sure that the XML that's generated is well formed and valid. Explicit mode's flexibility allows it to meet the needs for many industry-standard message specifications.

The EXPLICIT mode is implemented through UNION ALL queries, which essentially combine results of two or more queries. Each query must contain the same number of columns, and the corresponding columns in each query need to have compatible data types. The XML hierarchy is defined by the top or parent query.

The subsequent queries retrieve data for each of the XML nodes. The following listing shows an example of using the FOR XML EXPLICT mode:

```
SELECT Top 3
        1 as Tag, NULL as Parent,
        EmployeeID as [Employee!1!Employee_ID],
        NULL       as [Name!2!Last_Name!ELEMENT],
        NULL       as [Name!2!First_Name!ELEMENT]
FROM    HumanResources.Employee E, Person.Contact C
WHERE   E.ContactID = C.ContactID

UNION ALL

SELECT Top 3
        2 as Tag, 1 as Parent,
        EmployeeID,
        LastName,
        FirstName
FROM    HumanResources.Employee E, Person.Contact C
WHERE   E.ContactID = C.ContactID
ORDER BY [Employee!1!Employee_ID]
FOR XML EXPLICIT
```

This query describes a two-level hierarchy. The first query retrieves the values for the Employee element, and the second query retrieves the values for the Name element. The Top 3 clause is simply used to limit the size of the result set. In the first query you'll notice the ELEMENT directive is used to specify that the results are output as XML elements rather than attributes. The values prior to the ELEMENT directive state the parent element's name, the element level, and finally the element name that will be created.

As you can see in the following listing, the FOR XML EXCPLICIT mode gives you more control over the output of the query; however, you pay the price of added complexity:

```
<Employee Employee_ID="1">
  <Name>
    <Last_Name>Gilbert</Last_Name>
    <First_Name>Guy</First_Name>
  </Name>
</Employee>
<Employee Employee_ID="2">
```

```
<Name>
    <Last_Name>Brown</Last_Name>
    <First_Name>Kevin</First_Name>
  </Name>
</Employee>
<Employee Employee_ID="3">
  <Name>
    <Last_Name>Tamburello</Last_Name>
    <First_Name>Roberto</First_Name>
  </Name>
</Employee>
```

For more information about using the XML Explicit mode, see the SQL Server 2005 BOL.

Type Mode

When XML data types are returned using the FOR XML clause's Type mode, they are returned as XML data types. You can see an example of using the FOR XML clause with the XML Type directive here:

```
SELECT DocID, MyXMLDoc FROM MyXMLDocs
  WHERE DocID=1 FOR XML AUTO, TYPE
```

NOTE

This listing uses the example MyXMLDocs table that was created earlier in this chapter.

This query returns the relational DocID column along with the MyXMLDoc XML data type column. It uses the FOR XML AUTO clause to return the results as XML. The TYPE directive specifies that the results will be returned as an XML data type. You can see the results of using the Type directive here:

```
--------------------------------------------------
<MyXMLDocs DocID="1">
    <MyXMLDoc>
          <MyXMLDoc xmlns="http://MyXMLDocSchema">
          <DocumentID>1</DocumentID>
          <DocumentBody>Modified Body</DocumentBody>
          </MyXMLDoc>
    </MyXMLDoc>
</MyXMLDocs>

(1 row(s) affected)
```

> **NOTE**
>
> *The preceding listing was reformatted to make it more readable in the published page width.*

FOR XML Path

The new FOR XML PATH mode provides increased power to shape XML results than either the FOR XML AUTO or FOR XML RAW mode but without the complexity of the FOR XML EXCLICIT mode. The new PATH mode allows users to specify the path in the XML tree where an element or attribute can be added. Essentially, the new PATH mode is a simpler alternative to the FOR XML EXCPLICIT mode. It can accomplish most of the things the developers need with the use of universal tables and complex unions. However, it is more limited than the FOR XML EXPLICIT mode. You can see an example of using the FOR XML PATH mode in the following listing:

```
SELECT Top 3 title, FirstName, LastName from Person.Contact FOR XML PATH
```

This query uses the same Person.Contact table from the AdventureWorks database that the earlier FOR XML RAW and AUTO modes did, but with quite different results, which you can see here:

```
<row>
    <title>Mr.</title>
    <FirstName>Gustavo</FirstName>
    <LastName>Achong</LastName>
</row>
<row>
    <title>Ms.</title>
    <FirstName>Catherine</FirstName>
    <LastName>Abel</LastName>
</row>
<row>
    <title>Ms.</title>
    <FirstName>Kim</FirstName>
    <LastName>Abercrombie</LastName>
</row>
```

By default each of the results is enclosed in the set of <row> </row> tags. The output is close to the output that can be produced using FROM XML EXPLICIT.

However, the FOR XML PATH statement provides additional flexibility by making it possible to insert attributes and elements, enhancing the structure of the output. The following list shows how you can add the <Employee> element to this output using the For XML PATH mode:

```
SELECT Top 3
      title "Employee/Title",
      FirstName "Employee/First_Name",
      LastName "Employee/Last_Name"
 from Person.Contact FOR XML PATH
```

Much as when you use a standard SQL AS clause, you can add parent tags and rename the XML output elements by using the quoted string that you can see following each column in this FOR XML PATH example. The Employee tag, which you can see to the left of the / symbol, will be created when the result set is output. The name to the right of the / symbol will be used as a new name for the element. The output from this version of the FOR XML PATH mode can be seen in the following listing. Notice where the <Employee></Employee> tag has been added to the XML output:

```
<row>
  <Employee>
    <Title>Mr.</Title>
    <First_Name>Gustavo</First_Name>
    <Last_Name>Achong</Last_Name>
  </Employee>
</row>
<row>
  <Employee>
    <Title>Ms.</Title>
    <First_Name>Catherine</First_Name>
    <Last_Name>Abel</Last_Name>
  </Employee>
</row>
<row>
  <Employee>
    <Title>Ms.</Title>
    <First_Name>Kim</First_Name>
    <Last_Name>Abercrombie</Last_Name>
  </Employee>
</row>
```

Nested FOR XML Queries

SQL Server 2000 was limited to using the FOR XML clause in the top level of a query. Subqueries couldn't make use of the FOR XML clause. SQL Server 2005 adds the ability to use nested FOR XML queries, which are useful for returning multiple items where there is a parent-child relationship. One example of this type of relationship might be order header and order details records; another might be product categories and subcategories. You can see an example of using a nested FOR XML clause in the following listing:

```
SELECT (SELECT title, FirstName, LastName
        FROM Person.Contact
        FOR XML RAW, TYPE,ROOT('root')).query('/root[1]/row[1]')
```

Notice that the inner SELECT statement uses the TYPE mode to return a XML result. This result is then processed using a simple XQuery executed with the XML data type's query method. In this case the XQuery extracts the values from the first row in the result set, as is shown here:

```
<row title="Mr." FirstName="Gustavo" LastName="Achong" />
```

Inline XSD Schema Generation

SQL Server 2005's FOR XML support also has the ability to generate an XSD schema by adding the XMLSCHEMA directive to the FOR XML clause. You can see an example of using the new XMLSCHEMA directive in the following listing:

```
SELECT MyXMLDoc FROM MyXMLDocs WHERE DocID=1 FOR XML AUTO, XMLSCHEMA
```

In this case, because the XMLSCHEMA directive has been added to the FOR XML clause, the query will generate and return the schema that defines the specific XML column along with the XML result from the selected column.

The XMLSCHEMA directive works only with the FOR XML AUTO and FOR XML RAW modes. It cannot be used with the FOR XML EXPLICIT or FOR XML PATH mode. If the XMLSCHEMA directive is used with a nested query, it can be used only at the top level of the query. The XSD schema that's generated from this query is shown in the following listing:

```
<xsd:schema targetNamespace="urn:schemas-microsoft-com:sql:SqlRowSet2"
    xmlns:schema="urn:schemas-microsoft-com:sql:SqlRowSet2"
    xmlns:xsd="http://www.w3.org/2001/XMLSchema"
    xmlns:sqltypes="http://schemas.microsoft.com/sqlserver/2004/sqltypes"
    elementFormDefault="qualified">
```

```
<xsd:import namespace="http://schemas.microsoft.com
  /sqlserver/2004/sqltypes"
  schemaLocation="http://schemas.microsoft.com
  /sqlserver/2004/sqltypes/sqltypes.xsd" />
<xsd:import namespace="http://MyXMLDocSchema" />
<xsd:element name="MyXMLDocs">
  <xsd:complexType>
    <xsd:sequence>
      <xsd:element name="MyXMLDoc" minOccurs="0">
        <xsd:complexType sqltypes:xmlSchemaCollection=
              "[tecadb].[dbo].[MyXMLDocSchema]">
          <xsd:complexContent>
            <xsd:restriction base="sqltypes:xml">
              <xsd:sequence>
                <xsd:any processContents="strict" minOccurs="0"
                    maxOccurs="unbounded"
                    namespace="http://MyXMLDocSchema">
                </xsd:sequence>
              </xsd:restriction>
            </xsd:complexContent>
          </xsd:complexType>
        </xsd:element>
      </xsd:sequence>
    </xsd:complexType>
  </xsd:element>
</xsd:schema>
<MyXMLDocs xmlns="urn:schemas-microsoft-com:sql:SqlRowSet2">
  <MyXMLDoc>
    <MyXMLDoc xmlns="http://MyXMLDocSchema">
      <DocumentID>1</DocumentID>
      <DocumentBody>Modified Body</DocumentBody>
    </MyXMLDoc>
  </MyXMLDoc>
</MyXMLDocs>
```

The XMLSCHEMA directive can return multiple schemas, but it always returns
at least two: one schema is returned for the SqlTypes namespace, and a second
schema is returned that describes the results of the FOR XML query results. In the
preceding listing you can see the schema description of the XML data type column
beginning at: <xsd:element name="MyXMLDocs">. Next, the XML results can be
seen at the line starting with <MyXMLDocs xmlns="urn:schemas-microsoft-com:
sql:SqlRowSet2">.

NOTE

You can also generate an XDR (XML Data Reduced) schema by using the XMLDATA directive in combination with the FOR XML clause. However, the XDR schema has been deprecated in favor of XSD schema.

OPENXML

While the FOR XML clause essentially creates an XML document from relational data, the OPENXML keyword does the reverse. The OPENXML function provides a relational rowset over an XML document. To use SQL Server's OPENXML functionality, you must first call the sp_xml_preparedocument stored procedure, which parses the XML document using the XML Document Object Model (DOM) and returns a handle to OPENXML. OPENXML then provides a rowset view of the parsed XML document. When you are finished working with the document, you then call the sp_xml_removedocument stored procedure to release the system resources consumed by OPENXML and the XML DOM.

With SQL Server 2005 the OPENXML support has been extended to include support for the new XML data type and the new user-defined data type. The following example shows how you can use OPENXML in conjunction with a WITH clause and the new XML data type:

```
DECLARE @hdocument int
DECLARE @doc varchar(1000)
SET @doc ='<MyXMLDoc>
    <DocumentID>1</DocumentID>
    <DocumentBody>"OPENXML Example"</DocumentBody>
    </MyXMLDoc>'
EXEC sp_xml_preparedocument @hdocument OUTPUT, @doc
SELECT * FROM OPENXML (@hdocument, '/MyXMLDoc', 10)
  WITH (DocumentID  varchar(4),
        DocumentBody varchar(50))
EXEC sp_xml_removedocument @hdocument
```

At the top of this listing you can see where two variables are declared. The @hdocument variable will be used to store the XML document handle returned by the sp_xml_preparedocument stored procedure, while the @doc variable will contain the sample XML document itself. Next, the sp_xml_preparedocument stored procedure is executed and passed the two variables. This stored procedure uses XML DOM to parse the XML document and then returns a handle to the parsed document in the @hdocument variable. That document handle is then passed to the OPENXML keyword used in the SELECT statement.

The first parameter used by OPENXML is the document handle contained in the @hdocument variable. The second parameter is an XQuery that specifies the nodes in the XML document that will construct the relational rowset. The third parameter specifies the type of XML-to-relational mapping that will be performed. The value of 2 indicates that element-centric mapping will be used. (A value of 1 would indicate that attribute-centric mapping would be performed.) The WITH clause provides the format of the rowset that's returned. In this example, the WITH clause specifies that the returned rowset will consist of two varchar columns named DocumentID and DocumentBody. While this example shows the rowset names matching the XML elements, that's not a requirement. Finally, the sp_xml _removedocument stored procedure is executed to release the system resources.

This SELECT statement using the OPENXML feature will return a rowset that consists of the element values from the XML document. You can see the results of using OPENXML in the following listing:

```
DocumentID DocumentBody
---------- -----------------------------------------------------
1             "OPENXML Example"
(1 row(s) affected)
```

XML Bulk Load

There are several ways to bulk-load XML documents from disk. You can use the Bulk Copy Program (BCP) or SQL Server Integration Services. You can also do this programmatically by using the COM-based SQLXML object library from .NET or by using the bulk load functionality that Microsoft has added to the OPENROWSET function. You can see an example of using OPENROWSET to bulk-load an XML document in the following listing:

```
INSERT into MyXMLDocs(DocID, MyXMLDoc)
   Select 3 AS DocID, * FROM OPENROWSET
     (Bulk 'c:\temp\MyXMLDoc3.xml', SINGLE_CLOB) as DocumentID
```

In this example the INSERT statement is used to insert the results of the SELECT statement into the MyXMLDocs table. Here the value for the DocID column is supplied as a literal, but you could also use a variable for this value. The XML document is loaded into the MyXMLDoc column in the MyXMLDocs table using the * FROM OPENROWSET statement. The OPENROWSET function uses the bulk rowset provider to read data in from the file 'C:\temp\MyXMLDoc3.xml'. The SINGLE_CLOB argument specifies that the data from the file will be inserted into a single row. If you omit the SINGLE_CLOB argument, then the data from the file can be inserted into multiple rows. By default, the Bulk provider for the OPENROWSET function will split the rows on the Carriage Return character, which is the default row delimiter. Alternatively, you can specify the field and row delimiters using the optional FIELDTERMINATOR and ROWTERMINATOR arguments of the OPENROWSET function. You can see the contents of the MyXMLDoc.xml file in the following listing:

```
<MyXMLDoc xmlns="http://MyXMLDocSchema">
        <DocumentID>3</DocumentID>
        <DocumentBody>"The Third Body"</DocumentBody>
</MyXMLDoc>
```

If you execute this command from the SQL Server Management Studio, you need to remember that this will be executed on the SQL Server system, and therefore the file and path references must be found on the local server system. The following query shows the contents of the MyXMLDocs file after performing the bulk load:

```
select * from MyXMLDocs
```

These are the updated contents of the MyXMLDocs file:

```
DocID    MyXmlDoc
-------  ----------------------------------------------------------------
1        <MyXMLDoc xmlns="http://MyXMLDocSchema"><DocumentID>1</DocumentID>
            <DocumentBody>Modified Body</DocumentBody></MyXMLDoc>
2        <MyXMLDoc xmlns="http://MyXMLDocSchema"><DocumentID>2</DocumentID>
            <DocumentBody>"My text2"</DocumentBody></MyXMLDoc>
3        <MyXMLDoc xmlns="http://MyXMLDocSchema"><DocumentID>3</DocumentID>
            <DocumentBody>"The Third Body"</DocumentBody></MyXMLDoc>

(3 row(s) affected)
```

NOTE
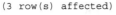
The preceding listing was reformatted to make it more readable in the published page width.

Native HTTP SOAP Access

Another new XML-related feature found in SQL Server 2005 is native HTTP SOAP support. This new feature enables SQL Server to directly respond to the HTTP/SOAP requests that are issued by Web services without requiring an IIS system to act as an intermediary. Using the native HTTP SOAP support, you can create Web services that are capable of executing T-SQL batches, stored procedures, and user-defined scalar functions. To ensure a high level of default security, native HTTP access is turned off by default. However, you can enable HTTP support by simply creating an HTTP endpoint and specify that it be started.

Creating SOAP Endpoints

SOAP endpoints essentially enable programmatic access via Web services to SQL Server objects like stored procedures and functions. In the following example you'll see how to create a SOAP endpoint that exposes the uspGetEmployeeManagers stored procedure in the sample AdventureWorks database. You can see the uspGetEmployeeManagers stored procedure in Figure 7-1.

Creating a new SOAP endpoint will create a Web services wrapper for that uspGetEmployeeManagers stored procedure, enabling it to be called by external processes. To create an SOAP endpoint, you need to use the CREATE ENDPOINT statement like the one shown in the following listing:

```
CREATE ENDPOINT MyAdWWebService
STATE = STARTED
AS HTTP(
    PATH = '/AdWWS',
    AUTHENTICATION = (INTEGRATED ),
    PORTS = ( CLEAR ),
    SITE = 'SQL2005-2'
    )
FOR SOAP (
    WEBMETHOD 'GetManagers'
      (name='AdventureWorks.dbo.uspGetEmployeeManagers',
       FORMAT = ROWSETS_ONLY),
    WSDL = DEFAULT,
    SCHEMA = STANDARD,
    DATABASE = 'adventureworks',
    NAMESPACE = 'http://AdWWS.com'
    );
```

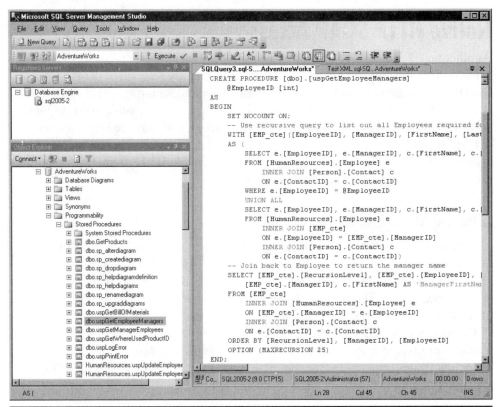

Figure 7-1 *AdventureWorks uspGetEmployeeManagers stored procedure*

This example illustrates creating a SOAP endpoint named MyAdWWebService for the stored procedure named GetProductName in the sample AdventureWorks database. The STATE keyword that you see in the beginning indicates that this endpoint will be started and available immediately after it is created. Other supported values include STOPPED and DISABLED.

There are basically two sections to the CREATE ENDPOINT command. The first half of the statement, beginning with the AS HTTP clause, describes the network access to the Web service. The second part, beginning with the FOR SOAP clause, describes the Web service itself. In the first part the PATH keyword specifies the URL for the Web service endpoint. This value will be appended to the local server name (e.g., http://server/AdWWS). The AUTHENTICATION keyword specifies the type of authentication to be used to access the Web service. This example uses INTEGRATED security, but values of BASIC, NTLM, and KERBEROS are also supported. The PORTS keyword specifies the TCP/IP port that will be used. Supported vales are CLEAR (default 80) or SSL (default port 443). CLEAR is used to respond to HTTP requests, while SSL requires HTTPS. Finally, the SITE keyword specifies the name of the host SQL Server system.

The FOR SOAP clause describes the Web service. The WEBMETHOD keyword specifies the name of the Web method that will be executed by the Web service. The name keyword is used to link the Web method to the stored procedure on the SQL Server system. In this example when the Web Service GetManagers method is executed, it will in turn call the uspGetEmployeeManagers stored procedure in the AdventureWorks database. The FORMAT key indicates the type of results that will be returned by the Web service. Support values are ALL RESULTS and ROWSETS_ONLY. If you want the client system to be able to consume the results of the Web service as a dataset, then you must specify the value of ROWSETS_ONLY. While this example uses a single Web method, you can specify multiple Web methods per endpoint. The WSDL keyword indicates whether the endpoint supports WSDL. The value of DEFAULT means that WSDL is supported. NONE indicated WSDL is not supported. Alternatively, you can provide a stored procedure name to implement a custom WSDL. The SCHEMA keyword specifies whether an inline XSD schema will be returned for the Web method. Supported values are NOE and SCHEMA. The DATABASE keyword specifies the name of the default database. The NAMESPACE keyword is used to supply a namespace for the endpoint.

Once the HTTP endpoint is created, it can be accessed via a SOAP request issued by an application. You can list the SOAP endpoints that have been created by displaying the contents of the sys.soap_endpoints system view.

```
select * from sys.soap_endpoints
```

You can use the ALTER ENDPOINT and DROP ENDPOINT DDL statements to manage SQL Server's HTTP endpoints. The new HTTP endpoints are also able to provide data stream encryption using SSL.

Using SOAP Endpoints

If the SOAP endpoint is created using the STATE value of STARTED, it can be accessed immediately after the command completes. However, before users can connect to the endpoint, they must be granted connect rights to that endpoint. The basic syntax for the CONNECT ON ENDPOINT statement follows:

```
{ GRANT | DENY | REVOKE } CONNECT ON ENDPOINT:: <EndPointName> TO <login>
```

The GRANT, DENY, and REVOKE permissions all work exactly like the standard SQL Server object security. GRANT allows access, DENY prohibits access, and REVOKE undoes the current permissions. The EndPointName identifies the endpoint, and the login identifies the database login.

For instance, the following command illustrate how you might use the GRANT CONNECT permission to enable the Sales group to connect to the MyAdWWebService:

```
GRANT CONNECT ON ENDPOINT:: MyAdWWebService to HR
```

Querying the Web Service Using WSDL

WSDL (Web Services Description Language) is used to create XML documents that describe a Web service. Such a document specifies the location of the service and the operations (or methods) the service exposes. WSDL provides the information necessary for a client to interact with a Web service. Tools such as Visual Studio .NET and JBuilder use the WSDL to generate proxy code that client applications can use to communicate with a Web service. If the endpoint has WSDL enabled, that endpoint will produce WSDL when it receives a request for it. For example, the following listing shows how to request the WSDL for our sample SOAP endpoint.

```
http://sql2005-2/AdwWS?wsdl
```

NOTE

You will need to replace the value of sql2005-2 with either the name of your server or the value of localhost if you are running the browser on the same system as your SQL Server 2005 instance.

In this example the value of sql2005-2 is the name of the SQL Server system where the Web service is located. The value of /AdWWS refers to the path or virtual directory for the Web service. This corresponds to the value used in the CREATE ENDPOINT statement's PATH keyword. You can see an example of the WSDL displayed in the browser in Figure 7-2.

Calling the Web Service

After the SOAP endpoint has been created and the users have been granted connect access to the endpoint, you call the Web service from your client applications. The following section illustrates how to build a VB.NET application that calls the Web service. You can see the sample application in Figure 7-3.

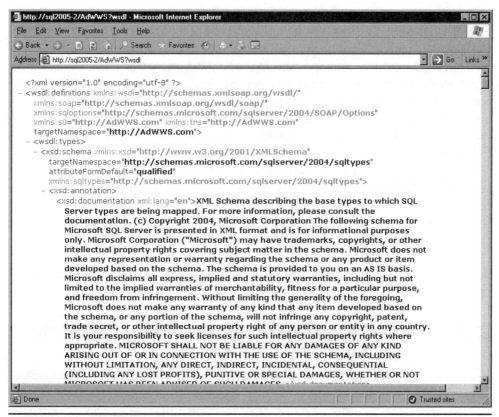

Figure 7-2   *Displaying the Web service's WSDL*

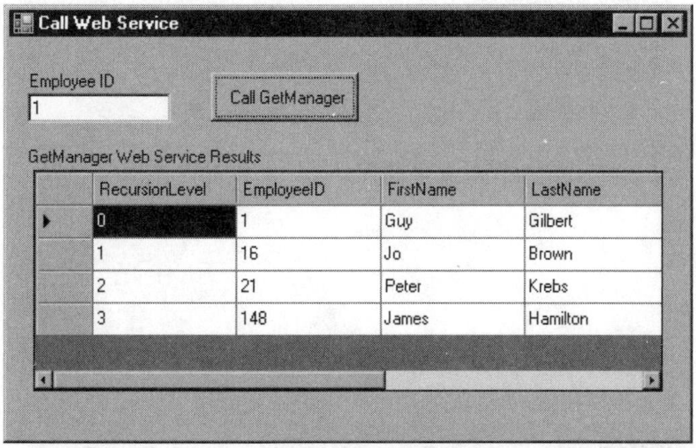

Figure 7-3   *The Web service client application*

To use the sample application to call the Web service and display the result in the grid, the user enters an employee ID number in the text box and then clicks the Call GetManager button to execute the Web service and display the result set in the grid.

To create this project, you open Visual Studio 2005 and select a new Visual Basic Windows Forms project. Open the designer and drag a Button control, a TextBox control, and a DataGridView control to the design surface. After arranging the interface elements, you need to add a reference to the Web service by selecting the Project | Add Web Reference option, which will display a dialog like the one shown in Figure 7-4.

In the URL prompt enter the same URL that you would use to display the Web services WSDL. Then click Go. If Visual Studio finds the Web service, it will be listed on the screen as you see in Figure 7-4. You can optionally rename the reference using the Web Reference Name text box. You add the Web reference to your project by clicking Add Reference.

After adding a reference to the Web service, you can create the code to execute the Web service. You can see the code that calls the GetManagers Web method and displays the results in the following listing:

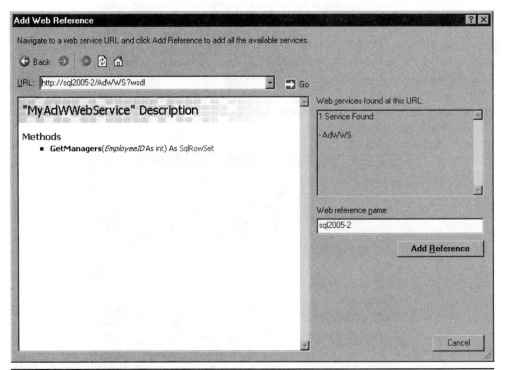

Figure 7-4   *Adding a Web reference*

```
Imports.System.Data

Private Sub Button1_Click(ByVal sender As System.Object, _
    ByVal e As System.EventArgs) Handles Button1.Click

    ' Create a new instance of the web service
    Dim MyAdWService As AdWWS.MyAdWWebService = New _
        AdWWS.MyAdWWebService()

    ' Authenticate to use the service
    MyAdWService.Credentials = _
        System.Net.CredentialCache.DefaultCredentials
    ' The web service results converted to a DataSet
    Dim ds As System.Data.DataSet = DirectCast _
        _(MyAdWService.GetManagers(TextBox1.Text), DataSet)

    ' Display the Results
    DataGridView1.DataSource = ds.Tables(0)
End Sub
```

To create a bit more readable code, I first renamed the Web reference from sql2005-2 to AdWWS by right-clicking the reference in the Solution Explorer window and then typing in the new name.

After the Web reference was renamed, the code that you see near the top of this listing creates a new instance of the Web service, named MyAdWService. Then the Credentials property of that object is assigned the value of System.Net. CredentialCache.DefaultCredentials, which causes the client program to pass the user's Windows credentials to the Web service for authentication. Next, a DataSet named ds is created to contain the results passed back from the Web service. The ds DataSet is then assigned the results of the GetManagers call. The call to GetManagers passes in the value that the user enters into a text box. After the DataSet is populated with the results from the Web service call, it is bound to a DataGridView object and the results are displayed to the end user.

Summary

The new XML data type adds a whole new level of relational database-XML integration capabilities to SQL Server 2005. In this chapter you saw how to declare and use both typed and untyped XML data values as well as how to use the FOR XML statement, how to bulk load XML data, and how to create HTTP and SOAP endpoints for XML Web Services.

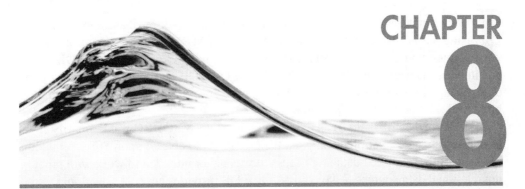

CHAPTER

8

Developing Database Applications with ADO

In this chapter, you will see how to develop SQL Server database applications using Visual Basic and ActiveX Data Objects (ADO). In the first part of this chapter, you get a brief overview of OLE DB, with a look at the OLE DB architecture, as well as the basic relationship of OLE DB and ADO. The second part of this chapter illustrates the basic ADO database programming techniques used to build SQL Server database applications.

Microsoft created OLE DB as the successor to ODBC. ODBC was primarily designed to handle relational data, and the ODBC API is based upon SQL. While it works well for relational database access, it was never intended to work with other, nonrelational data sources. Like ODBC, OLE DB provides access to relational data, but OLE DB extends the functionality provided by ODBC. OLE DB has been designed as a standard interface for all types of data. In addition to relational database access, OLE DB provides access to a wide variety of data sources, including tabular data such as Excel spreadsheets, ISAM files such as dBase, e-mail, Active Directory, and even IBM DB2 data. Using OLE DB, you can access many different and diverse data sources using a single interface.

An Overview of OLE DB

As its name implies, OLE DB is built on an OLE foundation. Unlike ODBC, which provides a DLL call-level interface, ADO provides a COM interface for OLE DB that allows it to be called from other OLE-compliant applications. OLE DB has been created with the understanding that business data is maintained in a variety of diverse data sources. OLE DB provides a similar interface to all sorts of data. OLE DB can be used to access any data that can be represented in a basic row and column format.

OLE DB Architecture Overview

Applications that use OLE DB are typically classified as either OLE DB providers or OLE DB consumers. Figure 8-1 illustrates the relationship between OLE DB providers and OLE DB consumers.

As you can see, OLE DB consumers are nothing more than applications that are written to use the OLE DB interface. In contrast, OLE DB providers are responsible for accessing data sources and supplying data to OLE DB consumers via the OLE DB interface. More specifically, there are actually two types of OLE DB providers: data providers and service providers. *Data providers* simply expose the data from a data source, while *service providers* both transport and process data. Service providers

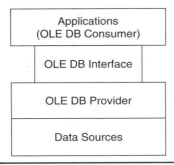

Figure 8-1   *OLE DB consumers and providers*

typically provide more advanced functions that extend the basic data access found in OLE DB data providers. Microsoft Query is an example of an OLE DB service provider, while the Microsoft OLE DB Provider for SQL Server is an example of a data provider. As you would expect from its ODBC roots, OLE DB provides different levels of functionality based on the capabilities of the different OLE DB providers. While all OLE DB drivers support a common interface, each individual driver is able to extend the basic level of OLE DB functionality. The following OLE providers are shipped with SQL Server 2005:

▶ Microsoft SQL Native Client OLE DB Provider

▶ Microsoft OLE DB Provider for ODBC

▶ Microsoft OLE DB Provider for Jet

▶ Microsoft OLE DB Provider for DTS Packages

▶ Microsoft OLE DB Provider for Oracle

Very similar to ODBC, each different OLE DB source uses its own OLE DB provider. Figure 8-2 illustrates how different OLE DB providers are required to access multiple data sources.

In this figure, you can see a high-level overview of how a Visual Basic application might use OLE DB to access several heterogeneous data sources. With the exception of ODBC databases, each different data source is accessed using a different OLE DB provider. For example, SQL Server databases are accessed using SQLOLEDB, Microsoft's SQL Server's OLE DB provider. Data contained in Microsoft Excel or Exchange is accessed using their respective OLE DB providers. ODBC is an exception to this one OLE DB provider-per-data-source rule. To provide maximum

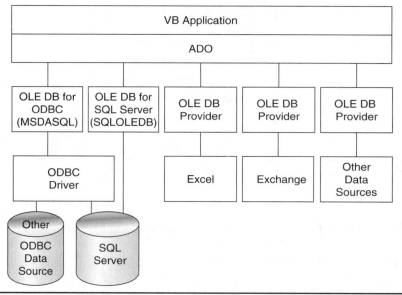

Figure 8-2   *OLE DB overview*

compatibility with existing ODBC data sources, Microsoft developed MSDASQL, the OLE DB provider for ODBC. Unlike most OLE DB providers, which provide direct database access, the MSDASQL OLE DB provider for ODBC accesses data using existing ODBC drivers. The MSDASQL OLE DB provider for ODBC maps OLE DB calls into their equivalent ODBC calls.

Each OLE DB provider delivers data access and reflects its capabilities through its exposed COM interfaces. However, the OLE DB COM interface is a low-level interface that requires support for pointers, data structures, and direct memory allocation. As a result, the direct use of OLE DB providers is unsuitable for development environments that don't support low-level functions like pointers, such as Visual Basic, VBA, VBScript, Java, JScript, JavaScript, and several others. This is where ADO fits in: ADO allows OLE DB providers to be accessed by interactive and scripting languages that need data access but don't support low-level memory access and manipulation.

ADO (ActiveX Data Objects)

ADO is essentially an OLE DB consumer that provides application-level access to OLE DB data sources. ADO is an OLE automation server that most OLE-compliant development and scripting environments can access. Both OLE DB and ADO are delivered as part of the SQL Server 2000 client components. ADO was delivered as part of the Visual Basic 6.0 and the older pre- .NET Visual Studio Enterprise Edition, which included Visual Basic 6.0 and Visual C++ 6.0. ADO has since been succeeded by ADO.NET and Visual Studio 2005, which you can read about in Chapter 7. However, there are still many COM-based ADO applications written in Visual Basic 6.0 that connect to SQL Server.

As you saw in Figure 8-2, OLE DB provides two distinctly different methods for accessing SQL Server data: the OLE DB for SQL Server provider and the OLE DB provider for ODBC. ADO can work with both of these OLE DB providers. ADO takes advantage of a multilevel architecture that insulates the applications using the ADO object framework from the underlying network protocols and topology. Figure 8-3 illustrates the relationship of ADO, OLE DB, ODBC, and the PCs networking support.

At the top of the figure, you can see the Visual Basic ADO application. The Visual Basic application creates and uses the various ADO objects. The ADO object framework makes calls to the appropriate OLE DB provider. If the ADO application is using the OLE DB provider for ODBC, then the MSDASQL OLE DB provider will be used. If the ADO application is using the OLE DB for SQL Server provider, then the SQLOLEDB provider will be used. When using the OLE DB provider for ODBC, ADO loads the msdasql.dll file, which, in turn, loads the ODBC Driver Manager. The OLE DB provider for ODBC maps the OLE DB calls made by ADO into ODBC calls, which are passed on to the ODBC Driver Manager.

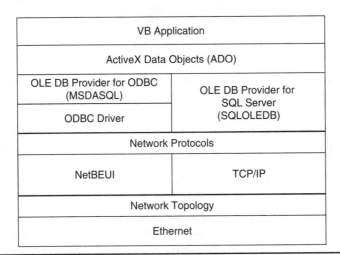

VB Application	
ActiveX Data Objects (ADO)	
OLE DB Provider for ODBC (MSDASQL)	OLE DB Provider for SQL Server (SQLOLEDB)
ODBC Driver	
Network Protocols	
NetBEUI	TCP/IP
Network Topology	
Ethernet	

Figure 8-3   *ADO Network architecture*

The ODBC Driver Manager handles loading the appropriate ODBC driver. The ODBC driver typically uses a network interprocess communication (IPC) method like Named Pipes, TCP/IP Sockets, or SPX to communicate to a remote IPC server that provides access to the target database. The native OLE DB provider for SQL Server doesn't use any additional middle layers. When using the OLE DB provider for SQL Server, ADO loads sqloledb.dll, which directly loads and uses the appropriate network IPC method to communicate with the database. The IPC client component establishes a communications link with the corresponding server IPC through the networking protocol in use. The network protocol is responsible for sending and receiving the IPC data stream over the network. The most common network protocol is TCP/IP. Finally, at the bottom of this stack is the physical network topology. The physical network includes the adapter cards and cabling that make the actual connections between the networked systems. Ethernet is the most common network topology.

OLE DB and ADO Files

Here is a summary of the client files used to implement ADO:

File	Description
msdasql.dll	OLE DB Provider for ODBC
Sqloledb.dll	OLE DB Provider for SQL Server
msado15.dll	ADO Object Library

ADO Architecture

As with several of the other data access object models, ADO is implemented using a hierarchical object framework. However, the ADO object model is simpler and flatter than Microsoft's previous data access object libraries, such as Data Access Objects (DAO) or Remote Database Objects (RDO) frameworks. In Figure 8-4, you can see an overview of ADO's object hierarchy.

The Connection, Recordset, and Command objects are the three primary objects in the ADO object model. The *Connection* object represents a connection to the remote data source. In addition to establishing the connection to a data source,

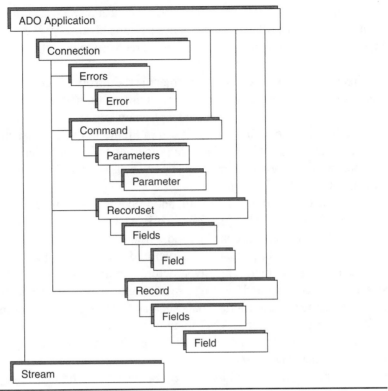

Figure 8-4   *ADO object hierarchy*

Connection objects can also be used to control the transaction scope. A Connection object can be associated with either a Recordset object or a Command object.

The *Recordset* object represents a result set returned from the data source. An ADO Recordset object can either use an open Connection object or establish its own connection to the target data source. Recordset objects let you both query and modify data. Each Recordset object contains a collection of Field objects, where each Field object represents a column of data in the Recordset.

The *Command* object is used to issue commands and parameterized SQL statements. Command objects can be used to call stored procedures and execute SQL action statements, as well as SQL queries that return recordsets. Like the ADO Recordset object, the Command object can either use an active Connection object or establish its own connection to the target data source. The Command object contains a Parameters collection, where each Parameter object in the collection represents a parameter the Command object uses. In the case where a Command object executes a parameterized SQL statement, each Parameter object would represent one of the parameters in the SQL statement.

Directly beneath the Connection object is the Errors collection. Each Error object contained in the Errors collection contains information about an error encountered by one of the objects in the ADO object framework.

In addition to the main objects shown in Figure 8-4, the Connection, Command, Recordset, and Field objects all have a Properties collection, which consists of a set of Property objects. Each Property object can be used to get or set the various properties associated with the object.

While the Connection, Command, and Recordset objects are the most commonly used objects in the ADO object framework, ADO also includes Record and Stream objects. The *Record* object can be used to represent a single record in a Recordset, or it can represent hierarchical tree-structured namespaces. The Record object can be used to represent hierarchically structured entities like folders and files in a file system, or directories and messages in an e-mail system. The Stream object is used to read or write stream-oriented data such as XML documents or binary objects.

While at first glance, the ADO framework may seem as hierarchically structured as DAO and RDO, that's not really the case. Unlike the older data access object frameworks that ADO essentially replaces, all the primary ADO objects (for example, Connection, Command, and Recordset) can be created on their own without needing to be accessed through a higher-level object. This makes the ADO object framework much flatter and more flexible than the other object models. For instance, the ADO object framework allows a Recordset object to be opened and accessed without first requiring an instance of the Connection object. The capability to use each object directly without first instantiating any higher-order objects tends to make ADO a bit simpler to work with than the other object frameworks. As you see in some of the code examples, however, ADO isn't always as straightforward in use as the other frameworks.

An Overview of Using ADO

ADO is built as a COM automation server, which makes accessing ADO functions from Visual Basic easier. Unlike when using ODBC or other DLL-based APIs, where you must manually declare their functions and parameters in a .bas or .cls module, with ADO you only need to add the ADO reference to your project, as explained in the next section. After adding the ADO reference to your Visual Basic development environment, you can readily use all the ADO objects. A summary of the steps required to use ADO from Visual Basic follows:

1. Make a reference in Visual Basic to the Microsoft ADO 2.8 object library.
2. Open a connection using the Connection, Command, or Recordset object.
3. Use the Command or Recordset object to access data.
4. Close the connection to the Connection, Command, or Recordset object.

Adding the ADO Reference to Visual Basic

Before you can use ADO from Visual Basic, you must set a reference to the ADO object library, also known as the *ADO automation server.* The files that provide the basic support for ADO 2.8 are installed on the system when you first download the ADO support from the Microsoft Web site or when you install one of the products containing ADO listed previously, in the section "ADO (ActiveX Data Objects)." Before you can begin using ADO in your Visual Basic projects, however, you need to set a reference to the ADO COM object library in Visual Basic's development environment. To add a reference to the ADO Objects 2.8 Library in Visual Basic 6, start Visual Basic, and then select Project | References to display the References dialog box shown in Figure 8-5.

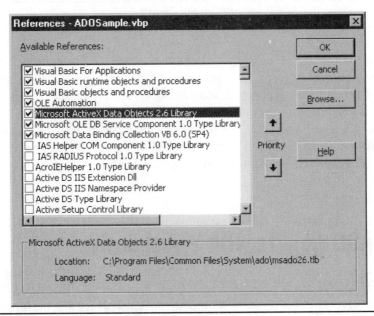

Figure 8-5   *Setting a reference to the ADO Object Library*

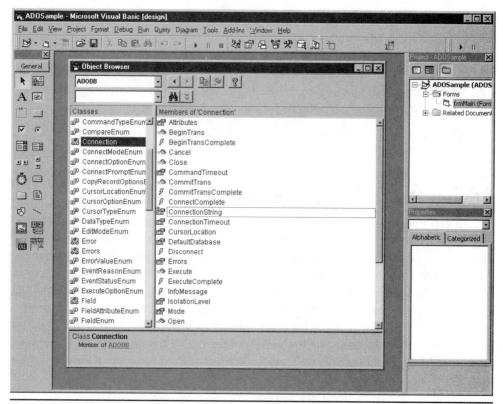

Figure 8-6   *Viewing the ADO classes from the Object Browser*

In the References dialog box, scroll through the Available References list until you see the Microsoft ActiveX Data Objects 2.8 Library option. Clicking the check box and then clicking the OK button adds the ADO Objects Library to Visual Basic's *Interactive Development Environment (IDE).* Unlike ActiveX Controls, adding a reference to Visual Basic's IDE doesn't create any visual objects in Visual Basic's Toolbox. To see the ADO objects, properties, and methods, you need to use Visual Basic's Object Browser. Figure 8-6 displays the ADO Objects Library using Visual Basic's Object Browser.

Using ADO Objects with Visual Basic

After adding a reference to the ADO object library in the Visual Basic development environment, you're ready to create Visual Basic applications using ADO. Unlike the DAO or RDO object models, ADO has no top-level object that must be created before you establish a connection to a data source. Using ADO, the first action your application takes is to open a connection using the Connection, Command, or Recordset object.

Connecting to SQL Server

ADO can connect to SQL Server using either the MSDASQL OLE DB provider for ODBC or the SQLOLEDB OLE DB provider for SQL Server. The MSDASQL provider allows the ADO object framework to be used with existing ODBC drivers, while the SQLOLEDB OLE DB provider connects directly to SQL Server. Both of these OLE DB providers can be used with the ADO Connection, Command, and Recordset objects. In the following section, you see how to establish a connection with SQL Server using both the OLE DB provider for ODBC and the OLE DB provider for SQL Server. You also see how to connect to SQL Server using the ADO Connection object, as well as making a connection directly using ADO Recordset object.

Opening a Connection with the OLE DB Provider for ODBC

If you're familiar with the DAO or RDO object frameworks, using the ADO Connection object with the OLE DB provider for ODBC to establish a connection to a SQL Server system is probably the most familiar starting point for beginning to build an ADO application. Like DAO and RDO, the MSDASQL OLE DB provider for ODBC uses an ODBC driver to access SQL Server. This means either the system running the application must have an existing ODBC driver for SQL Server and a *Data Source Name (DSN)* for SQL Server in the ODBC Administrator, or the application must use a DSN-less connection string.

The following code illustrates how to use the ADO Connection object and the MSDASQL provider to prompt the user to select an existing DSN that will be used to connect to SQL Server:

```
Private Sub Connect(sLoginID As String, sPassword As String)
    Dim cn As New ADODB.Connection
    ' DSN Connection using the OLE DB provider for ODBC - MSDASQL
    cn.ConnectionString = "DSN=" & _
        ";DATABASE=AdventureWorks;UID=" & sLoginID & _
        ";PWD=" & sPassword

    ' Prompt the user to select the DSN
    cn.Properties("Prompt") = adPromptComplete
    cn.Open
    cn.Close
End Sub
```

In the beginning of this code example, you can see where a new instance of the ADO Connection object named cn is created. Because ADO objects don't rely on upper-level objects, each object must generally have a Dim statement that uses Visual Basic's New keyword. Or, you could use late-binding and create the object at run time using the CreateObject statement. Next, the ConnectionString property of the cn Connection object is assigned an ODBC connection string. Like the normal ODBC connection string, the connection string used in the ADO ConnectionString property must contain a set of predefined keywords where each keyword and its associated value are separated from the other keywords and their values by semicolons. Because ADO is based on OLE DB rather than just ODBC, the keywords used in the connection string are a bit different than the keywords used in a standard ODBC connection string. Table 8-1 presents the ADO connection string keywords supported for all OLE DB providers.

 TIP

While this example uses uppercase to present the OLE DB connection string keywords, that isn't a requirement. The keywords aren't case-sensitive.

In addition to the generic OLE DB connection string keywords, each OLE DB provider also supports provider-specific connection string keywords. In the case of the OLE DB Provider for ODBC, the provider passes on any non-ADO connection

Keyword	Description
PROVIDER	This optional keyword can be used to identify the name of the OLE DB provider to be used. If no provider name is supplied, the connection uses the MSDASQL provider.
DATASOURCE or SERVER	The name of an existing SQL Server instance.
DATABASE or INITIAL CATALOG	The SQL Server target database name.
USER ID or UID	The login ID for the data source (used for SQL Server authentication).
PASSWORD or PWD	The password associated with the login ID (used for SQL Server authentication).
OLE DB Services	Used to disable specific OLE DB services. The value of −1 is the default that indicates all services are enabled; −2 disables connection pooling; −4 disables connection pooling and auto-enlistment; −5 disables client cursors; −6 disables pooling, auto-enlistment, and client cursors; 0 disables all services.

Table 8-1   *Common ADO Connection String Keywords*

parameters to the ODBC driver manager, which uses them with the target ODBC driver. Table 8-2 lists the connection string keywords supported by MSDASQL, provider for the Microsoft SQL Server ODBC driver. The most common keywords are presented at the top of the list, and the lesser-used keywords follow in alphabetical order.

Keyword	Description
DSN	The name of an existing data source created using the ODBC Administrator.
FILEDSN	The name of an existing file data source created using the ODBC Administrator.
DRIVER	The name of an existing ODBC driver.
SERVER	The name of an existing SQL Server system.
SAVEFILE	The name of a file data source that contains the saved connection information.
ADDRESS	The network address of the SQL Server system.
ANSINPW	Uses a value of YES or NO, where YES specifies that ANSI-defined behaviors are to be used for handling NULLs.
APP	Specifies the name of the client application.
ATTACHDBFILENAME	Specifies the name of an attachable database. The path to the data file must be included (for example, c:\mssql\Mydatabase.mdf). If the database was detached, it automatically becomes attached after the connection completes and the database then becomes the default database for the connection.
AUTOTRANSLATE	Uses a value of TRUE or FALSE, where FALSE prevents automatic ANSI/multibyte character conversions. The default value of TRUE automatically converts the values transfer between SQL server and the client.
FALLBACK	Uses a value of YES or NO, where YES specifies the ODBC driver should attempt to connect to the fallback server specified by an earlier SQLSetConnectAttr ODBC function call (SQL Server 6.5 only).
LANGUAGE	Specifies the SQL Server language name to be used for this connection.
NETWORK	Specifies the network library DLL to be used. The value used by this keyword should not include the path of the .dll file extension.
QUERYLOGFILE	Specifies the full path of the file used to store query logs.
QUERYLOG_ON	Uses a value of YES or NO, where YES specifies that long-running queries are to be logged to the query log file specified by the QUERYLOGFILE keyword.
QUOTEDID	Uses a value of YES or NO, where YES specifies that Quoted Identifiers will be set on for the connection.

Table 8-2   *OLE DB Provider for ODBC Provider-Specific Keywords for SQL Server*

Keyword	Description
REGIONAL	Uses a value of YES or NO, where YES specifies SQL Server uses client settings when converting date, time, currency, and data.
STATSLOGFILE	Specifies the full path of the file used to store ODBC driver performance statistics.
STATSLOG_ON	Uses a value of YES or NO, where YES specifies ODBC driver statistics are to be logged to the stats log file specified by the STATSLOGFILE keyword.
TRUSTED_CONNECTION	Uses a value of YES or NO, where a value of YES indicates Windows NT authentication is to be used and a value of NO indicates mixed or SQL Server authentication is to be used.
USEPROCFORPREPARE	Uses a value of YES or NO to indicate whether SQL Server should create temporary stored procedures for each prepared command (SQL Server 6.5 only).
WSID	Identifies the client workstation.

Table 8-2   *OLE DB Provider for ODBC Provider-Specific Keywords for SQL Server (Continued)*

After the OLE DB connection string is assigned to the Connection object's ConnectionString property, the Connection object's Prompt property is assigned the constant value of adPromptComplete. This value specifies the ODBC Driver Manager should prompt for any required connection information that's not supplied in the connection string.

TIP

The Properties collection of the ADO Connection, Command, and Recordset objects lets you get and set property values using named items in the Properties collection. In fact, some ADO properties like the Prompt property aren't exposed directly through the object framework and can only be accessed through the Properties collection. While this dynamic Properties collection gives the ADO object model more flexibility than DAO or RDO, it also hides properties, making it more difficult to find and work with properties than the more straightforward DAO or RDO object models. If you can't find an ADO property you think should exist, try searching for it by iterating through the Properties collection.

The Prompt property controls how the ODBC Driver Manager responds to the keyword and values contained in the connection string. Table 8-3 lists the valid values for the Prompt property.

In this example, the connection string doesn't use the PROVIDER keyword, so the OLE DB provider for ODBC—MSDASQL—is used by default. This means the connection to SQL Server takes place via an ODBC driver. In addition, the connection string doesn't specify a value for the DSN keyword. This means

Constant	Description
adPromptNever	The ODBC Driver Manager can only use the information provided by the connection string to make a connection. If sufficient information is not supplied, the connection fails.
adPromptAlways	The ODBC Driver Manager always displays the ODBC Administrator to prompt for connection information.
adPromptComplete	The ODBC driver determines if all the required connection information has been supplied in the connection string. If all the required information is present, the connection is made without further prompting. If any of the required information is missing, the ODBC Administrator prompts the user for the missing information.
adPromptCompleteRequired	This option behaves like adPromptComplete, except any prompts containing information that has already been supplied are disabled.

Table 8-3 *ADO MSDASQL Prompt Constants*

either the connection string must use the DRIVER keyword to make a DSN-less connection or the ODBC Driver Manager must prompt the user for the DSN to make a connection to SQL Server. In this example, the DRIVER keyword isn't used and the value of adPromptComplete is specified in the Prompt property. This allows the ODBC Driver Manager to prompt the user to select an existing ODBC data source.

After the user has responded to the ODBC Driver Manager prompt, the cn Connection object's Open method connects to SQL Server. The Connection object's Open method takes three optional parameters:

- ► The first optional parameter accepts a string that contains an OLE DB connection string. This parameter performs exactly the same function as the Connection object's ConnectionString property, and you can use this parameter as an alternative to setting the ConnectionString property.

- ► The second optional parameter accepts a String variable that contains a valid login ID for the target data source.

- ► The third optional parameter accepts a String variable that can contain the password for the target data source.

TIP

While both OLE DB connection strings and the second and third parameters of the Open method let you specify login information, don't use both at the same time. Because you normally need to use the OLE DB connection string to supply the name of the OLE DB provide anyway, supplying the login information as a part of the OLE DB connection string is usually simpler.

In this example, there's no other processing, so the Close method ends the connection.

Opening a DSN-less Connection with the OLE DB Provider for ODBC

The previous example illustrated how to establish a SQL Server connection using the MSDASQL provider and an existing DSN. Instances occur when your application may need to make an ODBC-based connection, however, without being able to rely on a DSN being preconfigured. Luckily, the MSDASQL OLE DB provider also supports using DSN-less connections. Using a DSN-less connection removes the requirement for an existing data source.

The following code illustrates how to use the ADO Connection object and the MSDASQL provider to make a DSN-less connection to SQL Server:

```
Private Sub DSNlessConnect _
    (sServer As String, sLoginID As String, sPassword As String)
    Dim cn As New ADODB.Connection
    ' DSNless Connection using the OLE DB provider for ODBC - MSDASSQL
    cn.ConnectionString = "DRIVER=SQL Server" & _
        ";SERVER=" & sServer & _
        ";UID=" & sLoginID & _
        ";PWD=" & sPassword & _
        ";DATABASE=AdventureWorks"
    cn.Open
    cn.Close
End Sub
```

Creating a new ADO Connection object named cn is the first action that takes place in this code example. Next, the ConnectionString property of the cn Connection object is assigned a connection string. As you might expect, because this connection string is intended to establish a DSN-less connection, it's quite a bit different than the connection string presented in the preceding example. Because the PROVIDER keyword isn't used, the MSDASQL provider for ODBC is used as the default. As you might guess, the DSN keyword isn't needed to establish a DSN-less connection. Instead, the DRIVER keyword has the value of "SQL Server" to indicate the SQL Server ODBC driver should be used.

NOTE
Optionally, the value used by the DRIVER keyword can be enclosed in {}, as in {SQL Server}, but this isn't a requirement.

In addition to specifying the ODBC driver to be used, a DSN-less ODBC connection string must also indicate the server and database to be used. These values are supplied by the SERVER and DATABASE keywords. Finally, the UID and PWD keywords, described in Table 8-1, supply the required SQL Server login information.

After setting the ConnectionString property with a DSN-less ODBC connection string, the Connection object's Open method starts a connection to the SQL Server system. Then the Connection object's Close method ends the connection.

Opening a Connection with the OLE DB Provider for SQL Server

The OLE DB provider for ODBC is primarily intended to enable ADO applications to access ODBC-compliant databases when no native OLE DB provider is available. While ODBC is certainly the established database access standard and is supported by virtually all popular databases, that's not the case with OLE DB, which is a newer technology. The SQL Server 2000 OLE DB provider is supplied in sqloledb.dll.

Using the OLE DB provider for SQL Server is similar to using the OLE DB provider for ODBC. Because the OLE DB provider for SQL Server doesn't use ODBC, there's no requirement for using a data source or an existing ODBC driver. However, you do need to specify the name of the OLE DB provider.

The following example illustrates how to make a connection to SQL Server using the ADO Connection object and the OLE DB provider for SQL Server:

```
Private Sub SQLOLEDBConnect _
   (sServer As String, sLoginID As String, sPassword As String)
    Dim cn As New ADODB.Connection
    ' Connect using the OLE DB provider for SQL Server - SQLOLEDB
    cn.ConnectionString = "PROVIDER=SQLOLEDB" & _
        ";SERVER=" & sServer & _
        ";UID=" & sLoginID & _
        ";PWD=" & sPassword & _
        ";DATABASE=AdventureWorks"
    cn.Open
    cn.Close
End Sub
```

As in the previous examples, an instance of the ADO Connection object is created. Then the ConnectionString property of the ADO Connection object is assigned an

OLE DB connection string. This connection string uses the PROVIDER keyword to specify the SQLOLEDB provider is used. Specifying the PROVIDER keyword is required to use the OLE DB provider for SQL Server. If you omit this keyword, the provider defaults to the value of MSDASQL (the OLE DB provider for ODBC). In addition, the SERVER and DATABASE keywords are also required. The SERVER keyword specifies the name of the SQL Server system that will be connected to, and the DATABASE keyword identifies the database to be used. The UID and PWD keywords provide the authentication values required to log in to SQL Server if you are connecting using mixed security. If you are connecting using NT Authentication, the UID and PWD keywords are ignored, as the login will use your Windows NT user name and password. Table 8-4 lists all the provider-specific keywords provided by Microsoft's OLE DB Provider for SQL Server.

TIP

As the preceding listing demonstrates, you can freely mix the provider-specific connection string keywords with the generic OLE DB connection string keywords in the connection string.

Keyword	Description
TRUSTED_CONNECTION	Uses a value of YES or NO to indicate where a value of YES indicates Windows NT authentication is to be used and a value of NO indicates mixed or SQL Server authentication should be used.
CURRENT LANGUAGE	Specifies the SQL Server language name to be used for this connection.
NETWORK ADDRESS	Specifies the SQL Server network address.
NETWORK LIBRARY	Specifies the network library DLL to be used. The value used by this keyword should not include the path of the .dll file extension.
USE PROCEDURE FOR PREPARE	Uses a value of YES or NO to indicate whether SQL Server should create temporary stored procedures for each prepared command.
AUTO TRANSLATE	Uses a value of TRUE or FALSE, where FALSE prevents automatic ANSI/multibyte character conversions. The default value of TRUE automatically converts the data transferred between the SQL server and the client.
PACKET SIZE	Used to alter the network packet size. Accepts values from 512 to 32767. If no value is specified, a default packet size of 4096 is used.
APPLICATION NAME	Identifies the current application.
WORKSTATION ID	Identifies the client workstation.

Table 8-4 *Connection String Keyword for the OLE DB Provider for SQL Server*

After setting the ConnectionString property, the Open method starts the connection. Once the connection has been established, other database access can be performed. In this example, there's no additional work, so the connection is closed using the Close method.

TIP

If you are connecting to a named instance of SQL Server 2005, you need to use the named instance name in conjunction with the SERVER keyword. For instance, to connect to a named instance other than the default instance, you would use the following format with the SERVER keyword: SERVER=computername\instancename. And to connect to the instance named TestServer on the computer named teca4, for example, you would use the following form of the SERVER keyword: SERVER=teca4\TestServer.

Opening a Trusted Connection using the OLE DB Provider for SQL Server

The preceding example illustrated how to establish a SQL Server connection using the SQLOLEDB Provider and SQL Server Security (aka *mixed security*). However, using NT Security, also known as *Integrated Security*, provides for a more secure connection because the same values used for the client's Windows login are also used for SQL Server authentication—there's no need to specify the user ID or the password from the application. In addition, Integrated Security can make administration easier by eliminating the need to create a set of SQL Server login IDs that are separate from the Windows NT/2000 User IDs. The following example illustrates how to make a trusted connection to SQL Server using the ADO Connection object and the OLE DB provider for SQL Server:

```
Private Sub SQLOLEDBTrustedConnect _
  (sServer As String, sLoginID As String, sPassword As String, _
  bIntegratedSecurity As Boolean)
    Dim cn As New ADODB.Connection
    ' Connect using the SQLOLEDB provider
    cn.ConnectionString = "PROVIDER=SQLOLEDB" & _
        ";SERVER=" & sServer & _
        ";DATABASE=AdventureWorks"
    ' Use the Trusted_Connection keyword for integrated security
    If bIntegratedSecurity = True Then
        cn.ConnectionString = cn.ConnectionString _
          & ";TRUSTED_CONNECTION=YES"
    Else
        ' Otherwise supply the LoginID and Password
        cn.ConnectionString = cn.ConnectionString & ";UID=" _
```

```
            & sLoginID & ";PWD=" & sPassword
      End If
      cn.Open
      cn.Close
End Sub
```

In the beginning of this subroutine, you can see where the server name, login ID, and password are passed in the subroutine as String values. In addition, the bIntegratedSecurity Boolean variable is used to indicate whether the SQL Server connection should be made using Integrated Security or SQL Server Security. A value of True indicates Integrated Security is to be used, while a value of False indicates the connection will use SQL Server Security.

Next, an instance of the ADO Connection object is created and the ConnectionString property is assigned. As in the previous example, the connection string uses the PROVIDER keyword to specify the SQLOLEDB provider, and the DATABASE keyword should set AdventureWorks as the default database.

Then the bIntegratedSecurity variable is tested for a value of True. If the bIntegratedSecurity variable is true, then Integrated Security is be used and the TRUSTED_CONNECTION=YES keyword is appended to the connection string. Otherwise, SQL Server Security is to be used, and the UID and PWD keywords are used to provide the SQL Server authentication information.

After the ConnectionString has been set up, the ADO Connection object's Open method is used to connect to SQL Server. In this example, after the connection has been established, it is immediately closed using the Connection object's Close method.

Open a Connection Using the Connection Object's Properties

All the previous examples have illustrated connecting to SQL Server using values supplied via the Connection object's ConnectionString property. While providing server and database connection information is certainly a requirement to establish an ADO connection to SQL Server, using the ConnectionString property is not. You can also provide all the required connection information using the ADO Connection object's Extended Properties. Unlike standard ADO object properties that can be viewed using the Object Browser, Extended Properties access provider-specific information that isn't explicitly available in the standard ADO Connection object. The following example illustrates how to set up a SQL Server connection using the ADO Connection object's extended properties:

```
Private Sub SQLOLEDBPropertiesConnect _
  (sServer As String, sLoginID As String, sPassword As String, _
  bIntegratedSecurity As Boolean)
```

```
    Dim cn As New ADODB.Connection
    ' Specify the OLE DB provider
    cn.Provider = "sqloledb"

    ' Set the extended connection properties
    cn.Properties("Data Source").Value = sServer
    cn.Properties("Initial Catalog").Value = "AdventureWorks"

    ' Check for Integrated security
    If bIntegratedSecurity = True Then
        cn.Properties("Integrated Security").Value = "SSPI"
    Else
        cn.Properties("User ID").Value = sLoginID
        cn.Properties("Password").Value = sPassword
    End If

    cn.Open
    cn.Close
End Sub
```

String variables containing the server name, login ID, and password are passed in to the beginning of this subroutine, followed by the bIntegratedSecurity Boolean variable, which indicates whether Integrated Security will be used. Like the previous example, a value of True indicates Integrated Security is to be used, while a value of False indicates the connection will use SQL Server security.

Next, an instance of the ADO Connection object is created and its Provider property is set to sqloledb, the name of the SQL Server OLE DB provider. After the Provider property is set, then the specific connection values are assigned to the Connection object's Extended Properties. Each Extended Property is located in the Properties collection by using its name. For instance, the Data Source property is identified using the "Data Source" string, and its value is set to the name of the SQL Server instance to which the application intends to connect. Next the Initial Catalog property is assigned the name of the AdventureWorks database, which causes AdventureWorks to be used as the default database.

TIP

While you can't see the available extended properties using the Object Browser, you can see them in the Debugger by adding an instance of the Connection object to the Watch List, and then expanding the Properties collection. Each Extended Property is listed as Item n (where n uniquely numbers each property). And as you might expect, the Name property contains the Extended Properties' name, while the Value property contains its value.

Then the bIntegratedSecurity variable is tested for a value of True. If the bIntegratedSecurity variable is True, then the Integrated Security property is set to a value of *Security Support Provider Interface (SSPI),* to specify Windows NT Authentication. Otherwise, the User ID and Password connection properties are assigned values and SQL Server Security is used for the connection authentication.

After the Connection object's Extended Properties have been assigned connection values, the Open method is used to connect to SQL Server. The connection is then closed using the Connection object's Close method.

Connecting to SQL Server Using a UDL File

A *Universal Data Link (UDL)* file is the OLE DB equivalent to an ODBC File DSN. Like an ODBC File DSN, a UDL file stores OLE DB connection information, such as the provider, server, database username, password, and other connection options you can use to establish an ADO connection. One of the advantages to using a UDL file is that an administrator or developer can centrally create the UDL file, which can then be distributed to all networked clients along with the application. From an application developer's standpoint, using a UDL file to connect to SQL Server is similar to using the standard OLE DB connection string. The following example illustrates how you can use an existing UDL file to connect to SQL Server.

```
Private Sub SQLOLEDBUDLConnect()
    Dim cn As New ADODB.Connection
    ' Connect using the OLE DB Provider for SQL Server - SQLOLEDB
    cn.ConnectionString = "FILE NAME=" & App.Path & \\udlSample.udl
    cn.Open
    cn.Close
End Sub
```

First an instance of the ADO Connection object is created, and then the ConnectionString property of the Connection object is assigned a string consisting of the FILE NAME= keyword, followed by the path and name of the UDL that contains the SQL Server connection information. In this example, the udlsample.udl file is located in the same directory as the VB database application. If the application were located in the c:\DBApp directory, the resolved connection string would then appear as follows:

```
"FILE NAME=C:\DBApp\udlsample.udl"
```

After the Connection object's ConnectionString property has been assigned the FILE NAME keyword and the path to the existing UDL, the Open method is used to connect to SQL Server. The connection is then closed using the Connection object's Close method.

Connecting to SQL Server Using the Data Link Dialog

Just as it's possible to cause the ODBC driver to prompt the user for any required connection parameters at run time, it's also possible to prompt for the required OLE DB connection values at run time. However, nothing that's inherently a part of either OLE DB or ADO lets you prompt for the connection attributes. Instead, OLE DB connection properties are captured at run time using the DataLink dialog, which is a part of the OLE DB Service object.

Adding a Reference to the OLE DB Service Object   Before you can use the Data Link dialog box from your Visual Basic application, you must add a reference to the Microsoft OLE DB Service Component 1.0 Type Library, as well as a reference to the Microsoft ActiveX Data Objects 2.8 Library. To add a reference to Visual Basic, select the References option from Visual Basic's Project menu. The References dialog box shown in Figure 8-7 is then displayed.

When the References dialog box is first displayed, scroll through the list of references until you see the Microsoft OLE DB Service 1.0 Type Library.

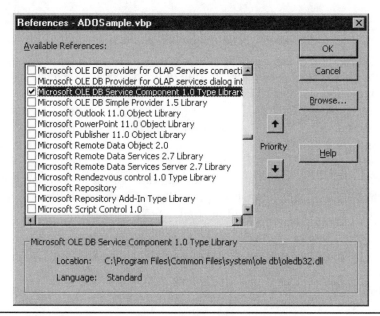

Figure 8-7   *Adding the OLE DB Service Component Type Library*

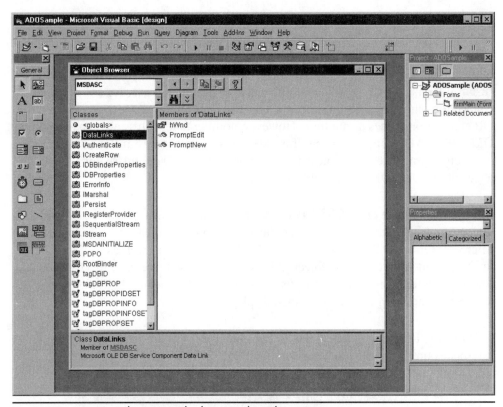

Figure 8-8 *Viewing the DataLink object in the Object Browser*

Clicking the check box immediately in front of the name, and then clicking the OK button adds a reference to the OLE DB Service Library to the current VB project. After a reference to the OLE DB Service Library has been added to your project, you can use Visual Basic's Object Browser to view the object's properties and methods, as shown in Figure 8-8.

After a reference to the OLE DB Service Component 1.0 Type Library is added to VB, you can then create an instance of the Data Link object in your application that displays the OLE DB connection prompts to the end user. The following code listing shows the code to display the Data Link dialog box:

```
Private Sub SQLOLEDBPromptConnect(cn As ADODB.Connection)
    Dim dl As New MSDASC.DataLinks

    ' Display the Data Link Dialog
    Set cn = dl.PromptNew
    On Error Resume Next
```

```
    'Check object for nothing
    If cn = "" Then
        MsgBox "No connection information has been entered"
        End
    Else
        cn.Open
        cn.Close
    End If

    dl = Nothing
End Sub
```

In the beginning of this listing, you can see where an instance of an existing ADO Connection object is passed into the subroutine as a parameter. This ADO Connection object is set to an instance of the Connection object that will be returned by the Data Link object. The following Dim statement then creates a new instance of the DataLinks object named dl. After the dl DataLinks object has been instantiated, you can then use the Data Link object's PromptNew method to display the Data Link dialog box, as shown in Figure 8-9.

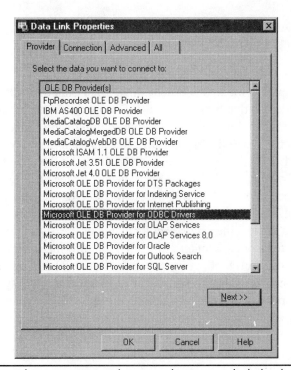

Figure 8-9 *Selecting the OLE DB Provider using the Data Link dialog box*

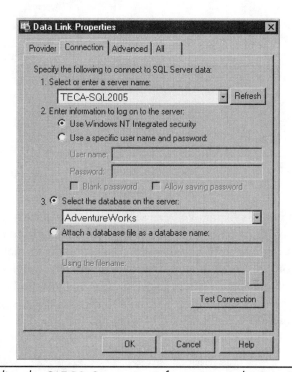

Figure 8-10 *Providing the OLE DB Connection information on the Data Link dialog box*

When the PromptNew method is executed, the Data Link dialog box initially displays the Provider tab that lists all the OLE DB providers that are installed on the system. The Data Link dialog box lets you both configure and connect to a target data source. To connect to SQL Server using the Data Link dialog box, the user must first select the OLE DB provider to be used from the list of the OLE DB providers displayed on the Provider tab. In Figure 8-9, you can see the OLE DB Provider for SQL Server has been selected. Clicking the Next button or selecting the Connection tab displays the OLE DB Connection information dialog box, as shown in Figure 8-10.

The Connection tab lets the user select the name of the SQL Server system that will be connected to, as well as enter authentication information and specify a default database. In Figure 8-10, you can see the Data Link dialog box is being used to connect to a system named teca-sql2005, that Integrated Security will be used, and AdventureWorks will be set as the default database. When all the connection information has been entered, clicking OK returns the connection information to the application.

To connect to SQL Server, the Data Links object contains its own ADO Connection object. An instance of that Connection object is returned by the PromptNew method. The previous listing shows the Connection object returned by the dl object's PromptNew method being assigned to the ADO Connection object named cn.

If the user clicks Cancel in the dialog box, however, then no Connection object is returned. Enabling VB's error handler allows the properties of the cn Connection object to be tested without generating a run-time error. The cn Connection object is checked to see if it contains a value. If the Connection object is equal to nothing, then the user clicked the Cancel button. The message is displayed and the program is ended using the End function. Otherwise, the cn Connection object's Open method is executed to establish a session with the SQL Server system identified in the Data Link dialog box. Then all the system resources used by the dl DataLinks object are released when the object is set to nothing before the subroutine is exited.

Ending a Connection

As the previous examples illustrate, before ending your application, you should use the Connection object's Close method to end the database connection. An example of the Close method follows:

```
Dim cn As New ADODB.Connection
'Perform work with the connect and then end it
cn.Close
```

Retrieving Data with the ADO Recordset

ADO lets you retrieve data using either the Recordset or the Command object. Both of these objects can be used with an active Connection object or can open their own connections. In the following section, you see how to retrieve data from SQL Server using the Recordset object. You learn about the differences between the various types of ADO Recordset objects, as well as how to traverse Recordset objects and work with column values using the ADO Fields collection.

ADO Recordset Types

Like the Recordset object found in DAO or RDO's Resultset object, the ADO Recordset object represents a result set that's returned from a database query. ADO Recordset objects support several different types of cursors that correspond to the different types of ODBC cursors. ADO provides support for forward-only, static, keyset, and dynamic Recordset objects. The type of cursor used in an ADO

Recordset object must be set before the Recordset is opened. If you don't specify the type of Recordset object you want to use, ADO automatically uses a forward-only cursor.

Forward-Only Cursors   As a default, ADO uses a forward-only cursor. The *forward-only* cursor provides the best performance and the least overhead of any of the ADO cursor types; however, it's also less capable than other ADO cursors. ADO Recordset objects that use forward-only cursors are updatable, but you can modify only the current row. Any changes in the base table that other users make aren't reflected in the Recordset object.

Static Cursors   A *static* cursor provides a snapshot of the data at the time the cursor was opened. ADO Recordset objects that use static cursors aren't updatable, and they don't reflect any changes made in the base tables unless the cursor is closed and reopened. Because of their static nature, Recordset objects created by static cursors are generally less resource-intensive than Recordset objects that use keyset or dynamic cursors. Because the static cursor makes a local copy of the data, however, you need to be careful about using this type of cursor with large result sets. Using a static cursor with an extremely large result set can definitely be a bigger resource drain than either a keyset or a dynamic cursor.

Keyset Cursors   *Keyset* cursors build a local set of keys where each key is an index to a row in the result set. When your application accesses a Recordset object that uses a keyset cursor, the key value from the local keyset retrieves the corresponding row from the base table. Recordset objects that use keyset cursors are updatable, but after they are fully populated, they don't dynamically reflect changes other users make in the base table. Keyset cursors are capable, but they are also relatively resource-intensive. This is because the client system must maintain the keys for the entire result set, as well as a buffer that contains a block of the actual data values.

Dynamic Cursors   *Dynamic* cursors are the most powerful and capable type of ADO cursors, but they are also the most resource-intensive. Dynamic cursors are similar to keyset cursors. Both use a local set of keys that correspond to each row in the result set, and both are fully updatable. However, unlike Recordset objects that use a keyset cursor, Recordset objects that use dynamic cursors can reflect any changes automatically that other applications make to the base tables. To maintain the result set dynamically, ADO Recordset objects that use dynamic cursors must refresh the result set each time a new fetch operation is performed, automatically updating the local result set with any changes.

Using a Forward-Only Recordset Object

The ADO Recordset object can be used with an existing Connection object, or it can optionally open a connection to the target data source on its own.

TIP

When an ADO Recordset object opens its own Connection object, the ADO object framework automatically creates a Connection object, but that object isn't associated with a Visual Basic program variable. This makes using the Recordset object quick and easy, but it also adds the overhead required to create the Connection object for each new Recordset object. If your application needs to create multiple Recordset objects that use the same database, it's much more efficient to use a Connection object and then associate each new Recordset object with the existing Connection object.

The following code listing illustrates how to use a Recordset object with an ADO Connection object:

```
Private Sub ForwardOnlyRecordset(cn As ADODB.Connection)
    Dim rs As New ADODB.Recordset
    ' Associate the Recordset with the open connection object
    rs.ActiveConnection = cn

    'Use the open method
    rs.Open "Select * From Sales.SalesPerson", , , , adCmdText

    'Display the results in a grid
    DisplayForwardGrid rs, hflxResults

    'Close the recordset & release its resources
    rs.Close
    Set rs = Nothing
End Sub
```

Before using the ADO Recordset object, you need to assign it to a Visual Basic variable. The Dim statement at the beginning of this subroutine creates a new ADO Recordset object named rs. Next, the ActiveConnection property of the rs Recordset object is set to the active Connection object named cn, which was passed into this subroutine as a parameter. Assigning the rs object's ActiveConnection property to an active Connection object associates the new Recordset object with the connected SQL Server system. The Connection object must have been previously instantiated and connected to SQL Server, using one of the connection methods illustrated in the prior Connection object examples. The ADO Connection object could use either the OLE DB Provider for ODBC or the OLE DB Provider for SQL Server. All the subsequent ADO coding for both OLE DB providers is the same.

After the ActiveConnection property is set, a forward-only cursor is opened using the Recordset object's Open method. The Recordset object's Open method takes five optional parameters.

The first parameter is a Variant data type, and as you might think, it can accept a number of different values, such as the name of an existing Command object, a SQL statement, a table name, or the name of a stored procedure. In the preceding example, the first parameter contains a simple SQL Select statement that creates a result set consisting of all the rows and columns contained in the Sales.SalesPerson table that's found in the AdventureWorks database.

The Open method's optional second parameter can be used to associate the Recordset object with an ADO Connection object. This parameter performs exactly the same function as the Recordset object's ActiveConnection property, and you can use this parameter as an alternative to setting the ActiveConnection property. This parameter can accept either a string that contains an OLE DB connection string or a variant that contains the name of an active ADO Connection object. If you specify an OLE DB connection string rather than the name of a Connection object, then ADO implicitly creates a Connection object and uses it to establish a link to the target data source.

The third optional parameter of the Open method specifies the cursor type the Recordset object is to use. If this parameter isn't designated, then the cursor type is set to forward-only by default, which is the simplest and also the best-performing option. Table 8-5 presents the ADO constants used to specify the cursor type an ADO Recordset object will use.

The fourth optional parameter specifies the type of locking the OLE DB provider is to use. If this parameter isn't designated, then the lock type will be set to read-only by default. Table 8-6 presents the ADO constants used to specify the lock type an ADO Recordset object is to use.

ADO Constant	Cursor Type
adOpenForwardOnly	Forward-only cursor (default)
adOpenStatic	Static cursor
adOpenKeyset	Keyset cursor
adOpenDynamic	Dynamic cursor

Table 8-5   *ADO Recordset Cursor Types*

Lock Type	Description
AdLockReadOnly	Read-only (default)
AdLockPessimistic	Pessimistic locking
AdLockOptimistic	Optimistic locking
AdLockBatchOptimistic	Optimistic locking using batch mode updates

Table 8-6   *ADO Recordset Lock Types*

The fifth optional parameter specifies the options of the Open method. The options parameter explicitly tells ADO how to handle the first parameter if the first parameter doesn't contain the name of an ADO Command object.

TIP

While this may seem a bit innocuous, specifying a value for the fifth parameter can result in improved performance because ADO doesn't need to test the data source to determine what type of value was supplied in the first parameter of the Open method. If you specify a constant for the fifth parameter that doesn't match the value supplied in the first parameter, however, then ADO generates an error.

Table 8-7 presents the ADO constants used to specify the options to be used by an ADO Recordset object.

After the Open method completes, the data in the Recordset object is available for processing. In the previous example, the DisplayForwardGrid subroutine is called to display the contents of the rs Recordset object in a grid. In the next section of code, you see how to move through the rows in the Recordset object, as well as how to

Option	Description
adCmdUnknown	The source is unknown and ADO must test for it (default).
adCmdFile	The source is the name of a file.
adCmdStoredProc	The source is the name of a stored procedure.
adCmdTable	The source is the name of a table.
adCmdText	The source is a command (or SQL statement).

Table 8-7   *Recordset Source Options*

access the column information in the Fields collection. The DisplayForwardGrid
subroutine is shown here:

```
Private Sub DisplayForwardGrid _
    (rs As ADODB.Recordset, hflxResults As MSHFlexGrid)
    Dim fld As ADODB.Field

    ' Setup the hflxResults
    hflxResults.Redraw = False
    hflxResults.FixedCols = 0
    hflxResults.FixedRows = 0
    hflxResults.Cols = rs.Fields.Count
    hflxResults.Rows = 1
    hflxResults.Row = 0
    hflxResults.Col = 0
    hflxResults.Clear

    'Setup the hflxResults headings
    For Each fld In rs.Fields
        hflxResults.Text = fld.Name
        hflxResults.ColAlignment(hflxResults.Col) = 1
        hflxResults.ColWidth(hflxResults.Col) = _
          Me.TextWidth(fld.Name & "AA")
        If hflxResults.Col < rs.Fields.Count - 1 Then
            hflxResults.Col = hflxResults.Col + 1
        End If
    Next fld

    ' Move through each row in the record set
    Do Until rs.EOF
        ' Set the position in the hflxResults
        hflxResults.Rows = hflxResults.Rows + 1
        hflxResults.Row = hflxResults.Row + 1
        hflxResults.Col = 0

        'Loop through all fields
        For Each fld In rs.Fields
            hflxResults.Text = fld.Value
            If hflxResults.ColWidth(hflxResults.Col) < _
              Me.TextWidth(fld.Value & "AA") Then
                hflxResults.ColWidth(hflxResults.Col) = _
                    Me.TextWidth(fld.Value & "AA")
            End If
```

```
            If hflxResults.Col < rs.Fields.Count - 1 Then
                hflxResults.Col = hflxResults.Col + 1
            End If
        Next fld

        rs.MoveNext
    Loop

    If hflxResults.Rows = 1 Then
        hflxResults.Rows = 2
    End If
    hflxResults.FixedRows = 1
    hflxResults.Redraw = True
End Sub
```

At the beginning of this subroutine, you can see where an instance of the ADO Recordset object named rs is passed as the first parameter and an instance of the MSHFlexGrid object is passed as the second parameter of the DisplayForwardGrid subroutine. This allows the same subroutine to be reused with many different Recordset and Grid objects. The Dim statement in this subroutine creates an instance of an ADO Field object named fld.

NOTE

Unlike the previous ADO examples, there's no need to use the New keyword to declare either the ADO Recordset object or the ADO Field object. This was because both of these variables are references to instances of the Recordset and Field objects that were already created and, subsequently, passed in to this subroutine.

After the ADO objects have been declared, the next portion of the DisplayForwardGrid subroutine sets up the grid to display the contents of the ADO Recordset object. First the grid's Redraw property is set to False to improve performance and prevent flicker while data is being added to the grid. Next, setting each property to 0 clears any existing FixedCols and FixedRows settings. Then the number of grid columns is set using the Count property of the Recordset objects Fields collection. Each column in the result set is represented by a Field object, and all the Field objects are contained in the Recordset object's Fields collection. Retrieving the Fields collection's Count property allows the grid to be displayed using one grid column per result set column. Next, the grid's Rows property is set up to have at least one row that will contain the column heading information. Then the grid's Row and Col properties are used to set the current grid cell at row 0 column 0 (the upper left-hand corner of the grid) and the grid's Clear method is executed to ensure no unwanted data is in the grid.

Once the initial preparation of the grid object is completed, the heading values and sizes for each of the grid's columns are set up. Every column in the result set has a corresponding Field object in the Recordset object's Fields collection. A For Each loop iterates through all the Field objects contained in the Fields collection. The first action within the For Each loop sets the current row to the first row in the grid. Then the Field object's Name property is used as heading text for the grid columns. Next, the grid's ColAlignment property for each column is set to left-align the cell text by setting the ColAlignment property to 1. To set the alignment of the current column, the ColAlignment property requires the index of the current grid column. In this case, the index is supplied using the hflxResults.Col property. Next, the column width of each column in the grid is set using the grid's ColWidth property. The ColWidth property must be assigned a value in *twips* (one twentieth of a printer's point); Visual Basic's TextWidth function is used to return the number of twips required to display the name of each Field object. The correct number of twips is determined by creating a placeholder string using the Field object's Name property (which contains the name of the column), plus two extra characters (AA) that help to prevent the grid columns from appearing too crowded. Finally, the current column is incremented by adding 1 to the value of the grid's current Col property.

NOTE

Because the ADO object framework doesn't provide an OrdinalPosition property like the DAO and RDO frameworks, you must either add additional code to track the current column position manually or use the value of the Field object's index in the Fields collection.

Next, a Do Until loop reads through all the columns in the Recordset object. The Do Until loop continues until the Recordset's *EOF (End of File)* property becomes true—which indicates all the rows in the Recordset have been read. Inside the Do Until loop, the grid's Rows property is incremented to expand the size of the grid for each row read from the Recordset, and the Row property is incremented to move the current position to the new grid row. Then the current grid column is set to 0, which is the first column, and a For Each loop is used to move the data values contained in the Fields collection to the grid columns. An If test ensures the code doesn't attempt to access an invalid grid column. After all the Field values have been processed, the Recordset object's MoveNext method moves the cursor to the next row in the Recordset object. You can see the contents of the ADO Recordset displayed in Figure 8-11.

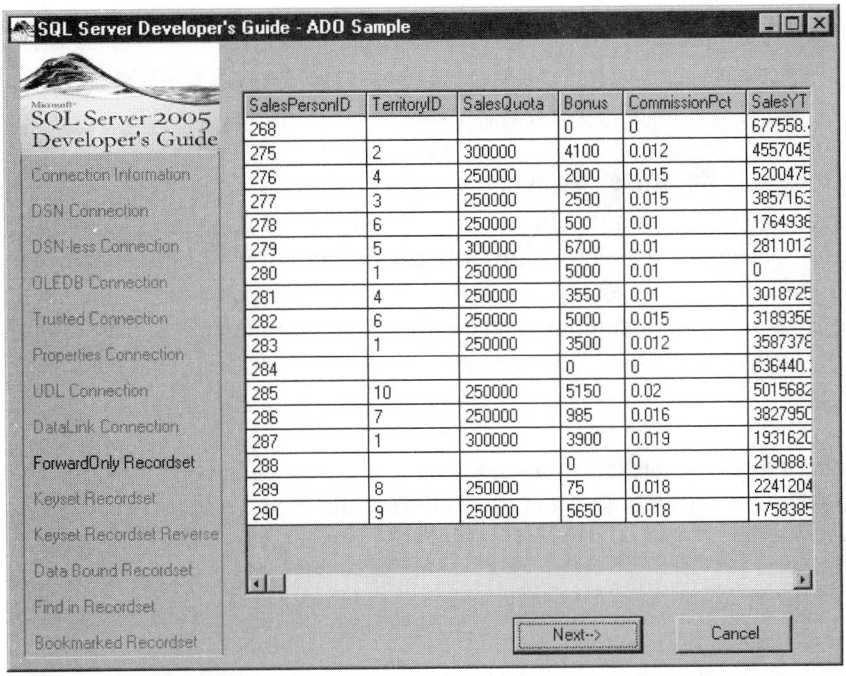

Figure 8-11 *Using a ForwardOnly Recordset*

After the DisplayForwardGrid subroutine completes, then all the data contained in the rs Recordset object is displayed in the grid. The end user can view the data and scroll through it using the navigation tools provided by the grid object. Once the Recordset object has been processed, control is returned to the calling routine. Then the Recordset object is closed and its resources are released by setting it to Nothing.

Closing a Recordset

Before ending your application, close any open Recordset objects using the Recordset object's Close method. An example of the Close method follows:

```
rs.Close
```

You could also close the connection by setting the Recordset object to nothing, as follows:

```
Set rs = Nothing
```

TIP

A good programming practice is to always close any open Recordset objects immediately as soon as they're no longer needed by your application.

Using a Keyset Recordset Object

The preceding code example illustrated how to use ADO to create a simple Recordset object that uses a forward-only cursor. The forward-only cursor is fast and efficient, but it's not as capable as the other cursor types. For instance, while the forward-only cursor can only make a single pass through a Recordset in forward order, a keyset cursor allows multiple passes, as well as forward and backward scrolling.

Processing a Keyset Recordset in Forward Order   The following code illustrates how to use an ADO Recordset object that uses a keyset cursor:

```
Private Sub KeysetRecordset(cn As ADODB.Connection)
    Dim rs As New ADODB.Recordset
    ' Associate the Recordset with the open connection
    rs.ActiveConnection = cn
    rs.Source = "Select * From Sales.SalesTerritory Order By TerritoryID"

    ' Pass the Open method the SQL and Recordset type parameters
    rs.Open , , adOpenKeyset, adLockReadOnly

    ' Display the recordset -- use a 1 to display in forward order
    DisplayKeysetGrid rs, hflxResults, 1

    rs.Close
    Set rs = Nothing
End Sub
```

In this example, a new ADO Recordset object named rs is created. Then the ActiveConnection property of the rs Recordset object is set to cn, which is the name of an existing ADO Connection object that has an active database connection. Next, the Recordset object's Source property is assigned a simple SQL Select statement that returns all the rows and columns from the Sales.SalesTerritory table, ordered according to the values of the TerritoryID column.

NOTE

For publication purposes, several of the examples in this chapter use simple, unqualified SQL Select statements. Unless you know the target tables are relatively small, however, you should try to keep your own result sets as small as possible by explicitly defining just the desired columns and using the SELECT statement's WHERE clause to retrieve only the rows your application will use.

Next, the Open method executes the source SQL statement on the target database. In this example, the first two parameters of the Open method needn't be specified, because they were already set using the Source and ActiveConnection properties of the Recordset object. The value of adOpenKeyset in the third parameter indicates this Recordset object will use a keyset cursor. The value of adLockReadOnly in the fourth parameter makes the Recordset read-only.

After the Open method has executed the query, the DisplayKeysetGrid subroutine displays the contents of the rs Recordset object in a grid. The DisplayKeysetGrid subroutine use three parameters: the name of an ADO Recordset object, the name of an MSHFlexGrid object, and an integer value that controls the direction in which the data will be displayed. Because the capabilities of the keyset cursor are greater than those of the forward-only cursor, this subroutine contains a couple of enhancements that can take advantage of those capabilities. The code for the DisplayKeysetGrid subroutine is shown here:

```
Private Sub DisplayKeysetGrid _
  (rs As ADODB.Recordset, hflxResults As MSHFlexGrid, _
  Optional nDirection As Integer)
    Dim fld As ADODB.Field
    Dim nForward As Integer
    Dim nReverse As Integer
    On Error Resume Next

    nForward = 1
    nReverse = 2

    'If the direction parameter is not provided use forward
    If IsMissing(nDirection) Then
        nDirection = nForward
    End If

    ' Setup the hflxResults
    hflxResults.Redraw = False
    hflxResults.Clear
    hflxResults.FixedCols = 0
    hflxResults.FixedRows = 0
```

```
hflxResults.Cols = rs.Fields.Count
rs.MoveLast
hflxResults.Rows = rs.RecordCount + 1
hflxResults.Row = 0
hflxResults.Col = 0

'Setup the hflxResults headings
 For Each fld In rs.Fields
    hflxResults.Text = fld.Name
    hflxResults.ColAlignment(hflxResults.Col) = 1
    hflxResults.ColWidth(hflxResults.Col) = _
      Me.TextWidth(fld.Name & "AA")
    If hflxResults.Col < rs.Fields.Count - 1 Then
        hflxResults.Col = hflxResults.Col + 1
    End If
Next fld

If nDirection = nForward Then
    ' Position at beginning
    rs.MoveFirst
Else
    ' Position at end
    rs.MoveLast
End If

' Check for either the beginning or the end of the recordset
Do Until rs.BOF Or rs.EOF
    ' Set the position in the hflxResults
    hflxResults.Row = hflxResults.Row + 1
    hflxResults.Col = 0

    'Loop through all fields
    For Each fld In rs.Fields
        hflxResults.Text = fld.Value
        If hflxResults.ColWidth(hflxResults.Col) < _
          Me.TextWidth(fld.Value & "AA") Then
            hflxResults.ColWidth(hflxResults.Col) = _
              Me.TextWidth(fld.Value & "AA")
        End If
        If hflxResults.Col < rs.Fields.Count - 1 Then
            hflxResults.Col = hflxResults.Col + 1
        End If
    Next fld
```

```
        ' Read according to direction
        If nDirection = nForward Then
            rs.MoveNext
        Else
            rs.MovePrevious
        End If
    Loop

    ' If there was no data returned set the grid to show 2 rows
    If hflxResults.Rows < 2 Then
        hflxResults.Rows = 2
    End If

    ' Set the fixed rows and redraw the grid
    hflxResults.FixedRows = 1
    hflxResults.Redraw = True
End Sub
```

As in the DisplayForwardGrid subroutine presented earlier, the parameters used by the DisplayKeysetGrid subroutine allow it to be reused by many different Recordset and Grid objects. However, because this subroutine is intended to be used with keyset cursors, which support both forward and backward scrolling, it uses an additional optional parameter that can control the direction the data is to be listed. The internals of this subroutine are also a bit different than the DisplayForwardGrid subroutine to allow it to take advantage of some of the additional capabilities provided the Keyset Recordset object.

At the beginning of this subroutine, an ADO Field object is declared, followed by two Integer variables. The ADO Field object is used to contain and manipulate the values of each column returned by the Recordset object. The Integer variables are used to determine the direction the data will be presented and to improve the readability of the code. Next, the optional parameter is tested to determine if it was supplied. If the parameter is missing, then the default Recordset processing direction is set to forward.

The section of code immediately following these variables sets up the grid. This section is similar to the DisplayForwardGrid shown earlier, but one notable difference exists. Because keyset cursors support backward movement, this subroutine is able to use the Recordset object's MoveLast method to move to the end of the Recordset. This populates the Recordset object, which can then be used to size the grid to the appropriate number of rows. This technique results in a slightly better performance because the grid needs to be sized only once rather than resized as each row is read. In this example, the grid is sized using the value from the Recordset's RecordCount property, plus one additional row for the column headings.

Next, the grid columns are sized and the column headings are set to the database column names for each Field object in the Recordset object's Fields collection. While this code is identical to the ForwardOnlyGrid subroutine, the next section of code after that illustrates how the keyset cursor's capability to scroll forward and backward is used. The value passed in to the third parameter of the DisplayKeysetGrid subroutine controls the direction the Recordset data is to be listed in the grid. A value of 1 lists the data in forward order, while a value of 2 causes the Recordset data to be listed in backward order. The If test compares the value of the nDirection variable to the value of the Integer variable named nForward. If the value is equal, then the Recordset is displayed in forward order and the cursor is positioned to the beginning of the Recordset object using the MoveFirst method. Otherwise, the contents of the Recordset are displayed in reverse order and the cursor is positioned to the last row in the Recordset using the rs Recordset object's MoveLast method.

The next section of code reads the contents of the Recordset object and is essentially the same as the code in the previous DisplayForwardGrid subroutine. A Do loop is used to read all the rows in the Recordset object. And for every row, a For Each loop copies each row's data from the Fields collection to the grid. Two notable differences exist, however. First, because the Recordset object may be processed either from front-to-back or back-to-front, the Do Until loop has been modified to check for either the BOF indicator or the EOF indicator. As you would expect, the EOF property contains a value of True when the last row in the Recordset has been read using the MoveNext method, while the BOF property contains a value of True when the first row in the Recordset object is read using the MovePrevious method. Second, after the For Each loop has been executed and all the Field values for the current row have been copied to the grid, the nDirection variable is checked again to determine which row is to be read next. If the nDirection variable indicates the Recordset object is being processed in a forward direction, then the MoveNext method is executed to read the next row. Otherwise, the rs Recordset object's MovePrevious method is executed to read the prior row.

After the DisplayKeysetGrid subroutine has completed, the contents of the Recordset object are displayed in the grid, allowing the end user to view the data. Then, the control is returned to the calling KeysetRecordset subroutine, where the Recordset object is closed and its resources are released by setting the Recordset object to Nothing.

Processing a Keyset Recordset in Reverse Order   While the DisplayKeysetGrid subroutine has the capability of displaying the data in a Recordset object in either forward or backward order, the preceding example only displayed the data in a forward fashion. The following subroutine illustrates how the DisplayKeysetGrid subroutine can be used with a Keyset type of Recordset to display the Recordset data in reverse order:

```
Private Sub KeysetRecordsetReverse(cn As ADODB.Connection)
    Dim rs As New ADODB.Recordset
    ' Pass the Open method the SQL and Recordset type parameters
    rs.Open "Select * From Sales.SalesTerritory", _
        cn, adOpenKeyset, adLockReadOnly, adCmdText

    ' Display the grid -- use a 2 to display in reverse order
    DisplayKeysetGrid rs, Grid, 2

    rs.Close
    Set rs = Nothing
End Sub
```

The example demonstrates a couple of significant differences from the previous examples. In addition to using the DisplayKeysetGrid subroutine to display the Recordset in reserve order, this subroutine also shows how to use the first and second parameters of the Recordset object's Open method to pass in the source and connection information. Using the first and second parameters of the Open method is an alternative to assigning values explicitly to the Recordset object's ActiveConnection and Source properties. The first parameter sets the Source property to the simple SQL Select statement that can retrieve all the rows from the Sales.SalesTerritory table. The second parameter sets the ActiveConnection to an existing Connection object named cn. The third parameter specifies a keyset cursor. The fourth parameter sets the lock type to read-only, and the fifth parameter identifies the first ("source") parameter as command text.

After the Open method completes, the DisplayKeysetGrid function is called. The name of the open Recordset object is passed into the first parameter, the name of an existing grid is used in the second parameter, and the value of 2 is used in the third parameter to set the display order to backward. You can see the Keyset Recordset object displayed in reserve order in Figure 8-12.

Using Data Bound Recordsets

The previous examples illustrated how to process the contents of a Recordset object manually and display them on a Hierarchical FlexGrid. Manually processing the Recordset object gives you complete control over how you want the data to be

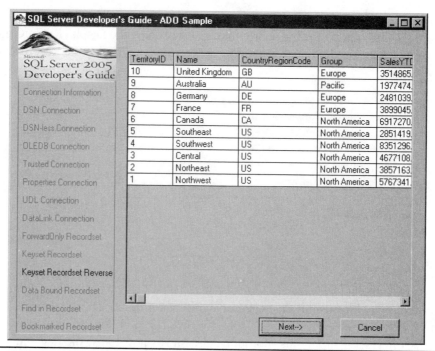

Figure 8-12   *Display a Keyset Recordset in reverse order*

presented, as well as how you want the grid to be displayed. For instance, the earlier examples illustrated presenting the column names at the top of the grid, dynamically resizing the grid columns according to the size of the data, and presenting the data in a different order than it was retrieved. Sometimes, however, these types of capabilities are more than is required and you might simply want to display a result set in a grid quickly. Using the Hierarchical FlexGrid's data-bound capabilities in conjunction with the ADO Recordset object lets you quickly display the contents of an ADO Recordset with little coding.

NOTE

Data binding *refers to creating an association between a database object like an ADO Recordset object and a grid. When an interface object is bound to an ADO object, changing the data that's displayed in the interface object automatically changes the data in the underlying database object. Data binding is also often used between an ADO Recordset object and a group of Text Boxes to create simple data entry forms.*

The listing that follows illustrates how to bind the Hierarchical FlexGrid to an ADO Recordset object:

```
Private Sub DataBoundGrid(cn As ADODB.Connection)
    Dim rs As New ADODB.Recordset
    ' Open the  recordset
    With rs
        ' Set the properties & open
        .Source = "Select * From Sales.SpecialOffer"
        .ActiveConnection = cn
        .CursorType = adOpenKeyset
        .LockType = adLockOptimistic
        .Open
    End With

    ' Populate the grid
    Set hflxResults.DataSource = rs
End Sub
```

As in the previous examples, in this example you can see a new instance of the Recordset object created at the top of the subroutine. And in this example, the Recordset object's important connection attributes are set inside a With block. The Source property is assigned a SQL statement that will retrieve all the rows and columns from the Sales.SpecialOffer table. The ActiveConnection property is assigned an instance of the cn ADO Connection object that's passed into the subroutine as a parameter. Next, the CursorType and LockType properties are set to adOpenKeyset and adLockOptimistic. The rs Recordset object's Open method is then executed to run the query and return the data to the Recordset object.

After the Recordset has been opened, it can then be assigned to the Hierarchical Flexgrids's DataSource property using the Set statement. As soon as the DataSource property is set to an open Recordset object, the grid is automatically populated with the contents of the Recordset. Figure 8-13 presents the sample results of using a data-bound grid.

Assigning the DataSource property of a Hierarchical FlexGrid is an extremely easy method for displaying the contents of the Recordset, but it lacks the control that's available when you manually assign the Recordset values to the grid. For instance, there's no way to control what's displayed in the grid column headings. There's also no way to size the grid columns, align the data in the cells, or control the formatting of the data displayed.

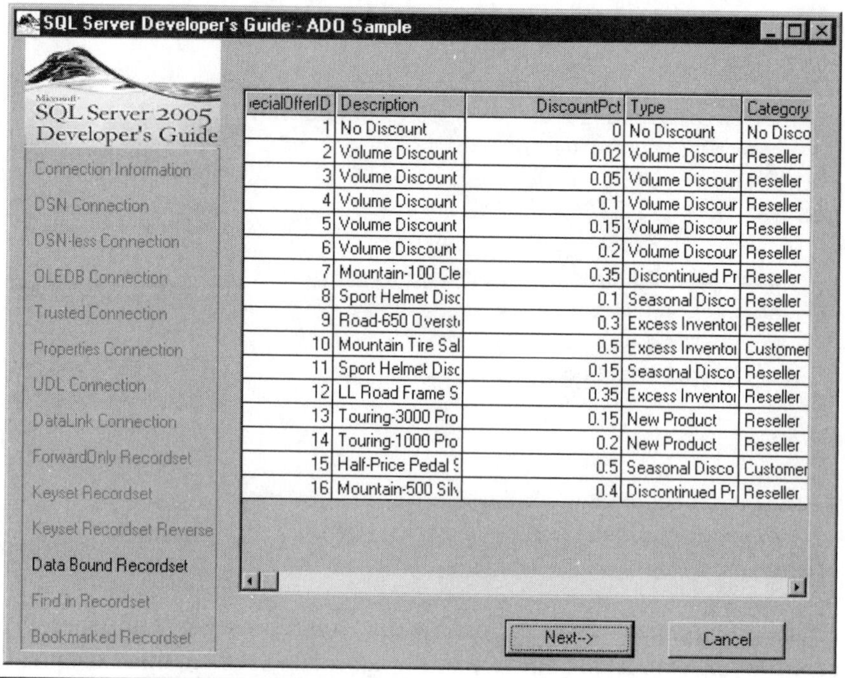

Figure 8-13 *Using a data-bound grid*

Finding and Bookmarking Rows

ADO Recordset objects support several methods for navigating through the contents of the Recordset. Previous examples have illustrated using the MoveFirst, MoveLast, MoveNext, and MovePrevious methods. All these methods are intended for sequential processing, where you read one record after another in the order in which they occur in the Recordset. However, ADO Keyset and Dynamic Recordsets objects also support several methods that provide random navigation through a Recordset. In the following example, you see how the Find method can be used to locate a given row, or group of rows, within a Recordset, as well as how a bookmark can be used to jump quickly to a specific row. An ADO Bookmark is a property of the Recordset object that returns a unique identifier for the current record. This unique record identifier doesn't change during the life of a Recordset. By setting this property to a valid bookmark, you can also use this property to move the pointer to a specified record. The following listing illustrates how to use the Find method and how to save an ADO Recordset bookmark:

```
Private Sub BookMarkFind(cn As ADODB.Connection, _
   rs As ADODB.Recordset, oBookMark As Variant)
     With rs
         .CursorLocation = adUseClient
         .Open "Select * from Sales.SpecialOffer Order By SpecialOfferID", cn
     End With

     ' Find Mountain Tire Sale and set a bookmark
     rs.Find "Description = 'Mountain Tire Sale'", , adSearchForward
     oBookMark = rs.Bookmark

     ' Find Volume Discount over 60, display the remainder of the resultset
     rs.Find "Description = 'Volume Discount over 60'", , adSearchBackward

     DisplayForwardGrid rs, hflxResults
End Sub
```

In the beginning of the BookmarkFind subroutine, you can see where instances of the ADO Connection and Recordset objects are passed into the subroutine. In addition, a Variant variable named oBookMark is used to pass back the bookmark to be set inside this routine.

Next, a With statement is used to assign values to properties of the rs Recordset object. Using a value of adUseClient indicates the Recordset will be maintained on the client system rather than on the SQL Server system. Using a local cursor typically provides much better performance for processing small and medium result sets consisting of a few hundred records. Then the Open method is used along with a SQL select statement that retrieves all the rows and columns from the Sales. SpecialOffer table and orders them by SpecialOfferID.

After the Open method has completed, the rs Recordset object will be populated and the Find method can then be used to locate specific records within the Recordset. In this code listing, the Find method is used twice. The first instance of the Find method is used to locate the first row in the Recordset where the Description column contains the value of Mountain Tire Sale. The first parameter of the Find method takes the search argument, which uses the same type of search criteria used in a typical Where clause. The ADO Find method search criteria can use a single field name with one comparison operator and a literal value to use in the search. The search parameter supports using equal, not equal, greater than, less than, and Like operators. The second parameter of the Find method isn't used in this example, but optionally, it indicates the number of records to skip before attempting to find the desired record. The third parameter indicates the direction of the search. The value of adSearchForward causes the search to move forward from the current pointer position, while the value of adSearchBackward causes the search to go backward from the current position in the Recordset. If the Find isn't successful, the EOF indicator will be set to True in the rs Recordset object. Likewise, if the pointer is at the end of the Recordset and another Find is executed, it will fail unless you reposition the pointer in the Recordset. After the row containing the value of Mountain Tire Sale is located using the Find method, then the Bookmark property of that row is assigned to the oBookmark variable to allow that row to be located easily later.

Next, the Find method is used a second time to locate the row in the Recordset object where the Description column contained the value of Volume Discount over 60. In this case, because Volume Discount over 60 occurs before Mountain Tire Sale in the Recordset set object, the adSearchBackward flag is used to search the Recordset object in reverse order. After the pointer is positioned in the Recordset object to Volume Discount over 60, the DisplayForwardGrid subroutine is called to display the remaining contents of the Recordset object. The results of the Find method are shown in Figure 8-14.

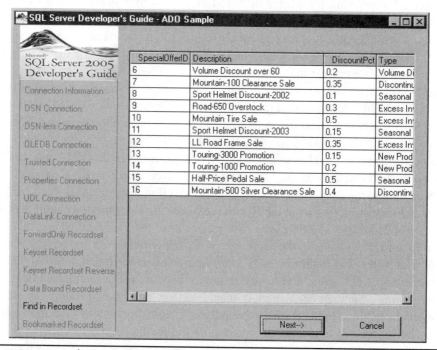

Figure 8-14 *Using the Recordset object's Find method*

After a bookmark has been saved, you can then use that saved bookmark to position the pointer quickly to the bookmarked row in the Recordset. In the previous code listing, the bookmark value of the row where the Description column contained the value of Mountain Tire Sale was saved in the Variant variable named oBookmark. In the next listing, you can see how to use that saved bookmark value to reposition the pointer in the Recordset.

```
Private Sub BookMarkJump(cn As ADODB.Connection, _
   rs As ADODB.Recordset, oBookMark As Variant)
     ' Jump to previous bookmark and display the result set
     rs.Bookmark = oBookMark
     DisplayForwardGrid rs, hflxResults
End Sub
```

In the BookMarkJump subroutine shown in this listing, you can see where instances of the ADO Connection and Recordset objects are passed into the subroutine, followed by the oBookMark Variant variable. In this example, the oBookMark variable contains the value of the bookmark that was saved in the earlier listing. This means it contains a value that uniquely identifies the row in the Recordset that contains the value of Mountain Tire Sale.

Assigning the .rsBookMark property with the saved bookmark value immediately repositions the pointer in the Recordset to the bookmarked row. Next, the DisplayForwardGrid subroutine is used to display the contents of the Recordset, beginning with the value of Mountain Tire Sale. You can see the results of using the bookmark in Figure 8-15.

Using Prepared SQL and the ADO Command Object

The capability to use prepared SQL statements and parameter markers is one of the features that enables ADO to be used in developing high-performance database applications. Using prepared statements in your database applications is one of those small changes that can result in big performance gains. Dynamic SQL statements must be parsed and a data access plan must be created each time the Dynamic SQL statement is executed—even if exactly the same statement is reused.

Although dynamic SQL works well for ad hoc queries, it isn't the best for executing the type of repetitive SQL statements that make up *online transaction processing (OLTP)*–type applications. *Prepared SQL,* or *static SQL,* as it's sometimes called, is better suited to OLTP applications where a high degree of SQL statement reuse occurs. With prepared SQL, the SQL statement is parsed and the creation of the data access

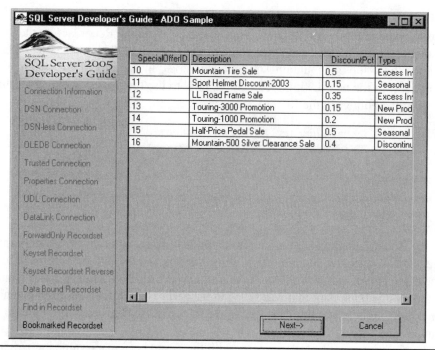

Figure 8-15 *Using an ADO Recordset bookmark*

plan is only performed once. Subsequent calls using the prepared statements are fast because the compiled data access plan is already in place.

TIP

For prepared SQL statements, SQL Server 2005 creates data access plans in the procedure cache. The procedure cache is a part of SQL Server's buffer cache, which is an area of working memory used by SQL Server. Although data access plans stored in the procedure cache are shared by all users, each user has a separate execution context. In addition, the access plans created for ad hoc SQL statement queries can also be stored in SQL Server procedure cache. However, they are stored only if the cost to execute the plan exceeds a certain internal threshold, and they are reused only under "safe" conditions. Unlike when using prepared SQL statements, you can't rely on the data access plans created for these dynamic SQL statements being maintained in the procedure cache.

The following code example shows how to create an ADO query that uses a prepared SQL statement:

```
Private Sub CommandPS(cn As ADODB.Connection)
    Dim cmd As New ADODB.Command
    Dim rs As New ADODB.Recordset
    With cmd
        .ActiveConnection = cn
        ' Set up the SQL statement
        .CommandText = "Select * From Sales.SalesOrderDetail" _
          & "Where SalesOrderID = ?"
        ' Add the parameter (optional)
        .CreateParameter , adInteger, adParamInput, 4
        'Set the parameter value
        .Parameters(0).Value = 43695
    End With

    'Set up the input parameter
    Set rs = cmd.Execute

    DisplayForwardGrid rs, Grid

    rs.Close
    Set rs = Nothing
End Sub
```

In the beginning of this subroutine, a new ADO Command object name cmd is created, along with an ADO Recordset object named rs. The Command object is used to create and execute the prepared SQL statement, while the Recordset object is used to hold the returned result set.

Next, the Visual Basic With block works with a group of the Command object's properties. The first line of code in the With block sets the Command object's ActiveConnection property to the name of an active ADO Connection object named cn. Then the CommandText property is assigned a string containing the SQL statement to be executed. This SQL statement returns all columns in the Sales.SalesOrderDetail table where the value of the SalesOrderID column equals a value to be supplied at run time. The question mark (?) is a parameter marker. Each replaceable parameter must be indicated using a question mark. This example SQL statement uses a single parameter in the Where clause, so only one parameter marker is needed. Next, the CreateParameter method defines the attribute of the parameter.

The CreateParameter statement accepts four parameters. The first optional parameter accepts a string that can be used to give the parameter a name. The second parameter accepts a Long variable, which identifies the data type to be used with the parameter. In the preceding example, the value of adInteger indicates the parameter will contain character data. The following table lists the ADO data type constants and matches them with their corresponding SQL Server data types:

SQL Server Data Type	ADO Data Type
Bigint	adBigInt
Binary	adBinary
Bit	adBoolean
Char	adChar
Datetime	adDBTimeStamp
Decimal	adNumeric
Float	adDouble
Image	adLongVarBinary
Int	adInteger
Money	adCurrency
Nchar	adWChar
Ntext	adWChar
Numeric	adNumeric
Nvarchar	adWChar
Real	adSingle
smalldatetime	adTimeStamp
Smallint	adSmallInt
smallmoney	adCurrency
sql_variant	adVariant
Sysname	adWChar
Text	adLongVarChar
Timestamp	adBinary
Tinyint	adUnsignedTinyInt
uniqueidentifier	adGUID
Varbinary	adVarBinary
Varchar	adVarChar

The third parameter of the CreateParameter statement specifies whether the parameter is to be used as input, output, or both. The value of adParamInput shows this is an input-only parameter. Table 8-8 lists the allowable values for this parameter.

ADO Direction Constant	Description
adParamInput	The parameter is input-only.
adParamOutput	The parameter is an output parameter.
adParamInputOutput	The parameter is to be used for both input and output.
adParamReturnValue	The parameter contains the return value from a stored procedure. This is typically only used with the first parameter (Parameters(0)).

Table 8-8 *ADO Parameter Direction Constants*

The fourth parameter specifies the length of the parameter. In the preceding example, a value of 4 indicates the parameter is four bytes long.

After the parameter characteristics have been specified, the value 43695 is placed into the Value property of the first (and in this case, only) Parameter object in the Parameters collection. Parameters(0) corresponds to the ? parameter marker used in the SQL Select statement. Assigning 43695 to the Parameter object's Value property essentially causes the SQL statement to be evaluated as

```
Select * From Sales.SalesOrderDetail Where SalesOrderID = 43695
```

Next, the Command object's Execute method runs the Select statement on SQL Server. Because this SQL Select statement returns a result set, the output of the cmd object is assigned to an ADO Recordset object. The rs Recordset object is then passed into the DisplayForwardGrid subroutine, which displays the contents of the Recordset object. Finally, the Recordset object is closed using the Close method. You can see the results of the prepared SQL statement code in Figure 8-16.

If this Command object were executed only a single time, there would be no performance benefits over simply using the ADO Recordset object to execute the query. Executing this Command object multiple times, however, results in improved performance because the SQL statement and access plan have already been prepared. To execute a Command object multiple times, you would simply assign a new value to the Parameter object's Value property, and then rerun the Command object's Execute method.

Executing Dynamic SQL with the ADO Connection Object

ADO can also be used to execute dynamic SQL statements on the remote database. Dynamic SQL can be used for a variety of both data management and data

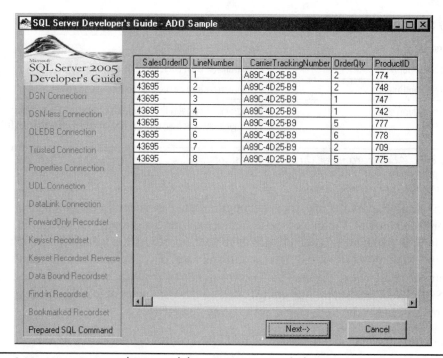

Figure 8-16 *Using Prepared SQL and the ADO Command object*

manipulation tasks. The following example illustrates how you can create a table named
Sales.SalesDepartment in the AdventureWorks database:

```
Private Sub CreateTable(cn As ADODB.Connection)
    Dim sSQL As String
    On Error Resume Next
    'Make certain that the table is created by dropping the table
    ' If the table doesn't exist the code will move on to the
    ' next statement
    sSQL = "Drop Table Sales.SalesDepartment"
    cn.Execute sSQL

    'Reset the error handler and create the table
    ' If an error is encountered it will be displayed
    On Error GoTo ErrorHandler
    sSQL = "Create Table Sales.SalesDepartment " _
        & "(Dep_ID Char(4) Not Null, Dep_Name Char(25), " _
        & "Primary Key(Dep_ID))"
```

```
        cn.Execute sSQL
        Exit Sub

ErrorHandler:
        DisplayADOError
End Sub
```

This CreateTable subroutine actually performs two separate SQL action queries. The first statement deletes a table, and the second statement re-creates the table. The SQL Drop statement ensures the table doesn't exist prior to running the SQL Create statement.

Near the beginning of the subroutine, Visual Basic's On Error statement enables error handling for this subroutine. In this first instance, the error handler is set up to trap any run-time errors and then resume execution of the subroutine with the statement following the error. This method traps the potential error that could be generated by executing the SQL Drop statement when there's no existing table.

Using the ADO Connection object's Execute method is the simplest way to perform dynamic SQL statements. In this example, an existing Connection object currently connected to SQL Server issues the SQL statement. The first parameter of the Execute method takes a string that contains the command to be issued. The first instance uses the SQL Drop Table statement that deletes any existing instances of the table named Sales.SalesDepartment.

Next, Visual Basic's error handler is reset to branch to the ErrorHandler label if any run-time errors are encountered. This allows any errors encountered during the creation of the Sales.SalesDepartment table to be displayed by the DisplayADOError subroutine. For more details about ADO error handling, see the section "Error Handling" later in this chapter. The SQL Create Table statement is then performed using the Connection object's Execute method.

NOTE

The Sales.SalesDepartment table isn't part of the example AdventureWorks database. The Sales. SalesDepartment table is created to illustrate database update techniques, without altering the contents of the original tables in the AdventureWorks database.

Modifying Data with ADO

You can modify data with ADO in a number of ways. First, ADO supports updatable Recordset objects that can use the AddNew, Update, and Delete methods to modify the data contained in an updatable Recordset object. ADO also supports updating data using both dynamic and prepared SQL. In the next part of this chapter, you see how to update SQL Server data using an ADO Recordset object, followed by several examples that illustrate how to update data using prepared SQL and the ADO Command object.

Updating Data with the ADO Recordset Object

In addition to performing queries, Recordset objects can also be used to update data. As you have probably surmised after seeing the various parameters of the Recordset object's Open method, however, not all ADO Recordset objects are updatable. The capability to update a Recordset depends on the type of cursor the Recordset object uses, as well as the locking type used. Both these factors can be specified as parameters of the Open method or by setting the Recordset object's CursorType and LockType properties before the Recordset is opened.

Both the CursorType and LockType properties influence the capability to update a Recordset object. Table 8-9 summarizes the Recordset object cursor and lock types and their capability to support data update methods.

The lock type parameter takes precedence over the cursor type parameter. For instance, if the lock type is set to adLockReadOnly, then the result set isn't updatable, no matter which cursor type is used.

Inserting Rows to a Recordset Object   You can use the Recordset object's AddNew method in combination with the Update method to add rows to an updatable ADO

Recordset Cursor Type	Updatable?
adOpenForwardOnly	Yes (current row only)
adOpenStatic	No
adOpenKeyset	Yes
adOpenDynamic	Yes
Recordset Lock Type	**Updatable?**
adLockReadOnly	No
adLockPessimistic	Yes
adLockOptimistic	Yes
adLockBatchOptimistic	Yes

Table 8-9   *ADO Recordset Cursor and Lock Types and Updates*

result set. The following code illustrates how you can add rows to a Recordset object that was created using a keyset cursor:

```
Private Sub CursorAdd(cn As ADODB.Connection)
    Dim rs As New ADODB.Recordset
    Dim i As Integer
    'Pass in the SQL, Connection, Cursor type, lock type and
    'source type
    rs.Open "Select Dep_ID, Dep_Name From Sales.SalesDepartment", _
      cn, adOpenKeyset, adLockOptimistic, adCmdText

    'Add 50 rows to the Sales.SalesDepartment table
    ' Note that the Bang ! notation is used to specify column names
    For i = 1 To 50
        rs.AddNew
        rs!Dep_ID = i
        rs!Dep_Name = "Department " & CStr(i)
        rs.Update
    Next

    'Display the new rows in a grid
    DisplayKeysetGrid rs, Grid, 1

    rs.Close
End Sub
```

The first parameter of the Recordset object's Open method accepts a string containing a SQL statement that defines the result set. In this case, the result set consists of the Dep_ID and Dep_Name columns from the Sales.SalesDepartment table created in the earlier dynamic SQL example. The second parameter of the Open method contains the name of an active Connection object named cn. The third parameter uses the constant adOpenKeyset to specify that the Recordset object will use a keyset cursor. The fourth parameter contains the value adLockOptimistic. These two parameters indicate this Recordset object set is updatable and will use optimistic record locking. After the result set has been opened, a For Next loop is used to add 50 rows to the Recordset object. Within the For Next loop, the AddNew method is called to create a row buffer that will contain the new row values. Unlike the earlier examples in this chapter that accessed columns by iterating through the Fields collection, this example illustrates how to access individual columns using the column name and Bang (!) notation.

The value of the Dep_ID column is set using a unique integer value obtained by using the loop counter. The Dep_Name column is set using the string formed by concatenating the literal "Department" and the string representation of the loop counter. After the row values have been set, the Update method is called to add the row to the Recordset object and the data source. Next, the DisplayKeysetGrid subroutine is called, which displays the new row values in a grid. Finally, the Close method is used to close the Recordset object.

Updating Rows with the Recordset The Recordset object's Update method can be used to update rows in an updatable ADO result set. The following code illustrates how you can update the rows in an ADO Recordset object created using a keyset cursor:

```
Private Sub CursorUpdate(cn As ADODB.Connection)
    Dim rs As New ADODB.Recordset
    Dim i As Integer
    Dim sTemp As String
    ' Pass in SQL, Connection, cursor type, lock type and source type
    rs.Open "Select Dep_ID, Dep_Name From Sales.SalesDepartment", _
        cn, adOpenKeyset, adLockOptimistic, adCmdText

    Do Until rs.EOF
        'Trim off the blanks - ADO doesn't truncate fixed char data
        sTemp = Trim(rs!Dep_Name)
        rs!Dep_Name = "Updated " & sTemp
        'Update the row
        rs.Update
        rs.MoveNext
    Loop

    'Display the updated rows in a grid
    DisplayKeysetGrid rs, Grid, 1

    rs.Close
End Sub
```

Again, the Recordset object's Open method is used to create a new ADO Recordset object named rs. The first parameter of the Open method accepts a string that specifies the result set. In this case, Recordset object consists of the Dep_ID and the Dep_Name columns from the Sales.SalesDepartment table. An active Connection object named cn is used in the second parameter. The adOpenKeyset and asLockOptimistic constants used in the third and fourth parameters indicate the Recordset object will use an updatable keyset cursor and optimistic record locking.

After the Recordset object set has been created, a Do Until loop reads through all the rows in the Recordset object. The loop ends when the Recordset object's EOF property turns true. Within the Do loop, the value of the Dep_Name column is set to a new string value that begins with the literal "Updated" concatenated with the current column value.

Then the Update method is called to update the row Recordset object, and the MoveNext method positions the cursor to the next row. After all the rows in the Recordset have been updated, the DisplayKeysetGrid function displays the contents of the updated Sales.SalesDepartment table. Finally, the Close method closes the Recordset object.

Deleting Rows from a Recordset Object   The Recordset object's Delete method removes rows in an updatable ADO Recordset object. The following code illustrates how you can delete rows in a forward-only type of result set:

```
Private Sub CursorDelete(cn As ADODB.Connection)
    Dim rs As New ADODB.Recordset
    'Pass in the SQL, Connection, cursor type, lock type and source
    'type. Note that this is a forward-only cursor but it can update
    ' the current row.
    rs.Open "Select Dep_ID, Dep_name From Sales.SalesDepartment", _
      cn, adOpenForwardOnly, adLockOptimistic, adCmdText

    'Delete all of the rows
    Do Until rs.EOF
        rs.Delete
        rs.MoveNext
    Loop

    'Display the empty Recordset in a grid
    DisplayForwardGrid rs, Grid

    rs.Close
End Sub
```

As in the previous examples, the Open method is used to create a new ADO Recordset object named rs that contains the Dep_ID and Dep_Name columns from the Sales.SalesDepartment table. The second parameter contains the name of an active Connection object named rs. The third and fourth parameters contain the constants adOpenForwardOnly and adLockOptimistic, which specify the result set will use a forward-only cursor that supports updates using optimistic record locking.

TIP

Forward-only record sets are often thought of as read-only because they don't support the same type of capabilities as keyset cursors. However, forward-only Recordset objects do support updating the current row, and in ADO, they provide much better performance than keyset or dynamic cursors. Any changes made to the data source won't be reflected in a forward-only Recordset object until it's refreshed.

After the Recordset object has been created, a Do Until loop reads through all the rows contained in the Recordset object. The rs Recordset object's Delete method deletes each row, and the MoveNext method positions the cursor on the next row in the result set. After all the rows have been deleted, the DisplayForwardGrid subroutine displays the (now empty) Sales.SalesDepartment table. Finally, the Close method closes the Recordset object.

Updating Data with the ADO Command Object

The preceding section showed how to update SQL Server databases using Recordset objects and cursors. However, while updating data using Recordset objects is easy to code, this method isn't usually optimal in terms of performance. Using prepared SQL statements to update data usually provides better performance—especially in OLTP-type applications where the SQL statements have a high degree of reuse. Next, you see how you can use prepared SQL statements and the ADO Command object's Execute method to insert, update, and delete data in a SQL Server table.

Inserting Rows with a Command Object and Prepared SQL   The SQL Insert statement adds rows to a table. The following example illustrates how to use the SQL Insert statement with an ADO Command object:

```
Private Sub PreparedAdd(cn As ADODB.Connection)
    Dim cmd As New ADODB.Command
    Dim rs As New ADODB.Recordset
    Dim i As Integer
    'Set up the Command object's Connection, SQL and parameter types
    With cmd
        .ActiveConnection = cn
        .CommandText = "Insert Into Sales.SalesDepartment Values(?,?)"
        .CreateParameter , adChar, adParamInput, 4
        .CreateParameter , adChar, adParamInput, 25
    End With
```

```
'Execute the prepared SQL statement to add 50 rows
For i = 1 To 50
    cmd.Parameters(0) = CStr(i)
    cmd.Parameters(1) = "Department " & CStr(i)
    cmd.Execute , , adExecuteNoRecords
Next

'Create a recordset to display the new rows
rs.Open "Select * From Sales.SalesDepartment", cn, , , adCmdText
DisplayForwardGrid rs, Grid

    rs.Close
End Sub
```

In this example, you create new ADO Command and Recordset objects. Then the ActiveConnection property of the Command object receives the name of an active Connection object named cn. Next, the CommandText property is assigned a SQL Insert statement that uses two parameter markers. The CreateParameter method is then used to specify the characteristics of each parameter. The first parameter contains a character value that is 4 bytes long, and the second parameter contains a character value that is 25 bytes long. As you would expect with an Insert statement, both parameters are input-only.

TIP

While this example simply refers to each parameter using its ordinal position within the Parameters collection, you can also name each parameter when it's created. Naming the parameters lets you refer to them in almost the same way as working with the Field objects contained in a Recordset. For instance, you can create a named parameter as follows:
```
cmd.CreateParameter "Dep_ID" , adChar, adParamInput, 4
```
You could then refer to the parameter as:
```
cmd.Paramters("Dep_ID") = CStr(i).
```

A For Next loop adds 50 rows to the table. Within the For Next loop, the values used by each parameter are assigned. The cmd.Parameter(0) object refers to the first parameter marker, while the cmd.Parameter(1) object refers to the second parameter marker. As in the earlier example that added rows using a cursor, the first parameter (the Dep_ID column) has a unique integer value based on the loop counter. The second parameter (the Dep_Name column) has a string that contains the literal "Department" in conjunction with a string representation of the loop counter. After you set the parameter values, the prepared statement executes using the Execute method.

The adExecuteNoRecords option specifies that the Execute method will not return a Recordset.

The DisplayForwardGrid subroutine displays the contents of the Sales. SalesDepartment table in a grid, and then the Recordset closes.

Updating Data with a Command Object and a Prepared SQL The SQL Update statement updates columns in a table. The following example illustrates using the SQL Update statement with an ADO Command object to update all the rows in the Sales. SalesDepartment table:

```
Private Sub PreparedUpdate(cn As ADODB.Connection)
    Dim cmd As New ADODB.Command
    Dim rs As New ADODB.Recordset
    Dim i As Integer
    'Set up the Command object's Connection, SQL and parameter types
    With cmd
        .ActiveConnection = cn
        .CommandText = _
          "Update Sales.SalesDepartment Set Dep_Name = ? Where Dep_ID = ?"
        .CreateParameter , adChar, adParamInput, 25
        .CreateParameter , adChar, adParamInput, 4
    End With

    ' Execute the prepared SQL statement to update 50 rows
    For i = 0 To 50
        cmd.Parameters(0).Value = "Updated Department " & CStr(i)
        cmd.Parameters(1).Value = CStr(i)
        cmd.Execute , , adExecuteNoRecords
    Next

    ' Create a recordset to display the updated rows
    rs.Open "Select * From Sales.SalesDepartment", cn, , , adCmdText
    DisplayForwardGrid rs, Grid

    rs.Close
End Sub
```

As in the previous insert example, new ADO Command and Recordset objects are created in the beginning of the subroutine. The ActiveConnection property method of the Command object has the name of an active Connection object named cn. Here, the CommandText property has a SQL Update statement that uses two parameter markers. In this case, the first parameter refers to the Dep_Name column, and the second parameter refers to the Dep_ID column. Then the CreateParameter method specifies the characteristics of each parameter.

A For Next loop updates each of the 50 rows in the Sales.SalesDepartment table. Within the For Next loop, the values used by each parameter are assigned and the Update statement is run using the Command object's Execute method.

After the updates are finished, a Recordset object is created and displayed in a grid using the DisplayForwardGrid subroutine.

Deleting Data with a Command Object and Prepared SQL   As with Insert and Update operations, ADO Command objects can be used to delete one or more rows in a remote data source. The following code listing illustrates how to delete rows from a SQL Server database using a prepared SQL Delete statement and a Command object:

```
Private Sub PreparedDelete(cn As ADODB.Connection)
    Dim cmd As New ADODB.Command
    Dim rs As New ADODB.Recordset
    Dim i As Integer
    'Set up the Command object's Connection and SQL command
    With cmd
        .ActiveConnection = cn
        .CommandText = "Delete Sales.SalesDepartment"
    End With

    'Execute the SQL once (that's all that is needed)
    cmd.Execute , , adExecuteNoRecords

    'Create a recordset to display the empty table
    rs.Open "Select * From Sales.SalesDepartment", cn, , , adCmdText
    DisplayForwardGrid rs, Grid

    rs.Close
End Sub
```

Thanks to SQL's set-at-time functionality, this example is a bit simpler than the previous insert and update examples. SQL's capability to manipulate multiple rows with a single statement allows one SQL Update to be used to update all 50 rows in the table. As in those examples, first new ADO Command and Recordset objects are created, and then the ActiveConnection property method of the Command object gets the name of an active Connection object. Next, a SQL statement is assigned to the Command object's CommandText property. In this case, the SQL Delete statement doesn't use any parameters. Because no Where clause is contained

in this statement, the Delete operation is performed on all rows in the Sales.
SalesDepartment table when the Execute method is run.

> **NOTE**
>
> *Use caution when you employ SQL action statements without a Where clause. This powerful technique can easily and inadvertently modify more rows than you intend.*

After the updates are finished, a Recordset object is created and displayed in a grid
using the DisplayForwardGrid subroutine, and then the Recordset object is closed.

Executing Stored Procedures with Command Objects

Stored procedures provide the fastest mechanism available for accessing SQL Server
data. When a stored procedure is created, a compiled data access plan is added to
the SQL Server database. By using this existing data access plan, the application
foregoes the need to parse any incoming SQL statements, and then creates a
new data access plan. This results in faster execution of queries or other data
manipulation actions. SQL Server automatically shares stored procedures among
multiple users.

Stored procedures can also be used to implement a more robust database security
than you can achieve by setting permissions directly on target files. For example,
you can restrict all direct access to SQL Server tables and only permit access to
the stored procedures. When centrally controlled and administered, the stored
procedures can provide complete control over SQL Server database access.

Using ADO, stored procedures are called in much the same way as are prepared
SQL statements. The Command object calls the stored procedure, and a question
mark denotes each stored procedure's input and output parameters. The following
example is a simple stored procedure that accepts one input parameter and returns
one output parameter:

```
Create Procedure CountOrderQty
(
    @SalesOrderID Char(4),
    @OrderQty int Output
)
As
Select @OrderQty = Select Sum(OrderQty) From Sales.SalesOrderDetail
    Where SalesOrderID = @SalesOrderID
GO
```

The CountOrderQty stored procedure in this example accepts a character argument containing the SalesOrderID as input and returns an integer value containing the total of the OrderQty column for all the rows in the sales table that matched the supplied SalesOrderID. In this example, the SQL Select sum() function is used to sum up the values contained in the OrderQty column.

NOTE

The variable names used in the stored procedure don't need to match the column names in the source table.

The following code example shows how you can call the CountOrderQty stored procedure using an ADO Command object:

```
Private Sub CallSP(cn As ADODB.Connection)
    Dim cmd As New ADODB.Command
    Dim parm0 As New ADODB.Parameter
    Dim parm1 As New ADODB.Parameter
    Dim sSQL As String
    On Error GoTo ErrorHandler
    cmd.ActiveConnection = cn
    cmd.CommandType = adCmdStoredProc
    cmd.CommandText = "CountOrderQty"

    parm0.Direction = adParamInput
    parm0.Type = adInteger
    parm0.Size = 4
    cmd.Parameters.Append parm0

    parm1.Direction = adParamOutput
    parm1.Type = adInteger
    parm1.Size = 4
    cmd.Parameters.Append parm1

    parm0.Value = 43675
    cmd.Execute

    Label_Mid.Caption = " Total Qty for Sales Order 43675: "
    Text_Mid.Text = parm1.Value
ErrorHandler:
    DisplayADOError cn
End Sub
```

In the beginning of this subroutine, you can see where an ADO Command object named cmd and two ADO Parameter objects named parm0 and parm1 are created. Using Parameter objects is an alternative to using the CreateParameter method illustrated earlier in this chapter, in the section "Using Prepared SQL and the Command Object." Both techniques can be used to specify the characteristics of a parameter marker, and either method can be used to execute prepared SQL, as well as stored procedures.

Next, the ActiveConnection property of the Command object is assigned the name of an existing Connection object named cn. This associates the Command object with a target data source. Then the Command object's CommandType property is assigned the value of adCmdStoredProc, and the CommandText property is assigned the name of the stored procedure to be executed. Because the CommandType property tells ADO this Command object is used to call a stored procedure, no need exists to set up a SQL string that contains an ODBC Call statement.

The next section of code shows how Parameter objects are initialized. For each Parameter object, the Direction, Type, and Size properties are set. Then the Append method of the Parameters collection is used to add the Parameter object to the Parameters collection.

NOTE

You must add each Parameter object to the Parameters collection in the same order as the parameter is used by the stored procedure or prepared SQL statement. In other words, you must use the Append method for the first Parameter object, which represents the first parameter, before you execute the Append method for the second Parameter object, which represents the second parameter.

After the Parameter objects have been added to the Command object's Parameters collection, the Value property of the first parameter is assigned a string that contains a valid SalesOrderID value. This value is passed to the first parameter of the CountOrderQty stored procedure. Then the Command object's Execute method is used to call the stored procedure. When the call to the stored procedure has completed, the value of the output parameter is available in the Value property of the second Parameter object (parm1). In the previous example, this value is assigned to a text box to be displayed.

Error Handling

Run-time errors that are generated using the ADO object framework are placed in the ADO Errors collection. When an ADO run-time error occurs, Visual Basic's error handler is fired, enabling you to trap and respond to run-time errors. This tight integration with Visual Basic makes it easy to handle ADO errors. The following ShowError subroutine illustrates how ADO's error handling can be integrated with Visual Basic's On Error function:

```
Private Sub ShowError(cn As ADODB.Connection)
    Dim rs As New ADODB.Recordset
    On Error GoTo ErrorHandler

    rs.Open "Select * From no_such_table", cn
    rs.Close

    Exit Sub

ErrorHandler:
    DisplayADOError cn
End Sub
```

Here, the ShowError function attempts to open a Recordset object against a nonexistent table. At the beginning of this function, the On Error statement enables Visual Basic's error handler. In this case, the On Error statement causes the program to branch to the ErrorHandler label when a trappable error is encountered.

Executing the Open method with a nonexisting table causes the ADO object framework to generate a run-time error, which, in turn, causes the program execution to resume with the first statement following the label. In this example, the DisplayADOError subroutine is executed following the invalid Open attempt.

The following code listing shows how the DisplayDAOError subroutine uses DAO's Error object and Errors collection to display information about an ADO error condition in a simple message box:

```
Private Sub DisplayADOError(cn As ADODB.Connection)
    Dim er As ADODB.Error

    For Each er In cn.Errors
        MsgBox "Number: " & er.Number & vbCrLf & _
        "Source: " & er.Source & vbCrLf & _
        "Text: " & er.Description
    Next

End Sub
```

Figure 8-17   *ADO error handling*

In this subroutine, an ADO Connection object is passed in as a parameter. The ADO Errors collection is contained in the Connection object. Next, a new ADO Error object named er is declared, and a For Each loop iterates through the ADO Errors collection. The loop is required because the ADODB Errors collection can contain multiple Error objects where each Error object represents a different error condition. With the For Each loop, the values of the Number, Source, and Description properties are displayed in a message box. The Number property of the ADO Error object contains the ADO error message number, while the Source property identifies the source object that fired the error. As you might expect, the Description property contains the error condition's text description. Figure 8-17 shows the message box that the DisplayADOError subroutine displays.

Advanced Database Functions Using ADO

You've now seen how to use the basic ADO Connection, Recordset, and Command objects to query and update the SQL Server database. In this section, you see how to use some of the more advanced ADO functions, such as how to perform updates with batch cursors and commit and roll back transactions.

Batch Updates

Batch updates allow all the changes made to a Recordset object to be written back to the data source all at once. Batch updates are most useful when you are working with disconnected Recordset sets such as you might use in Web-based applications. With batch updates, the Recordset object is updated using the normal AddNew, Update, and Delete methods. After all the changes have been made to the Recordset object, the BatchUpdate method is used to post the entire batch of changes to the database. The client Batch cursor library generates a SQL query to synchronize the local Recordset object and the data on the remote SQL Server system. The following example illustrates how to use the ADO Recordset object's BatchUpdate method:

```
Private Sub BatchUpdate(cn As ADODB.Connection)
    Dim rs As New ADODB.Recordset
    Dim i As Integer
    'Pass in the SQL, Connection, Cursor type,
    '  lock type and source type
    rs.Open "Select Dep_ID, Dep_Name From Sales.SalesDepartment", _
       cn, adOpenKeyset, adLockBatchOptimistic, adCmdText

    'Add 50 rows to the Sales.SalesDepartment table
    For i = 1 To 50
        rs.AddNew
        rs!Dep_ID = i
        rs!Dep_Name = "Add Batch Department " & CStr(i)
        rs.Update
    Next

    rs.UpdateBatch

    'Display the new rows in a grid
    DisplayKeysetGrid rs, Grid, 1

    rs.Close
End Sub
```

This code is much like the standard ADO cursor update example presented earlier in this chapter in the section "Updating Rows with a Recordset." However, one important difference exists. The Recordset object's lock type parameter is assigned the constant adLockBatchOptimistic. This tells ADO the Recordset object will use a batch cursor. After the Recordset object is opened, the AddNew and Update methods are used to add 50 rows to the local Recordset. Important to note is that unlike a standard keyset cursor, which immediately propagates the new rows to the data source, the batch cursor doesn't update the data source until the UpdateBatch method executes. Then all the updated rows are written to the base tables.

TIP

The CancelBatch method can be used to cancel all the pending changes that would be performed by an UpdateBatch operation.

Using Transactions

Transactions enable you to group together multiple operations that can be performed as a single unit of work. This helps to ensure database integrity. For instance, transferring funds from your savings account to your checking account involves multiple database operations, and the transfer cannot be considered complete unless all the operations are successfully completed. A typical transfer from your savings account to your checking account requires two separate, but related, operations: a withdrawal from your savings account and a deposit to your checking account. If either operation fails, the transfer is not completed. Therefore, both these functions are considered part of the same logical transaction. In this example, both the withdrawal and the deposit would be grouped together as a single transaction. If the withdrawal operation succeeded, but the deposit failed, the entire transaction could be rolled back, restoring the database to the condition it had before the withdrawal operation was attempted. SQL Server supports transactions, but not all databases do.

Rolling Back Transactions

In ADO, transactions are enabled in the Connection object. The Connection object's RollbackTrans method can be used to restore the database to the state it was in before the transaction occurred. The following example shows how to use the RollbackTrans method:

```
Private Sub TransRollBack(cn As ADODB.Connection)
    Dim rs As New ADODB.Recordset
    'Start a transaction using the existing Connection object
    cn.BeginTrans

    'Execute SQL to delete all of the rows from the table
    cn.Execute "Delete Sales.SalesDepartment"

    'Now Rollback the transaction - the table is unchanged
    cn.RollbackTrans

    'Create a recordset to display the unchanged table
    rs.Open "Select * From Sales.SalesDepartment", cn, , , adCmdText
    DisplayForwardGrid rs, Grid
    rs.Close
End Sub
```

In this example, executing the BeginTrans method of the Connection object named cn signals to the database that a transaction is about to begin. Then the

Connection object's Execute method is used to issue a SQL Delete statement that deletes all the rows in the Sales.SalesDepartment table. Instead of committing that change to the database, however, the Connection object's RollbackTrans method is used to undo the transaction, restoring the original contents of the Sales. SalesDepartment table. A rollback would also be performed if a network failure or system crash prevented the Commit from being successfully executed. A Recordset object is created and displayed to illustrate that the table's contents were unchanged after the RollBackTrans method.

TIP

SQL Server maintains database modifications in a transaction log file, which contains a serial record of all the modifications that have been made to a database. The transaction log contains both before and after images of each transaction.

Committing Transactions

When a transaction is successfully completed, the Connection object's CommitTrans method writes the transaction to the database. In the following example, you see how to use ADO to begin a transaction and then commit that transaction to the SQL Server database:

```
Private Sub TransCommit(cn As ADODB.Connection)
    Dim rs As New ADODB.Recordset
    'Start a transaction using the existing Connection object
    cn.BeginTrans

    'Execute SQL to delete all of the rows from the table
    cn.Execute "Delete Sales.SalesDepartment"

    'Commit the transaction and update the table
    cn.CommitTrans

    'Create a recordset to display the empty table
    rs.Open "Select * From Sales.SalesDepartment", cn, , , adCmdText
    DisplayForwardGrid rs, Grid
    rs.Close
End Sub
```

Again, executing the BeginTrans method of the Connection object signals to the database that a transaction is about to begin, and the Execute method is used to issue a SQL Delete statement. This time, however, the changes are committed to the database using the Connection object's CommitTrans method. Finally, a Recordset object is opened to illustrate that the table's contents were deleted following the CommitTrans method.

Summary

While ADO provides similar functionality to both the older DAO and RDO object frameworks, ADO's more-flexible object model allows it to be used effectively for a wider range of applications. The DAO object model was primarily designed around the Jet engine, and the RDO object model was primarily designed for ODBC data access; however, the ADO object model was built around OLE DB. Unlike Jet and ODBC, which are both geared toward database access, OLE DB is intended to provide heterogeneous data access to a number of different data sources. OLE DB provides access to a variety of data sources, including Excel spreadsheets, Active Directory, and Exchange, in addition to relational databases such as SQL Server.

Bear in mind that ADO is best suited for maintaining older COM-based applications. Microsoft recommends that all new SQL Server 2005 applications be written using ADO.NET and the .NET Framework as you saw in Chapter 7.

Reporting Services

One of the most exciting enhancements found in SQL Server 2005 is Reporting Services. Reporting Services was first introduced as an add-on to SQL Server 2000 and provided customers with a comprehensive reporting platform. Because SQL Server has always been an easy-to-implement relational database platform, it has been very popular for department-level implementations as well as a database platform for small and medium-sized businesses. However, SQL Server had no built-in tools that were capable of generating reports, so many companies started using desktop reporting tools like Microsoft Access. Many medium- and larger-sized organizations adopted more powerful third-party reporting products such as Business Object's Crystal Reports.

The inclusion of Reporting Services in SQL Server 2005 has changed all of that. Reporting Services is a server-based reporting service that goes beyond the capabilities of simple reporting solutions like Access. Reporting Services provides an extensive environment for designing, managing, and deploying reports to local departments or the entire organization. You can build reports based on relational or multidimensional data from SQL Server, Analysis Services, any Microsoft .NET data provider such as ODBC or OLE DB, or even Oracle. You can create ad hoc reports that use predefined models and data sources, or create tabular, matrix, and free-form reports. Reporting Services not only provides the ability to graphically design reports but also enables you to securely deploy those reports across the enterprise rendered in a variety of different formats, including Web-based HTML reports, Windows-based rich client reports, and reports rendered for mobile devices. In the first part of this chapter, you'll get an overview of the architecture used by SQL Server 2005's Reporting Services. In the second part of this chapter, you get a look at how you design reports using the report designer and report wizard. Then you see how to manage and deploy reports using Reporting Services.

Reporting Services Architecture

SQL Server 2005's Reporting Services isn't just a report design tool. Instead, it's a complete reporting platform that enables the creation of reports, stores report definitions, provides secure access to reports, renders reports in a variety of different output formats, schedules report delivery, enables the deployment of those reports, and allows for programmability and extensibility features.

Reporting Services provides a middle-tier server that runs under IIS (Internet Information Services). If IIS is not present on the system running the installation, the option to install Reporting Services will not be present on SQL Server 2005's installation dialogs. While Reporting Services can be installed on the same server system as the SQL Server database engine, for improved scalability it's usually better to install Reporting Services on a separate server.)

NOTE

Reporting Services is licensed as a part of SQL Server 2005 and does not require any separate licensing for use on a single system. However, it does require an additional license if you implement it on a separate system.

SQL Server 2005 Reporting Services includes several applications. It's a server-based subsystem that's designed to enable the creation, management, and deployment of reports across the enterprise. You can see an overview of the Reporting Service architecture shown in Figure 9-1.

Reporting Services Components

As you can see in Figure 9-1, Reporting Services consists of a variety of interrelated components. These components include processing components, graphical and command-prompt tools, and programmatic interfaces that facilitate development of reports in a managed environment.

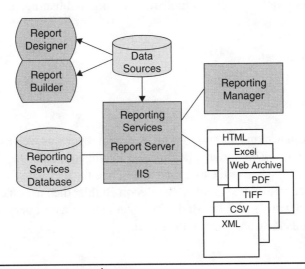

Figure 9-1   *Reporting Services architecture*

Report Server

The Report Server is the core component in Reporting Services. The Report Server processes report requests and renders reports in the desired output format. Report Server functions also include processing of report models, distribution of reports, security enforcement, and controlling user access to items and operations.

Report Manager

The Report Manager is a Web-based application that enables the DBA or reporting administrator to control the security and overall management attributes of the reports created using Reporting Services. The Report Manager is used to specify report change authority as well as report access authority. It can also be used to set up delivery schedules for Reporting Services reports.

Reporting Services Configuration and Management Tools

Reporting Services includes two configuration tools you can use to configure, deploy, upgrade, and manage local or remote report server instances:

▶ The Reporting Services Configuration tool

▶ The Report Server command-prompt utilities

Report Authoring Tools

Reporting Services includes several tools for creating, publishing, and managing reports.

▶ The Report Designer

▶ The Report Model Designer

▶ The Report Builder

The Report Designer enables you to visually design reports as well as control their deployment and is accessed through the Business Intelligence (BI) Development Studio. The Report Model Designer is the tool used to describe the metadata from a data source that is incorporated into ad hoc reports. The Report Builder then uses the report model definitions created with the Report Model Designer to generate a query to retrieve the requested data, and create and publish the report.

Programmability

Reporting Services provide a full range of APIs that developers can use to incorporate Reporting Services functions into custom Web or Windows applications. You can also develop your own components and extensions to perform specialized functions relevant to your own business needs.

Installing Reporting Services

Reporting Services contains both server-side components and client-side components. Even though clients that connect to SQL Server require a client access license, the client-side components of Reporting Services can be installed on any computer. The server-side components require a SQL Server license. SQL Server 2005 provides two ways to install Reporting Services components: you can use the SQL Server Installation Wizard, or you can install Reporting Services from a command prompt.

Installing from the SQL Server Installation Wizard

To install Reporting Services using the SQL Server Installation Wizard, you select Reporting Services on the Components To Install page. To install the default configuration of Reporting Services, you also need to select the SQL Server Database Services option. The Components To Install page is used to specify a Report Server installation and does not include authoring or administering tools that a Report Server needs for deployment. On the Components To Install page, click the Advanced button to display the Feature Selection page, where you can choose which components to install. You can choose to install server-side components or client-side components or both.

Server Components   The following lists the server-side components that are included with the installation of Reporting Services.

▶ **Report Server**   The Report Server stores metadata and definitions for objects in a report server database. When the Report Server component is installed, the two services that make up its implementation, a Microsoft Windows service and an ASP.NET Web service that runs on Microsoft Internet Information Services (IIS), are employed on the host computer.

▶ **Report Server Database** Two SQL Server databases are used for internal storage for a Report Server instance. One database, named ReportServer, stores data that is used on an ongoing basis; the other database, called ReportServerTembDB, is used for temporary storage.

▶ **Report Manager** The Report Manager, installed by default with Report Server, is used to manage one instance of Report Server.

▶ **Report Builder** The Report Builder tool is used to create ad hoc reports in a Web-based, visual environment. The Report Builder is available when the Enterprise, Developer, or Evaluation Edition of SQL Server 2005 is installed.

▶ **Reporting Services Configuration** The Reporting Services Configuration tool is installed with a Report Server instance and is used to customize or deploy a Report Server installation.

Client Components The following list describes the Reporting Services client-side components that can be installed on client computers and do not require a SQL Server license.

▶ **Report Designer** The Report Designer is a visual tool that allows you to create, edit, and publish reports to the Report Server. This tool runs within Visual Studio 2005.

▶ **Model Designer** The Model Designer is a tool that allows you to specify data relationships that will be used to create reporting models for ad hoc reports. This tool runs within Visual Studio 2005.

▶ **Command-prompt utilities** Several command-line tools are available to help you configure and manage a Reporting Services installation. The following tools can be installed to perform Report Server administration tasks from the command line:

rsconfig	Used to change Report Server Database connection settings
rs	Scripting host used to process Visual Basic scripts
rskeymgmt	Used to back up and restore the Report Server encryption keys

▶ **SQL Server Management Studio** The Management Studio is a management environment that allows you to manage your SQL Server components servers from a common place.

▶   **SQL Server Configuration Manager**   The SQL Server Configuration Manager allows you to set and manage properties of the Report Server Windows service. You can use the Configuration Manager for initialization and scheduling of Report Server actions.

Installing from the Command Prompt

A Setup.exe program is supplied that allows you to install Reporting Services from a command-line prompt. You can customize the way Reporting Services is installed by specifying properties on the command line or in an .ini file. The following output lists the syntax, and the available properties for the command-line or .ini file installation are shown in Tables 9-1 and 9-2.

```
Setup /?

Setup
    [/i package_file | package_code]
    {/settings ini_file | property1=setting1 property2=setting2 ...}
    [{/qn}]
    [/l*v log_file]

setup
    /x package_code
    [/qn]
    [/l*v log_file]
```

Syntax	Description
/?	Displays syntax help for arguments.
/i package_file | package_code	Package_file names the Windows installation file (an .msi file) to use for Reporting Services installation. Package_code names the .msi file to use when setup is run in maintenance mode.
/settings ini_file | property1=setting1 property2=setting2	Ini_file names the .ini file that contains the property settings for the installation.
/qn	Specifies to run the setup unattended; no user interface displayed.
/l*v log_file	Log_file specifies the path and name of a verbose log file for the Windows Installer log options. If omitted, no log file is created.
/x package_code	Package_code names the .msi file to use when uninstalling Reporting Services.

Table 9-1   *Reporting Services Command-Line Installation Options*

Property	Description
INSTALLDIR=*"RS_exec_folder_path"*	Names folder for installed files.
USERNAME=*"user_name"*	User registering product.
COMPANYNAME=*"company_name"*	Company registering product.
REINSTALL=All	Installs all previously installed features of Reporting Services.
REINSTALLMODE={ omus | amus }	Sets level of processing to perform by Setup. O Reinstall file if missing or newer A Reinstall all files M Rewrite required Registry entries for hives HKEY_LOCAL_MACHINE or HKEY_CLASSES_ROOT U Rewrite required Registry entries for hives HKEY_CURRENT_USER or HKEY_USERS S Reinstall shortcuts and icons
PERSEAT=*"per_seat_lic"*	Number of per-seat licenses purchased. Cannot be used with PERPROCESSOR property.
PERPROCESSOR=*"per_proc_lic"*	Number of processor licenses purchased. Cannot be used with PERSEAT property.
PIDKEY=*cdkey*	REQUIRED. The 25-character product ID key.
RSACCOUNT=*"domain\logon_name"*	Optional. Applies to the RS_Server feature. The domain is limited to 254 characters, and the logon_name is limited to 20 characters. Default value assigned by current operating system: Windows 2000 Local System Windows XP Local System Windows Server 2003 Network Service
RSPASSWORD=*"password"*	Optional. Applies to the RS_Server feature. Corresponds to the user name specified for the RSACCOUNT property. Limited to 255 characters. Default value is null.
RSCONFIGURATION={ default | filesonly }	Optional. Specifies how a report server instance is installed. The default installation requires a local database engine instance and cannot be installed as a virtual server. The files only installation installs the program files and minimally configures a report server installation.
RSAUTOSTART={ 1 | 0 }	Optional. Applies to the RS_Server feature. Specifies whether to start the Report Server automatically at Windows startup. 1=true, 0=false. Default value is 1=true.

Table 9-2   *Reporting Services Setup .ini File Options*

Property	Description
RSVIRTUALDIRECTORYSERVER= "*virtualdirectory*"	Optional. Applies to the RS_Server feature. Specifies the virtual directory for Report Server. Limited to 50 characters. Default value is ReportServer. Characters not valid in virtual directory names:

\ (backslash)	" (quotation mark)
/ (slash mark)	< > (angle brackets)
: (colon)	| (vertical bar)
* (asterisk)	; (semicolon)
? (question mark)	@ (at sign)
= (equal symbol)	& (ampersand)
+ (plus sign)	$ (dollar sign)
{ } (braces)	^ (circumflex)
[ ] (brackets)	` (accent grave)
, (comma)	. (period)

Property	Description
RSVIRTUALDIRECTORYMANAGER= "*virtualdirectory*"	Optional. Applies to the RS_Server feature. Specifies the virtual directory for Report Manager. Default value is Reports.
RSDATABASESERVER= "*servername\instancename*"	Optional. Applies to the RS_Server feature. Specifies the SQL Server instance that hosts the report server database. Default value is the default instance of SQL Server on the local machine.
RSDATABASENAME= "*ReportServerDatabase*"	Optional. Applies to the RS_Server feature. Specifies the name of the ReportServer database that the Report Server will use to store its metadata. Minimum limit of 1 character, maximum limit of 117 characters. Default value is ReportServer. Rules for name generation: 1. First character of name must be a letter or an underscore "_" character. The characters "@" and "#" cannot be used in the first position. 2. Subsequent characters can be letters, decimal numbers, or the "@", "$Embedded spaces or special characters are not allowed.
RSDATABASEDATAFILELOCATION= "*database_file_location*"	Optional. Applies to the RS_Server feature. Specifies the folder where the ReportServer database data file is stored. Must exist on the same computer that hosts the SQL Server instance that is hosting the report server database.
RSDATABASELOGFILELOCATION= "*database_logfile_location*"	Optional. Applies to the RS_Server feature. Specifies the folder where the report server database log files are stored. Must exist on the same computer that hosts the SQL Server instance that is hosting the report server database.
RSSETUPACCOUNT="*logon_name*"	Optional. Applies to the RS_Server feature. Specifies the SQL Server logon that is used by Setup. Default value is the credentials of the user running Setup. The account must belong to an administrator and must have permissions to create logins, create roles, create databases, and assign permissions to users.

Table 9-2   *Reporting Services Setup .ini File Options (continued)*

Property	Description
RSSETUPPASSWORD=*"password"*	Optional. Applies to the RS_Server feature. Required if RSSETUPACCOUNT property is specified. Specifies the password for SQL Server logon. Default value is null.
RSSQLACCOUNT=*"domain \logon_name"*	Optional. Applies to the RS_Server feature. The domain is limited to 254 characters, and the logon_name is limited to 20 characters. If RSSQLACCOUNT is a SQL login, the RSDATABASESECURITYMODE property must be set to "SQL".
RSSQLPASSWORD=*"password"*	Optional. Applies to the RS_Server feature. Required if RSSQLACCOUNT property is specified. Limited to 255 characters. Specifies the password for the SQL Server credentials specified in RSSQLACCOUNT.
RSDATABASESECURITYMODE="SQL"	Optional. Applies to the RS_Server feature. If omitted, RSSQLACCOUNT is assumed to be a Windows user account.
RSEMAILSMTPSERVER=*"servername"*	Optional. Applies to the RS_Server feature. Specifies the SMTP server that is used to deliver reports.
RSEMAILFROM=*"from@ext.com"*	Optional. Applies to the RS_Server feature. Specifies the e-mail address that appears in the From line.
RSREDIRECTTOMANAGER={ 0	1 }	Optional. Applies to the RS_Manager feature. Specifies whether Setup will add redirection from the top-level Web site to the Report Manager virtual directory. 1=true, 0=false. Default value is 0=false.
RSUSESSL={ 0	1 }	Optional. Applies to the RS_Server feature. Specifies whether the report server requires Secure Sockets Layer (SSL) connections. 1=true, 0=false. Default value is 0=false.
RSSAMPLESFILELOC=*"path"*	Optional. Applies to the RS_Samples feature. Path where the samples are installed. Default value is the Reporting Services installation directory.
RSSAMPLESDATABASESERVER= *"servername\instance"*	Optional. Applies to the RS_AdventureWorks feature. Default location is the value specified in RSDATABASESERVER.
RSWEBFARMSERVER=*servername\ instancename*	Optional. Applies to the RS_Server feature. Specifies the computer running the Report Server installation using the existing ReportServer database.
RSWEBFARMACCOUNT=*"domain\ username"*	Optional. Specifies the Windows account permission specified in the RSWEBFARMSERVER property.
RSWEBFARMPASSWORD=*"password"*	Optional. Applies to the RS_Server feature. Specifies the password for the username specified in the RSWEBFARMACCOUNT property.
ADDLOCAL=*"feature_selection"*	Specifies the features to be installed for an installation in the form of a comma-delimited list.
REMOVE=*"feature_selection"*	Specifies the features to be removed.

Table 9-2   *Reporting Services Setup .ini File Options (continued)*

Component	Feature Value	Properties
Report Server Web service, Report Server Windows service, Reporting Services Configuration tool	RS_Server	RSACCOUNT, RSPASSWORD, RSAUTOSTART, RSCONFIGURATION, RSVIRTUALDIRECTORYSERVER, RSDATABASESERVER, RSDATABASENAME, RSDATABASEFILELOCATION, RSDATABASELOGFILELOCATION, RSSETUPACCOUNT, RSSETUPPASSWORD, RSSQLACCOUNT, RSSQLPASSWORD, RSEMAILSMTPSERVER, RSEMAILFROM, RSDATABASESECURITYMODE, RSUSESSL, RSWEBFARMSERVER, RSWEBFARMACCOUNT, RSWEBFARMPASSWORD
Report Manager	RS_Manager	RSVIRTUALDIRECTORYMANAGER, RSREDIRECTTOMANAGER
Report Designer, Report Model Designer	SQL_WarehouseDevWorkbench	None
Reporting Services command-line utilities	RS_Tools	None
Administration tools	RS_Admin_Tools	None
Product documentation	RS_BooksOnline_<language>	None
Sample reports, sample applications	RS_Samples	RSSAMPLESFILELOC
AdventureWorks OLTP database	RS_AdventureWorks	RSSAMPLESDATABASESERVER

Table 9-3 *Parameters Used with the ADDLOCAL and REMOVE Properties*

The *feature_selection* parameters used with the ADDLOCAL and REMOVE properties are listed in Table 9-3.

You can also specify Setup command-prompt properties using an .ini file. Use the /settings *ini_file* argument on the command line to specify your installation .ini file. The first entry in the .ini file must contain the string "[Options]".

The following listing shows an example .ini file that sets some of the Reporting Services arguments:

```
[Options]
USERNAME=DOTECA
COMPANYNAME=TECA_Inc
ADDLOCAL=RS_Server
RSAUTOSTART=1
RSEMAILFROM="Denielle@teca.com"
```

Report Server

The Report Server is the central component of Reporting Services. The Report Server is the primary rendering and distribution engine; processing report requests and retrieving report formatting, data, and properties. The Report Server uses the Report Definition Layout (RDL) files that are created by the Report Designer and renders the report into the desired output format. Figure 9-2 shows an overview of the functionality provided by the Reporting Services Report Server.

The Report Server is implemented as two services, a Web service and a Windows service. The Web service is an ASP.NET-based application that exposes an HTTP SOAP endpoint that allows client applications to access the Report Server. The Windows service provides report delivery services and scheduling services. These two services working together make up a single Report Server instance.

The Report Server handles all of the essential report generation and distribution tasks. When a user requests a report or a report is deployed to an end user, the Report

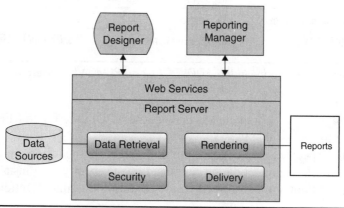

Figure 9-2   *Report Server overview*

Server checks the report's security attributes to ensure that the user has permissions to the report itself as well as to the database objects that are used by the report. If the user has the required permissions, then the Report Server will retrieve the report definition from the ReportServer database and render the report according to the format specified in the RDL. As the report is rendered, the Report Server will access all of the required data sources, retrieve the data, and build the report. Once the report has been created, the Report Server handles distributing the report to all of its predefined delivery targets. The Report Server caches the retrieved results in an intermediate format for a predefined amount of time. When the reports are cached, all of the required data retrieval and rendering steps have already been completed and the Report Server simply needs to distribute the cached report to the end user.

The Report Server contains subcomponents that include processors and extensions. Processors cannot be modified or extended, as they are used to support the consistency of the reporting system. Extensions are processors that perform specific functions. Default extensions are provided, but third-party developers can create additional extensions to replace or extend the processing ability of the Report Server.

Report Server Processors

There are two types of Report Server processors: a Report Processor and a Scheduling and Delivery Processor. The Report Processor retrieves a requested report definition or model, combines data from the data source with the layout information, and renders it in the desired format. The Scheduling and Delivery Processor runs reports that are triggered from a schedule and delivers the reports to target destinations.

Report Processor

The Report Processor handles two types of processes: report processing and model processing.

Report Processing   When a request for a report that has been saved in the ReportServer database is made, the Report Processor retrieves the report from the ReportServer database, initializes any variables or parameters, and performs preliminary preparations to the report for the incoming data in accordance with the report definition. A connection is then made to the data source and the data is retrieved. The Report Processor combines the report data being retrieved with the predetermined report layout. For each section in the report, the data is processed by row, including header and footer sections, group sections, and detail sections. Also at this time, any aggregate functions or expressions are processed. The report is then paginated and rendered in the appropriate format.

Model Processing *Model processing* occurs when a user has built an ad hoc report, also known as a model-based report, using the Report Builder tool. Ad hoc reporting uses report models that specify metadata and data source connection information. When a user requests to preview a model-based report, the report layout is displayed, showing how the report data will look. To actually retrieve the data, the Report Processor builds a query based on the report model and the report layout. The Report Processor then binds the data and processes the query, and finally, it merges the data and report layout to render the report. When a model-based report is published to the Report Server, the Report Processor creates a report definition based on the report model information and the report layout information. After it has been published to the Report Server, the report's execution is then handled by the Report Processor.

Scheduling and Delivery Processor

The Schedule and Delivery Processor supports scheduled operations using the delivery extensions to push reports to destinations like e-mail boxes and shared folders. Reporting Services uses the SQL Server Agent service for this purpose. The instance of SQL Server that hosts the ReportServer database provides the SQL Server Agent service that the Report Server uses. When a schedule is created, the Report Server creates a job in the SQL Server Agent based on specified date and time values. When the job runs, a report processing request is added to a queue in the ReportServer database. The Report Server polls the queue regularly for report processing requests, and if any are found, it will process them immediately in the order they were received. Scheduled report processing operations are handled by the Report Server Windows service, instead of the Report Server Web service.

For scheduled report processing to run smoothly, it needs both the SQL Server Agent service and the Report Server Windows service to be running. If the SQL Server Agent service is stopped, report processing requests will not be placed on the queue in the ReportServer database. When the SQL Server Agent service is restarted, report processing request jobs are resumed, but the requests made during the time the service was stopped will be lost. If the Report Server Windows service is stopped, the SQL Server Agent service will continue to place report processing requests on the queue, but no actual processing of the request will take place. When the Report Server Windows service is started, the Scheduling and Delivery Processor begins processing the requests in the order in which they were received.

Report Server Extensions

Report Server Extensions are also processors, but they do very specific functions. A Report Server requires that at least one Extension of each type of the default

Extensions be deployed. You can create additional Extensions that perform operations specific to your own needs and business practices. The required Extension types are: Security Extensions, Data Processing Extensions, Rendering Extensions, Report Processing Extensions, and Delivery Extensions.

Security Extensions

It is the Security Extension's function to authenticate users and groups to a Report Server. You can create a custom Security Extension to replace the default Security Extension, but only one Security Extension can be used in each installation of Reporting Services. Windows authentication is used in the default Security Extension.

Data Processing Extensions

Data Processing Extensions query a data source and return a tabular result set. Reporting Services provides Data Processing Extensions for SQL Server, Oracle, Analysis Services, OLE DB, and ODBC data sources. You can also develop your own Data Processing Extensions. Reporting Services can also use any ADO.NET data provider.

Query requests from the Report Processor are processed with the Data Processing Extensions and perform tasks such as: opening a connection, analyzing or running a query, returning a list of field names or a rowset, iterating through rows or rowsets, passing parameters to a query, and retrieving metadata information.

Rendering Extensions

Rendering Extensions do the work of transforming the retrieved data and layout information from the Report Processor into a device-specific format. Reporting Services includes seven rendering extensions:

- ► **HTML Rendering Extension** The Report Server uses the HTML Rendering Extension to render the report, when a report is requested through a Web browser.

- ► **Excel Rendering Extension** The Excel Rendering Extension is used to render reports that can be viewed and changed in Microsoft Excel 2000 or later.

- ► **CSV Rendering Extension** The Comma-Separated Value (CSV) Rendering Extension is used to render reports in comma-delimited plain text files.

- ► **XML Rendering Extension** The XML Rendering Extension is UTF-8 encoded and renders reports in XML files.

▶ **Image Rendering Extension** The Image Rendering Extension renders reports to bitmaps or metafiles and can render reports in the following formats: BMP, EMF, GIF, JPEG, PNG, TIFF, and WMF. The default image rendered is in TIFF format.

▶ **PDF Rendering Extension** The PDF rendering extension renders reports in PDF files. Adobe Acrobat 6.0 or later is used to open or view these reports.

Report Processing Extensions

The Report Server uses Report Processing Extensions to process report items such as tables, charts, text boxes, lists, images, lines, rectangles, and even subreports. You can add custom Report Processing Extensions to handle specialized report items or actions pertinent to your business operations.

Delivery Extensions

The Delivery Extensions are used by the Scheduling and Delivery Processor to deliver reports to various locations. Reporting Services includes two Delivery Extensions:

▶ **E-mail Delivery Extension** This extension sends an e-mail message via the Simple Mail Transport Protocol (SMTP) and can include the report or a URL link to the report. You can also send notices that do not include the report or URL link to devices such as pagers or telephones.

▶ **Shared Folder Delivery Extension** This extension sends reports to a shared folder on your network and allows you to specify a location, filename, format, and overwrite options for the file.

You can use Delivery Extensions to work in combination with subscriptions. You can create a subscription and choose a Delivery Extension for report delivery.

Report Manager

The Report Manager is the primary tool for accessing and managing Reporting Services reporting solutions. The Report Manager is an ASP.NET Web-based application and is accessed by pointing your Web browser to http://<servername>/ reports. You can see the Report Manager in Figure 9-3.

You can use the Report Manager to manage the content of the Report Server instance such as the folder hierarchy and security access settings. The Report

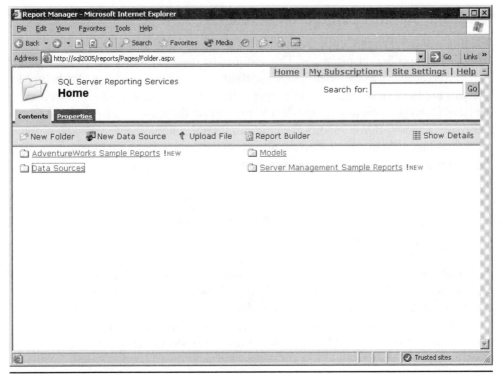

Figure 9-3   *Reporting Services Report Manager*

Manager enables you to view and manage all of the reports that have been deployed
to the Report Server. Using the Report Manager, you can create and manage data
sources and connection strings, folders, report models, linked reports, report history,
schedules, and subscriptions. The Report Manager allows the Reporting Services
Administrator to set up the security and manage role definitions for the reports that
can be accessed using Reporting Services. You can also launch the Report Builder
design tool to create or modify model-based reports.

Reporting Services Configuration
and Management Tools

Reporting Services includes a visual tool called the Reporting Services Configuration
tool, as well as several command-line utilities, that allow you to deploy, upgrade, and
manage Report Servers.

Reporting Services Configuration Tool

The Reporting Services Configuration tool is a visual utility that allows you to configure Report Server instances. This tool can be used to modify the settings of a Report Server that was installed with the default configuration and can also be used to configure local or remote Report Server instances. You can also use the Reporting Services Configuration tool to update a ReportServer database to a new format from a previous version. If you modify the configuration through other tools, such as the command-line utilities, the Reporting Services Configuration tool will automatically detect those changes when you connect to the instance of Report Server.

NOTE

If you installed a Report Server in an offline state, you need to use this tool to configure the server so that it can be used.

To start the Reporting Services Configuration tool, go to Start | Programs | Microsoft SQL Server 2005 | Configuration Tools. Then click the Reporting Services Configuration option. An Instance Selection dialog will be displayed like the one in Figure 9-4.

After selection of an instance of Report Server to configure, the Report Server Configuration Manager will be displayed. Figure 9-5 shows the Report Server Configuration Manager.

As you can see in Figure 9-5, each of the Report Server components is shown on the left side of the dialog, and each component that is already configured includes a green check mark next to it. Each of the components that need to be configured has

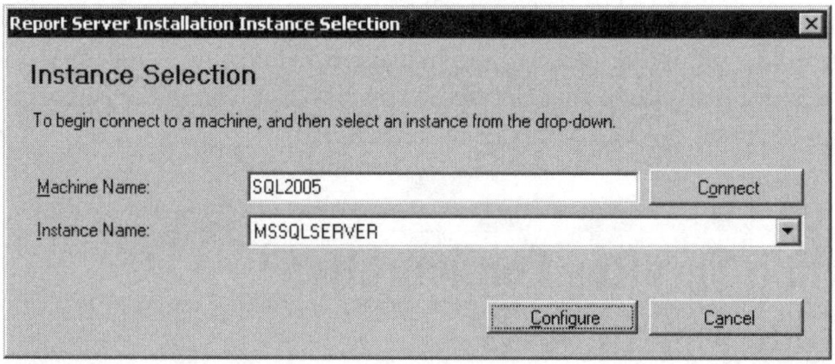

Figure 9-4   *Report Server installation instance selection*

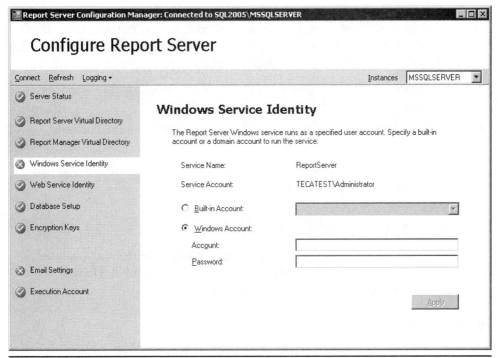

Figure 9-5   *Report Server Configuration Manager*

a red *x*-mark next to it. You can select each of the components regardless of whether they have been configured already or not, and make changes to their settings.

▶ **Server Status**   This displays the Report Server instance information and properties.

▶ **Report Server Virtual Directory**   This allows you to specify a virtual directory for the Report Server. You can also create a new virtual directory and optionally require Secure Socket Layer (SSL) connections.

▶ **Report Manager Virtual Directory**   This allows you to specify a virtual directory for the Report Server reports. You can also create a new virtual directory.

▶ **Windows Service Identity**   This allows you to specify the user account under which the Report Services Windows service runs.

▶ **Web Service Identity**   This allows you to specify the account under which the Report Services Web service runs. For those machines running IIS 5 or older, the specified account is a ASP.NET Machine account, and for those running IIS 6 or later, the Web service runs under the context of the application pool.

▶ **Database Setup** Here you can select the ReportServer database and connection permissions that are used by this instance of Report Server. You can also create the database if it does not already exist, verify a ReportServer database version, set the DSN, and grant user access rights from this display.

▶ **Encryption Keys** This option lets you back up, restore, and manage the encryption keys for the Report Server instance.

▶ **Email Settings** This allows you to set the e-mail address and delivery method for the Report Server to send e-mail notifications.

▶ **Execution Account** Use this option to set the account to use if the Report Server is to perform unattended operations.

Report Server Command-Prompt Utilities

When you install a Report Server, three command-prompt utilities that you can use to administer the Report Server are also automatically installed. They are the rsconfig utility, the rs utility, and the rskeymgmt utility.

The rsconfig Utility

The rsconfig utility is a tool that allows you to configure and manage a Report Server connection to the ReportServer database. It also permits you to configure an account that the Report Server can use for unattended report processing. The rsconfig utility stores connection and account values in an RSReportServer.config file.

You can run the rsconfig utility on a local or remote instance of Reporting Services, but you need to be a local administrator on the computer that hosts the Report Server you are configuring and Windows Management Instrumentation (WMI) must be installed on the computer that you are configuring. To use the rsconfig utility, you execute the rsconfig.exe program that is located in the \Program Files\Microsoft SQL Server\90\Tools\Binn directory. The following shows an example, and the arguments that can be used with the rsconfig utility are listed in Table 9-4.

```
rsconfig -?
rsconfig -e -u <DOMAIN\ACCOUNT> -p <PASSWORD> -t
```

The rs Utility

The rs utility is a tool you can use to run VB .NET scripts and perform scripting operations to publish reports and create or copy items in ReportServer databases. The script file must be written in VB .NET code and stored in a Unicode or UTF-8 text file with an .rss file extension.

Command-Line Switch	Requirement	Description
{–?}	Optional	Displays syntax help.
{–c}	Required if –e argument is not used	Indicates the connection string and data source values to connect a Report Server to the ReportServer database, will be included in arguments –m, –s, –i, –d, –a, –u, –p, or –t.
{–e}	Required if –c argument is not used	Indicates that the unattended report execution account will be included with arguments –u and –p, or –t.
{–m computername}	Required if configuring a remote Report Server instance	Name of the computer hosting Report Server. Default value is localhost.
{–i instancename}	Required if you are using named instances	The named instance of the ReportServer database.
{–s servername}	Required	The SQL Server instance that hosts the ReportServer database.
{–d databasename}	Required	The name of the ReportServer database.
{–a authmethod}	Required	The Report Server authentication method for connection to the ReportServer database. Values can be Windows or SQL (not case-sensitive).
{–u [domain\]username}	Required with –e, optional with –c	A user account for the ReportServer database connection.
{–p password}	Required if –u is specified	The password to use with the –u argument. Can be blank, is case-sensitive.
{–t}	Optional	Outputs error messages to the trace log.

Table 9-4 *Arguments to rsconfig*

To run the rs utility, you need to have the proper authority to connect to the Report Server instance you are running the script against. To use the rs utility, run the rs.exe file located in the \Program Files\Microsoft SQL Server\90\Tools\Binn directory.

The following code shows example uses of rs, and the arguments that can be used with the rs utility are listed in Table 9-5.

```
rs -?
rs -i c:\script_copy.rss -s http://localhost/reportserver
```

The rskeymgmt Utility

The rskeymgmt utility is an encryption key management tool that you can use to back up, delete, or restore the key set that is defined during Setup. You can also use

Command-Line Switch	Requirement	Description
{–?}	Optional	Displays syntax help.
{–i input_file}	Required	The .rss file to execute.
{–s serverURL}	Required	The Web server name and Report Server virtual directory name.
{–u [domain\]username}	Optional	A user account for the ReportServer connection. If omitted, the default is the current Windows user account.
{–p password}	Required if –u is specified	The password to use with the –u argument. Is case-sensitive.
{–l time_out}	Optional	The number of seconds before server connection times out. Default is 60. A value of 0 specifies no timeout.
{–b}	Optional	Sets commands in the file to run in batch mode.
{–v globalvar}	Optional	Global variables that are used in the script.
{–t}	Optional	Outputs error messages to the trace log.

Table 9-5   *Arguments to rs*

this tool to attach a report server instance to a shared report server database. You can use the rskeymgmt utility in database recovery operations, and if the keys cannot be recovered, the rskeymgmt tool provides a way to delete the encrypted content that is no longer useful.

The rskeymgmt tool can be run only on a computer that hosts the Report Server, and you need to be a local administrator on that computer. You cannot use the rskeymgmt utility to manage the encryption keys of a remote Report Server instance, but it can be used it to join a remote Report Server instance to a Report Server Web farm.

To run the rskeymgmt utility, you need to have the proper authority to connect to the Report Server instance you are running the script against. To use the rskeymgmt utility, run the rskeymgmt.exe file located in the \Program Files\Microsoft SQL Server\90\Tools\Binn directory.

The following code shows an example, and the arguments that can be used with the rskeymgmt utility are shown in Table 9-6.

```
rskeymgmt -?
rskeymgmt -a -f a:\backupkey\keys -p <password>
```

Command-Line Switch	Requirement	Description
{–?}	Optional	Displays syntax help.
{–e}	Optional	Extracts key for encryption/decryption for copying to a file. Requires –f and –p arguments.
{–a}	Optional	Applies a saved copy of the key to a report server instance. Requires –f and –p arguments.
{–d}	Optional	Deletes all encrypted data in a Report Server database and identifiers from the public key table for a Report Server instance.
{–s}	Optional	Generates a new key and re-encrypts all content using the new key.
{–j}	Optional	Joins a remote Report Server instance to an existing Report Server Web farm.
{–r installationID}	Optional	Removes the installationID (GUID) value for a Report Server instance.
{–f file}	Required if –e or –a is specified	Path to the file that stores a backup copy of the keys. For –e argument, file is written to a file. For –a argument, key value stored in the file is applied to the Report Server instance.
{–p password}	Required if –f is specified	The password used to back up or restore a key. Cannot be empty.
{–i instancename}	Required if you are using named instances	A local Report Server instance.
{–m computername}	Optional	Name of the remote computer hosting Report Server that you are joining to a Web farm.
{–n servername}	Required if you are using named instances	The name of the Report Server instance on a remote computer.
{–u useraccount}	Optional	The administrator account on the remote computer that you are joining to the Web farm.
{–v password}	Required if –u is specified	The password to use with the –u argument.
{–t}	Optional	Outputs error messages to the trace log.

Table 9-6 *Arguments to rskeymgmt*

Authoring Tools

'rvices reports are created using the Report Designer or the Report Builder.
Designer has a fully graphical design surface and interface program using
the Visual Studio 2005 shell to enable you to interactively design and test reports. The
Report Builder is a client-side report designer that allows end users to create ad hoc
reports based on a report model and then deploy them to the server or export them to
a local computer. Another tool, the Report Model Designer, is used to define the report
models that the Report Builder uses.

After a report is designed, the report definitions are stored in the ReportServer
database. Reporting Services reports are stored in a new XML-based data format
called Report Design Layout (RDL). By default, these RDL definitions are stored
in SQL Server 2005's ReportServer database. In addition to the report's RDL
specifications, the ReportServer database also stores information about a report's
security and destination.

Report Designer

Report Designer is a graphical tool with design surfaces used to preview and publish
reports. Within the Report Designer environment, tabbed windows are provided that
allow you to interactively design reports, including data panes, layout panes, report
elements, and preview panes. Tools such as query builders, an Expression editor, and
wizards are also included to help you step through the process of creating a simple
report.

There are several ways you can create a report using the Report Designer. The
Report Wizard is a tool that will guide you through the steps necessary to create
a simple tabular or matrix-type report. You can create a blank report using the Report
Project template in the development environment and add data queries and layout
information to it.

Using the Report Wizard to Create a Report

To use the Report Wizard to create a report, you open up SQL Server 2005's
Business Intelligence Development Studio and then select the File | New | Project.
On the New Projects dialog, click the Business Intelligence Projects options from the
Project Types list box to view the installed BI project templates and select the Report
Project Wizard template. Type a name and location for the project and click OK.

A series of wizard dialog boxes will be displayed to step you through the report
creation process. The first wizard dialog will prompt you for a data source. The next

wizard dialog will ask you to design a query to execute to retrieve the data for your report. A Query Builder button allows you to interactively create your query statement. Next, you will be prompted to select a report type, tabular or matrix. The next dialog asks how you would like your report grouped. A list of available fields is displayed for you to select and assemble according to Page, Group, or Detail sections on your report pages. You then choose the layout of your report and the style of your report.

After you select your report data, groupings, and layout, a summary dialog will be displayed where you can name your report and optionally choose to preview the report. The Report Wizard Summary is shown in Figure 9-6.

If you have chosen to preview your report, clicking the Finish button on the Report Wizard Summary page executes the query and generates the report to a preview pane in the BI Development Studio environment as shown in Figure 9-7.

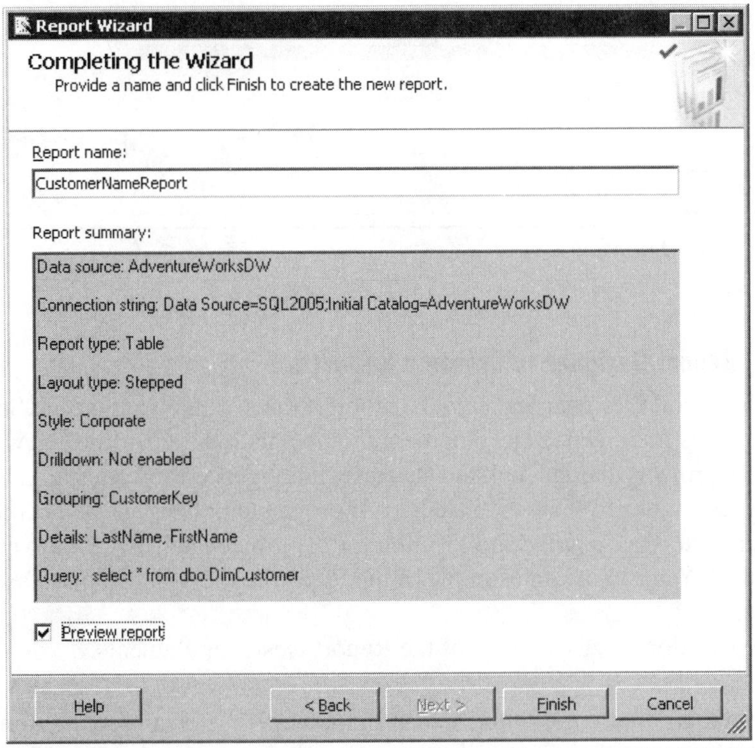

Figure 9-6 *Report Wizard summary*

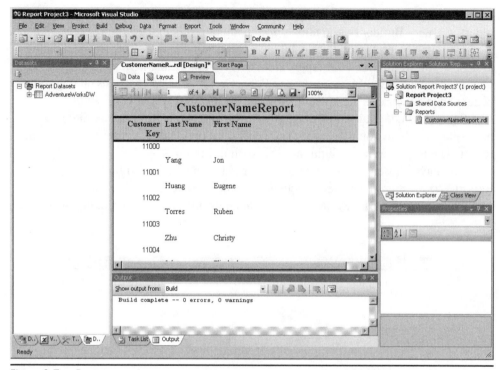

Figure 9-7   *Report preview*

Using the Report Designer to Create a Report

To start the Report Designer and create a report project, you open up SQL Server 2005's Business Intelligence Development Studio and then select File | New | Project. On the New Projects dialog, click the Business Intelligence Projects options from the Project Types list box to view the installed BI project templates and select the Report Project template. Type a name and location for the project and click OK to create the report project. You can see an example of the Reporting Services Report Designer in Figure 9-8.

The next section discusses each of the Report Designer elements.

Design Surface   In the center of the screen in Figure 9-8 you can see the Report Designer's *design surface*. The design surface presents three tabs: Data, Layout, and Preview. To create a report, you must first define a dataset by clicking the Data tab to reveal the Data pane. You create datasets in the Data pane to access data sources to include in your report. When you create a dataset in your project, the dataset is added

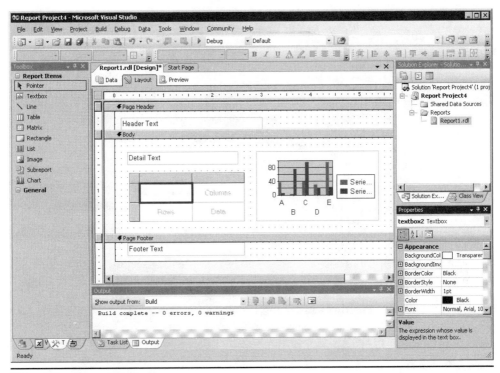

Figure 9-8 *Report Designer*

to the Dataset window located on the left side of the design environment. The dataset is built by selecting New Dataset from the drop-down box at the top of the Data pane. A Dataset dialog will then be displayed prompting you to specify the dataset name, data source, command type, and query statement. If you leave the query section of the Dataset dialog blank and click the OK button, a blank dataset will be created. You can then click the Generic Query Designer button, which causes the query builder tool to be displayed in the Data pane and allows you to interactively build a query for your dataset. You can see an example of the interactive query builder in Figure 9-9.

The Layout tab is where you design your report. You design the report by dragging and dropping items from the Toolbox window (which is located on the left side of the design environment) onto the Layout pane and then moving and resizing them. As you can see in Figure 9-8, the Layout pane shows all of the Reporting Services controls that have been added to the report.

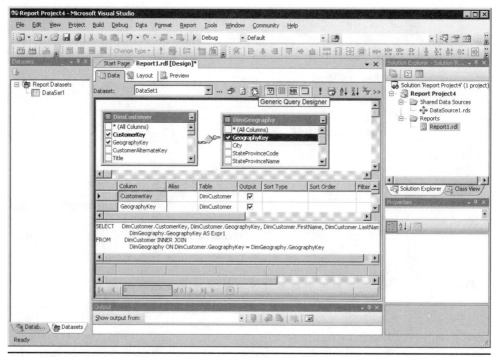

Figure 9-9   *Data pane – Interactive Query Builder*

The Preview tab allows you to preview what the rendered report will look like. When you click the Preview tab, the Report Designer will execute the report and display it in the Preview tab. The Preview doesn't allow you to make changes to the way the report looks. In order to change the report, you need to use the Layout tab.

Toolbox   The Toolbox window in the Reporting Services Report Designer is shown on the left side of the screen in Figure 9-8. The Toolbox is used to drag and drop components onto their respective design surfaces. The general report controls are listed here:

▶ **Textbox**   The Textbox control enables you to display textual data on your report. The text box can be placed anywhere on the report and can contain column data, labels, and calculated fields.

▶ **Line**   The Line control enables you to draw a line on the report layout.

▶ **Table**   The Table control enables you to bind a table to the report layout.

▶ **Matrix**   You can use the Matrix control to display a grid on the report layout. You can bind the Matrix control to the report's dataset.

▶ **Rectangle**   The Rectangle control is primarily used as a container for other report elements. It can also be used as a graphical element by the Line control.

▶ **List**   The List control enables you to place a list on your report layout. The list can be bound to fields in your dataset.

▶ **Image**   The Image control enable you to bind binary images to the report layout. The supported formats are BMP, JPG, GIF, and PNG.

▶ **Subreport**   The Subreport control is used to link a section of the report to another, previously defined report. The Subreport can either be a stand-alone report or be expressly designed to run within another report.

▶ **Chart**   The Chart control draws a chart on the report layout. The Chart control can be bound to the report's dataset and supports a large number of different chart types, including: columns, bar, line, pie, scatter, bubble, area, doughnut, radar, stock, and polar.

Solution Explorer   You can see the Report Designer's Solution Explorer in the upper right-hand corner of Figure 9-8. The Solution Explorer provides a hierarchical tree view of the different projects and files that are included in a Business Intelligence Development Studio solution. The top item in the Solution Explorer hierarchy is the solution name. Under the solution, you can have one or more projects.

Properties   The Report Designer's Properties window is located in the bottom-right corner of Figure 9-8. The Properties window can be used to set the attributes of each of the elements of the project, including the report layout items at design time and the location and filenames of the solution, data sources, and reports.

Output   The Report Designer also provides an Output window that shows the results of building and deploying reports. After a report is designed, it must be built and then deployed before it can be used. The Build process creates a .NET assembly, while the Deploy process takes that assembly and installs it in the ReportServer database. The result of these actions is shown in the Output window that you can see in the bottom of Figure 9-8.

Report Model Designer

The Report Model Designer is used to create a report model. A *report model* is a description of the metadata from a data source and its relationships. The report model is used by the Report Builder tool to search and select the data that users can employ to create reports from the data source. The Report Builder tool will use the report model definitions to generate a query to retrieve the requested data. The report model is contained in a report model project, which consists of data source files, data source view files, and report model files. Each report model file can reference only one data source file and one data source view file. Report model project can be generated only from SQL Server and Analysis Services databases. The Report Model Designer is shown in Figure 9-10.

To build a report model, you open up SQL Server 2005's Business Intelligence Development Studio and then select File | New | Project. On the New Projects dialog, click the Business Intelligence Projects options from the Project Types list box to view the installed BI project templates and select the Report Model Project template. Type a name and a location for the project and click OK.

A blank project will be started that contains elements like the Report Designer elements discussed previously, including the Solution Explorer window, the Properties window, and the design surface. However, the items inside each of these windows reflect the file types that are needed for this type of project. For example,

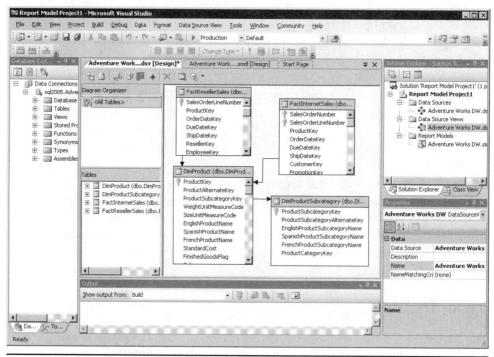

Figure 9-10   *Report Model Designer*

the Solution Explorer window shows a tree hierarchy that includes the folders Data Sources, Data Source Views, and Report Models; whereas the Report Designer's Solution Explorer window included folders for Shared Data Sources and Reports.

The first thing to do in the report model project is to add a data source to the project. Right-click the Data Sources folder in the Solution Explorer window and select the Add New Data Source option. A wizard will prompt you to select a server and a database name. Next, you need to add a data source view. Right-click the Data Source View folder in the Solution Explorer window and select the Add New Data Source View option. Another wizard will prompt you to select a data source and then tables and views to include in your data source view. You can open a data source view file and edit it interactively in the design surface. The data source view is displayed as a list of tables and a diagram showing the relationships of the tables. In the design surface you can add or remove tables, add new relationships, create named queries, replace tables, explore table data, and delete the table from the data source view. You can see an example of a data source view in Figure 9-11.

After a data source and a data source view have been created, you create a report model. A report model specifies the business entities, data fields, and roles that will

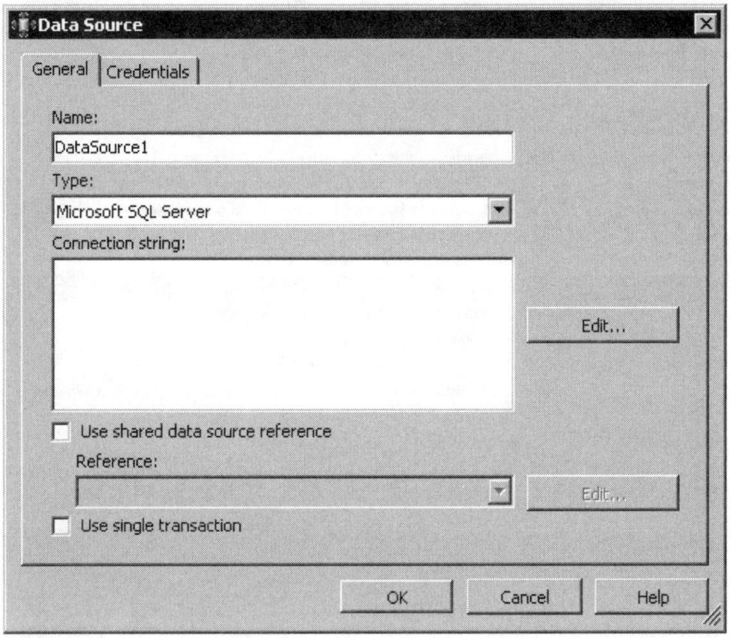

Figure 9-11 *Data source view*

be used in the report. Right-click the Report Model folder in the Solution Explorer window and select the Add New Report Model option. A wizard will start, prompting you to select a data source view. The next screen displays a list of options that allows you to choose the rules that will be used to generate the metadata information from the data source to produce the report model. Figure 9-12 shows the prompt to select report model generation rules.

After the report model is created, it needs to be published to the server before the Report Builder tool can use it to actually create a report. When a report model is published to the server, the data source and data source view are included in the publication. To publish the report model to the server, right-click the Report Model Project in the Solution Explorer and select the Deploy option. This will build the project and deploy it to your server.

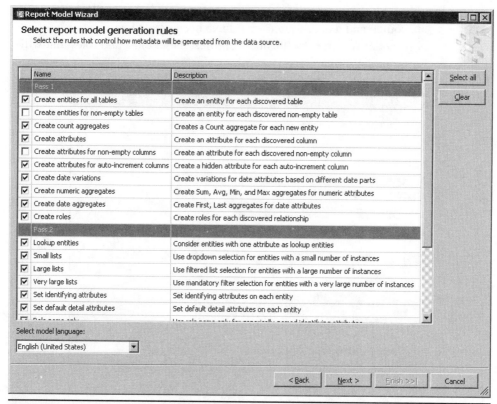

Figure 9-12 *Report model generation rules*

Report Builder

Once a report model has been created and published to the server, the Report Builder tool can be used to design and run a report based on the report model. Using the Report Builder, users can create table, matrix, or chart reports; use a report layout template; and select a predefined report model. Users can also add text and formatting to the report; create new fields and perform calculations to add to the report; and preview, print, and publish the completed report to the server. Using the report model information, the Report Builder will automatically generate a query that will retrieve all the requested data to include in the report.

The Report Builder is accessed through the Report Manager. To launch the Report Builder, point your Web browser to http://<servername>/reports, and then click the Report Builder button. A dialog will be displayed allowing you to choose a source of data for your new report. Select a data source and click OK to start the Report Builder interface. Figure 9-13 shows the Report Builder interface.

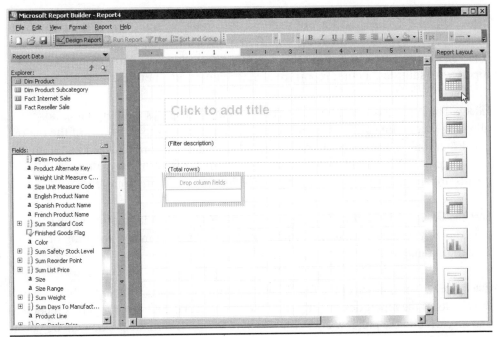

Figure 9-13 *Report Builder*

Report Builder Elements

The next section discusses the Report Builder elements.

Explorer   The Report Builder Explorer window, which is shown on the left side of Figure 9-13, displays the tables and items in your data source that are available to your report. Selecting one of the items in the Explorer window will display the fields associated with that item listed in the Fields window.

Fields   The Fields window is shown in Figure 9-13, below the Explorer window on the left side of the Report Builder environment. You can drag and drop fields from the Fields window onto the design surface of the Report Builder.

Design Surface   The design surface is displayed in the middle of the Report Builder and shows a grid layout for placing fields and items on your report. Areas on the design surface are predefined to accept the dragged and dropped fields, according to the Report Layout template chosen.

Report Layout   The Report Layout window, shown on the right side of the Report Builder, allows you to select from six different predefined report layout templates. You can choose a table report, a table report with subtitles, a matrix report, a matrix report with subtitles, a chart report, or a chart report with subtitles.

Filter   The Filter icon on the Report Builder toolbar displays a Filter dialog box allowing you to drag and drop fields onto a Filter pane on the right side of the dialog. The Filter dialog box is used to narrow the data results that are returned and used in your report. When fields are dropped onto the Filter pane in the dialog, the filter results are automatically created for you and incorporated into your report.

Sort and Group   The Sort and Group icon on the Report Builder toolbar allows you to organize your report data into groups and to sort the data in an ascending or descending manner.

Run Report   You can select the Run Report icon on the Report Builder toolbar to see the results of the report design populated with your actual data. Your report is rendered and displayed in the preview area of the Report Builder. From the preview mode you can view individual pages, filter your report, export your report, or print your report. To return to design mode, select the Design Report option from the main menu.

Programmability

Reporting Services is an extensible reporting platform, complete with a set of APIs that allow developers to design and build reporting solutions. Reporting Services can be integrated into custom applications in two ways: using URL access and using the Reporting Services Simple Object Access Protocol (SOAP) API. The programming method you choose depends on the functionality you need in your application. URL access is best used when users only need to view or navigate through rendered reports through a Web browser. The Reporting Services SOAP APIs allow more complex operations, such as creating and managing reports and subscriptions, data sources, and Report Server database items. There are also times when a combination of these two methods most effectively meets your business needs.

You can also develop and manage extensions consumed by the Reporting Services components using the available managed code API. You can create assemblies using the Microsoft .NET Framework that add new Reporting Services functionality to meet your specialized business tasks.

Using URL Access in a Window Form

Even though accessing your reports using URL links is best suited for Web environments, you can also launch a report by starting your Internet Explorer programmatically from a Windows form, or you can use a Web browser control to display a report on your Windows form.

Starting Internet Explorer from a Windows Form

Internet Explorer can be started from a Windows form using the Process class of the System.Diagnostics namespace. The Process class is used for controlling applications on your computer. To view a report in your ReportServer database, you set the arguments of the Process.Start function with the IExplore.exe application and the URL of the report. The following code shows launching the IExplore process to display a report when a user clicks a button on a Windows form:

```
Imports System.Diagnostics

Public Class Form1

    Private Sub Button1_Click(ByVal sender As System.Object, _
        ByVal e As System.EventArgs) Handles Button1.Click
        Process.Start("iexplore.exe", _
            "http://localhost/ReportServer/Pages/" & _
            "ReportViewer.aspx?%2fProducts+Report")
    End Sub
End Class
```

Notice how, at the top of the code, the Imports declaration is used to include the System.Diagnostics namespace. When the user clicks the Button1 button, the Internet Explorer browser is started and the Products report is displayed.

Embedding a Browser Control on a Windows Form

You can add a Web browser control to your Windows form for viewing your report. The Web browser control is included in the Internet Controls Library, shdocvw.dll.

To add the Web browser control to your Windows form:

1. Create a Windows form application in one of the .NET framework languages.

2. Select the Web Browser control from the Toolbox and drag it onto the design surface of your Windows form.

3. Right-click the Web browser control and select the Properties option from the pop-up menu.

4. Set the URL property to the URL access string for your report. In our example, the URL string is: http://localhost/ReportServer/Pages/ReportViewer .aspx?%2fProducts+Report.

When the application is run, the report will automatically be generated and displayed in the Web browser as shown in Figure 9-14.

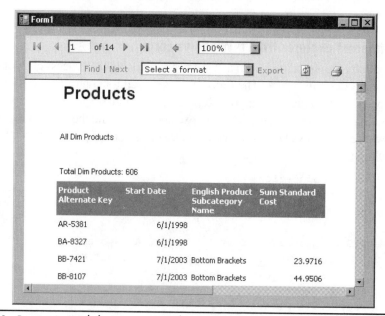

Figure 9-14 *Report in Web browser control*

Integrating Reporting Services Using SOAP

While you can view reports in your Windows programs using URL access, the Reporting Services SOAP APIs expose the full set of management functions, allowing you to develop customized business reporting solutions. All of the administrative actions of the Report Manager are available to the developer through the SOAP APIs.

Using the SOAP API in a Windows Application

A Web service object is provided that allows you to call the Reporting Services functions from your Windows form application code. To use the Web service object, you declare the object in your program code as follows:

```
Dim RepSrv As New ReportingService()
```

Then you can set the properties and use the methods just as you would for any other object. The ReportingService object allows you to manage actions such as catalog item retrieval, data sources, events, extensions, jobs, policies, roles, schedules, subscriptions, and tasks. The following code example shows how to list the items in a ReportServer database:

```
' Create a new Web service object
Dim RepSrv As New ReportingService()
RepSrv.Credentials = _
  System.Net.CredentialCache.DefaultCredentials

' Return the list of items in My Reports
Dim CatItms As CatalogItem() = _
  RepSrv.ListChildren("/My Reports", False)

Dim CatItm As CatalogItem
For Each CatItm In  items
    catalogComboBox.Items.Add(CatItm.Name)
End If
Next CatItm
```

Extensions

You can extend specific features of Reporting Services and its components by using the managed code API that is available. The Reporting Services Extension Library is a set of classes, interfaces, and value types that are included in Reporting Services.

You can use this library to access system functionality; it is designed to be the foundation on which .NET Framework applications can be used to extend Reporting Services components. You can build custom extensions to add functionality in areas such as data processing, delivery, rendering, and security. The extension functions are included in namespaces that you can import into your .NET applications. The extensions library namespaces are as follows:

Microsoft.ReportingServices.DataProcessing	Classes and interfaces to extend the data processing capability of Reporting Services
Microsoft.ReportingServices.Interfaces	Classes and interfaces to extend delivery extensions, and security extensions for Reporting Services
Microsoft.ReportingServices.ReportRendering	Classes and interfaces to extend the rendering capabilities of Reporting Services

RDL

The Report Definition Language (RDL) is composed of Extensible Markup Language (XML) elements that describe report layout and query information. RDL conforms to the XML grammar created for Reporting Services. It defines a common schema that enables the interchange of report definitions as a standard way of communicating using reports. RDL can be generated from an application using the .NET Framework classes of the System.Xml namespace.

Accessing Reports

You can access and manage your reports through the Report Manager tool or by pointing your browser directly to a report URL link. Report Manager is a Web-based tool you can use to view published reports, run reports, and subscribe to reports. Administrators can also use the Report Manager to configure permissions and manage report distribution. You access the Report Manager through your browser using the URL http://<servername>/reports.

Using URL Access

You access reports through a report server URL request that enables you to access the reports, resources, and other items in the report server database. Report parameters for your report, the rendering output, and device settings are contained in the query string of the URL. You can embed the hyperlink URL to your reports and report server items into Web or Windows applications.

URL Access Through a Web Application

The easiest method for accessing reports in a Web application is by directly pointing your browser to a URL address. An example of directly accessing a URL is shown here:

```
<a
href="http://localhost/ReportServer/Pages/ReportViewer.
aspx?%2fProducts+Report&rs:Command=Render&rc:LinkTarget=main" target="main" >
Click here for the Products report</a>
```

While this method is quite straightforward, it has some limitations, in that some servers and browsers have a 256-character limit. To get around this, you can use the POST request on a submission form.

URL Access Through a Form POST Method

By using the METHOD="POST" on a forms submission, an application can access reports without allowing the user to modify the URL query string. The following code shows an example of using the POST method:

```
<FORM id="frmRender"
action=http://server/reportserver?/SampleReports/Products
    method="post" target="_self">
    <INPUT type="hidden" name="rs:Command" value="Render">
    <INPUT type="hidden" name="rc:LinkTarget" value="main">
    <INPUT type="hidden" name="rs:Format" value="HTML4.0">
    <INPUT type="submit" value="Button">
</FORM>
```

Report Authoring

In the first part of this chapter you learned about the various components that make up SQL Server 2005's Reporting Services. In the second half of this chapter you'll get a more detailed look at the steps required to design and deploy a simple report.

Development Stages

To develop a simple Reporting Services application, you begin by using the Report Designer to define the report's data sources and layout. You then need to build and deploy the report to the Report Server. Finally, you need to make the report available to end users by either embedding the report within an application or adding subscriptions for the report.

Designing the Reporting Solution

To create Reporting Services solution using one of the interactive tools, you first create a reporting project and select a dataset that defines the data that will be used in the report. Then you lay out the individual data fields on the report. To handle stock reports that are presented in a tabular or matrix format, the Report Wizard steps you through the process of creating a data source and laying out the report. For more complex reports, use the Report Designer to define data sources, design specialized report layouts, and include custom items, such as images.

Building and Deploying the Reporting Solution

Once the report has been designed, you need to build the report and then deploy it to the Report Server. Building the report creates a .NET assembly that will run the report. Deploying the report essentially takes this assembly and copies it to the Reporting Services Report Server. While you can perform this sequence manually, the Report Designer has built-in options to both build and deploy reports to the Report Server.

Making the Report Available to End Users

After the report has been deployed to the Report Server, you can then make the report available to end users via several different mechanisms. You can allow access to the reports by embedding them in an application, via their URLs, or by creating a subscription that will push the report to the end user. Report subscriptions can be set up to be delivered at a certain time, or they can be data driven.

Now that you have an overview of the Reporting Services development process, the next section will take you through the steps of developing and deploying a simple report using SQL Server 2005's Reporting Services.

Creating a Reporting Services Report

You begin using the Report Designer either by starting the Report Wizard and using it to create your initial report or by starting with a blank design surface and then adding your own report definition elements. In either case, defining a dataset is the first thing you need to create a report. In this example, we'll look at how to build a report using the Report Designer.

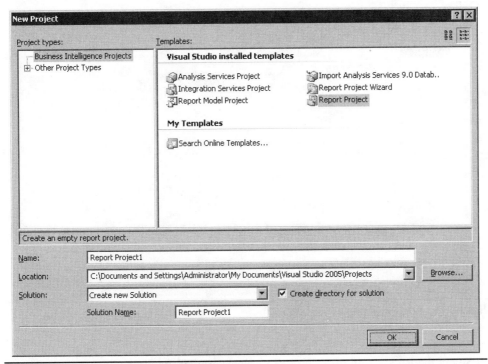

Figure 9-15   *Creating a new report: New Project*

To build a Reporting Services application, first open the Business Intelligence Development Studio and then select the File | New | Project option to display the New Project dialog that's shown in Figure 9-15.

To create a new Reporting Services report using the Report Designer, select the Business Intelligence Projects option from the Project Types list. Then in the Templates list shown in the right side of the screen select the Report Project option. Fill in the boxes at the bottom of the dialog, setting the name and location for your project. Clicking OK creates the project and displays the Report Designer. In the Solution Explorer to the right of the screen, you will see the Report Project with two folders in its directory structure: the Shared Data Sources folder and the Reports folder.

Right-click the Reports folder. A pop-up menu displays the options Add New Report, Add >, and Properties. If you select the Add New Report option, the Report Wizard will start to guide you through creating a simple tabular or matrix report. Here we will select the Add > | New Item option, which displays the Add New Item dialog as shown in Figure 9-16.

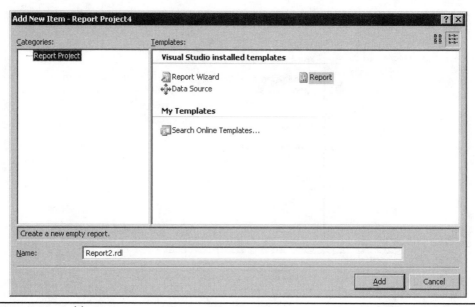

Figure 9-16 *Add New Item*

Select the Report option from the Templates area of the dialog and click the Add button to add the report file to your project and start the Report Designer. The design surface in the center of the environment presents three tabs: Data, Layout, and Preview. You define a dataset by clicking the Data tab to reveal the Data pane. You create datasets in the Data pane to access data sources to include in your report. Click the Datasets drop-down box and select the <New Dataset> option. This starts the Dataset dialog shown in Figure 9-17, which allows you to define your connection to the database.

Type a name for your data source in the Name text box. This name is used only for identification and can be anything you choose. Next, use the Type drop-down to select the type of database system that the data source will use. The default value is Microsoft SQL Server, but you can also choose OLE DB, Microsoft SQL Server Analysis Services, Oracle, or ODBC. Next, in the Connection String box input the connection string that's required to connect to the target database. If you're unfamiliar with the connection string values, you can click Edit to display the Data Link dialog, which will step you through the creation of the Data Source.

Next, de-select the Generic Query Designer button. The interactive Query Builder tool will be loaded into the design surface under the Data tab. The Query Builder

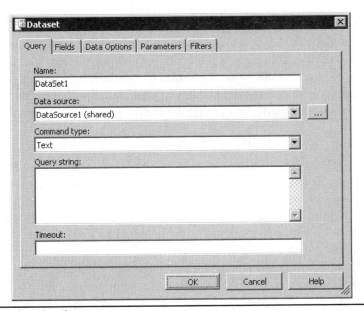

Figure 9-17   *Select the data source*

is a query design tool that enables you to build SQL queries without needing to be
a SQL expert. However, to effectively use the Query Design tool, you still need
to have a good basic knowledge of your database's design and scheme. You can
select tables from your database by right-clicking in the top portion of the Query
Builder and then selecting Add Table from the pop-up menu to display the Add
Tables dialog. There you can select one or more tables (multiple tables are selected
by holding down the CTRL key and clicking the desired table). The Query Builder
will automatically detect any relationships between the tables in terms of matching
column names and data types and will draw links between the tables visually
showing the relationships.

   After selecting the tables, you then select the desired columns from each table by
putting a check in the check box that precedes the column name. Checking the * (All
Columns) entry will automatically select all of the columns from the table. As you
interactively select the tables and columns and define the relationships between the
tables, the Query Designer automatically builds the SQL statement that will retrieve
data for your report. You can test the query by clicking the exclamation icon (!)
shown in the toolbar.

Parameterized Queries

The Query Builder can also be used to build parameterized queries where the end user supplies a value to the query at run time. To build a parameterized query using the Query Builder, you simply type a question mark into the Filter column that's in the row of the database column name that you want to use with a parameter. The Query Builder will automatically convert the question mark character to the =@ Param value.

After you've completed designing the query, click the Layout tab to display the report layout in the design surface area. Click the Toolbox tab on the left side of the environment to display a list of report items that you can drag and drop onto the report design surface. The standard report items that you can place on your report are: Textbox, Line, Table, Matrix, Rectangle, List, Image, Subreport, and Chart. Figure 9-18 shows an example of the report layout design area with several report items added to it.

You can associate the report items with fields from the data source by right-clicking the report item and selecting the Properties option from the pop-up menu. A Properties dialog will be displayed allowing you to customize the report item.

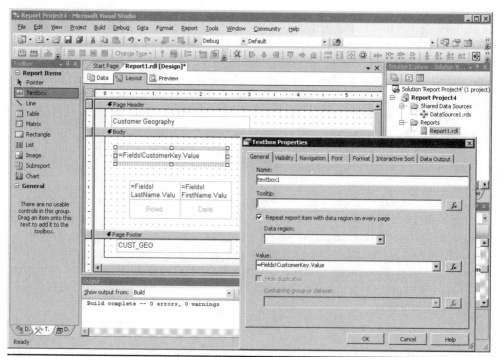

Figure 9-18 *Report layout design*

Click the Value drop-down box to list the fields available from the data source and select the field you want to relate to the report item. You can see in Figure 9-18 that the textbox1 item has been related to the field CustomerKey.Value.

After your report design is completed and the appropriate report items have been linked to fields in the data source, you can select the Preview tab to render the report for you to view in the Report Designer's Preview window. When you are satisfied with your report design, you can then generate and deploy your report to the Report Server.

Deploying a Reporting Services Report

After the report has been created, the next step in creating a Reporting Services application is to build the report and deploy it to the Report Server. Building the report creates a .NET DLL assembly, and deploying the report copies that assembly to the Reporting Services Report Server. You can deploy reporting solutions from the Report Designer by selecting the Build | Deploy Reports option from the main menu.

If you select one of the deployment options and the report has been changed, the Report Designer will automatically build the report before it is deployed. The output from the build and deployment processes is shown in the Output window that you can see at the bottom of Figure 9-18. Any errors or problems will be listed in the window. Likewise, if the report deployment succeeds, then the success message is listed in the Output window.

Running a Reporting Services Report

Reporting Services reports can be run by accessing their URL, through the Report Manager, or by embedding them in your applications. You can access and run Reporting Services reports using the URL, by pointing your browser to http://<servername>/ reportserver, where all of the Reporting Services reports and directories are listed. The ReportServer URL lists all of the reports that have been deployed to the Report Server. Each different solution is stored in its own subdirectory. Figure 9-19 shows the ReportServer Web page.

You can also access reports through Report Manager Web-based tool. Point your browser to the http://<servername>/reports directory to start the Report Manager. The Report Manager not only lets you view reports, but you can also update and manage reports with it. Figure 9-20 shows the Report Manager.

To test the reports that have been deployed, simply click the link and the Report Server will render the report inside the browser. Figure 9-21 shows the example report in the browser.

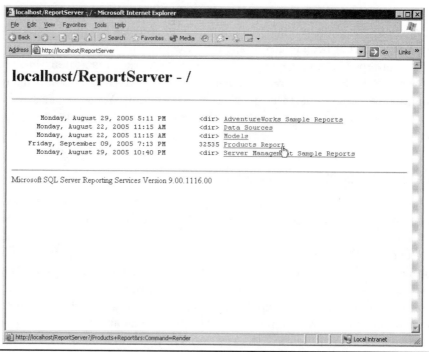

Figure 9-19   *Accessing Reporting Services reports from a URL*

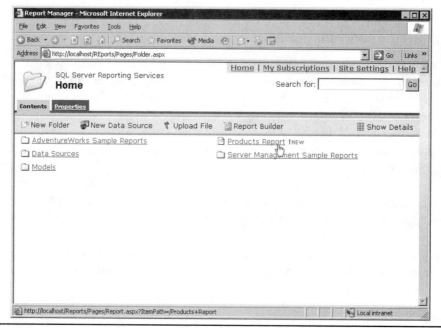

Figure 9-20   *Accessing Reporting Services reports from the Report Manager*

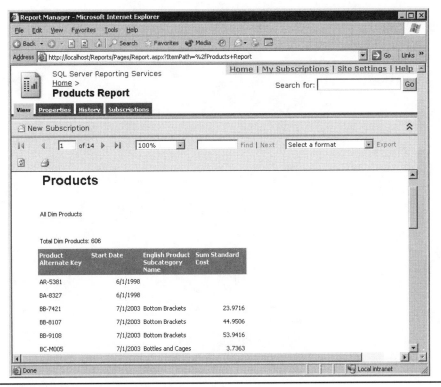

Figure 9-21 *Running Reporting Services reports*

The report that's rendered in the browser follows the format that was set up in the report design phase. Running the reports directly from the Reporting Services URL is great for testing, but when your application goes live, you'll want to embed the report URL in your application or access the Report Server via Web services calls.

Summary

The inclusion of Reporting Services is one of the most welcome enhancements found in SQL Server 2005. By providing an extensive environment for designing, managing, and deploying reports, Reporting Services goes beyond the possibilities of simple reporting solutions like Access. In this chapter, you saw the Reporting Services integrated development environment and learned about the SQL Server 2005 built-in tools capable of generating powerful, flexible reports for your organization.

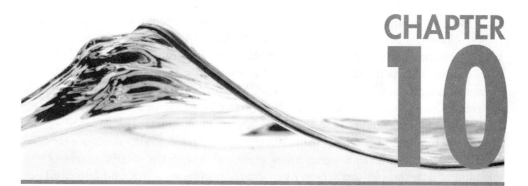

SQL Server Integration Services

IN THIS CHAPTER

An Overview of SQL Server Integration Services

Creating Packages

Deploying Packages

Programming with the SQL Server Integration Services APIs

S QL Server Integration Services is an all-new subsystem for SQL Server 2005. With SQL Server 2005 Microsoft has replaced the old Data Transformation Services (DTS) with the all-new SQL Server Integration Services (SSIS). It's important to understand that SSIS isn't a reworked version of DTS. Instead, Microsoft rewrote SSIS from the ground up. Microsoft's goal for SQL Server 2005's Integration Services was to make it an enterprise ETL platform for Windows on a par with any of the stand-alone enterprise-level ETL products. The new SSIS is completely redesigned and built using managed .NET code, giving it a more robust foundation. The new SSIS features a new graphical designer, a greatly enhanced selection of data transfer tasks, better support for programmability and improved run-time. In this chapter you'll learn how to develop data integration packages using SSIS. First, this chapter will start off by giving you an overview of the new SSIS. Next, you'll learn about how to create and deploy packages using the SSIS Designer. Then this chapter will wrap up by showing you how you can create and run SSIS packages programmatically using the Microsoft.SqlServer.Dts namespace.

NOTE

Don't be confused by the DTS moniker in the namespace. SSIS is not built on top of DTS, nor does it use any of the old DTS code. Microsoft simply didn't get around to renaming the APIs to match the name of the new subsystem.

An Overview of SQL Server Integration Services

The new Integration Services architecture is divided into two main sections: the Data Transformation Pipeline (DTP) and the Data Transformation Runtime (DTR). The split is designed to make a clear delineation between data flow and control flow. In the previous versions of DTS, the data flow engine was stronger than the control flow capabilities. This new division essentially makes the control flow portion of SSIS a first-class component on the same level as the data flow component. The new DTP essentially takes the place of the old DTS Data Pump that was used in the SQL Server 7 and 2000. Its primary function is to handle the data flow between the source and target destinations. The DTR is essentially a job execution environment that controls the control flow that's used in an SSIS package. Each of these components exposes its own distinct object model that you can program against. In Figure 10-1 you can see an overview of the new SQL Server Integration Services architecture.

The new Integration Services DTP and DTR are discussed in more detail in the following sections. More information about the new Integration Services tool set is also presented later in this chapter.

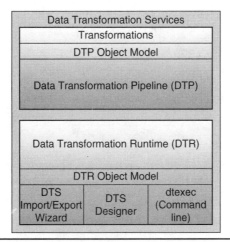

Figure 10-1 *Integration Services architecture*

Data Transformation Pipeline (DTP)

The DTP takes care of the data flow and transformations that take place as rows are moved between the data source and the data target. DTP uses data adapters to connect to the source and destination data sources. As you can see in Figure 10-1, the DTP engine is accessed using the DTP Pipeline object model. This object model is the API that is used by both the built-in transformations supplied by Microsoft and any user-created custom transformations. Transformations move and optionally manipulate row data as they move data from the source columns to the destination columns. You can get a more detailed look at the new DTP architecture in Figure 10-2.

SQL Server 2005 provides a number of source and destination data adapters. Out of the box, SQL Server 2005's Integration Services comes with adapters for SQL Server databases, XML, flat files, and other OLE DB–compliant data sources. While the job of the data adapters is to make connections to the data's source and destination endpoints, the job of the transformations is to move and optionally manipulate the data as it's moved between the source and destination endpoints. Transformation can be as simple as a one-to-one mapping between the source columns and the target columns, or it can be much more complex, performing such tasks as selectively moving columns between the source and target, creating new target columns using one-to-many mappings, or computing derived columns. SQL Server 2005's Integration Services comes with a substantial number of built-in transformations. In addition to these built-in transformations, you can build your own custom transformations by taking advantage of the DTP object model API.

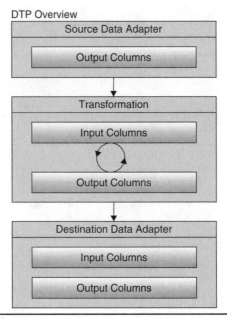

Figure 10-2 *Data Transformation Pipeline components*

Data Transformation Runtime (DTR)

The DTR consists of the DTR engine and the DTR components. DTR components are objects that enable you to govern the execution of SSIS packages. The DTR components are used to build work flows, containers provide structured operations, tasks provide data transfer and transformation functionality, and constraints control the sequence of a work flow in a package. You can see an overview of the new DTR architecture in Figure 10-3.

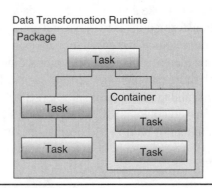

Figure 10-3 *Data Transformation Runtime overview*

The primary DTR components are packages, containers, and tasks. *Tasks* are collections of DTR components; each task is composed of data sources and target destinations as well as data transformations. *Containers* are used to organize and structure related tasks. These containers and tasks are grouped together to form packages. The Integration Services *package* is the physical unit that groups together all of the functions that will be performed in a given transfer operation. Packages are executed by the DTR to perform data transfers. Integration Services packages can be easily rerun or even moved to a different system and executed stand-alone.

The primary purpose of the DTR engine is to control the execution of Integration Services packages. The DTR controls the work flow of the tasks contained in an Integration Services package. In addition, the DTR engine stores package layout; runs packages; and provides debugging, logging, and event handling services. The DTR engine also enables you to manage connections and access Integration Services package variables.

The DTR is accessed using the DTR object framework. The DTR run-time object framework is the API that supports the Integration Services Import/Export Wizard and the Integration Services Designer in addition to the command-line dtexec tool. The Import/Export Wizard and the Designer are used to create packages. Programs that use the DTR object model can automate the creation and execution of Integration Services packages as is shown later in this chapter.

Creating Packages

You can create SSIS packages in three ways: using the SSIS Import and Export Wizard, using the SSID Designer, or programmatically using the DTR object model. In the next section of this chapter you'll see how to create SSIS interactively, first by using the SSIS Import and Export Wizard and then by using the SSIS Designer.

Using the SSIS Import and Export Wizard

The SQL Server 2005 Integration Services SSIS Import and Export Wizard provides a series of dialogs that lead you through the process of selecting the data source, the destination, and the objects that will be transferred. The wizard also allows you to optionally save and execute the SSIS package. Saving the packages generated with the Integration Services Import/Export Wizard and then editing them in the Integration Services Designer is a great way to learn more about Integration Services—especially if you're just getting started with Integration Services or if you're transitioning to the new SQL Server 2005 Integration Services from one of the earlier versions.

You can start the Integration Services Import/Export Wizard by entering **dtswizard** at the command line. The wizard steps you through the process of creating a package. The first action is choosing a data source. In the Data Source drop-down, you select the provider that you want to use. The connection options change depending on the provider that you select. If you select the Microsoft OLE DB Provider for SQL Server, you select the server that you want to connect to and then the database and the type of authentication that you need to use. Clicking Next leads you through the subsequent wizard dialogs. The next dialog allows you to select the data destination, which is essentially identical to the data source dialog except that it defines where the data will be transferred to. After you select the data source and destination, the wizard prompts you to select the data to be transferred and then to optionally save and execute the Integration Services package. As each task in the package executes, the transfer window is dynamically updated, showing the Integration Services package's transfer progress.

Using the SSIS Designer

While the Integration Services Import/Export Wizard is useful for simple ad hoc transfers, ETL (extraction, transformation, and loading) tasks typically require significantly more sophistication and complex processing than the SSIS Import and Export Wizard exposes. By their nature, ETL tasks are far more than just simple data transfers from one destination to another. Instead, they often combine data from multiple sources, manipulate the data, map values to new columns, create columns from calculated values, and provide a variety of data cleanup and verification tasks. That's where the new Integration Services Designer comes into play. The Integration Services Designer is a set of graphical tools that you can use to build, execute, and debug SSIS packages.

Package Overview

In this example the package will be performing an FTP transfer; the results of that FTP transfer will be a flat file; that flat file in turn will be transferred to a SQL Server database. As the flat file is being transferred to the SQL Server database, a lookup operation will occur that matches the incoming vendor product ID numbers to product IDs contained in the AdventureWorks products table. If the lookup succeeds, then the record with the corrected product ID will be written to the destination table. Otherwise, if the lookup fails, the data will be written to a log file.

To build the SSIS package, you first start the SSIS Designer using the Business Intelligence Development Studio (BIDS).

NOTE

Don't be confused by the fact that the SSIS Designer is started from the Business Intelligence Development Studio. SSIS is not limited to just Analysis Services projects. The projects developed in the Business Intelligence Development Studio are fully capable of working with relational data.

Open the BIDS and then select the File | New | Project option to open the New Project dialog. To create a new Integration Services project, select Business Intelligence Projects from the Project Types list and then Integration Project from the list of templates, as is shown in Figure 10-4. When the SSIS Designer first starts, you're presented with a blank design surface like the one shown in Figure 10-5.

Defining Tasks   At this point, to build an SSIS package, you need to drag and drop tasks from the Control Flow toolbox onto the design surface that represent the actions that you want the package to perform. To construct the sample package, you need to use an FTP task, a SQL task, and a Data Flow task. As you might imagine,

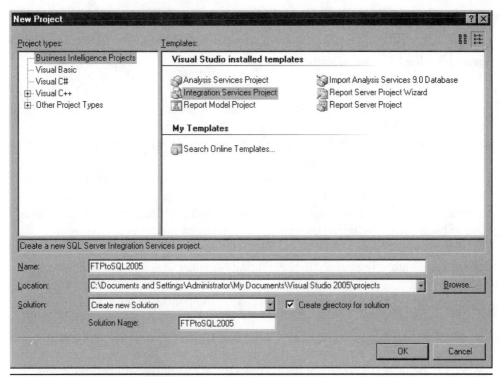

Figure 10-4   *Opening a data transformation project*

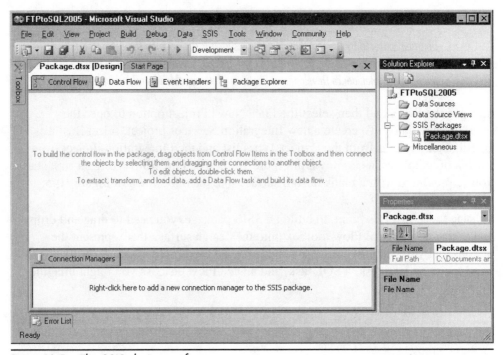

Figure 10-5 *The SSIS design surface*

the FTP task will transfer the file from the remote system. The SQL task will be used to create a new task to store the FTP data, and the Data Flow task will transfer the data from the flat file to the SQL Server table and will also perform the lookups. You can see these tasks laid out on the SSIS design surface in Figure 10-6.

You might notice in Figure 10-6 that the tasks are all marked with a red *x*. This indicates that the task has not yet been defined. At this point two things need to happen: the precedence between the tasks needs to be defined, and the tasks each need to be defined. To define the precedence between the tasks is easy.

Defining Precedence   The precedence essentially defines which task will be executed first, which second, and so on. To define precedence, click each task. This causes a green arrow indicating precedence to appear at the bottom of the task. First click the FTP task and drag the green arrow to the SQL task. Then click the SQL task and drag the green arrow to the Data Flow task. This forces the FTP task to complete before the SQL task is performed. Likewise, the SQL task must be performed before the Data Flow task. If you do not define precedence, the tasks will be executed in parallel.

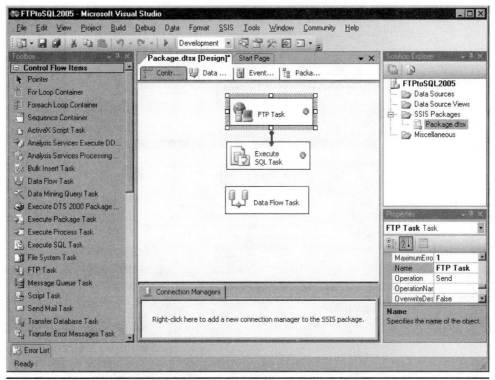

Figure 10-6 *The SSIS package tasks*

Defining Connections and Tasks Next the connections that will be used for each task must be defined. In our example, the FTP task will need an FTP connection to the remote host, the SQL task will need an OLE DB connection to the target database, and the data flow task will need a flat file connection for the resulting FTP file and an OLE DB connection to transfer the data to the SQL Server table. To create the FTP connection, right-click in the Connection Manager pane that you can see in the bottom of Figure 10-6 and then select the New Connection option to display the Add SSIS Connection dialog that you can see in Figure 10-7. To define the FTP connection, select FTP from the list of connection types and then click Add to display the FTP Connection Manager that is illustrated in Figure 10-8.

Enter the name of the FTP server in the Server Name prompt and the authentication information that is required to connect to the FTP server in the Credentials group. You can also optionally change the port from the default FTP port of 21 as well as the time-out values. Clicking Test Connection allows you to verify that the values that you've entered are correct. Click OK to save the FTP connection information.

After creating the FTP Connection Manager, you can now finish defining the FTP task. Double-click the FTP Task in the SSIS Designer to display the FTP Task Editor.

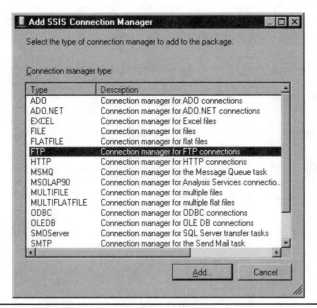

Figure 10-7   *The FTP connection*

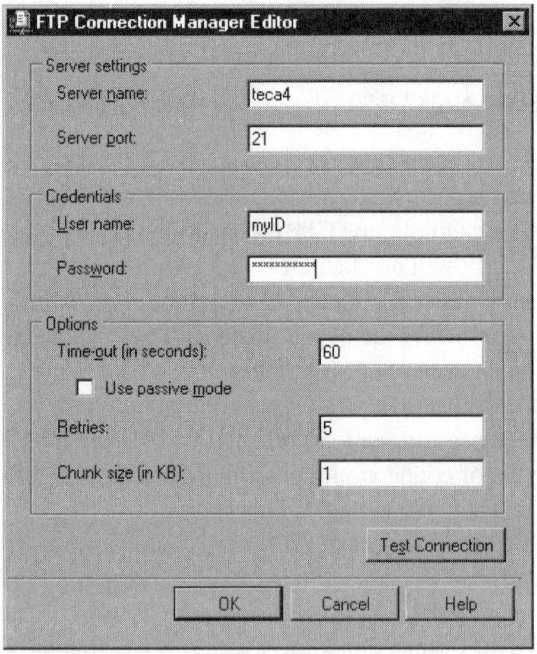

Figure 10-8   *FTP Connection Manager*

On the General screen select the FTP Connection Manager that you just created at the Ftp Connection prompt. Then click the File Transfer item to describe the transfer that will take place. You can see the File Transfer properties in Figure 10-9.

Under the Operation property select Receive Files from the drop-down list to execute an FTP Get operation. Next, under the RemotePath property enter the remote server directory where the file to download will be found. In this example you can see that the file that will be transferred is named /wwwroot/MyData.csv. Next, set the LocalPath property to the directory on the system where you want to receive the file. In Figure 10-9 the value of temp is used, which indicates that the file will be received in the c:\temp directory. Select a value of True for OverwriteFileAtDest if you want to recreate the file each time it is transferred regardless of the presence of an existing file. Click OK to save the settings in the FTP task.

After the FTP connection is defined, you can test it by right-clicking the task in the SSIS designer and then selecting the Execute Task option from the pop-up menu. Running the task will result in an FTP transfer, and the file MyData.csv will be created in the c:\temp directory.

Next, the Execute SQL task must be defined. As with the FTP task, you first need to create a connection for the task to use in order to connect to the desired database to execute a SQL Create Table command. To create an OLE DB connection for SQL

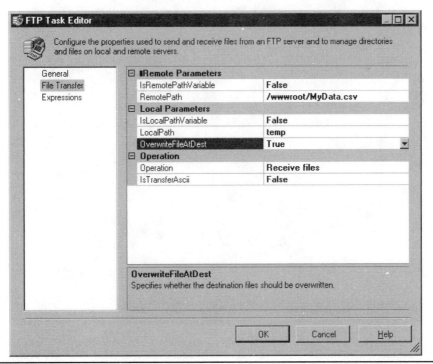

Figure 10-9 *FTP file transfer task properties*

Server, right-click in the Connection Manager and select New OLE DB Connection from the list. Then click New to create a new OLE DB connection. This will display the Connection Manager dialog shown in Figure 10-10.

NOTE

You could have selected an ADO.NET Connection type as well. However, most SSIS transformations can use only the OLE DB Connection type. Therefore, selecting the OLE DB connection enables the package to reuse the same connection for a variety of operations.

The Provider drop-down box should show .Native OLE DB\SQL Native Client. Fill in the server name, the required authentication information for the server, and the target database. Here you can see that this connection will use the server SQL2005-2. It will connect using Windows authentication, and AdventureWorks will be the default database. Click OK and then OK again to create a new OLE DB connection.

After defining the OLE DB connection, double-click the SQL task to assign values to the SQL task properties. Here you need to fill in the ConnectionType, Connection,

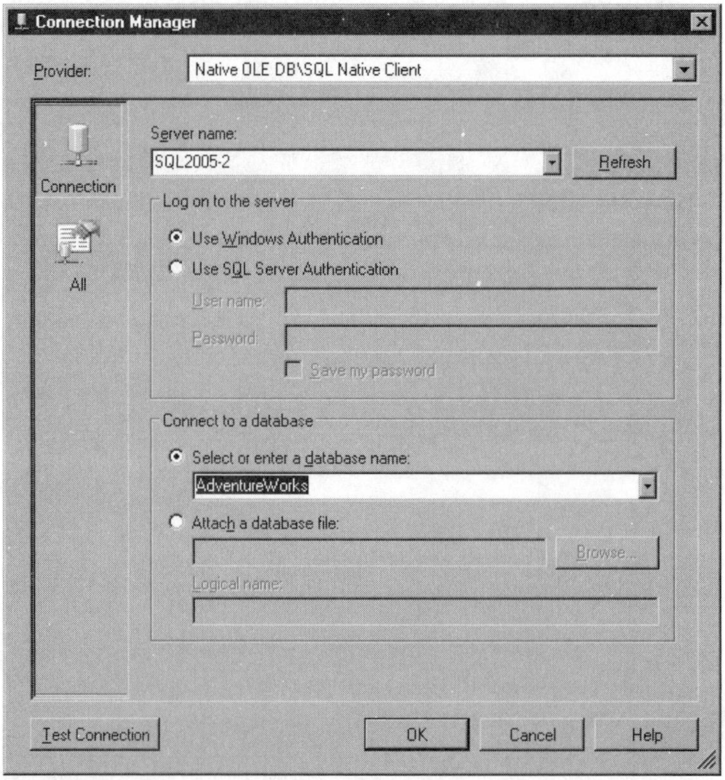

Figure 10-10   *OLE DB Connection Manager*

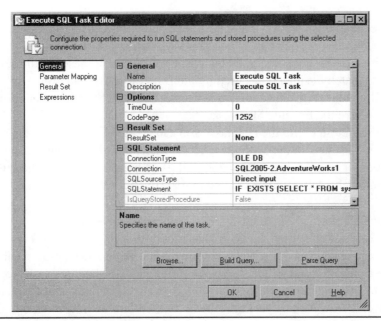

Figure 10-11 *SQL task properties*

and SQLStatement properties. You can see the completed Execute SQL Task properties shown in Figure 10-11.

As you can see in Figure 10-11, the ConnectionType property has been set to OLE DB, and the Connection property has been assigned the name of the OLE DB connection that was created earlier, in this case, SQL2005-2.AdventureWorks1. Next, the SQLStatement property must be assigned a SQL command. This example will use a SQL statement that first drops and then creates the destination table. You can see the complete SQL statement in the following listing:

```
IF  EXISTS (SELECT * FROM sys.objects WHERE object_id =
OBJECT_ID(N'[Purchasing].[ProductShipments]') AND type in (N'U'))
  DROP TABLE [Purchasing].[ProductShipments]
GO

CREATE TABLE [Purchasing].[ProductShipments](
  [ShipProductID] [varchar](15) NOT NULL,
  [AdwProductID] [int] NOT NULL,
  [Name] [varchar](50) NOT NULL,
  [ProductNumber] [varchar](25) NOT NULL,
  [ShipDate] [datetime] NULL,
  [Units] [int] NOT NULL
) ON [PRIMARY]
GO
```

The SQL code in this listing will create a table called Purchasing.ProductShipments in the AdventureWorks database. The columns here pass on the values that are provided by the FTP transfer. Take note of the data types of these columns, as they will need to match the data types used by the Data Flow task later on.

After filling out the ConnectionType, Connection, and SQLStatement properties, click OK to save the Execute SQL task.

As you saw earlier with the FTP task, you can test the Execute SQL task by right-clicking the task in the SSIS designer and selecting the Execute Task option from the pop-up menu. This will run the SQL statement; in this case, the Purchasing .ProductShipments table will be created in the AdventureWorks database.

Defining the Data Flow   Next, the Data Flow task needs to be defined. Double-click the Data Flow task to switch the SSIS Designer to the Data Flow tab. This will cause the toolbox to change from the Control Flow toolbox to the Data Flow toolbox. While the Control Flow toolbox shows the different tasks that are available, the Data Flow toolbox shows the available data sources, transformations, and destinations. To define the data flow for this package, first drag the Flat File Source onto the design surface from the Data Flow Source portion of the toolbox. Next, go to the Data Flow Transformations section of the toolbox and drag the Lookup transformation onto the designer. Then go to the Data Flow Destination section of the toolbox and drag the SQL Server Destination onto the SSIS data flow design surface. The design surface should appear like the one shown in Figure 10-12.

You assign precedence and values to each of the data flow elements in the same way that you did to the control flow tasks. To assign precedence to the data flow elements, first click the Flat File Source item and drag the green arrow to the Lookup transformation. Next, click the Lookup transformation and drag the green arrow to the SQL Server Destination item. This will cause the data flow to start with the flat file source, perform a lookup, and then move on to the SQL Server destination. To define each of the data flow elements, double-click the element that you want to work with to open the editor and then assign the appropriate value.

To define the Flat File Source, double-click the Flat File Source transformation to display the Flat File Source Editor. There, click New to create a new Flat File Manager. This will display the Flat File Connection Manager shown in Figure 10-13.

In the Flat File Connection Manager name the connection by filling in the Connection Manager Name property. This example uses the value of FTP File Output. Then tell the Flat File Manager about the file that you will be using as input by filling in the File Name property with the name of the file that will be read. In Figure 10-13 you can see that the Flat File Manager will be reading the file c:\temp\ Mydata.csv. If you know that the incoming data will have header values in the first row, as many csv files do, then check the Column Names In The First Data Row check box. Click OK to save the settings.

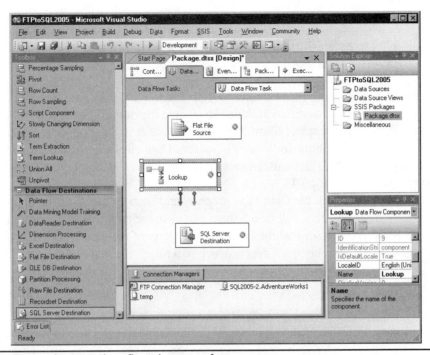

Figure 10-12 The SSIS data flow design surface

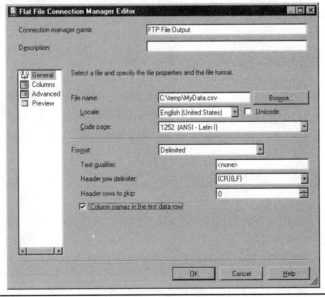

Figure 10-13 Flat File Connection Manager

NOTE

Testing the earlier FTP task will produce a file that you can use to connect to and preview with the Flat File Connection Manager.

Each of the output data types should be changed to match the data types that are used in the SQL Server destination table. To change the output data types, right-click the Flat File Source and select Show Advanced Editor from the pop-up menu to display the Advanced Editor for Flat File Source. Then click the Output Properties tab and expand the Flat File Source | Output Columns node to display a dialog like the one shown in Figure 10-14.

For each column, click the Data Type property and change the type from DT_STR (the default) to the type that will match the columns in the target table. For instance, in Figure 10-14 you can see that the Data Type property of the AdwProductID column has been changed to a four-byte integer, which will match the required output column.

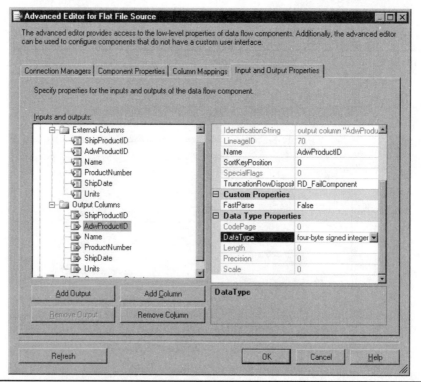

Figure 10-14 *Modify the Flat File output column data types*

In this case, it will also match the ProductID column of the Product table, which will later be used to perform a data lookup. After all of the data type changes have been made, click the OK button to save the Flat File property changes.

The next step is to set up the database lookup that will be used to verify that the vendor-supplied product numbers are correct. In this example, the AdventureWorks product number is supplied in the AdWProductID field that's found in the FTP output file. If the value for the AdWproductID matches a value from the Production .ProductID column, then the data will be written to the SQL Server destination table. Otherwise, the data will be written to an error file. To define the Lookup, double-click the Lookup transformation on the data flow design surface. This will display the Lookup Transformation Editor shown in Figure 10-15.

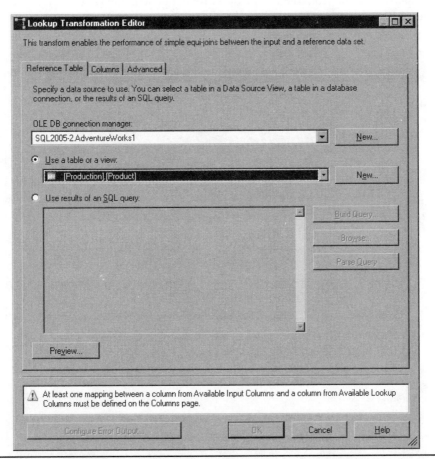

Figure 10-15 *Lookup Transformation Editor: Select Connection Manager*

Under the Reference Table tab use the drop-down box to select the OLE DB Connection Manager that was created earlier. Here you can see that the OLE DB Connection Manager is set to SQL2005-2.AdventureWorks1. After assigning the connection, the next step is to specify the table or query that will be used for the lookup operation. This example uses the table Production.Product from the AdventureWorks database. After selecting the table, the next step is to specify the columns that will be used in the lookup. To select the columns, click the Columns tab as is shown in Figure 10-16.

On the Columns tab first select the column from the list of Available Input columns that you will use to perform the lookup. Then drag that column over to the matching column in the Available Lookup Columns list. In Figure 10-16 you can see that the value from the incoming AdWProductID column will be used to look up values in the ProductID column from the Production.Product table that was selected earlier. If you only want to perform a lookup operation, you can stop here. Click OK to save the Lookup Transformation settings.

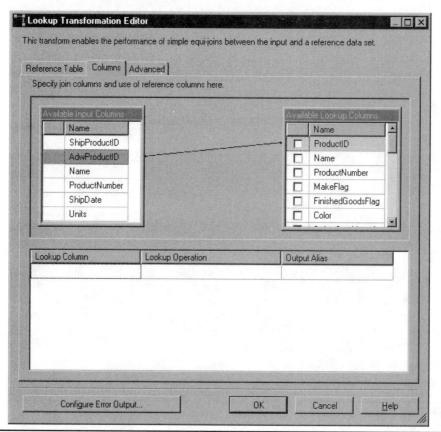

Figure 10-16 *Lookup Transformation Editor: Match Columns*

However, if you also want to build an error log to report lookup failures, then you should add a new Flat File Connection Manager that will allow you to output the Lookup transformation error output. As you saw earlier, to add a Flat File Connection, right-click in the Connection Manager pane in the SSIS Designer and then select New Flat File Connection from the pop-up menu to display the Flat File Connection Manager as shown in Figure 10-17.

Give the Flat File connection a name. In this example it is named Product Lookup Errors. Next, use the File Name prompt to specify the folder and file that will be used to write the output. In Figure 10-17 you can see that the lookup errors will be written to the file lookuperrors.csv in the c:\temp directory. The remainder of the prompts control the formation of the output data. In Figure 10-17 all of the defaults have been accepted, which will result in the creation of a comma-separated value (csv) file. Click OK after specifying the properties for the Product Lookup Errors Flat File connection to save the values.

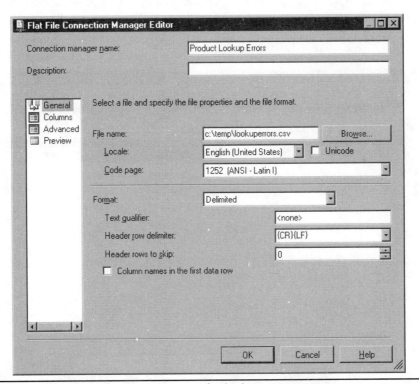

Figure 10-17 *Flat File Connection Manager for lookup error output*

After creating the new Flat File Connection Manager, drag a new Flat File Destination from the data flow toolbox onto the design surface. Double-click the new Flat File Destination to open the editor and then select the Product Lookup Errors connection for the Connection property. Finally, drag the red line from the Lookup Transformation to the Flat File Destination to connect the flat file to the Error Lookup Transformation's error output.

Next, to tell the Lookup Transformation to direct error rows to the flat file, double-click the transformation to open the Lookup Transformation Editor. Then click the Columns tab followed by the Configure Error Output button to display the Configure Error Output dialog shown in Figure 10-18.

On the Configure Error Output dialog use the drop-down beneath Error and select the Redirect Row option. This will redirect any error output to the flat file that was defined using the Flat File Connection Manager. Then click OK.

The final step to complete the configuration of the SSIS package's data flow is the definition of the SQL Server destination. On the data flow design surface double-click the SQL Server Destination object to open up the SQL Destination Editor that's shown in Figure 10-19.

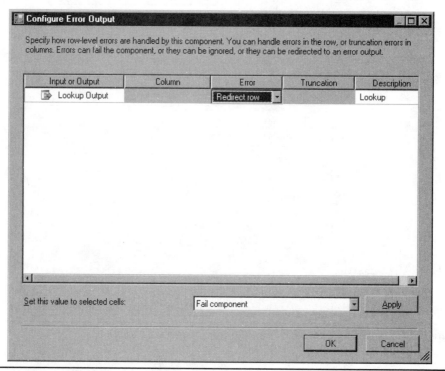

Figure 10-18 *Configure Error Output*

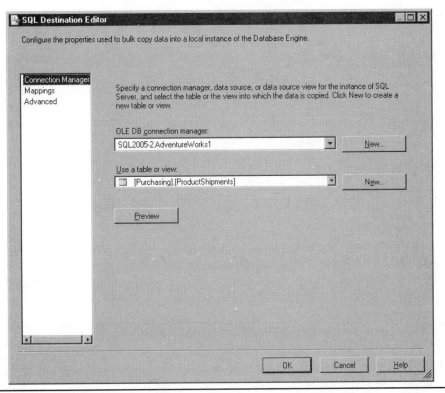

Figure 10-19 *SQL Destination Editor*

The first step in defining the OLE DB Destination is to select the appropriate OLE DB Connection Manager. Click the OLE DB Connection Manager drop-down and then select the SQL2005-2.AdventureWorks1 OLE DB Connection Manager. Next, in the Use A Table Or View drop-down select the table that will store the output. In Figure 10-19 you can see that the Purchasing.ProductShipments table has been selected.

NOTE

Testing the Execute SQL task that was previously created will produce a Purchasing .ProductsShipments table that you can use to define the OLE DB Connection Manager.

At this point the configuration of the SSIS package has been completed. You can optionally change the column mappings or view the contents of the ProductsShipments file. Clicking OK will save the properties configurations of the OLE DB Destination and close the SQL Destination Editor. The completed data flow is shown in Figure 10-20.

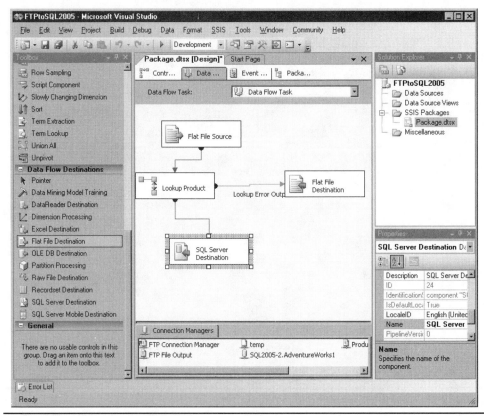

Figure 10-20   *The completed data flow*

The elements on the data flow designer reflect the flow of events that will happen when the SSIS package executes the Data Flow task. Here you can see that the Flat File source (which points to the c:\temp\MyData.csv file) will be read as input. For each row read a lookup to the AdventureWorks Production.Products table will be performed. If a match for the incoming ProductID is found in the Production.Products table, then the data will be written to the Purchasing.ProductShipments table in the AdventureWorks database. If the incoming ProductID has an error and doesn't match any rows in the Products table, then the data will be written to the Flat File Destination (which points to the c:\temp\lookuperrors.csv file).

NOTE

If you want to view the data that's being sent between any of the sources, transformations, or destinations on the data flow designer, you can click either the green or red connection line to display the Edit Data Path dialog. From the Edit Data Path dialog select Data Viewers and Add. When data flows over the selected data path, it will be displayed in the data viewer.

Running the Package

After the SSIS package has been designed, you can run it from the SSIS Designer by clicking the green arrow on the toolbar, pressing F5, or selecting the Debug | Start Debugging option from the menu.

In order to execute the package, a file must be available for import that can be found on the remote FTP server. The following listing shows the contents of the sample import file that is capable of testing the SSIS package:

```
ShipProductID,AdwProductID,Name,ProductNumber,ShipDate,Units
10-504,504,Cup-Shaped Race,RA-2345,,38055
10-505,505,Cone-Shaped Race,RA-7490,,38055
10-506,506,Reflector,RF-9198,,38055
10-507,507,LL Mountain Rim,RM-M464,,38055
10-508,508,ML Mountain Rim,RM-M692,,38055
10-509,509,HL Mountain Rim,RM-M823,,38055
10-510,510,LL Road Rim,RM-R436,,38055
10-511,511,ML Road Rim,RM-R600,,38055
10-512,512,HL Road Rim,RM-R800,,38055
10-514,594,LL Mountain Seat Assembly,SA-M198,,38055
10-515,595,ML Mountain Seat Assembly,SA-M237,,38055
10-516,596,HL Mountain Seat Assembly,SA-M687,,38055
10-517,597,LL Road Seat Assembly,SA-R127,,38055
10-518,518,ML Road Seat Assembly,SA-R430,,38055
```

Four rows in this test file will produce error output. These are the rows with the values 594, 595, 596, and 597, as there are no matching values for these in the Production.Products table.

Running the SSIS package from the designer will show you the package's run-time status under the Execution Results tab as is shown in Figure 10-21, where you can see the status of each of the different tasks that compose the FTPtoSQL2005 package. The FTP task was completed first, at 11:20:52, followed by the Execute SQL task, which was completed at 11:20:53, and the Data Flow task was completed last.

Using Breakpoints

The SSIS Designer provides a fully interactive development environment, and in addition to being able to create SSIS packages it also offers the ability to debug them. You can use the SSIS Designer to set breakpoints at the package level, the container level, or the individual tasks level of an SSIS package.

Integration Services provides ten break conditions that you can enable on all tasks and containers. In addition, some tasks and containers include additional task-specific

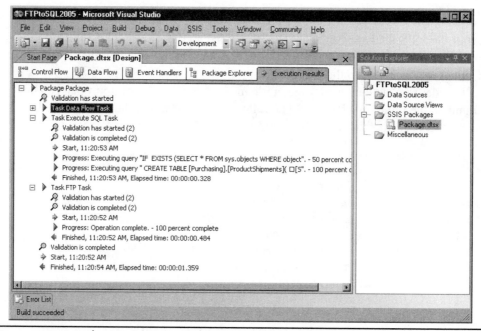

Figure 10-21 *Package execution results*

breakpoint conditions. When a breakpoint is encountered, the package halts execution and you can examine the contents of variables and other elements in the package. To set a task breakpoint in an SSIS package, right-click the task and select the Edit Breakpoints option from the pop-up menu to display the Set Breakpoints dialog that you can see in Figure 10-22.

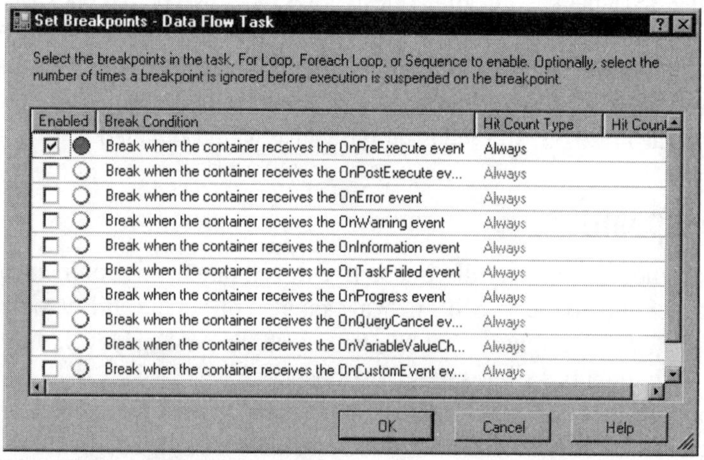

Figure 10-22 *Set Breakpoints*

You can set breakpoints on one or more of the conditions by placing a check mark in the Enabled box. In addition, you can use the Hit Count to control if and how frequently encountering the breakpoint will result in the halting of the packages. The default value is Always, meaning the package will always stop when the condition is encountered. However, by specifying a hit count, you can control how many times the condition must be encountered before the package execution is paused.

Using Checkpoints

Checkpoints enable a failed SSIS package to be restarted at the spot where the execution was ended. Using checkpoints can significantly improve the recoverability of packages that contain complex operations. In addition, they can provide considerable time savings for the recovery of packages that contain long-running tasks because the package doesn't need to reprocess all of the tasks prior to the checkpoint. When checkpoints are enabled, information about the package's execution is written to a checkpoint file. SSIS will use the data in this file to determine which control flow tasks in the package have been executed. If a package that is using checkpoints fails, the SSIS DTR engine can use the checkpoint file to restart the package at the point of failure.

Checkpoints apply to the package's control flow, not to the data flow. Control-flow containers are the basic unit of checkpoint restartability. When the execution of a package that uses checkpoints is restarted, the package execution begins with the failed control flow task. If that control flow task uses any data flow within that task, then the data flow will be rerun in its entirety—the task will not pick up from the last row transferred. Even with this minor limitation, checkpoints offer a great improvement in package recoverability.

Checkpoints are enabled by setting the package's SaveCheckpoints property to True in the SSIS package properties. You can see the SaveCheckpoints property in Figure 10-23.

Once checkpoints are enabled, you also need to tell the SSIS package where to write the checkpoint data. To do this, you must supply a filename to the CheckpointFileName property. In addition, the way SSIS treats running packages where there is an existing checkpoint file is controlled by the CheckpointUsage property. The CheckpointUsage property supports the following values:

CheckpointUsage Value	Description
Never	The checkpoint file is not used, and the package always starts from the beginning of the control flow.
Always	The checkpoint file is always used, and the package restarts from the point of the previous execution failure. The package's execution will fail if the checkpoint file is not present.
IfExists	The package restarts from the point of the previous execution failure if the checkpoint file exists. If there is no checkpoint file, execution starts at the beginning of the control flow.

Figure 10-23   *Enabling checkpoints*

Using Transactions

SSIS also supports database transactions. When using transactions, the database changes performed by a package can be committed as a unit if a package runs successfully, or the changes can be rolled back as a unit if the package execution fails. Transactions can be enabled for all SSIS container types, including packages, containers, loops, and sequence containers. You enable transaction support using the container's TransactionOption property, which you set using the SSIS Designer or programmatically. The TransactionOption property supports the following values:

TransactionOption Values	Description
Not Supported	The container does not start a transaction and will not join an existing transaction that was initiated by a parent container.
Supported	The container does not start a transaction but will join an existing transaction that was started by a parent container.
Required	The container starts a transaction. If an existing transaction has already been started by the parent container, the container will join it.

Package Security

SSIS packages can contain sensitive authentication information, and saving those packages opens up the possibly of a security exposure. To protect against this possibility, SSIS supports the encryption of sensitive information. SSIS uses the Triple Data Encryption Standard (3DES) cipher algorithm with a key length of 192 bits, and packages are encrypted either when they are created or when they are exported. SSIS package encryption is controlled using the package's ProtectionLevel property, which supports the following values:

ProtectionLevel Value	Description
DontSaveSensitive	Sensitive data is not saved in the package. When the package is opened, the sensitive data will not be present and the user will need to provide the sensitive data.
EncryptSensitiveWithUserKey	Sensitive data is saved as a part of the package and is encrypted with a key that's based on the user who created or exported the package. Only that user will be able to run the package. If another user opens the package, the sensitive data will not be available.
EncryptSensitiveWithPassword	Sensitive data is saved as a part of the package and is encrypted with a user-supplied password. When the package is opened the user must provide a password to access the sensitive data. If the password is not provided, the package will be opened without the sensitive data.
EncryptAllWithPassword	The entire contents of the package will be encrypted with a user-supplied password. When the package is opened, the user must provide the package's password. If the password is not provided, the package will not be able to be opened.
EncryptAllWithUserKey	The entire contents of the package will be encrypted with a key that's based on the user key for the user who created or exported the package. Only the user who created the package will be able to open it.
ServerStorage	The package is not encrypted. Instead, the package's contents are secured according to the database's object access security. If the ServerStorage value is used, the package must be saved to the sysdtspackages90 table in the msdb database. It cannot be saved to the file system.

Deploying Packages

SSIS supports the deployment of packages through the use of the package configurations and the ability to easily deploy packages using the package deployment utility. In the next section you'll see how to create a configuration for an SSIS package as well as how to use the package deployment utility.

Creating Configurations

Configuration information enables an SSIS package to automatically load external information at run time. You can use configurations to pass in variable values and connection information to an SSIS package at run time. For variables, the Value property is assigned with the value that is passed in when the package is run. Likewise, for connection information the Connection Manager's properties such as ConnectionString, ServerName, and InitialCatalog can be assigned to dynamically change the server system that will be used by an SSIS package.

SSIS configurations are created by using the Package Configuration Organizer, which is started from BIDS. To create a package configuration for an Integration Services project, select the SSIS | Package Configurations option in BIDS. This will start the Package Configurations Organizer tool that is shown in Figure 10-24.

You can create multiple configurations for a single package. The configurations are applied to the package in the order that they are displayed in the Package Organizer. You can use the directional arrows shown on the right side of Figure 10-24 to move a configuration up or down in the list.

You can also create a single configuration that can be applied to multiple packages. For example, if you want to deploy a package to several systems where the only difference in the package properties is the server name, you could create a configuration that uses an environment variable to supply the server name.

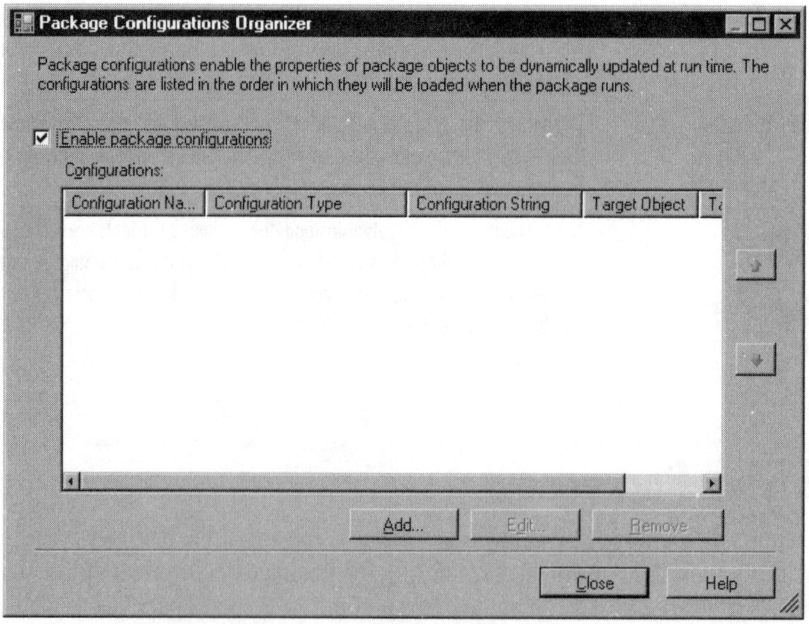

Figure 10-24 *The Package Configuration Organizer*

To create a configuration, first check the Enable Package Configurations check box and then click Add to start the SSIS Configuration Wizard. The Configuration Wizard steps you through creating a package configuration. Click past the Wizard welcome screen to display the Configuration Type dialog shown in Figure 10-25.

The Configuration Type drop-down enables you to select the data source that will be used by the configuration. SSIS package configuration supports the following configuration types:

- ▶ XML configuration file
- ▶ Environment variable
- ▶ Registry entry
- ▶ Parent package variable
- ▶ SQL Server

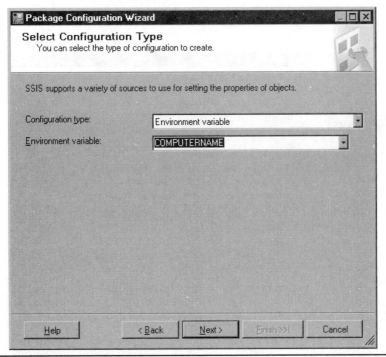

Figure 10-25 *Configuration Type*

In Figure 10-25 you can see that the type of Environment variable has been selected, along with the COMPUTERNAME variable. XML file configurations and SQL Server configurations support the selection of multiple properties in a single configuration object. The other configuration types permit only one configurable property per configuration. Click Next to display the dialog shown in Figure 10-26, which shows where you select the package's properties or variables that will have their values set by the configuration when the package is run.

In Figure 10-26 you can see that the properties for the OLE DB Connection Manager named SQL2005-2.AventureWorks1 have been expanded and that the ServerName property has been selected. This will enable the COMPUTERNAME environment variable to be substituted for the OLE DB Connection Manager's ServerName in the connection string when this package attempts to use the OLE DB connection. Clicking Next displays the configuration summary screen, which allows you to view and confirm your selections. If you need to make changes, you can use the Back button to page back through the Configuration Wizard and make any needed changes. Otherwise, clicking Next adds the configuration to the package and will display the Package Configuration Organizer with your configuration as you can see in Figure 10-27.

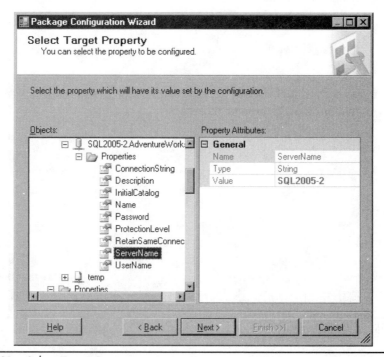

Figure 10-26 *Select Target Property*

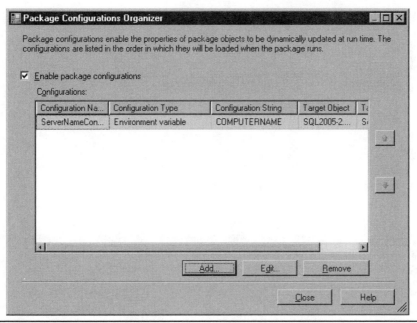

Figure 10-27   *The completed package configuration*

Later if you need to modify a configuration, click Edit to rerun the Configuration Wizard and select different objects and different properties.

Using the Package Deployment Utility

SSIS contains a handy feature called the Package Deployment Utility that allows you to assemble your SSIS packages, package configurations, and supporting files into a deployment folder and build an executable setup file to install your packages. To create the Package Deployment Utility, right-click the project properties in the BIDS Solution Explorer pane and then select the Properties option to display the Property Pages dialog box as shown in Figure 10-28.

Set the CreateDeploymentUtility option to True on the project property page. Then build your project by selecting the Build Solution option on the BIDS menu. Building the project creates the DTSDeploymentManifest.xml file and copies the project along with the DTSInstall.exe utility to the bin/Deployment folder or to the location specified in the DeploymentOutputPath property. The DTSDeploymentManifest.xml file lists the packages and the package configurations in the project. The DTSInstall.exe program runs the Package Installer Wizard.

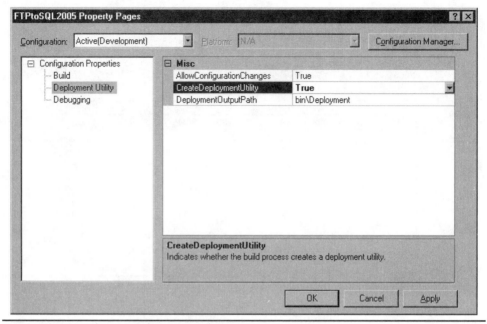

Figure 10-28 *Package Deployment Utility*

Programming with the SQL Server Integration Services APIs

In addition to providing a graphical development environment, SSIS also provides an object model API for both the DTR and the DTP that enables you to programmatically create and execute SSIS packages. Programming the data flow engine enables you to automate the creation and configuration of the SSIS tasks, transformations, and data flow tasks, and to create custom components. The run-time engine is exposed both as a native COM object model and as a fully managed object model. The SSIS data flow engine is written in native code, but it can be controlled programmatically using a managed .NET object model. In this next section you'll see an example of how you can use the SQL Server Integration Services API in a console application to create and execute a new SSIS package.

The SQL Server Integration Services API is located in a number of different assemblies: Microsoft.SqlServer.ManagedDTS.dll, SqlServer.DTSPipelineWrap .dll, and SqlServer.DTSRuntimeWrap.dll. To use these assemblies in your program, you need to add references for each of them in your project. Then you can use the Integration Services classes to create both SSIS DTP and DTR objects in your application. To add references to your project, select the Project | Add Reference menu option to display the Add Reference dialog. Scroll through the list until you see the Microsoft.SqlServer.DTSPipelineWrap, Microsoft.SqlServer.DTSRuntimeWrap, and Microsoft.SqlServer.ManagedDTS assemblies listed in the Component Name list. Select these assemblies as is illustrated in Figure 10-29. Click OK to add the references to your project.

Next, add import directives for the SSIS assembly namespaces to the Declarations section of your project. Using import directives enables you to use the classes in the imported namespaces without having to fully qualify the names. The following code listing shows how to create import directives for the SSIS namespace:

```
Imports Microsoft.SqlServer.Dts.Runtime
Imports Microsoft.SqlServer.Dts.Pipeline.Wrapper
Imports SSISRuntime = Microsoft.SqlServer.Dts.Runtime.Wrapper
```

NOTE

To avoid compile-time errors due to common object names, it's best to use an alternative import name when importing both Microsoft.SqlServer.DtsPipeline.Wrapper and Microsoft.SqlServer .DtsRuntime.Wrapper. That's why the third Imports statement uses the name SSISRuntime.

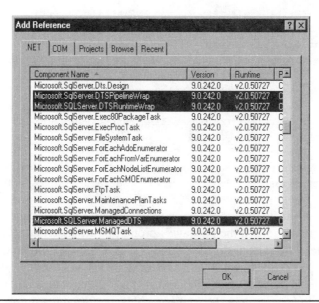

Figure 10-29   *Adding references to SSIS assemblies*

After adding the SSIS references to your project and import directives for the appropriate namespaces, you're ready to begin using the SSIS APIs in your application. The following code sample shows how you can create a package using the SSIS APIs:

```
Module CreateSSISPackage
    Sub Main()
        ' Create the Package
        Console.WriteLine("Creating the MySSIS Package")
        Dim myPackage As New Package()
        myPackage.PackageType = DTSPackageType.DTSDesigner90
        myPackage.Name = "MySSISPackage"
        myPackage.Description = "Created using the SSIS API"
        myPackage.CreatorComputerName = System.Environment.MachineName
        myPackage.CreatorName = "Otey"

        'Add the OLE DB and Flat File Connection Managers
        Console.WriteLine("Creating the MyOLEDBConnection")
        Dim cnOLEDB As ConnectionManager = _
          MyPackage.Connections.Add("OLEDB")
        cnOLEDB.Name = "MyOLEDBConnection"
        cnOLEDB.ConnectionString = _
          "Provider=SQLNCLI;Integrated Security=SSPI;" _
          & "Initial Catalog=AdventureWorks;Data Source=SQL2005-2;"

        Console.WriteLine("Creating the MyFlatFileConnection")
        Dim cnFile As ConnectionManager = _
          myPackage.Connections.Add("FLATFILE")
        cnFile.Properties("Name").SetValue(cnFile, "MyFlatFileConnection")
        cnFile.Properties("ConnectionString").SetValue _
          (cnFile, "c:\temp\MySSISFileExport.csv")
        cnFile.Properties("Format").SetValue(cnFile, "Delimited")
        cnFile.Properties("ColumnNamesInFirstDataRow") _
          .SetValue(cnFile, False)
        cnFile.Properties("DataRowsToSkip").SetValue(cnFile, 0)
        cnFile.Properties("RowDelimiter").SetValue(cnFile, vbCrLf)
        cnFile.Properties("TextQualifier").SetValue(cnFile, """")
```

Near the top of this listing you can see where a new SSIS package object named myPackage is created. Next, the package's properties are assigned values. The most important of these are the PackageType and Name properties, where the values of DTSpackageType.DTSdesigner90 and MySSISPackage are used.

After creating the package object, the next step is to create Connection Managers for the package. In this example, the package will be performing a simple export from SQL Server to the file system, which requires two Connection Managers: an OLE DB

Connection Manager to connect to SQL Server, and a Flat File Connection Manager to write the export file. First, the OLE DB Connection Manager is created and named MyOLEDBConnection. The Connection's Add method is then used to add the new ConnectionManager object to the package's Connections collection. Then the OLE DB ConnectionManager's ConnectionString property is assigned a connection string that will connect to the AdventureWorks database on the server named SQL2005-2 using integrated security. After that, a similar process creates a Flat File ConnectionManager object named MyFlatFileConnection and adds it to the package's Connections collection. Then the ConnectionString property of the MyFlatFileConnection is assigned the value of c:\temp\MySSISFileExport.csv. The following property assignments set up a delimited file type for the export operation.

After the creation of the package and Connection Manager objects, the next step to the creation of a Data Flow task is shown in the following code listing:

```
'Add a Data Flow Task
Console.WriteLine("Adding a Data Flow Task")
Dim taskDF As TaskHost = _
  TryCast(myPackage.Executables.Add("DTS.Pipeline"), TaskHost)
taskDF.Name = "DataFlow"

Dim DTP As MainPipe
DTP = TryCast(taskDF.InnerObject, MainPipe)

' Add the OLE DB Source
Console.WriteLine("Adding an OLEDB Source")
Dim DFSource As IDTSComponentMetaData90
DFSource = DTP.ComponentMetaDataCollection.New()
DFSource.ComponentClassID = "DTSAdapter.OLEDBSource"
DFSource.Name = "OLEDBSource"

' Connect, populate the Input collections and disconnect
Dim SourceInst As CManagedComponentWrapper = _
  DFSource.Instantiate()
SourceInst.ProvideComponentProperties()
DFSource.RuntimeConnectionCollection(0).ConnectionManagerID _
    = myPackage.Connections("MyOLEDBConnection").ID
DFSource.RuntimeConnectionCollection(0).ConnectionManager _
    = DtsConvert.ToConnectionManager90 _
      (myPackage.Connections("MyOLEDBConnection"))
SourceInst.SetComponentProperty("OpenRowset", "[Sales].[Customer]")
SourceInst.SetComponentProperty("AccessMode", 0)
SourceInst.AcquireConnections(Nothing)
SourceInst.ReinitializeMetaData()
SourceInst.ReleaseConnections()
```

Near the top of this listing you can see where a new Data Flow task named taskDF is created. Here the Data Flow task must be set up to read from the OLE DB Connection Manager that will be the source of the data and then write to the flat file connection that acts as the data destination. After creation of the Data Flow task, an OLE DB data adapter for the source data is created that's named DFSource. The DFSource object's ComponentClassID is set to DTSADpater.OLEDBSource, defining it as an OLE DB connection, and the Name of the data flow source is set to OLEDBSource. Next, an instance of the DFSource object is created in order to populate the input connections. This enables the downstream data flow components to see the input metadata. Here the OLE DB connection is set to the Sales.Customer table from the AdventureWorks database. After the input metadata has been collected, the connection is released.

The next step is to define the data flow destination as is shown in the following listing:

```
' Add the Flat File Destination
Console.WriteLine("Adding a Flat File Destination")
Dim DFDestination As IDTSComponentMetaData90
DFDestination = DTP.ComponentMetaDataCollection.New()
DFDestination.ComponentClassID = _
  "DTSAdapter.FlatFileDestination"
DFDestination.Name = "FlatFileDestination"

' Create an instance of the component
Dim DestInst As CManagedComponentWrapper = _
  DFDestination.Instantiate()
DestInst.ProvideComponentProperties()
DFDestination.RuntimeConnectionCollection(0).ConnectionManagerID _
    = myPackage.Connections("MyFlatFileConnection").ID
DFDestination.RuntimeConnectionCollection(0).ConnectionManager _
    = DtsConvert.ToConnectionManager90 _
        (myPackage.Connections("MyFlatFileConnection"))

' Map a connection between the source and destination
DTP.PathCollection.New().AttachPathAndPropagateNotifications _
  (DFSource.OutputCollection(0), DFDestination.InputCollection(0))

' Add columns to the FlatFileConnectionManager
Dim MyFlatFilecn As _
  SSISRuntime.IDTSConnectionManagerFlatFile90 = Nothing
For Each cm As ConnectionManager In myPackage.Connections
    If cm.Name = "MyFlatFileConnection" Then
        MyFlatFilecn = TryCast(cm.InnerObject, _
          SSISRuntime.IDTSConnectionManagerFlatFile90)
        DtsConvert.ToConnectionManager90(cm)
    End If
Next
```

```vb
' Get the columns from the source
Dim InColumns As IDTSVirtualInputColumnCollection90 _
    = DFDestination.InputCollection(0).GetVirtualInput() _
.VirtualInputColumnCollection()

Dim col As SSISRuntime.IDTSConnectionManagerFlatFileColumn90
Dim name As SSISRuntime.IDTSName90
For cols As Integer = 0 To InColumns.Count - 1 Step 1
    col = MyFlatFilecn.Columns.Add()
    ' Set the last column delimiter to CRLF
    If cols = InColumns.Count - 1 Then
        col.ColumnDelimiter = vbCrLf
    Else
        col.ColumnDelimiter = ","
    End If
    col.ColumnType = "Delimited"
    col.DataType = InColumns(cols).DataType
    col.DataPrecision = InColumns(cols).Precision
    col.DataScale = InColumns(cols).Scale
    name = TryCast(col, SSISRuntime.IDTSName90)
    name.Name = InColumns(cols).Name
Next

DestInst.AcquireConnections(Nothing)
DestInst.ReinitializeMetaData()

Dim wrapper As CManagedComponentWrapper = _
    DFDestination.Instantiate()
Dim vInput As IDTSVirtualInput90 = _
    DFDestination.InputCollection(0).GetVirtualInput()
For Each vColumn As IDTSVirtualInputColumn90 In _
    vInput.VirtualInputColumnCollection
        wrapper.SetUsageType(DFDestination _
            .InputCollection(0).ID, vInput, vColumn.LineageID, _
            DTSUsageType.UT_READONLY)
Next

' Match the input and output columns
Dim exCol As IDTSExternalMetadataColumn90
For Each InCol As IDTSInputColumn90 In _
    DFDestination.InputCollection(0).InputColumnCollection
        exCol = DFDestination.InputCollection(0) _
            .ExternalMetadataColumnCollection(InCol.Name)
        wrapper.MapInputColumn(DFDestination _
            .InputCollection(0).ID, InCol.ID, exCol.ID)
Next
DestInst.ReleaseConnections()
```

Here the data flow destination named DFDestination is created. Its ComponentClassID is set to DTSAdapter.FlatFileDestination, defining it as an OLE flat file in the file system, and the Name of the data flow source is set to FlatFileDestination. Next, an instance of the DFDestination object name DestInst is created in order to map the input columns to the columns in the destination output file.

You create the precedence between the data flow source and destination using the DTP object's AttachPathAndPropagateNotifications method. The next section of code adds the column to the FlatFile ConnectionManager. It does this by reading the metadata that was previously retrieved from the OLE DB Source connection. The DFDestination object's GetVirtualInput method populates the input collection, and then a For-Each loop is used to set the attributes for each of the output columns.

Once the collection of the columns has been created, the next step is to map the input columns from the OLE DB Source to the flat file output columns. Here a one-to-one mapping is used, and a simple For-Each loop reads through the input metadata, associating each column to the corresponding output column. After the mappings have been set up, the connection is released using the ReleaseConnections method.

This completes the code needed to create the SSIS package. In the next section of code you can see how to validate, save, and execute the package:

```
' Validate the package
Console.WriteLine("Validating the MySSISPackage")
Dim pkgStatus As DTSExecResult = myPackage.Validate _
  (Nothing, Nothing, Nothing, Nothing)
System.Console.WriteLine("Validation result: " & _
  pkgStatus.ToString())

' Save the package
Console.WriteLine("Saving the MySSISPackage")
Dim SSISExe As New Application()
SSISExe.SaveToXml("c:\temp\MySSISPAckage.dtsx", myPackage, Nothing)

' Execute the Package
If pkgStatus = DTSExecResult.Success Then
    Console.WriteLine("Executing the MySSISPackage")
    Dim pkgResult As DTSExecResult = myPackage.Execute()
    Console.WriteLine("MySSISPackage results: " _
      & pkgResult.ToString)
Else
    Console.WriteLine("Package validation failed")
End If
Console.ReadKey()
End Sub

End Module
```

Calling the SSIS package object's Validate method causes the SSIS engine to parse the package, ensuring that all of the settings are valid. Here the results of the Validate method are assigned to the status variable.

Next, regardless of the status, the package is saved to the file system by creating an instance of the SSIS Application object and then using that object's SaveToXML method. The first argument of the SaveToXML method specifies the filename to save the package under, and the second argument passes in an instance the package object.

Finally, the contents of the pkgStatus object are checked to ensure that the package was valid. If it is, then the package's Execute method is called to run the SSIS package and perform the data export. The execution results are returned in the pkgResult variable.

After the SSIS package has been successfully executed, a file containing the exported data named MySSISFileExport.csv along with an SSIS package named MySSISPAckage.dtsx will be found in the c:\temp directory. Double-clicking the MySSISPackage.dtsx package in the file system will launch the Execute Package Utility that you can see in Figure 10-30. The Execute Package Utility allows you to browse the package's properties, optionally changing properties and variables, as well as to execute the package.

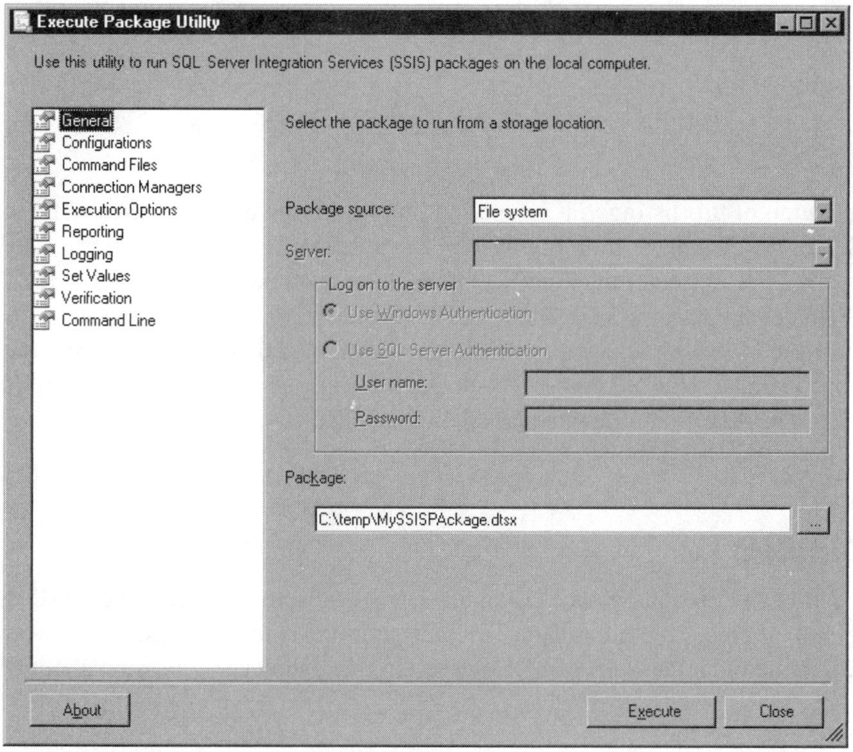

Figure 10-30 *The newly created SSIS package*

The previous example illustrated creating and running an SSIS package. However, as you can see in the following listing, if you just want to execute an existing SSIS package, the code is much simpler. The following code listing shows how to execute an SSIS package from a console application that has a reference added for the Microsoft.SqlServer.Dts.Runtime assembly:

```
Imports Microsoft.SqlServer.Dts.Runtime

Module Module1

    Sub Main()
        Dim sPath As String
        Dim oPkg As New Package
        Dim oApp As New Application
        Dim oResults As DTSExecResult

        sPath = "C:\temp\MySSISPackage.dtsx"
        pkg = oApp.LoadPackage(sPath, Nothing)
        oResults = oPkg.Execute()
        Console.WriteLine(oResults.ToString())
        Console.ReadKey()

    End Sub

End Module
```

At the top of this listing you can see an import directive for the Microsoft .SqlServer.Dts.Runtime assembly. Within the Sub Main procedure you can see where the DTS Application object's LoadPackage method is used to load the MySSISPackage.dtsx package file to the c:\temp directory in the file system. In this example the MySSISPackage.dtsx package was created using the code from the previous listings. After loading the package, the Execute method is used to run the package. The results are then displayed on the console.

Summary

SQL Server Integration Services is an all-new subsystem in SQL Server 2005 that completely replaces the older Data Transformation Services subsystem that was present in the older versions of SQL Server. In this chapter you learned about SSIS's simple SSIS Import and Export Wizard for performing basic data transfer operation as well as how to create more complex, multistep packages using the SSIS Designer. You saw how to use package checkpoints for recoverability and transactions to ensure data integrity, as well as how to create configurations for flexible package deployments. In addition, you also saw how to use the SSIS APIs to programmatically create SSIS packages from a .NET application.

CHAPTER 11

Developing BI Applications with ADOMD.NET

ADOMD.NET is a .NET data provider that enables the development of database applications that communicate with multidimensional data sources, such as SQL Server 2005 Analysis Services. SQL Server Analysis Services (SSAS) delivers online analytical processing (OLAP) and data mining functions for Business Intelligence (BI) applications using server and client components. SSAS allows you to analyze your data so as to look for patterns and trends that will help you serve your customers and meet your business plans and goals.

The server component of SSAS runs as a Windows service. Clients communicate with SSAS using a SOAP-based protocol, XML for Analysis (XMLA), which issues commands and receives responses and is exposed as a Web service. A managed provider, ADOMD.NET includes client objects to be used in applications, allowing interaction with XMLA and SSAS.

In this chapter, you will see how to develop SQL Server database applications using ADOMD.NET. The first part of the chapter provides you with a brief overview of the Analysis Management Objects (AMO) used by the SSAS server-side Windows service. Then an overview of the ADOMD.NET features and architecture will be presented. In the second section of this chapter, you'll get an understanding of classes used by ADOMD.NET.

Analysis Services Overview

SQL Server 2005 Analysis Services provides OLAP analysis, Key Performance Indicator (KPI) checks, and data mining functionality for your business data, which allows you to more quickly and efficiently supply information to your users. Using SSAS, you can show trends and summarized data, giving a clearer picture of how your organization is meeting its business goals and in turn how to facilitate making better business decisions. In Figure 11-1, you can see an overview of SQL Server 2005 Analysis Services.

Clients communicate with SSAS using the XML for Analysis (XMLA) protocol over a TCP or HTTP connection. XMLA is used for issuing commands and receiving responses and is exposed as a Web service. SSAS provides client object models that you can use over XMLA, including a managed provider called ADOMD.NET. You can issue query commands against an XMLA data source using SQL, Multidimensional Expressions (MDX), or Data Mining Extensions (DMX).

Multidimensional data sources are different from other types of data sources in that they use multiple, hierarchically structured dimensions to organize data. For example, relational database tables each represent two-dimensional data. At the intersection

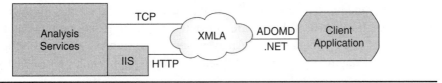

Figure 11-1   *SQL Server 2005 Analysis Services overview*

of each row and column in the table, a single element of data is represented. With multidimensional data sources, data can be represented by structures of more than two dimensions. This structured data assumes a form called cubes that have multiple dimensions and consist of measures based on one or more fact tables.

You can access and manipulate multidimensional objects and data using Multidimensional Expressions (MDX). MDX is a statement-based scripting language and has features that allow you to manage scope, context, and control flow within an MDX script.

XML for Analysis

XML for Analysis (XMLA) is a Simple Object Access Protocol (SOAP)–based XML protocol that allows you to access a multidimensional data source. XMLA is used for all communications between a client application and an instance of Analysis Services. XMLA is also used by both AMO and ADOMD.NET to interact with the instance of Analysis Services. XMLA has two standard, accessible methods: a Discover method and an Execute method.

The Discover method is used to retrieve metadata or detailed information about objects in SSAS. Using the Discover method, you can obtain information including lists of available data sources, lists of cubes, or metadata that describes the existing objects in the data source.

The Execute method is used for executing commands against an XMLA data source. The Execute method can execute SQL, MDX, or DMX statements and returns data from the multidimensional data source in the form of a CellSet or AdomdDataReader. These objects are discussed later in this chapter.

Analysis Management Objects (AMO) Overview

Analysis Management Objects (AMO) provides the ability to perform administrative tasks on an Analysis Services instance. You can use AMO in a managed client application to create or modify Analysis Services objects, such as databases, cubes, dimensions, and mining structures, using the interfaces in the Microsoft .NET Framework. It is also useful for retrieving and manipulating data from the underlying data sources, and for managing an Analysis Services instance by setting configuration properties, managing instance security, and controlling the Windows service for the Analysis Services instance.

ADOMD.NET Overview

ADOMD.NET is a .NET data provider built using managed code from the Microsoft .NET Framework, which means you can use the .NET execution time environment to build BI applications. ADOMD.NET consists of a set of classes within the .NET Framework that provide data access and management capabilities to .NET applications. Client applications can use ADOMD.NET to connect to multidimensional data sources for retrieving, analyzing, and manipulating data and metadata. ADOMD.NET can also be used for manipulating key performance indicators (KPIs) and data mining models.

Key Performance Indicators

Key performance indicators (KPIs) are used to measure and evaluate business goals. KPIs are collections of calculations and are associated with either a single measure group in a cube or with all measure groups in a cube. KPIs also contain metadata to provide information about how client applications should show the results of the KPI's calculations. KPIs in Analysis Services are server-based, giving you the performance benefit of executing sometimes complex calculations on the server rather than on each client computer.

AMO Hierarchy

The AMO library provides a complete set of .NET Framework classes for managing SSAS objects. It can also be used for administering security, processing cubes, and mining data models.

The Server Class

The Server class is the main class in the AMO architecture and handles the methods for connecting and disconnecting to Analysis Services, as well as adding or restoring databases from a backup.

The Database Class

The Database class is used for processing and updating databases in Analysis Services. You can use the Add method to add DataSources, DataSourceViews, Dimensions, and Cubes to the database.

The DataSource Class

The DataSource class defines and interacts with the DataSources available in Analysis Services.

The DataSourceView Class

A DataSourceView contains a list of data pertinent to its underlying data source. The DataSourceView class is used to associate a data source with a data source view, assign table schemas, and save data source views to Analysis Services.

The Dimension Class

The Dimension class allows you to set the source of a dimension, process the dimension, and save the dimension to Analysis Services. Dimensions are essentially an additional layer of metadata you can place over a table or set of tables to define hierarchical relationships between columns.

The Cube Class

The Cube class allows you to set the source of a cube, process the cube and the objects contained in the cube, add MeasureGroups to a cube, and save the cube and its contents to Analysis Services. Cubes store results of data at different summary levels, resulting in efficient multidimensional query actions.

ADOMD.NET Object Model

ADOMD.NET data provider is a .NET Framework data provider that you can use to communicate with multidimensional data sources from a client application.

AdomdConnection

The AdomdConnection class is used to open a connection to a multidimensional data source. It can also be used to connect to the multidimensional data source metadata, for example, a local cube (.cub) file. You can review the local cube file to learn about the metadata properties that represent the cube on the multidimensional data source. Each AdomdConnection is associated with an XMLA session. The AdomdConnection objects are not automatically destroyed when they go out of scope. This means that you must explicitly close any open ADOMD.NET Connection objects in your applications. If the AdomdConnection is not closed, it remains open and can be used by other AdomdConnections.

AdomdCommand

The AdomdCommand class is used to execute a command against a multidimensional data source that's associated with the active AdomdConnection object. AdomdCommand supports six types of commands: Execute, ExecuteCellSet, ExecuteNonQuery, ExecuteReader, ExecuteScalar, and ExecuteXmlReader. The ExecuteCellSet command returns a CellSet, the ExecuteReader command returns an AdomdDataReader object, and the Execute command returns either a CellSet or an AdomdDataReader. The ExecuteXmlReader command returns an XmlReader object, and the ExecuteNonQuery command is used to execute the command statements without returning any results. The ExecuteScalar will be implemented in the future.

AdomdDataReader

The AdomdDataReader class returns a forward-only result set from the multidimensional data source that's associated with the active AdomdConnection object. Unlike objects of most other ADOMD.NET classes that are instantiated by calling the constructor, objects created from the AdomdDataReader class are instantiated by calling the ExecuteReader method of the AdomdCommand object.

AdomdDataAdapter

The AdomdDataAdapter class is used to retrieve data from a multidimensional data source and fill a CellSet. The AdomdDataAdapter class is responsible for both filling up the CellSet as well as sending changes made in the CellSet back to the data source. You can employ the InsertCommand, UpdateCommand, and DeleteCommand properties to manipulate the data at the data source.

CellSet

The CellSet object represents a multidimensional result set returned as a result of running an MDX statement or query command. The Execute or ExecuteCellSet method of the AdomdCommand object returns a CellSet and contains collections of cells that are organized along multiple dimensions or axes.

Several other objects in the ADOMD.NET object hierarchy support additional data and metadata information about these main objects.

AdomdParameter

The AdomdParameter class is used to represent a parameter that's passed to an AdomdCommand object. AdomdParameter objects have properties that define their attributes.

AdomdTransaction

The AdomdTransaction class represents SQL transactions that allow multiple database transactions to be treated as a unit where an entire group of database updates either can be posted to the database or can all be undone as a unit. The AdomdTransaction object uses the BeginTransaction method to specify the start of a transaction and then either the Commit method to post the changes to the database or the Rollback method to undo the pending transaction. An AdomdTransaction object is attached to the active AdomdConnection object.

AdomdError

The AdomdError object is raised by the provider during the execution of a statement or query and represents an XML for Analysis error. The AdomdError objects are contained within the Errors property of an AdomdErrorResponseException and so are not directly raised in ADOMD.NET.

AdomdException

The AdomdException class throws an exception if an error occurs with the AdomdConnection while information is being retrieved from a data source.

CubeDef

The CubeDef represents only the metadata of a cube. The CubeDef is referenced from the AdomdConnection, allowing you to retrieve information, such as the dimensions, measures, and the properties of the cube, that is stored in a multidimensional data source.

Building a BI Application with ADOMD.NET

In the first part of this chapter you learned about the various components that make up SQL Server 2005's Analysis Services. In this part of the chapter you'll get a more detailed look at the steps required to develop a BI application with ADOMD.NET.

You begin building a client application by starting the Visual Studio 2005 development environment and creating a Windows forms project. In this example, we'll step through a sample program that connects to the AdventureWorksDW database and displays data and metadata for a sample cube.

To build a Windows forms application, first open Visual Studio and then select the File | New | Project option to display the New Project dialog as shown in Figure 11-2.

This example uses the VB.NET language, so as you can see in the figure, in the Project Types area of the dialog the Visual Basic | Windows option has been selected, and in the Templates area of the dialog the Windows Application option has been selected. Fill in the boxes at the bottom of the dialog, setting the name and location

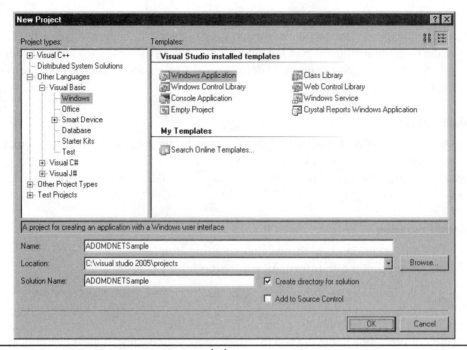

Figure 11-2   *ADOMD.NET New Project dialog*

for your project. Clicking OK creates the project and displays the Visual Studio design environment with a default Windows form created for you.

In the design environment of this VB.NET project, items from the Toolbox have been added and formatted on the Windows form to create a wizard-like program that steps through the basic ADOMD.NET events. Figure 11-3 shows the ADOMDNETSample application form.

Now that the screen has been designed, the next step is to add code to execute the ADOMD.NET actions.

Adding a Reference for ADOMD.NET

Before you can use the ADOMD.NET data provider in your code, you must first add a reference to the SSAS .DLL and also specify an import directive for the Microsoft .AnalysisServices.AdomdClient namespace in your project. To add a reference to the SSAS .DLL, you select Project | Add Reference from the Visual Studio's main menu. In the Add Reference dialog that is displayed, scroll through the list of available .NET components until you see Microsoft.AnalysisServices.AdomdClient option. Highlight the option and click the OK button to add the .DLL reference to your project. The

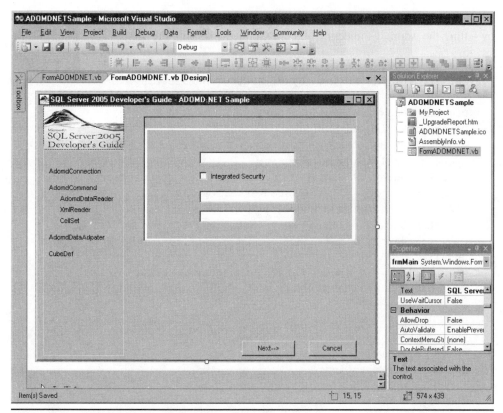

Figure 11-3   *ADOMDNETSample screen design*

Microsoft.AnalysisServices.AdomdClient namespace contains all of the related SSAS
connection and data access classes. Next, to add an import directive for the Microsoft
.AnalysisServices.AdomdClient to a VB.NET project, you would add the following code
to the declaration section of your source file:

```
Imports Microsoft.AnalysisServices.AdomdClient
```

Using the AdomdConnection Object

After adding an import directive to your code, you're ready to begin using the different
classes contained in the Microsoft.AnalysisServices.AdomdClient namespace. The most
basic of the classes is the AdomdConnection class. The Microsoft.AnalysisServices
.AdomdClient AdomdConnection class is used to connect to a multidimensional data

source on SQL Server 2005. The following example illustrates how to make a connection by setting the AdomdConnection object's ConnectionString Property:

```
Private Sub AdomdConnect(ByRef sServer As String, _
  ByRef sLoginID As String, ByRef sPassword As String)

    Dim cn As New AdomdConnection()
    Dim sConnString As String = _
      "Provider=SQLNCLI.1;Data Source=" & sServer & ";"
    ' Check for Integrated security
    If chkIntegratedSecurity.CheckState = CheckState.Checked Then
        sConnString += "Integrated Security=SSPI;"
    Else
        sConnString += "User ID=" & sLoginID & ";Password=" & _
          sPassword & ";"
    End If
    sConnString += "Initial Catalog=AdventureWorksDW"

    cn.ConnectionString = sConnString

    Try
        cn.Open()
    Catch ex As Exception
        MessageBox.Show(ex.Message)
    End Try

End Sub
```

In this case string variables containing the name of the SQL Server system to connect to along with the user ID and password are passed into the top of the routine. Next, a new instance of the Microsoft.AnalysisServices.AdomdClient AdomdConnection object named cn is created. Then the ConnectionString property of the Microsoft .AnalysisServices.AdomdClient AdomdConnection object is assigned. The connection string uses the Data Source keyword to identify the SQL Server system that will be connected to. The User ID and Password keywords provide the authentication values required to log in to SQL Server if you are connecting using mixed security. A User ID and Password are not required in the connection string if you are connecting using a trusted connection. A complete list of the valid ADOMD.NET Data Provider connection string keywords is presented in the next section. After the ConnectionString property has been assigned the appropriate connection string, a Try-Catch block is used to execute the cn AdomdConnection object's Open method. If a connection could not be made to the data source, the Catch block will be executed and a message box will be displayed showing the error information.

The ADOMD.NET Data Provider Connection String Keywords

The ADOMD.NET connection string is much like the connection strings used by ADO.NET. When an application calls the Open method of the AdomdConnection object, the connection string is parsed and each of the properties are evaluated. If the AdomdConnection object supports the property provided in the connection string, the value for that property is validated. However, if the value is invalid or is not supported, an exception is thrown. Table 11-1 shows the connection string keywords that are directly supported by the AdomdConnection object.

Keyword	Description
AutoSyncPeriod	Sets the time, in milliseconds, before objects are automatically synchronized with the server.
Catalog – or - Initial Catalog – or - Database	Sets the database for the AdomdConnection to connect to.
Character Encoding	Sets how characters are encoded. The default is a UTF-8 string.
ClientProcessID	Sets the process ID of the application associated with connection. If not set, and SspropInitAppName is set, it will automatically be set to the process ID retrieved from the client operating system.
Compression Level	Sets compression level. Values range from 0 to 9.
Connect Timeout	The time to wait before terminating a connection attempt and throwing an exception.
Connect To	Sets the method used to connect to the server. **8.0:** Connection uses in-process XMLA. **9.0:** Connection uses XMLA. **Default:** Connection first tries XMLA and then attempts to use in-process XMLA.
CreateCube	Sets the CREATE CUBE statement used during the creation of a local cube.
Data Source –or- DataSourceLocation	Sets the instance or local cube (.cub) file of the AdomdConnection connection.
DataSourceInfo	Sets the provider-specific information that is required to access the data source.
Encryption Password	Sets the password used to decrypt local cubes.
Extended Properties	Sets the connection string properties. Supports unlimited nesting.
Impersonation Level	Sets the level of impersonation the server is allowed when impersonating the client. Available settings are Anonymous, Identify, Impersonate, and Delegate. Default is Impersonate.
Integrated Security	Sets the connect access to use. **SSPI:** An SSPI-supported security package is used for user authentication. **Basic:** The UserName and Password settings are required for connection. HTTP connections can only use the Basic setting.
LocaleIdentifier	Sets the Locale ID for the client application.

Table 11-1 *ADOMD .NET Connection String Keywords*

Keyword	Description
Location	Sets server name.
Packet Size	Sets network packet size in bytes. The value must between 512 and 32767. The default is 4096.
Password —or-PWD	Sets the password for the AdomdConnection.
Persist Security Info	Sets if security information will be persisted. If 'true', security-related information can be obtained from the connection after the connection has been opened.
ProtectionLevel	Sets the level of protection for the provider to sign or encrypt the connection. **NONE:** Performs no authentication of data sent to the server. **CONNECT:** Authenticates when the client establishes the connection with the server. **PKT INTEGRITY:** Authenticates that complete and unchanged data is received from the client. **PKT PRIVACY:** Encrypts the data and authenticates that complete and unchanged data is received from the client.
Protocol Format	Sets the format of the XML sent to the server. Settings can be Default, XML, or Binary.
Provider	Sets the name of the provider for the data source. Default is MSOLAP.
Restricted Client	Sets client restriction. If 'true', the client is restricted from using local cube and local mining model functions.
Safety Options	Sets the safety level for how security for user-defined functions and actions is handled.
SessionID	Sets the session identifier for the connection.
SSPI	Sets the security package to use for user authentication. Settings are Negotiate, Kerberos, NTLM, or Anonymous User. Default is Negotiate.
SspropInitAppName	Sets the name of the application to be associated with connection.
Timeout	The time to wait for a command to run before terminating the attempt and throwing an exception.
Transport Compression	Sets if connection will communicate with compression. **None:** No compression is used. **Compressed:** Compression is used. **GZIP:** Compresses HTTP connections. **Default:** Compression is used over HTTP connections; otherwise, no compression.
Use Encryption for Data	Sets encryption between the client and server. If 'true', all data sent between the client and server is encrypted with SSL encryption. Server needs certificate installed.
UseExistingFile	Set to use or overwrite the existing file. If 'true', the local file must already exist, and the cube is either created if the cube does not exist or used if the cube does exist. If 'false', the existing local cube is overwritten. Default is 'false'.
UserName -or-UID —or -User ID — or - Authenticated User	Sets the login ID for the AdomdConnection.

Table 11-1   *ADOMD .NET Connection String Keywords (continued)*

Using the AdomdCommand Object

After a connection has been established to a multidimensional data source, you can use the AdomdCommand object to execute commands that return data or metadata information from the multidimensional data source. The format of data or metadata that is returned depends on the execution method you call from the AdomdCommand object. These are the AdomdCommand execution methods:

▶ **Execute**   The Execute method runs the command contained in the AdomdCommand object and returns either an AdomdDataReader or a CellSet. If the results of the command cannot be formatted into an AdomdDataReader or a CellSet, the Execute method returns a null value.

▶ **ExecuteCellSet**   The ExecuteCellSet method runs the command contained in the AdomdCommand object and returns a CellSet. If the results of the command cannot be formatted into a CellSet, an exception is thrown.

▶ **ExecuteNonQuery**   The ExecuteNonQuery method is used to execute commands that do not return any data or metadata.

▶ **ExecuteReader**   The ExecuteReader method runs the AdomdCommand command and returns an AdomdDataReader object. While the AdomdDataReader is in use and being served by the AdomdConnection and AdomdCommand objects, only the Close method can be performed on the AdomdConnection and AdomdCommand objects. Once the Close or Dispose method is called on the AdomdDataReader object, other operations can be performed on the AdomdConnection and AdomdCommand objects.

▶ **ExecuteXmlReader**   TheExecuteXmlReader method returns an XmlReader object in response to the AdomdCommand object's command. The XmlReader object directly references the XMLA response to the command in its native XML format. Like the AdomdDataReader, the AdomdConnection object can only be closed until the Close method for the XmlReader is called.

Let's take a closer look at how to use several of these execution methods using the example program.

Using the AdomdDataReader Object

The AdomdDataReader class is the implementation of the System.Data.IDataReader interface for ADOMD.NET and is used as a quick way to read forward-only result sets. To create an AdomdDataReader, you must call the ExecuteReader method of the AdomdCommand, instead of directly using a constructor. The following code listing shows creating an AdomdDataReader and outputting the results to a ListView control:

```
Private Sub AdomdDataReader(ByRef cn As AdomdConnection)

    Dim cmd As New AdomdCommand("SELECT NON EMPTY " & _
        "[Dim Time].[English Month Name].MEMBERS ON COLUMNS, " & _
        "NON EMPTY {[Dim Employee].[Last Name].MEMBERS} ON ROWS " & _
        "FROM [AdventureWorksDW]", cn)
    Dim dr As AdomdDataReader
    Dim lvItem As ListViewItem

    ' Clear the ListView
    rstListView.Items.Clear()
    rstListView.Columns.Clear()

    Try
        ' Execute the query and return AdomdDataReader
        dr = cmd.ExecuteReader()
        dr.Read()
        rstListView.Columns.Add("", 80, HorizontalAlignment.Left)
        ' Add the column names
        For iColName As Integer = 1 To dr.FieldCount - 1
            rstListView.Columns.Add _
                (ParseColName(dr.GetName(iColName)), 60, _
                HorizontalAlignment.Left)
        Next iColName

        ' Read the DataReader
        Do
            ' Init the new ListViewItem
            If (Not dr.IsDBNull(0)) Then
                lvItem = New ListViewItem(dr(0).ToString())
            Else
                lvItem = New ListViewItem(String.Empty)
            End If

            ' Add the column items
            For iField As Integer = 1 To dr.FieldCount - 1
                If (Not dr.IsDBNull(iField)) Then
                    lvItem.SubItems.Add(dr(iField).ToString())
                Else
```

```
                lvItem.SubItems.Add(String.Empty)
            End If
        Next iField

        ' Add the item to the listview
        rstListView.Items.Add(lvItem)
    Loop While (dr.Read())

    ' Close the DataReader
    dr.Close()
    Catch ex As Exception
        MessageBox.Show(ex.Message)
    End Try

End Sub
Private Function ParseColName(ByRef sColName As String) As String
    Dim sShortName As String
    Dim iFound As Integer = sColName.LastIndexOf("[") + 1
    sShortName = sColName.Substring(iFound, sColName.Length() - _
        (iFound + 1))
    Return sShortName
End Function
```

At the top of the subroutine, you can see that an AdomdConnection object is passed in. The next statement creates a new AdomdCommand object named cmd and uses an MDX SELECT statement as a parameter on the constructor. This very simple MDX SELECT statement, when executed, will set the column and row dimensions of the multidimensional results with employee last names and English name months. The NON EMPTY keywords are used, so that only the nonempty data will be selected. Next, an AdomdDataReader is initialized to receive the multidimensional data, and a ListViewItem object is initialized.

The next two lines clear the Items and Columns from the ListView control that was placed on the Windows form at the program design phase. The AdomdCommand's ExecuteReader method is then called and returns the AdomdDataReader named dr. As you can see from the code listing, the ExecuteReader is called inside the Try-Catch loop. Any exceptions that may occur are trapped by the Try-Catch loop, and a message will be displayed to the user.

After the data has been retrieved with the ExecuteReader method and output to the dr AdomdDataReader object, the Read method of the dr object is called to read the first data and set up the column names for output to the ListView control. The next few lines of code use a For Next loop to add columns to the ListView control. In this example, the dr object's GetName method is used to set the column text with the names of the retrieved columns. Because the GetName method returns the complete name of the column, including the dimension hierarchy, we use a simple ParseColName function to strip the column name of unwanted characters. For example, the dr.GetName method returns the value of '[Dim Time].[English Month Name].&[April]'. We want only the month name to appear on the column heading of the ListView control, so we pass the whole string to the ParseColName function and strip out the unwanted hierarchy description, returning the short text value of 'April'. The ParseColName function is included in the code listing.

Once each of the columns has been added to the ListView control and the column names have been added to the column text, a Do While is used to initialize a new ListViewItem and read each element of the AdomdDataReader. Inside the Do While loop, a For Next loop iterates through each of the dr object's row items and adds them to the new ListViewItem. The Do While loop then reads the next row item of the dr object using the dr.Read method, and adds a ListViewItem to the ListView control until all of the rows of the dr object have been read.

The dr AdomdDataReader object is then closed using the dr.Close method, and the results are displayed to the user, as shown in Figure 11-4.

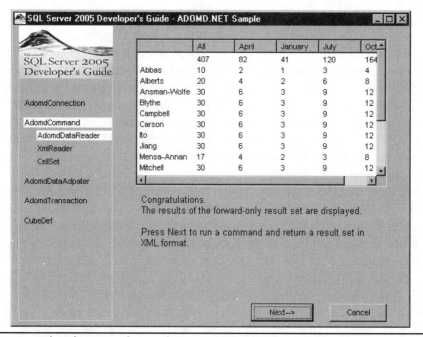

Figure 11-4 *AdomdDataReader results*

Using the XMLReader Object

The AdomdCommand object also allows returned multidimensional data to be displayed in XML format. To view data in XML format, the AdomdCommand's ExecuteXmlReader method is used that returns an XmlReader object. The next subroutine shows retrieving data to an XmlReader and displaying it in a Listbox control:

```
Private Sub XMLReader(ByRef cn As AdomdConnection)

    Dim cmd As New AdomdCommand("SELECT NON EMPTY " & _
      "[Dim Time].[English Month Name].MEMBERS ON COLUMNS, " & _
      "NON EMPTY {[Dim Employee].[Last Name].MEMBERS} ON ROWS " & _
      "FROM [AdventureWorksDW]", cn)
    Dim xmlReader As System.Xml.XmlReader

    Try
        ' Execute the XML query
        xmlReader = cmd.ExecuteXmlReader()

        xmlReader.MoveToContent()
        While xmlReader.Read()
            Select Case xmlReader.NodeType
                Case XmlNodeType.Element
                    rstListBox.Items.Add("<{0}>" & xmlReader.Name)
                Case XmlNodeType.Text
                    rstListBox.Items.Add(xmlReader.Value)
                Case XmlNodeType.CDATA
                    rstListBox.Items.Add("<![CDATA[{0}]]>" & _
                       xmlReader.Value)
                Case XmlNodeType.ProcessingInstruction
                    rstListBox.Items.Add("<?{0} {1}?>" & _
                       xmlReader.Name & xmlReader.Value)
                Case XmlNodeType.Comment
                    rstListBox.Items.Add("<!--{0}-->" & _
                       xmlReader.Value)
                Case XmlNodeType.XmlDeclaration
                    rstListBox.Items.Add("<?xml version='1.0'?>")
                Case XmlNodeType.Document
                Case XmlNodeType.DocumentType
                    rstListBox.Items.Add("<!DOCTYPE {0} [{1}]" & _
                       xmlReader.Name & xmlReader.Value)
                Case XmlNodeType.EntityReference
                    rstListBox.Items.Add(xmlReader.Name)
```

```
                         Case XmlNodeType.EndElement
                             rstListBox.Items.Add("</{0}>" & xmlReader.Name)
                    End Select
                End While
                xmlReader.Close()

        Catch ex As Exception
            MessageBox.Show(ex.Message)
        End Try

End Sub
```

As you can see at the top of the listing, an AdomdConnection object is passed in to the subroutine. The next statement creates the AdomdCommand object using the MDX SELECT statement in its constructor. The next line shows the creation of an XmlReader object. The XmlReader is found in the System.Xml namespace; therefore, this line of code shows the creation of the XmlReader using the fully qualified namespace hierarchy.

The AdomdCommand's ExecuteXmlReader is then executed and returns the xmlReader object. The Try-Catch loop is employed here to catch any exceptions that may occur and displays the exception message to the user. The next statement calls the xmlReader's MoveToContent method that skips over random XML markup. The xmlReader's Read method is called in a While loop to read through each retrieved row in the xmlReader. Inside the While loop a Select Case statement is used to format the information and add it to the Listbox control found on the Windows form.

When all of the rows have been read from the xmlReader, it is closed and the resulting Listbox is displayed to the user.

Using the CellSet Object

The ExecuteCellSet method of the AdomdCommand object is called to return multidimensional results to a CellSet. A CellSet is similar to a DataSet; however, a DataSet can contain only two-dimensional relational data, but a CellSet can contain multidimensional data. A CellSet's contents consist of a collection of cells that are organized along multiple dimensions. The code listing that follows shows creating a CellSet with an AdomdCommand's ExecuteCellSet method and displays the retrieved information in a Listbox:

```
Private Sub CellSet(ByRef cn As AdomdConnection)

    Dim cmd As New AdomdCommand("SELECT NON EMPTY " & _
        "[Dim Time].[English Month Name].MEMBERS ON COLUMNS, " & _
        "NON EMPTY {[Dim Employee].[Last Name].MEMBERS} ON ROWS " & _
```

```
        "FROM [AdventureWorksDW]", cn)
Dim cs As CellSet

' Clear the ListBox
rstListBox.Items.Clear()

Try
    ' Execute the query and return a cellset
    cs = cmd.ExecuteCellSet()

    rstListBox.Items.Add("The cellset has " & cs.Cells.Count & _
      " cells organized along " & cs.Axes.Count & " axes")

    Dim axCol As Axis = cs.Axes(0)
    Dim axRow As Axis = cs.Axes(1)
    Dim posRow As Position, posCol As Position

    For Each posRow In axRow.Positions
        Dim sCell As String = 0
        For Each posCol In axCol.Positions
            sCell += cs(posCol.Ordinal, _
                posRow.Ordinal).FormattedValue() & vbTab
        Next

        ' Add the item to the listbox
        rstListBox.Items.Add(sCell)
    Next
Catch ex As Exception
    MessageBox.Show(ex.Message)
End Try

End Sub
```

Again, an AdomdConnection object is passed in at the top of the subroutine and an AdomdCommand object is created using the SELECT MDX statement. A CellSet object is then created, and the Windows form Listbox control is cleared of any leftover information.

The next statement shows calling the AdomdCommand's ExecuteCellSet method and returning the results to the CellSet. The CellSet now contains a collection of query axes, which help to organize the information within the CellSet, and a collection of cells. In this example, there are two axes in the CellSet Axes collection, one for the columns in the CellSet and one for the rows in the CellSet. The next statements initialize variables for the Axes collections and Position variables to select and output the coordinates of the

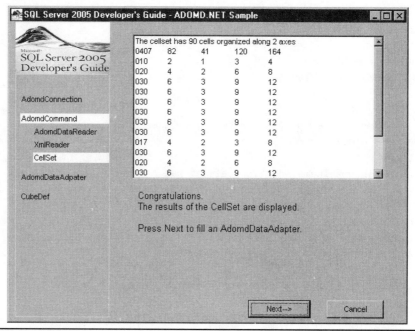

The cellset has 90 cells organized along 2 axes

0407	82	41	120	164
010	2	1	3	4
020	4	2	6	8
030	6	3	9	12
030	6	3	9	12
030	6	3	9	12
030	6	3	9	12
030	6	3	9	12
030	6	3	9	12
017	4	2	3	8
030	6	3	9	12
020	4	2	6	8
030	6	3	9	12

Congratulations.
The results of the CellSet are displayed.

Press Next to fill an AdomdDataAdapter.

Figure 11-5   *CellSet results*

cells in the CellSet. Nested For Next loops are set up next, to iterate through the axes and add the cells to the Listbox according to the position coordinates of the cells.

The final results are displayed to the user as shown in Figure 11-5.

Using the AdomdDataAdapter Object

The AdomdDataAdapter is used in combination with the AdomdConnection object and the AdomdCommand object to fill a CellSet with multidimensional data and then resolve the information back to a SQL Server database.

The following example illustrates how to use an AdomdConnection, create an AdomdCommand object, and populate a new DataTable with the AdomdDataAdapter. The contents of the DataTable will then be displayed to the user in a grid:

```
Private Sub AdomdDataAdapter(ByRef cn As AdomdConnection)

    Dim cmd As New AdomdCommand("SELECT NON EMPTY " & _
      "[Dim Time].[English Month Name].MEMBERS ON COLUMNS, " & _
      "NON EMPTY {[Dim Employee].[Last Name].MEMBERS} ON ROWS " & _
      "FROM [AdventureWorksDW]", cn)
    Dim da As New AdomdDataAdapter(cmd)
    Dim dt As New DataTable
```

```
Try
    da.Fill(dt)
    rstDataGridView.DataSource = dt
Catch ex As Exception
    MessageBox.Show(ex.Message)
End Try

End Sub
```

An instance of the AdomdConnection object is passed in at the top of the subroutine. The next statement creates an AdomdCommand object and sets its CommandText property to the SELECT MDX statement and Connection property to the previously passed-in AdomdConnection object. Next, an instance of a AdomdDataAdapter is created and its SelectCommand property is set to the AdomdCommand object. An empty DataTable is then created, which will be populated with the results of the SELECT query command. The DataTable is then filled using the AdomdDataAdapter's Fill method, which is executed inside a Try-Catch block. If the Fill method fails, the code in the Catch block is executed and a message box appears showing the error message. Finally, a DataGrid's DataSource property is set to the DataTable and displayed to the user as shown in Figure 11-6.

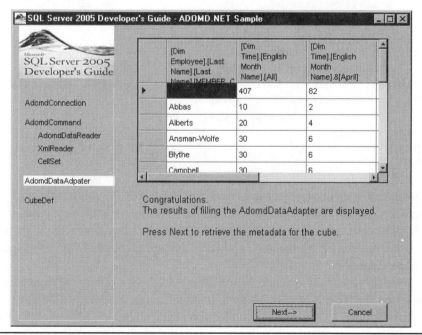

Figure 11-6   *AdomdDataAdapter results*

Using the CubeDef Object

Using the CubeDef object in ADOMD.NET, you can retrieve metadata information about a cube, including its dimensions, measures, and named sets. The CubeDef object contains only metadata information and no actual cell data. The AdomdConnection object contains a collection of cubes that are in the database specified for the AdomdConnection object.

The following code listing shows how to display some metadata information from a cube in a Listbox control:

```
Private Sub CubeDef(ByRef cn As AdomdConnection)

    Dim cubDef As CubeDef = cn.Cubes(0)

    ' Clear the Listbox
    rstListBox.Items.Clear()

    rstListBox.Items.Add("  **  Measures  **  ")
    For Each meas As Measure In cubDef.Measures
        rstListBox.Items.Add("Name        : " & meas.Name)
        rstListBox.Items.Add("Description : " & meas.Description)
        rstListBox.Items.Add("Expression  : " & meas.Expression)
        rstListBox.Items.Add("Units       : " & meas.Units)
    Next
    rstListBox.Items.Add("  **  Dimensions  **  ")
    For Each dimen As Dimension In cubDef.Dimensions
        rstListBox.Items.Add("Name        : " & dimen.Name)
        rstListBox.Items.Add("Description : " & dimen.Description)
        rstListBox.Items.Add("Hierarchy   : " & _
            dimen.Hierarchies(0).ToString())
    Next

End Sub
```

The AdomdConnection object is passed in at the top of the subroutine, and a CubeDef object is created and set with the information from the first cube in the AdomdConnection's Cubes collection. The CubeDef contains collections for Dimensions, Measures, NamedSets, and KPIs that are associated with each specified cube in the database.

The next statements in the code listing clear the Listbox of any previous items, and then two For Next loops are set up to iterate through the Measures collection of the CubeDef and the Dimensions collection of the CubeDef, adding each of the collection elements to the Listbox for display to the user.

Summary

ADOMD.NET is a database provider that allows you to develop database applications that communicate with multidimensional data sources. In this chapter you learned about some of the SQL Server Analysis Services capabilities as well as how to develop BI applications that access some of those capabilities. SSAS allows you to analyze your data to determine trends and patterns to meet your business goals. Developing visual applications with ADOMD.NET to show those trend and patterns can increase the usability of that information.

Summary

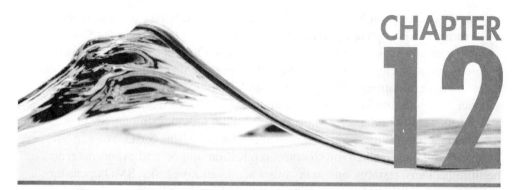

Developing with SMO

In this chapter, you learn how you can manage SQL Server programmatically from VB.NET by taking advantage of SQL Management Objects (SMO). Like its predecessor, Distributed Management Objects (SQL-DMO), SMO enables you to develop custom SQL Server management applications that you can tailor to your environment. Using SMO with VB.NET or any other .Net language, you can create custom SQL Server management interfaces that let you perform all the functions SQL Server's Management Studio provides. In fact, SMO is the foundation for SQL Server's Management Studio. Using SMO, you can list databases and tables; add logins; control replication; import and export data; and perform backups, restores, and many other administrative tasks. SMO opens up SQL Server to a number of custom programs that can both display and manipulate SQL Server and all of its databases and objects.

In this chapter, you get an overview of SMO, as well as a look at its underlying architecture. Then, you see how to use SMO from VB.NET. In this section, you see how to add the SMO object library to the Visual Basic Integrated Development Environment (IDE). You also see how to perform some common tasks with SMO. Finally, this chapter finishes by presenting a sample SQL Server management utility that's built using VB.NET and SMO.

Using SMO

To get programmatic access to management functions of other database platforms, you might need to master low-level networking and system interfaces—if it's available at all. However, SMO provides a .NET framework solution that makes SQL Server's database management functions easy to access. The hierarchy for the SMO objects used in the .NET framework is discussed in the next section of this chapter. SQL Server's SMO functions can be used by a programming language that is supported by the Common Language Runtime (CLR), such as Visual Basic.NET and Visual C#.NET.

To use SMO from VB.NET, follow these basic steps:

1. Add a reference to the SMO assemblies and then import the namespaces that are required so that your program can recognize the SMO types.

2. Create an instance of the Server object.

3. Establish a connection to the instance of the Server object to SQL Server.

4. Use the Server object.

5. Disconnect from SQL Server.

The following section of the chapter walks you through the basic steps needed to build a project using SMO. The project presented is a Winforms project built in Visual Basic, but you can follow these steps to build an ASP project or even a command-line project.

Adding SMO Objects to Visual Studio

Before you can begin to use the SMO objects in Visual Basic's development environment, you need to incorporate the SMO assemblies into your Visual Basic project. The files that provide the basic support for SMO are copied to your client system when you first install the SQL Server client. However, you still need to set a reference to them in Visual Studio's development environment to enable their use from your applications. To add the SMO references to your Visual Studio project, you must select the Add Reference option from the Project menu. This action displays the References dialog box you can see in Figure 12-1.

Select the .NET tab and scroll through the References dialog box until you see the SMO assemblies: Microsoft.SqlServer.ConnectionInfo, Microsoft.SqlServer.Smo, Microsoft.SqlServer.SmoEnum, and Microsoft.SqlServer.SqlEnum. Selecting these items and then clicking OK adds the references to Visual Basic's Interactive

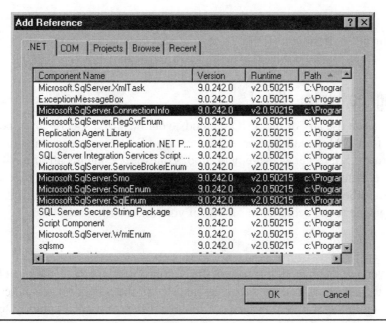

Figure 12-1 *Adding references to SMO*

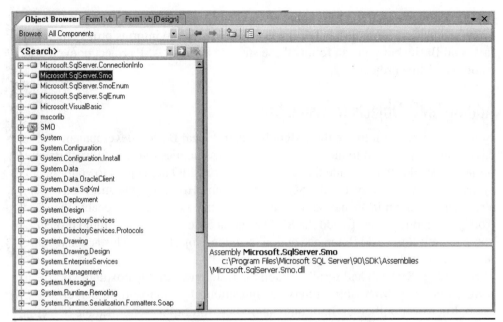

Figure 12-2 *Viewing an SMO assembly from the Object Browser*

Development Environment (IDE). To see the SMO properties and methods, you must use Visual Basic's Object Browser, shown in Figure 12-2.

Creating the Server Object

Before you can use any of the SMO methods, you must first specify an import directive for the Microsoft.SqlServer.Management.Smo Namespace in your project. The Microsoft.SqlServer.Management.Smo Namespace contains all of the related SQL Server connection and data access classes. To add an import directive for the Microsoft.SqlServer.Management.Smo to a VB.NET project, you would add the following code to the declaration section of your source file:

```
Imports Microsoft.SqlServer.Management.Smo
```

Next, you must create an instance of the Server object, which is the most basic object in the SMO set. You can create an instance of the Server object and establish a connection to the SQL Server instance in three different ways: explicitly setting the connection information through the Server object properties, passing the SQL Server instance name to the Server object constructor function, or using the ServerConnection object to provide the connection information.

To explicitly set the connection information through the Server object properties, you simply declare the Server object variable using the default constructor. If you do not set any of the Server object's properties, the Server object attempts to connect to the local instance of SQL Server with the default connection settings. To connect to a remote or named instance of SQL Server, set the name property and any other properties that affect the connection settings, such as authentication mode, logins, and passwords, as shown here:

```
Dim oSQLServer As New Server()
oSQLServer.ConnectionContext.LoginSecure = false
oSQLServer.ConnectionContext.Login = "username"
oSQLServer.ConnectionContext.Password = "password"
```

To pass the SQL Server instance name to the Server object, you first declare the Server object variable and pass the SQL Server instance name as a string parameter in the constructor, as shown here:

```
Dim oSQLServer As Server = New Server("SQL2005")
```

To use the ServerConnection object, you need to specify an import directive for the Microsoft.SqlServer.Management.Common namespace. The import directive for Microsoft.SqlServer.Management.Common is added to the declaration section of your source file:

```
Imports Microsoft.SqlServer.Management.Common
```

In order to use the ServerConnection object to provide the connection information to the Server object, you declare a ServerConnection object variable and set the connection information, such as the SQL Server instance name and the authentication mode into its properties. You then pass the ServerConnection object as a parameter to the Server object constructor. Here is an example of this method:

```
Dim oServerConn As ServerConnection = New ServerConnection()
oServerConn.ServerInstance = "SQL2005"
oServerConn.LoginSecure = True
Dim oSQLServer As New Server(oServerConn)
```

NOTE

One advantage to using the ServerConnection object is that the connection information can be reused. SMO removes the association between the application object and the Server object, allowing you to release the application state. In other words, you can instantiate a Server object by reusing an existing connection, perform your application processes, and then release the reference to the Server object. This lets you write a program that use memory efficiently by controlling when you want to release an object's state.

Using SMO Properties

A SQLServer object has more than 1000 different properties that can be accessed from your application. The SMO hierarchy section later in this chapter will show some of the most common SMO objects. The SQL Server Books Online help file lists all the SMO object properties and notes whether they are read-only or read/write.

TIP

You can use the Object Browser to list the properties for each SQLServer object from Visual Studio's IDE.

Getting Property Values

You can retrieve the property values for all the properties that are standard data types using the Visual Basic assignment operator ("="), as shown here:

```
Dim sInstanceName As String
sInstanceName = oSQLServer.InstanceName
```

Here, you can see that a string named sInstanceName is first declared using the Visual Basic Dim statement. Then the Visual Basic assignment operator is used to fill the sInstanceName string variable with the contents of the oSQLServer .InstanceName property. This technique works for all the standard Visual Basic data types, including String, Long, and Integer. Object properties are treated a little differently, however, as you can see in following example:

```
Dim oJobServer As Microsoft.SqlServer.Management.Smo.Agent.JobServer
oJobServer = oSQLServer.JobServer
```

To retrieve the contents of SMO object properties, you assign an object reference to a variable. In this case, the Dim statement is used to declare an object of the Smo .Agent.JobServer data type named oJobServer. Then you assign the contents of the oSQLServer.JobServer object to the oJobServer object.

Setting Property Values

You can set the value of SMO read/write properties from Visual Basic by using the assignment operator ("="). The following example shows how to set the SQLServer object's ApplicationName property:

```
Dim boolDefaultTextMode As Boolean
boolDefaultTextMode = True
oSQLServer.DefaultTextMode = boolDefaultTextMode
```

In this example, you can see the oSQLServer.DefaultTextMode property is set using the Visual Basic assignment operator to the value of "True", which is contained in the boolDefaultTextMode Boolean variable.

TIP

While you can set only properties that use standard data types—such as String, Boolean, or Long—you cannot set any of the SMO properties that are object data types. Object properties are always read-only.

SMO Property Collections

SMO's core object hierarchy makes extensive use of *object collections*, which are basically groups of related objects. For instance, the Databases collection in the Server object is a collection of Database objects.

TIP

Collection objects typically end with an s. For instance, Databases indicates a collection of Database objects.

Table 12-1 lists the object collections that are part of the Server object.

Like objects, collections are all contained within a parent object. In the case of the object collections shown in Table 12-1, all the object collections belong to the SQLServer core object.

A collection object is actually an object that has its own set of properties and methods. The following list shows the different properties and methods contained in the Databases collection:

> Count property
>
> IsSynchronized property
>
> Item property

SMO Server Object Collection	Description
BackupDevices	Listing of backup devices available
Credentials	Listing of credential objects
Databases	Listing of databases
Endpoints	Listing of endpoints defined
Languages	Listing of supported languages
LinkedServers	Listing of registered linked servers
Logins	Listing of login IDs
Roles	Listing of roles defined on SQL Server
SystemDataTypes	Listing of system data types defined
SystemMessages	Listing of system messages
Triggers	Listing of triggers defined
UserDefinedMessages	Listing of user-defined messages

Table 12-1 *SMO Server Object Collections*

> ItemByID method
> Parent property
> Refresh method

You can see that the properties and methods of the Databases collection objects are all oriented toward working with the group of databases. For instance, the Count property reports on the number of Database objects contained in the collection, while the ItemByID method returns a specific Database object in the Databases collections. Because all collection objects contain and manage multiple objects, the properties and methods for all collections are similar.

In contrast, the following list shows a selection of some of the primary properties of an individual Database object:

> CreateDate property
> DataSpaceUsage property
> Defaults collection
> Drop method
> FileGroups collection

Name property

Owner property

Rename method

SpaceAvailable property

StoredProcedures collection

Tables collection

Views collection

You can see that the properties and methods of the Database object are all directly related to a SQL Server database. For instance, the Drop method drops the database from the server, while the Owner property contains the name of the database owner. Notice that some of the Database object properties are also other Collection objects. For instance, the StoredProcedures property is a collection of the stored procedures in the database. Likewise, the Tables property is a collection of the tables contained in the database.

Iterating Through Collections

To use SMO effectively, one of the first things you should know is how to work with the collection objects. Iterating through a collection can be accomplished using the following code:

```
Dim oServerConn As ServerConnection = New ServerConnection()
oServerConn.ServerInstance = "SQL2005"
oServerConn.LoginSecure = True
Dim oSQLServer As New Server(oServerConn)

For Each oDatabase As Database In oSQLServer.Databases
    Debug.Print (oDatabase.Name)
Next
```

Visual Basic's For Each statement automatically loops through all the objects in a collection. This example prints a list of all the database names contained in the Databases collection of the oSQLServer object. The code within the For Each block refers to the current object in the collection.

Getting a Specific Collection Object

You also need to understand how to reference a specific object in a collection. You can refer to individual objects within a collection either by the object name or by the ordinal value within the collection. For example, to refer to a Database object by name, you could use the following:

```
Dim oServerConn As ServerConnection = New ServerConnection()
oServerConn.ServerInstance = "SQL2005"
oServerConn.LoginSecure = True
Dim oSQLServer As New Server(oServerConn)

oSQLServer.Databases("SMOSample")
```

or

```
Dim oServerConn As ServerConnection = New ServerConnection()
oServerConn.ServerInstance = "SQL2005"
oServerConn.LoginSecure = True
Dim oSQLServer As New Server(oServerConn)

oSQLServer.Databases.Item("SMOSample")
```

or

```
Dim oServerConn As ServerConnection = New ServerConnection()
oServerConn.ServerInstance = "SQL2005"
oServerConn.LoginSecure = True
Dim oSQLServer As New Server(oServerConn)

Dim sDatabaseName As String
sDatabaseName = "SMOSample"
oSQLServer.Databases.Item(sDatabaseName)
```

All these examples are equivalent. In each case, they reference the database named "SMOSample" in the oSQLServer object. Because the Item method is the default, you can optionally omit the use of the "Item" method. In other words, to reference an individual collection object by name, you pass the Item method a string containing the object's name.

NOTE

This code implicitly uses the Item method of the collection object. The Item method is the default method in a collection; therefore, you needn't explicitly code oSQLServer.Databases.Item("SMOSample"). The Item method can accept either a string or an ordinal number.

To refer to the first database object by ordinal number, you use the following code:

```
Dim oServerConn As ServerConnection = New ServerConnection()
oServerConn.ServerInstance = "SQL2005"
oServerConn.LoginSecure = True
Dim oSQLServer As New Server(oServerConn)

oSQLServer.Databases(0)
```

Again, this code implicitly uses the Item method of the Databases collections. In this case, the Item method is passed the first ordinal value, instead of a string containing the name of the database. The ordinal value of 0 returns the first database in the oSQLServer object. Similarly, the ordinal value of 1 returns the second database, and so on.

SMO Hierarchy

The SMO object model extends and supplants its predecessor, the SQL-DMO object model. Unlike the SQL-DMO object framework, which was based on COM, the newer SMO object model is based on the .NET framework. This means that SMO requires the .NET framework to be installed on the systems that are used to run SMO management applications. SMO can be used to manage SQL Server 7 and SQL Server 2000, as well as SQL Server 2005, allowing you to easily manage a multiversion environment. SQL-DMO will also continue to be supported by SQL Server 2005, allowing backward compatibility for your applications, but SQL-DMO has not been enhanced to include the new features found in the new release. In other words, SQL-DMO is limited to supporting only those features that were found in the previous releases of SQL Server. The new SMO object framework contains over 150 new classes, enabling your custom management application to take advantage of the new features found in SQL Server 2005.

The SMO object model consists of a hierarchy of objects contained in several namespaces and .dll files. The different SMO namespaces represent different areas of functionality within SMO. Table 12-2 lists the namespaces and their relative functionality.

The core SMO namespace, Microsoft.SqlServer.Management.Smo, is implemented as a .NET assembly. This means that the Common Language Runtime (CLR) must be installed before using the SMO objects. The main SMO namespace contains classes that are divided into two categories: *instance* classes and *utility* classes.

Namespace	Function
Microsoft.SqlServer.Management.Smo	Contains instance classes, utility classes, and enumerations that are used to programmatically control SQL Server.
Microsoft.SqlServer.Management.Common	Contains the classes that are common to Replication Management Objects (RMO) and SMO.
Microsoft.SqlServer.Management.Smo.Agent	Contains classes that represent the SQL Server Agent.
Microsoft.SqlServer.Management.Smo.Wmi	Contains classes that represent the WMI Provider.
Microsoft.SqlServer.Management.Smo.RegisteredServers	Contains classes that represent Registered Server.
Microsoft.SqlServer.Management.Smo.Mail	Contains classes that represent Database Mail.
Microsoft.SqlServer.Management.Smo.Broker	Contains classes that represent the Service Broker.
Microsoft.SqlServer.Management.Smo.NotificationServices	Contains classes that represent Notification Services.

Table 12-2 *SMO Namespaces*

Utility Classes

The utility classes in SMO provide programmatic control over certain SQL Server objects and perform specific tasks, such as backup and restore, and transfer of schema and data. The utility classes are shown here:

▶ **Backup**   Provides programmatic access to SQL Server backup operations.

▶ **BackupDevice**   Provides programmatic access to SQL Server backup devices.

▶ **BackupDeviceItem**   Provides programmatic access to named SQL Server backup devices.

▶ **BackupRestoreBase**   A base class that represents functionality that is common to both backup and restore operations.

▶ **DatabaseActiveDirectory**   Provides programmatic access to the Active Directory settings for a database.

▶ **FullTextService**   Allows programmatic access to the Search Full Text settings.

▶ **PartitionFunction**   Provides programmatic access to partition functions.

▶ **PartitionFunctionParameter**   Provides programmatic access to partition function parameters.

▶ **PartitionScheme**   Provides programmatic access to partition schemes.

▶ **PartitionSchemeParameter**   Provides programmatic access to partition scheme parameters.

► **ProgressReportEventArgs**   Provides programmatic access to the arguments used to report the progress of an operation that works through an object hierarchy, such as discovering dependencies in scripting operations.

► **Property**   Provides programmatic access to the properties of SMO objects.

► **Protocol**   Provides programmatic access to the protocols supported by SQL Server.

► **RelocateFile**   A programmatic tool that allows an .mdf or .ldf file to be relocated.

► **Restore**   Provides programmatic access to restore operations.

► **Rule**   Provides programmatic access to a SQL Server rule.

► **Scripter**   The overall, top-level object for managing scripting operations.

► **ScriptingErrorEventArgs**   Provides programmatic access to the arguments used to report the errors that occur during scripting operations.

► **ScriptingOptions**   Provides programmatic options to the options that can be set for scripting operations.

► **ServerActiveDirectory**   Provides programmatic access to Active Directory functionality.

► **ServerEventArgs**   Provides programmatic access to the arguments used to report all types of events that occur on an instance of SQL Server.

► **SmoEventArgs**   Provides programmatic access to the arguments used to report the events that occur in SMO applications.

► **SoapMethodCollectionBase**   A base class that is inherited by the SoapMethodCollection class and provides programmatic access to the collection of SOAP methods that exist in the SOAP configuration.

► **SoapMethodObject**   A base class that is inherited by the SoapMethod class and provides programmatic access to the referenced SOAP method.

► **TcpProtocol**   Provides programmatic access to the protocols supported by SQL Server.

► **Transfer**   A tool object that provides programmatic control over copying of schemas and data to other instances of SQL Server.

► **Urn**   Provides programmatic access to Uniform Resource Name (URN) addresses that uniquely identify SQL Server objects.

► **VerifyCompleteEventArgs**   Provides programmatic access to the arguments used to report the details of the event that occurs when a backup verification operation completes.

Instance Classes

The instance classes embody SQL Server objects such as servers, databases, and tables and are organized into a hierarchical format.

> **NOTE**
>
> *An important optimization that SMO has over SQL-DMO is called **delayed instantiation**. As your applications run, SMO retrieves the objects and properties only as they are needed. Unlike SQL-DMO, which gets everything up front, instead SMO makes many small round-trips to the server. SMO also lets you prefetch collections and retrieve objects using predefined properties. This lets you have control over SMO's behavior as you build applications.*

SMO Server Object Hierarchy

The Server object is the primary SMO object. The other SMO instance class objects reside under the Server object:

► **ActiveDirectory**   Returns a Microsoft.SqlServer.Management.Smo .ServerActiveDirectory object that specifies the Active Directory settings for the database.

► **Configuration**   Returns a Microsoft.SqlServer.Management.Smo.Configuration object that specifies the configuration options for the instance of SQL Server.

► **ConnectionContext**   Returns Microsoft.SqlServer.Management.Common .ServerConnection object that specifies the details of the current connection to the instance of SQL Server.

► **Events**   Returns a Microsoft.SqlServer.Management.Smo.ServerEvents object that represents the server events.

► **FullTextService**   Returns a Microsoft.SqlServer.Management.Smo .FullTextService object that specifies the full-text service implementation on the instance of SQL Server.

► **Information**   Returns a Microsoft.SqlServer.Management.Smo.Information object that specifies information about the instance of SQL Server.

► **JobServer**   Returns a Microsoft.SqlServer.Management.Smo.Agent.JobServer object that specifies the SQL Server Agent associated with the instance of SQL Server.

► **ProxyAccount**   Returns a Microsoft.SqlServer.Management.Smo .ServerProxyAccount object that specifies the proxy account associated with the instance of SQL Server.

▶ **ServiceMasterKey**   Returns a Microsoft.SqlServer.Management.Smo
.ServiceMasterKey object that specifies the service master key associated
with the instance of SQL Server.

▶ **Settings**   Returns a Microsoft.SqlServer.Management.Smo.Settings object
that specifies modifiable settings for the instance of SQL Server.

▶ **UserOptions**   Returns a Microsoft.SqlServer.Management.Smo.UserOptions
object that specifies user options for the current connection to the instance of
SQL Server.

NOTE

*This list only represents most of the objects in the SMO Server object hierarchy; the Server object
collections are listed later in this section. Many of these objects also contain their own objects,
properties, and collections.*

SMO Database Object Hierarchy

The SMO Database objects let you work with the various SQL Server database
objects such as defaults, rules, tables, and stored procedures. The following SMO
objects and collections are contained in the SMO Database object hierarchy:

Database Object Properties

▶ **ActiveDirectory**   Returns a Microsoft.SqlServer.Management.Smo
.DatabaseActiveDirectory object that specifies the Active Directory settings
for the database.

▶ **CompatibilityLevel**   Returns a Microsoft.SqlServer.Management.Smo
.CompatibilityLevel object value that specifies the compatibility level of the
database.

▶ **DatabaseOptions**   Returns a Microsoft.SqlServer.Management.Smo
.DatabaseOptions object value that contains database configuration options.

▶ **Events**   Returns a Microsoft.SqlServer.Management.Smo.DatabaseEvents
object that represents the database events.

▶ **LogReuseWaitStatus**   Returns a Microsoft.SqlServer.Management.Smo
.LogReuseWaitStatus that specifies the type of operation on which the reuse of
transaction log space is waiting.

▶ **MasterKey**   Returns a Microsoft.SqlServer.Management.Smo.MasterKey
system object value that specifies the master key used to encrypt the private
keys of certificates.

- ▶ **MirroringSafetyLevel**   Returns a Microsoft.SqlServer.Management.Smo .MirroringSafetyLevel object value that specifies the mirroring safety level.

- ▶ **MirroringStatus**   Returns a Microsoft.SqlServer.Management.Smo .MirroringStatus object value that specifies the status of the database and mirroring session.

- ▶ **MirroringWitnessStatus**   Returns a Microsoft.SqlServer.Management.Smo .MirroringWitnessStatus object value that specifies the status of the mirroring witness server.

- ▶ **Parent**   Returns a Microsoft.SqlServer.Management.Smo.Server object that is the parent of the Microsoft.SqlServer.Management.Smo.Database object.

- ▶ **ReplicationOptions**   Returns a ReplicationOptions object value that specifies the active replication settings for the database.

- ▶ **Status**   Returns a Microsoft.SqlServer.Management.Smo.DatabaseStatus object value that specifies the status of the database.

Database Collections

- ▶ **ApplicationRoles**   Returns a Microsoft.SqlServer.Management.Smo .ApplicationRoleCollection object that represents all the application roles defined on the database.

- ▶ **Assemblies**   Returns a Microsoft.SqlServer.Management.Smo .SqlAssemblyCollection object that represents all the assemblies defined on the database.

- ▶ **AsymmetricKeys**   Returns a Microsoft.SqlServer.Management.Smo .AsymmetricKeyCollection object that represents all the asymmetric keys defined on the database.

- ▶ **Certificates**   Returns a Microsoft.SqlServer.Management.Smo .CertificateCollection object that represents all the certificates defined on the database.

- ▶ **Defaults**   Returns a Microsoft.SqlServer.Management.Smo.DefaultCollection object that represents all the defaults defined on the database.

- ▶ **ExtendedProperties**   Returns a Microsoft.SqlServer.Management.Smo .ExtendedPropertyCollection object that specifies the extended properties of the Microsoft.SqlServer.Management.Smo.Database object.

- ▶ **ExtendedStoredProcedures**   Returns a Microsoft.SqlServer.Management.Smo .ExtendedStoredProcedureCollection object that represents all the extended stored procedures defined on the database.

► **FileGroups**   Returns a Microsoft.SqlServer.Management.Smo .FileGroupCollection object that represents all the filegroups defined on the database.

► **FullTextCatalogs**   Returns a Microsoft.SqlServer.Management.Smo .FullTextCatalogCollection object that represents all the full-text catalogs defined on the database.

► **LogFiles**   Returns a Microsoft.SqlServer.Management.Smo.LogFileCollection object that represents all the log files defined on the database.

► **PartitionFunctions**   Returns a Microsoft.SqlServer.Management.Smo .PartitionFunctionCollection object that represents all the partition functions defined on the database.

► **PartitionSchemes**   Returns a Microsoft.SqlServer.Management.Smo .PartitionSchemeCollection object that represents all the partition schemes defined on the database.

► **Roles**   Returns a Microsoft.SqlServer.Management.Smo.DatabaseRoleCollection object that represents all the roles defined on the database.

► **Rules**   Returns a Microsoft.SqlServer.Management.Smo.RuleCollection object that represents all the rules defined on the database.

► **Schemas**   Returns a Microsoft.SqlServer.Management.Smo.SchemaCollection object that represents all the schemas defined on the database.

► **StoredProcedures**   Returns a Microsoft.SqlServer.Management.Smo .StoredProcedureCollection object that represents all the stored procedures defined on the database.

► **SymmetricKeys**   Returns a Microsoft.SqlServer.Management.Smo .SymmetricKeyCollection object that represents all the symmetric keys defined on the database.

► **Synonyms**   Returns a Microsoft.SqlServer.Management.Smo .SynonymCollection object that represents all the synonyms defined on the database.

► **Tables**   Returns a Microsoft.SqlServer.Management.Smo.TableCollection object that represents all the tables defined on the database.

► **Triggers**   Returns a Microsoft.SqlServer.Management.Smo.TriggerCollection object that represents all the triggers defined on the database.

► **UserDefinedAggregates**   Returns a Microsoft.SqlServer.Management.Smo .UserDefinedAggregateCollection object that represents all the user-defined aggregates defined on the database.

▶ **UserDefinedDataTypes**   Returns a Microsoft.SqlServer.Management.Smo
.UserDefinedDataTypeCollection object that represents all the user-defined data
types on the database.

▶ **UserDefinedFunctions**   Returns a Microsoft.SqlServer.Management.Smo
.UserDefinedFunctionCollection object that represents all the user-defined
functions on the database.

▶ **UserDefinedTypes**   Returns a Microsoft.SqlServer.Management.Smo
.UserDefinedTypeCollection object that represents all the user-defined types
on the database.

▶ **Users**   Returns a Microsoft.SqlServer.Management.Smo.UserCollection
object that represents all the users defined on the database.

▶ **Views**   Returns a Microsoft.SqlServer.Management.Smo.ViewCollection
object that represents all the views defined on the database.

▶ **XmlSchemaCollections**   Returns a Microsoft.SqlServer.Management.Smo
.XmlSchemaCollectionCollection object that represents all the XML schemas
defined on the database.

NOTE

*This list represents only some of the objects and collections in the SMO Database object hierarchy.
Many of these objects also contain their own objects, properties, and collections.*

SMO Table Object and View Object Hierarchy

The SMO Table and View objects let you drill down to the data level and work
with the information on your SQL Server system. The following SMO objects and
collections are contained in the SMO Table and View object hierarchy:

Table Objects

▶ **Events**   Returns a Microsoft.SqlServer.Management.Smo.TableEvents object
that represents the table events.

▶ **Parent**   Returns a Microsoft.SqlServer.Management.Smo.Database object
value that is the parent of the Microsoft.SqlServer.Management.Smo.Table
object.

▶ **Checks**   Returns a Microsoft.SqlServer.Management.Smo.CheckCollection
object that represents all the check constraints defined on the table.

▶ **ForeignKeys**   Returns a Microsoft.SqlServer.Management.Smo .ForeignKeyCollection object that represents all the foreign keys defined on the table.

▶ **PartitionSchemeParameters**   Returns a Microsoft.SqlServer.Management .Smo.PartitionSchemeParameterCollection object that represents all the partition scheme parameters defined on the table.

View Objects

▶ **Events**   Returns a Microsoft.SqlServer.Management.Smo.ViewEvents object that represents the view events.

▶ **Parent**   Returns a Microsoft.SqlServer.Management.Smo.Database object value that specifies the parent of the Microsoft.SqlServer.Management.Smo .View object.

TableViewBase Objects

▶ **FullTextIndex**   Returns a Microsoft.SqlServer.Management.Smo .FullTextIndex object that represents a Microsoft Search full-text index.

▶ **Columns**   Returns a Microsoft.SqlServer.Management.Smo .ColumnCollection object that represents all the columns in the table.

▶ **ExtendedProperties**   Returns a Microsoft.SqlServer.Management.Smo .ExtendedPropertyCollection object that represents all the extended properties defined on the table or view.

▶ **Indexes**   Returns a Microsoft.SqlServer.Management.Smo.IndexCollection object that represents all the indexes defined on the table or view.

▶ **Statistics**   Returns a Microsoft.SqlServer.Management.Smo.StatisticCollection object that represents all the statistic counters defined on the table or view.

▶ **Triggers**   Returns a Microsoft.SqlServer.Management.Smo.TriggerCollection object that represents all the triggers defined on the table or view.

SMO JobServer Object Hierarchy

The SMO JobServer objects let you control SQL Servers Agent functions such as tasks, jobs, and alerts. The primary object of the SMO Agent objects is the JobServer object. The JobServer object controls SQL Server's tasks and scheduling functions.

JobServer Object Properties

▶ **AgentLogLevel**   Returns a Microsoft.SqlServer.Management.Smo.Agent
.AgentLogLevel object value that specifies the type of messages that are logged
by SQL Server Agent.

▶ **AlertSystem**   Returns a Microsoft.SqlServer.Management.Smo.Agent
.AlertSystem object value that stores information about all the alerts defined on
SQL Server Agent.

▶ **JobServerType**   Returns a Microsoft.SqlServer.Management.Smo.Agent
.JobServerType object value that specifies the type of job server.

▶ **Parent**   Returns a Microsoft.SqlServer.Management.Smo.Server object value
that specifies the parent of the Microsoft.SqlServer.Management.Smo.Agent
.JobServer object.

JobServer Collections

▶ **AlertCategories**   Returns a Microsoft.SqlServer.Management.Smo.Agent
.AlertCategoryCollection object that represents all the alert categories defined
on SQL Server Agent.

▶ **Alerts**   Returns a Microsoft.SqlServer.Management.Smo.Agent
.AlertCollection that represents the alerts defined on SQL Server Agent.

▶ **JobCategories**   Returns a Microsoft.SqlServer.Management.Smo.Agent
.JobCategoryCollection that represents the job categories defined on SQL
Server Agent.

▶ **Jobs**   Returns a Microsoft.SqlServer.Management.Smo.Agent.JobCollection
that represents the jobs defined on SQL Server Agent.

▶ **OperatorCategories**   Returns a Microsoft.SqlServer.Management.Smo
.Agent.OperatorCategoryCollection that represents the operator categories
defined on SQL Server Agent.

▶ **Operators**   Returns a Microsoft.SqlServer.Management.Smo.Agent
.OperatorCollection that represents the operators defined on SQL Server Agent.

▶ **ProxyAccounts**   Returns a Microsoft.SqlServer.Management.Smo.Agent
.ProxyAccountCollection that represents the proxy accounts defined on SQL
Server Agent.

▶ **SharedSchedules**   Returns a Microsoft.SqlServer.Management.Smo.Agent
.JobScheduleCollection that represents the shared schedules defined on SQL
Server Agent.

▶ **TargetServerGroups**   Returns a Microsoft.SqlServer.Management.Smo
.Agent.TargetServerGroupCollection that represents the target server groups
defined on SQL Server Agent.

▶ **TargetServers**   Returns a Microsoft.SqlServer.Management.Smo.Agent
.TargetServerCollection that represents the target server defined on SQL Server
Agent.

NOTE

This list represents only the major objects in the SMO JobServer object hierarchy. Many of these objects also contain their own objects, properties, and collections.

Building the SMO Sample Application

In the first part of this chapter, you had an overview of SMO objects, followed
by an explanation of some of the most important SMO collections, methods, and
properties. In the next part of the chapter, you learn how you can put SMO to work
in a sample VB.NET program. Figure 12-3 presents the main screen of an example
SMO application name SMOSample.exe that was built using VB.NET.

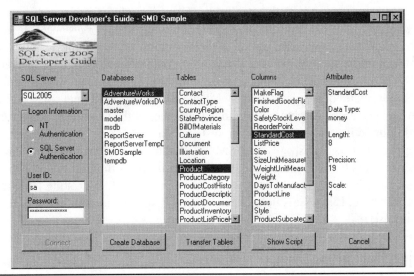

Figure 12-3 *A sample VB.NET SMO application*

This sample application demonstrates many of the essential techniques required to use SMO, including:

- Creating the Server object
- Connecting to a SQL Server system
- Using collections
- Getting specific objects from a collection
- Creating new database objects
- Copying existing database objects
- Disconnecting from a SQL Server system

The sample application lists the registered SQL Server systems in a drop-down box, enabling the user to select the desired system to connect to. After selecting the desired SQL Server system, the user selects the appropriate authentication type. If SQL Server Authentication is selected, then the user is prompted to enter the Login ID and Password. If Windows Authentication is chosen, the user simply clicks the Connect button. Following a successful connection, the sample application lists all the databases the user is authorized to use. Lists showing the tables and columns for the first database in the list are filled in automatically. The Columns list is automatically filled in with the column names from the first table. Likewise, the Attributes list is filled in with the attributes of the first column in the list.

Clicking any of the list items updates all the dependent lists. For instance, clicking a different database name causes the list of tables, columns, and column attributes to be updated with information from the newly selected database. And clicking a different item in the Tables list causes the Columns and Attributes lists to be updated with the column names and attributes of the selected table. Likewise, clicking a different entry in the column list updates the Attributes list with the attributes of the newly selected column.

In addition to listing the SQL Server system's databases schema, the sample SMO application also illustrates how SMO is capable of performing basic database management functions. Clicking Create Database prompts the user to create a new database. Clicking Copy Table lets the user create a copy of an existing table in the selected database. Likewise, clicking Show Keys displays the keys where a given column is used.

Creating the Server Object

The first thing the sample application needs to do is create an instance of the Server object. In the sample application, the Server object is shared by all the objects on the form, so it has been created using the following code in the Declarations section of the main Visual Basic form:

```
Dim oSQLServer As New Server()
```

Listing the Registered SQL Systems

After a new global instance of the SMO object is instantiated in the project's Declarations section, the list of registered SQL Server systems is retrieved during the initial Form_Load subroutine and displayed in a combo box enabling the user to select a specific SQL Server system. The code illustrating how to use SMO to retrieve the list of registered SQL Server systems is shown in the following listing:

```
Private Sub Form_Load(ByVal sender As System.Object, _
    ByVal e As System.EventArgs) Handles MyBase.Load
  Dim oRegisteredServers As RegisteredServers.RegisteredServer() = _
      SmoApplication.SqlServerRegistrations.EnumRegisteredServers()

  ' Add each name to the combobox
  For Each oRegisteredServer As RegisteredServers.RegisteredServer _
      In oRegisteredServers
    cboServer.Items.Add(oRegisteredServer.ServerInstance)
  Next
End Sub
```

In the beginning of the Form_Load subroutine, you can see where an instance of the RegisteredServer object is created and filled using the EnumRegisteredServers method of the SqlServerRegistrations class. Using this method is a vast improvement over SQL-DMO, as there is no longer any need to use a recursive loop through the servers and server groups to list the registered servers.

Next, you see the For Each Loop read through all the individual SQL Server system names contained in the RegisteredServers collection. The registered systems objects are assigned to the oRegisteredServer object, and the Items.Add method of the cboServer combo box is used to add the value of the oRegisteredServer .ServerInstance property to the combo box's drop-down list.

Connecting to the Selected SQL Server System

After an oSQLServer object is created, you can use the ServerConnection object's connect method to establish a connection to a SQL Server system. In the sample application, the SQL Server connection is started after the user selects the name

of the appropriate SQL Server system, then enters the appropriate authentication
information, and then clicks Connect. Clicking Connect executes the following code
in the cmdConnect_Click subroutine:

```
Private Sub cmdConnect_Click(ByVal sender As System.Object, _
    ByVal e As System.EventArgs) Handles cmdConnect.Click
   ResetScript()
   Dim oServerConn As New ServerConnection()
   oServerConn.ServerInstance = cboServer.Text
   oServerConn.LoginSecure = False
   Dim oDatabase As Database

   Try
       ' Setup a secure login for NT security
       If Me.optNTSecurity.Checked = True Then
           oServerConn.LoginSecure = True
       Else
           oServerConn.Login = txtLogin.Text
           oServerConn.Password = txtPwd.Text
       End If


       ' Connect to the selected SQL Server system
       oServerConn.Connect()
       oSQLServer = New Server(oServerConn)
       ' Disable the Connect button
       cmdConnect.Enabled = False
       ' List the databases
       For Each oDatabase In oSQLServer.Databases
           If oDatabase.Status <> DatabaseStatus.Inaccessible Then
               lstDatabases.Items.Add(oDatabase.Name)
           End If
       Next oDatabase


       ' Populate the other list boxes
       lstDatabases_Click(sender, e)
       ' Enable all of the other buttons
       cmdCreateDB.Enabled = True
       cmdTransferTables.Enabled = True
       cmdShowScript.Enabled = True
   Catch
       SQLSMOError()
   End Try
End Sub
```

In the beginning of this routine, an instance of Database is declared and named oDatabase. Next, the SMO ServerConnection object is declared and the server name from the cboServer drop-down box is put to the ServerInstance property. The ServerConnection object is also set with the LoginSecure type and Login and Password properties based on the security type selected by the user. Next, the oServerConn object is then passed as a parameter to the oSQLServer object's constructor. If the user chose to use Windows Authentication, then the LoginSecure property of the oServerConn object is set to True, indicating that a trusted connection between SQL Server and NT will be used to authenticate the client.

The Connect method could fail if the user enters an invalid SQL Server name or other invalid login information. As you can see in the cmdConnect_Click subroutine, a Try/Catch loop is used around the Connect method of the SMO objects. If the Connect method fails, a run-time error is generated and Visual Basic's error handler is invoked. This causes control of the cmdConnect_Click subroutine to jump to the Catch portion of the Try/Catch loop, where the SQLSMOError function is executed. Handling SMO errors and the SQLSMOError subroutine is discussed later in this chapter.

Listing Databases

If the Connect method is successful, the cmdConnect_Click subroutine continues and the cmdConnect button is disabled, preventing the user from attempting to connect a second time. Next, the For Each loop is executed, which fills the list of databases on the SMO example program with the database names from the connected SQL Server system.

The Databases property of the oSQLServer object contains a collection of the database names for the connected SQL Server. In the cmdConnect_Click subroutine shown previously, you can see how Visual Basic's For Each operation is used to loop through the collection of database names and add each name to the list of databases.

Each iteration of the For Each loop addresses a different Database object in the Databases collection. For instance, the first time the For Each loop is executed, the first Database object in the Databases collection is the current object. The second time the For Each loop is executed, the second Database object in the Databases collection is the current object. Within the For Each loop, first the database is tested to ensure that it's accessible. For instance, the user running the application might not have permission to access the database. Next, the database name contained in the Name property of the current oDatabase object is added to the lstDatabases ListBox object using the Items.Add method. The For Each loop executes once for each object contained in the Databases collection.

To fill out the Tables list, the Columns list, and the Columns attributes automatically, the cmdConnect_Click subroutine then executes the lstDatabases_Click subroutine, which retrieves a list of tables contained in the first database in the oDatabases collection.

Listing Tables

The code that retrieves the database table information for the sample application is executed either automatically at the end of the cmdConnect_Click subroutine or when the user clicks one of the database names in the list of databases. Both cases execute the lstDatabases_Click subroutine shown here:

```
Private Sub lstDatabases_Click(ByVal sender As Object, _
    ByVal e As System.EventArgs) Handles lstDatabases.Click
    ResetScript()
    Dim oCurDatabase As Database
    Dim oTable As Table

    Try
        ' Get the selected database name
        If lstDatabases.SelectedIndex >= 0 Then
            oCurDatabase = oSQLServer.Databases(lstDatabases.SelectedIndex)
        Else ' otherwise pick the first database
            oCurDatabase = oSQLServer.Databases(0)
            lstDatabases.SetSelected(0, True)
        End If

        ' Clear the dependant objects
        lstTables.Items.Clear()
        lstColumns.Items.Clear()
        txtAttributes.Text = vbNullString

        ' Add the table names to the list
        For Each oTable In oCurDatabase.Tables
            lstTables.Items.Add(oTable.Name)
        Next oTable

        ' Populate the dependant objects
        lstTables_Click(sender, e)
    Catch
        SQLSMOError()
    End Try
End Sub
```

At the top of the lstDatabases_Click subroutine, you can see where instances of the SMO Database object and the Table object are created. Next, the Try/Catch loop is set up to transfer control to the Catch tag and the SQLSMOError function to trap any run-time errors. Next, the SelectedIndex property of the lstDatabases list is checked to determine if this subroutine was evoked automatically by the cmdConnect_Click subroutine or by the user's clicking one of the database names in the list of databases. If the value of the lstDatabases.SelectedIndex property is 0 or greater, then the user clicked one of the database list items and the program should display the tables for the selected database. Otherwise, if the lstDatabases .SelectedIndex property value is less than 0 (actually –1), then no user selection was made. The oCurDatabase object is set to the SelectedIndex property value of the Database objects contained in the oSQLServer.Databases collection. In other words, if the user clicks the fifth item in the lstDatabases ListBox, the lstDatabase .SelectedIndex property value will be used to set the oCurDatabase object to the fifth Database object in the oSQLServer.Databases collection. If no selection was made, the oCurDatabase object is set to the first Database object in the collection.

Next, all the information currently displayed in the dependent interface objects is cleared. Then, Visual Basic's For Each operation is used to list the members of the Tables collection. The For Each operation loops through the collection of SQL Server table names contained in the oCurDatabase object. Inside the For Each loop, the name of each member of the Tables collection is added to the lstTables list using the Items.Add method.

Listing Columns

After all the table names have been added to the list of tables, the lstTables_Click subroutine is executed to refresh the list of column names. The code that retrieves the names of the columns contained in a given table is executed either automatically at the end of the lstTables_Click subroutine or when the user clicks one of the table items displayed in the Tables list. In both instances, the lstTables_Click subroutine shown here is executed:

```
Private Sub lstTables_Click(ByVal sender As Object, _
    ByVal e As System.EventArgs) Handles lstTables.Click
    ResetScript()
    Dim oCurDatabase As Database
    Dim oCurTable As Table
    Dim oColumn As Column

    Try
        ' Get the selected table name
        If lstTables.SelectedIndex >= 0 Then
            oCurDatabase = oSQLServer.Databases(lstDatabases.SelectedIndex)
            oCurTable = oCurDatabase.Tables(lstTables.SelectedIndex)
        Else ' otherwise pick the first table
```

```
            oCurDatabase = oSQLServer.Databases(0)
            oCurTable = oCurDatabase.Tables(0)
            lstTables.SetSelected(0, True)
        End If

        ' Clear the dependant objects
        lstColumns.Items.Clear()
        txtAttributes.Text = vbNullString

        ' Add the column names to the list
        For Each oColumn In oCurTable.Columns
            lstColumns.Items.Add(oColumn.Name)
        Next oColumn

        ' Populate the dependant objects
        lstColumns_Click(sender, e)
    Catch
        SQLSMOError()
    End Try
End Sub
```

The lstTables_Click subroutine is structured much like the lstDatabases_Click subroutine. The first thing the lstTables_Click subroutine does is to make instances of the SMO Database, Table, and Column objects named oCurDatabase, oCurTable, and oColumn. Next, the lstTables_Click subroutine sets up the Try/Catch loop used to catch any errors generated and, subsequently, execute the SQLSMOError function.

Then the lstTables.SelectedIndex property is tested to determine if this subroutine has been evoked automatically from the lstDatabases_Click subroutine or if this subroutine has been evoked by the user's clicking one of the items in the lstTables list. If the lstTables_Click subroutine was called by the user's clicking an entry in the lstTables list, then the oCurDatabase and oCurTable objects are assigned the value of the selected list items. Otherwise, the oCurDatabase and oCurTable variables are set to the first entry in each of their respective lists.

After the variables containing the parent Database and Table names have been set, the old values in the lstColumns list and txtAttributes text box interface objects are cleared. This ensures that the lstColumns list and the txtAttributes text box will contain the values from the user's new selection.

Like the Databases and Tables collections, a For Each loop is used to iterate through the collection of Column objects. As the For Each loop progresses, the name of each current Column object is added to the lstColumns ListBox object. After all the names from the Columns collection have been added to the lstColumns list, the lstColumns_Click subroutine is called to retrieve a subset of the specific attributes of a selected column.

Retrieving Column Attributes

The code that retrieves the attributes of a specific column is executed either automatically at the end of the lstColumn_Click subroutine or when the user clicks an item in the Columns list. The lstColumns_Click subroutine shown here is executed for both of these actions:

```
Private Sub lstColumns_Click(ByVal sender As Object, _
    ByVal e As System.EventArgs) Handles lstColumns.Click
    ResetScript()
    Dim oCurDatabase As Database
    Dim oCurTable As Table
    Dim oColumn As Column

    Try
        ' Get the selected column name
        If lstColumns.SelectedIndex >= 0 Then
            oCurDatabase = oSQLServer.Databases(lstDatabases.SelectedIndex)
            oCurTable = oCurDatabase.Tables(lstTables.SelectedIndex)
            oColumn = oCurTable.Columns(lstColumns.SelectedIndex)
        Else ' otherwise pick the first column
            oCurDatabase = oSQLServer.Databases(0)
            oCurTable = oCurDatabase.Tables(0)
            oColumn = oCurTable.Columns(0)
            lstColumns.SetSelected(0, True)
        End If

        ' Clear the dependant objects
        txtAttributes.Text = vbNullString
        ' Add the attributes to the textbox
        txtAttributes.Text = oColumn.Name.ToString() _
        & vbCrLf & vbCrLf _
        & "Data Type:" & vbCrLf _
        & oColumn.DataType.ToString() & vbCrLf & vbCrLf _
        & "Length:" & vbCrLf _
        & oColumn.Properties.Item("Length").Value.ToString() _
        & vbCrLf & vbCrLf _
        & "Precision:" & vbCrLf _
        & oColumn.Properties.Item("NumericPrecision").Value.ToString() _
        & vbCrLf & vbCrLf _
        & "Scale:" & vbCrLf _
        & oColumn.Properties.Item("NumericScale").Value.ToString()
    Catch ex As Exception
        SQLSMOError()
    End Try
End Sub
```

Again, the lstColumns_Click subroutine starts by declaring instances of the SMO Database, Table, and Column objects.

Like the other subroutines, the lstColumns_Click subroutine then determines if the user has clicked an entry in the lstColumns list or if the lstColumns_Click subroutine was called automatically from the lstTables_Click subroutine. If the user has clicked one of the lstColumn items, then the oCurDatabase, oCurTable, and oColumn variables are assigned the select list items. Otherwise, the oCurDatabase, oCurTable, and oColumn variables are assigned the first item in each of the respective lists.

Next, the txtAttributes.Text property is cleared. You might notice that unlike the other subroutines, the lstTables_Click subroutine doesn't use a list box or iterate through a collection. Instead, the lstColumns_Click subroutine displays a selection of properties from one specific member of the Columns collection. The following properties of the Column object are displayed:

▶ Name

▶ DataType

▶ Length

▶ NumericPrecision

▶ NumericScale

The txtAttributes text box has the Multiline property enabled, which allows multiple lines to be displayed in the text box. Each line is separated by CR + LF characters, which are represented by the vbCrLf constant.

Creating Databases

The earlier examples in this chapter illustrated how to list the various SQL Server database objects using SMO collections. SMO is capable of far more than listing databases or tables, however. SMO's extensive object framework lets you perform virtually any management function that can be performed using the SQL Server Enterprise Manager. The following example illustrates how SMO can be used to create a new SQL Server database programmatically. The cmdCreateDB_Click subroutine is executed when the user clicks the Create Database button provided by the SMOSample application, shown earlier in Figure 12-3. The code for the cmdCreateDB_Click subroutine is shown in the following listing:

```
Private Sub cmdCreateDB_Click(ByVal sender As System.Object, _
    ByVal e As System.EventArgs) Handles cmdCreateDB.Click
    ResetScript()
    Dim sDatabaseName As String

        'Input the database name
        sDatabaseName = InputBox("Enter the new database name", _
            "New Database")
    Try
        Dim oDatabase As New Database(oSQLServer, sDatabaseName)
        oDatabase.Create()
        'Add the DB name to the list
        lstDatabases.Items.Add(oDatabase.Name)
    Catch
        SQLSMOError()
    End Try
End Sub
```

This subroutine begins by declaring a string object called sDatabaseName.
The Visual Basic InputBox method is then called to prompt the user to enter a new
database name to create, and the result is placed into the newly created string
sDatabaseName. A new Database object is then instantiated using the current SQL
Server instance and sDatabaseName string as parameters. To create the new database
on the server, the database object's Create method is called. The Create method
creates the new database using default property settings; however, you can also set
the database object properties before calling the Create method.

Last, the list of databases displayed by the SMOSample application is updated
with the new name by using the lstDatabases object's Items.Add method to add the
name of the new database to the list of databases.

Transferring Tables

In addition to creating and manipulating databases, SMO is capable of creating and
managing tables and other databases objects. Using the SMOSample application,
a user can copy tables in the selected database to another database on the server by
clicking the Transfer Tables button. Clicking the Transfer Tables button executes the
cmdTransferTables_Click event subroutine that you can see in the following listing.

NOTE

*To use the Transfer utility class functions from a client system, the DTS run time needs to be
installed on the client system.*

The code in the cmdTransferTables_Click subroutine shows how the SMO Transfer utility class can be used to copy tables from one database to another database within a SQL Server system.

```
Private Sub cmdTransferTables_Click(ByVal sender As System.Object, _
    ByVal e As System.EventArgs) Handles cmdTransferTables.Click
    ResetScript()
    Dim oCurDatabase As Database
    Dim oTrans As New Transfer()

    Try
        ' Set the database object from the current list selection
        If lstDatabases.SelectedIndex >= 0 Then
            oCurDatabase = oSQLServer.Databases(lstDatabases.SelectedIndex)
        Else
            oCurDatabase = oSQLServer.Databases(0)
        End If
        oTrans.Database = oCurDatabase
        ' Prompt for new table name
        oTrans.DestinationDatabase = InputBox( _
            "Enter the destination database name:", "Destination Database")
        oTrans.DestinationServer = cboServer.Text
        oTrans.DestinationLoginSecure = False
        ' Setup a secure login for NT security
        If Me.optNTSecurity.Checked = True Then
            oTrans.DestinationLoginSecure = True
        Else
            oTrans.DestinationLogin = txtLogin.Text
            oTrans.DestinationPassword = txtPwd.Text
        End If
        oTrans.CopyAllTables = True
        oTrans.CopyData = True
        oTrans.CopySchema = True
        oTrans.TemporaryPackageDirectory = "c:\temp"

        oTrans.TransferData()
    Catch
        SQLSMOError()
    End Try
End Sub
```

At the beginning of the cmdTransferTables_Click subroutine, you can see where the Database object oCurDatabase is declared, which represents the current database selected on the SMOSample dialog. A new oTrans object is then instantiated. The VB Try/Catch loop is enabled, and then the oCurDatabase object is assigned to correspond to the database name that's currently selected on the dialog. If the user has previously clicked a database, then that database is used. Otherwise, the first database in the list is assigned as the current database. The oTrans.Database property is then set with the selected database. The Database property of the Transfer object is the source database from which the schema and/or data is transferred to the target location.

Next, the user is prompted to input a destination database name using the InputBox function, and the value keyed by the user is assigned to the oTrans.DestinationDatabase property. The cmdTransferTables_Click subroutine then continues to set the other destination properties—DestinationServer, DestinationLoginSecure, DestinationLogin, and DestinationPassword—with the appropriate values displayed on the SMOSample application dialog.

In the SMOSample application, all tables, including data and the schema, are to be transferred to the destination database; therefore, the oTrans object properties of CopyAllTables, CopyData, and CopySchema are all set to True. The next line in the subroutine sets the TemporaryPackageDirectory property to the c:\temp directory on the local hard drive. When the oTrans.TransferData method is called, several files will be generated and placed into the temporary directory. The following files and file types are generated:

- **Prologue**   SQL file
- **NonTransactable**   SQL file
- **Epilogue**   SQL file
- **CompensatingAction**   SQL file
- **TransferMetadata**   XML document
- **InnerPackage**   SSIS package file

Each of the SQL files contains T-SQL statements that are generated in accordance with the Transfer object's properties, the XML document contains the metadata information based on the Transfer object's properties, and the SSIS package file is used to execute the transfer of the schema and/or data to the destination location. An example of the TransferMetadata file is shown in Figure 12-4.

The oTrans.TransferData method is then called and the tables are copied from the selected database to the destination database. After the transfer completes, the files in the temporary directory are automatically deleted.

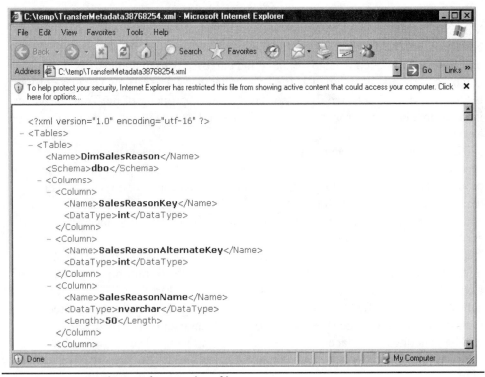

Figure 12-4 *A sample TransferMetadata file*

Showing T-SQL Script for Tables

Another one of the handy utility classes found in SMO is the Scripter class. The Scripter class allows you to programmatically create a hierarchical tree object that represents the parent or child dependent relationships of SQL Server objects. You can also generate Transact-SQL scripts that can be used to re-create SQL Server objects. In the example SMOSample application, selecting a table name from the tables list and clicking the Show Script button displays a text box showing the T-SQL script that can be used to re-create the table object. The cmdShowScript_ Click subroutine is shown in the following listing:

```
Private Sub cmdShowScript_Click(ByVal sender As System.Object, _
    ByVal e As System.EventArgs) Handles cmdShowScript.Click
    Dim oCurDatabase As Database
    Dim oCurTable As Table
    Dim sScript As String
```

```
    ' Clear the dependant objects, reset the textbox
    txtAttributes.Text = vbNullString
    Label4.Text = "Script"
    Label5.Visible = False
    txtAttributes.Width = 220
    txtAttributes.Left = 379
    Try
        ' Set the database object from the current list selection
        If lstDatabases.SelectedIndex >= 0 Then
            oCurDatabase = oSQLServer.Databases(lstDatabases.SelectedIndex)
            oCurTable = oCurDatabase.Tables(lstTables.SelectedIndex)
        Else ' otherwise pick the first table
            oCurDatabase = oSQLServer.Databases(0)
            oCurTable = oCurDatabase.Tables(0)
            lstTables.SetSelected(0, True)
        End If
        For Each sScript In oCurTable.Script()
            txtAttributes.Text += sScript & vbCrLf
        Next sScript
    Catch
        SQLSMOError()
    End Try
End Sub
```

At the top of the cmdShowScript_Click subroutine, you can see where two SMO objects are declared. The oCurDatabase object contains an instance of the current database object selected in the database list. Likewise, the oCurTable object can contain an instance of the current table object selected in the list of tables displayed by the SMOSample application. Next, a string variable named sScript is created.

The next few lines of code reset the labels and text box that are displayed on the VB Windows form so that the generated script can be easily read. After all the working objects and variables have been declared, objects that represent the current database and table selected by the user are assigned. Essentially, this code determines the item in the lstDatabases and lstTables list boxes the user clicked, or it selects the first item if no selection has been made.

Next, you can see where the Script function of the oCurTable object is called. The Script function returns a collection of string objects representing the T-SQL that is used to create the current table. A For Each loop is used to read each of the string items contained in the collection and then add each string object to the text box. Appending a vbCrLf character to each string object causes the contents of the text box to be presented to the end user as a list.

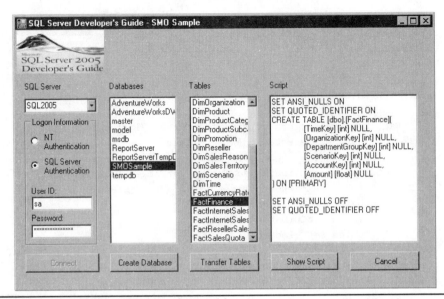

Figure 12-5 *Showing a T-SQL script for a table*

After the list of T-SQL strings has been added to the text box, it is displayed to the end user. Figure 12-5 shows the SMOSample application displayed by the cmdShowScript_Click subroutine.

SMO Error Handling

Errors that the SMO methods generate can be trapped using Visual Basic's standard error handling. If an error is raised by one of the SMO methods and Visual Basic's error handling is not implemented, the user sees a Visual Basic run-time error and the application is terminated.

TIP

Make use of Visual Basic's built-in error handler to trap any SMO errors and prevent unexpected application errors from terminating the application.

All the subroutines presented in the sample SMO application make use of the common SQLSMOError subroutine shown here:

```
Public Function SQLSMOError()

    Dim sErrorMsg As String

    sErrorMsg = Err.Source & " Error: " & _
                Err.Number - vbObjectError & ": " & Err.Description

    SQLSMOError = MsgBox(sErrorMsg, vbOKOnly, "SMO Error")

End Function
```

The SQLSMOError function is a relatively simple function, which displays a message box to the user that provides more information about any error conditions encountered. SMO errors can be displayed using the Visual Basic Err object. The Err.Source property contains the name of the SMO component that raised the error. Subtracting the vbObjectError constant from the Err.Number property results in the SMO error number. The Err.Description property contains a text description of the error.

Summary

As you can see from the code examples, SMO opens the power of SQL Server's management functions to Visual Basic, and its .NET implementation makes it easy to use from Visual Basic and other .NET programming languages. The examples in this chapter illustrated a small section of the capabilities provided by SMO, which is capable of performing virtually every function you can manually perform using the SQL Server Management Studio.

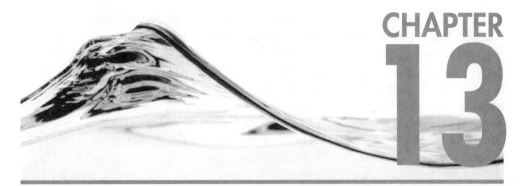

CHAPTER 13

Using sqlcmd

A nother new development tool that's provided with SQL Server 2005 is the new sqlcmd utility, which is essentially a replacement for the older command-line osql and isql utilities found in the earlier releases of SQL Server. The old isql program used the now-deprecated SQL Server DB-library to connect to SQL Server, while the osql program used an ODBC interface. For backward compatibility, the osql utility is still shipped with SQL Server 2005; however, isql has been dropped. Like those tools, the sqlcmd utility is run from the command prompt and enables you to enter and execute T-SQL statements, stored procedures, and T-SQL batches. However, it connects to SQL Server using OLE DB and extends the power that was provided in those earlier command-line tools by adding support for variables and extended commands.

sqlcmd Components

The sqlcmd utility consists of four primary components: the sqlcmd command shell, its command-line parameters, and the built-in commands and variables that are supported by the sqlcmd shell, which enables to you build and execute batches of T-SQL commands. The command-line parameters enable you to pass in run-time information to the SqlCmd shell as well as run T-SQL commands and other sqlcmd scripts. The built-in variables enable your sqlcmd scripts to access system and environment information, while the built-in commands enable you to add extended control flow to your scripts.

Command Shell

Much like its earlier counterparts, isql and osql, sqlcmd uses a command shell to submit T-SQL commands to SQL Server. Entering **sqlcmd** at the command prompt starts the sqlcmd command shell. When the command shell is active, each line in the batch will be numbered until the batch is executed. The first line in the batch will be labeled with 1> prompt. You build the batch by entering T-SQL commands and then pressing the ENTER key following each command. The sqlcmd shell will add the line to the batch and increment the line number for the next command. Entering the T-SQL Go command will execute all of the commands in the current batch. You can see a simple example of using the sqlcmd shell in the following listing:

```
C:\temp>sqlcmd
1> use adventureworks
2> select DepartmentID, Name from HumanResources.Department
3> go
Changed database context to 'AdventureWorks'.DepartmentID Name
----------- ------------------------------------------------------
```

```
12 Document Control
 1 Engineering
16 Executive
14 Facilities and Maintenance
10 Finance
 9 Human Resources
11 Information Services
 4 Marketing
 7 Production
 8 Production Control
 5 Purchasing
13 Quality Assurance
 6 Research and Development
 3 Sales
15 Shipping and Receiving
 2 Tool Design

(16 rows affected)
```

Here you can see how the sqlcmd command is executed to start the sqlcmd command shell. Then two T-SQL commands are added to the batch. The first command sets the current database to the sample AdventureWorks database, and the next command performs a simple T-SQL query that returns the DepartmentID and Name columns from the HumanResources.Department table in the Adventureworks database.

Command-Line Parameters

The sqlcmd utility supports a number of command-line parameters that influence how the utility works. The following listing shows the complete set of command-line parameters that are supported by the sqlcmd utility:

```
C:\temp>sqlcmd /?
Microsoft (R) SQL Server Command Line Tool
Version 9.00.1187.07 NT INTEL X86
Copyright (C) 2004 Microsoft Corporation.  All rights reserved.

usage: sqlcmd         [-U login id]        [-P password]
  [-S server]         [-H hostname]        [-E trusted connection]
  [-d use database name] [-l login timeout] [-t query timeout]
  [-h headers]        [-s colseparator]    [-w screen width]
  [-a packetsize]     [-e echo input]      [-I Enable Quoted Identifiers]
  [-c cmdend]         [-L[c] list servers[clean output]]
  [-q "cmdline query"]  [-Q "cmdline query" and exit]
```

```
[-m errorlevel]            [-V severitylevel]        [-W remove trailing spaces]
[-u unicode output]        [-r[0|1] msgs to stderr]
[-i inputfile]             [-o outputfile]           [-z new password]
[-f <codepage> | i:<codepage>[,o:<codepage>]] [-Z new password and exit]
[-k[1|2] remove[replace] control characters]
[-y variable length type display width]
[-Y fixed length type display width]
[-p[1] print statistics[colon format]]
[-R use client regional setting]
[-b On error batch abort]
[-v var = "value"...]   [-A dedicated admin connection]
[-X[1] disable commands, startup script, environment variables [and exit]]
[-x disable variable substitution]
[-? show syntax summary]
```

NOTE

sqlcmd command-line switches are case sensitive.

The most important and commonly used parameters are explained in the following section.

Listing SQL Server Systems: –L

Use the –L switch to list all of the registered SQL Server systems, as is shown here:

```
C:\temp>sqlcmd -L

Servers:
    SQL2005
    SQL2005-2
    TECA4
```

SQL Server System/Instance: –S

You can use the –S switch to specify the registered SQL Server system that you want to connect to. The following example shows using the –S switch to connect to the SQL Server system named SQL2005:

```
sqlcmd -S sql2005
```

To connect to a named instance, you need to append the instance name using the slash. For example, the following example shows how to connect to SQLInstance1:

```
sqlcmd -S sql2005/SqlInstance1
```

User Logon ID and Password: –U –P

While it's usually preferable to connect using integrated security, sqlcmd also supports connections that use SQL Server authentication via the –U and –P switches. As you might expect, the –U parameter enables you to pass in the SQL Server Login ID, while the –P parameter enables you to supply the password.

NOTE

Unlike the other command line parameters, the –U and –P parameters must not have a space between the switch and its value. The following illustrates using the –U and –P command-line parameters:

```
sqlcmd -S sql2005 -Usa -Pmy1stStrongSAPwd!
```

To accommodate login IDs and passwords that have embedded spaces, you need to surround the value supplied to the –U or –P switch with double quotes (""), as shown in the following listing:

```
sqlcmd -S sql2005 -U"sa" -P"my1stStrongSAPwd!"
```

Database Name: –d

The –d parameter can be used to specify the database that you want the sqlcmd utility to connect to. In the following example, you can see how to use the –d switch to connect to the AdventureWorks database on the SQL Server system named SQL2005:

```
sqlcmd -S sql2005 -d AdventureWorks
```

Query: –Q

The –Q (or –q) switch enables you to submit a query from the command line. This can be useful when you want to execute an ad hoc query or when you want to dynamically build a query in a batch file. The following example illustrates using the –q switch:

```
C:\temp>sqlcmd -q"select Name from AdventureWorks.Production.Product
where ProductID = 777"
Name
--------------------------------------------------
Mountain-100 Black, 44

(1 rows affected)
```

In this example, the –q switch is used to send a select statement to the SQL Server system. Since the SELECT statement can contain spaces, it needs to be enclosed in double quotes("").

Input Source: –i

While directly passing a query as a command-line parameter is a great way to execute simple queries or ad hoc queries that are built into your script, this approach obviously has some shortcomings when it comes to executing more complex sets of instructions. That's where the –i switch comes in, enabling you to direct the sqlcmd utility to use the contents of a script as its input source. Here is an example of using the –i switch:

```
sqlcmd -S sql2005 -i c:\temp\MySqlCmdScript.sql
```

The contents of the file specified with the –i switch will include a combination of T-SQL statements and sqlcmd extended commands and variables. More information about how you write SqlCmd scripts is presented later in this chapter, in the section titled "Developing sqlcmd Scripts."

Output Destination: –o

Much as the –i switch is used to redirect the input source that's used by the sqlcmd utility, the –o switch can be used to redirect the output of sqlcmd from the screen to a file. Here is an example of using the –o switch:

```
sqlcmd -S sql2005 -i c:\temp\MySqlCmdScript.sql -o c:\temp\MyOutput.txt
```

Here the output that's generated by MySqlCmdScript.sql will be written to the file MyOutput.txt in the c:\temp directory. The default output format is plain text. However, you can also use the –s switch to change the column separator character, which is useful for creating comma- or tab-delimited files.

Performance Statistics: –p

Another useful switch is –p, which outputs the performance statistics for the result set. The following listing illustrates using the –p switch in conjunction with the –q switch:

```
C:\temp>sqlcmd -q"select Name from AdventureWorks.Production.Product
where ProductID = 777" -p
Name
--------------------------------------------------
```

```
Mountain-100 Black, 44

(1 rows affected)

Network packet size (bytes): 4096
1 xact[s]:
Clock Time (ms.): total        16   avg    16.00 (62.50 xacts per sec.)
```

Administrative Mode: –A

One important feature that the sqlcmd utility has in addition to the ability to execute commands is the fact that it can connect to the database using SQL Server 2005's Dedicated Administrative Connection (DAC). The DAC permits you to connect and run at a higher priority than any other SQL Server process, enabling you to terminate any runaway process. To use the DAC, you must start the sqlcmd utility using the –A switch, as is shown here:

```
sqlcmd -S sql2005 -A
```

Variable Values: –v

In addition to supporting the execution of standard T-SQL statements, the sqlcmd utility also supports a number of scripting extensions that enable you to include flow control and variables in your scripts. You can use the –v switch to define scripting variables, or you can set them using the command-shell setvar command. The following example shows how to define a variable using the –v parameter and assign it a value:

```
sqlcmd -S Sql2005 -d AdventureWorks -v ProductID="11" -i MyScript.sql
```

In this example, the –S and the –d parameters are used to connect sqlcmd to the AdventureWorks database on the SQL Server system named Sql2005. Then the –v parameter is used to define a variable named ProductID and to assign the value of 11 to that variable. Next the –i parameter is used to execute the script named MyScript .sql. This script can make use of the ProductID variable and pass its value to a SQL query embedded in the script. More detailed examples showing how to use the –v switch are provided later in this chapter.

Online Help: /?

You can get a full listing of the supported command-line switches by entering **sqlcmd /?** at the command prompt.

sqlcmd Extended Commands

To enable the creation of scripts that are able to execute complex logic, the sqlcmd utility provides a number of control commands. To make a clear distinction between sqlcmd commands and T-SQL statements, all sqlcmd commands must be prefixed with a colon (:). The extended sqlcmd commands are listed in Table 13-1.

sqlcmd Variables

In addition to providing for user-defined variables, the sqlcmd utility also includes a set of built-in variables that can be used with sqlcmd scripts. Table 13-2 lists the built-in variables supported by the sqlcmd utility and the command-line switches that can be used to supply values for those variables.

Command	Description
:GO [count]	Signals the end of a batch and executes the cached statements. Adding an optional count value executes the statements a given number of times.
:RESET	Clears the statement cache.
:ED	Starts the next edit for the current statement cache.
:!!	Executes operating system commands.
:QUIT	Ends the sqlcmd utility.
:EXIT (results)	Uses the value of a result set as a return value.
:r <filename>	Includes additional sqlcmd statements from the specified file.
:ServerList	Lists the configured SQL Server systems.
:List	Lists the contents of the statement cache.
:Error <filename>	Redirects error output to the specified file.
:Out <filename>	Redirects query results to the specified file.
:Perftrace <filename>	Redirects performance statistics to the specified file.
:Connect [timeout]	Connects to a SQL Server instance.
:On Error [exit |retry	ignore]	Specifies the action to be performed when an error is encountered.
:XML [ON	OFF]	Specifies whether XML results will be output as a continuous stream.

Table 13-1   *sqlcmd Commands*

Variable	Command-Line Switch
SQLCMDUSER	−U
SQLCMDPASSWORD	−P
SQLCMDSERVER	−S
SQLCMDWORKSTATION	−H
SQLCMDDBNAME	−d
SQLCMDLOGINTIMEOUT	−l
SQLCMDSTATTIMEOUT	−t
SQLCMDHEADERS	−h
SQLCMDCOLSEP	−s
SQLCMDCOLWIDTH	−w
SQLCMDPACKETSIZE	−a
SQLCMDERRORLEVEL	−m

Table 13-2 *sqlcmd Built-in Variables*

Developing sqlcmd Scripts

The preceding section presented the basics of the sqlcmd tool. In this section you'll see some examples of sqlcmd in action. First, this section will cover some of the tools for building sqlcmd scripts. Then you'll see some sqlcmd scripts illustrating how to use variables, nested scripts, and flow control for building database scripts with sqlcmd.

Developing sqlcmd Scripts with Query Editor

You can develop sqlcmd scripts using any text editor like Notepad or TextPad. However, you may not realize that SQL Server Management Studio also has the capability of creating sqlcmd scripts. To develop sqlcmd scripts using Query Editor, you first need to open the Query Editor window and then click the sqlcmd icon as is shown in Figure 13-1.

Query Editor has the following features that can be helpful in developing sqlcmd scripts:

▶ Color-coded syntax

▶ Syntax parsing

▶ Script execution

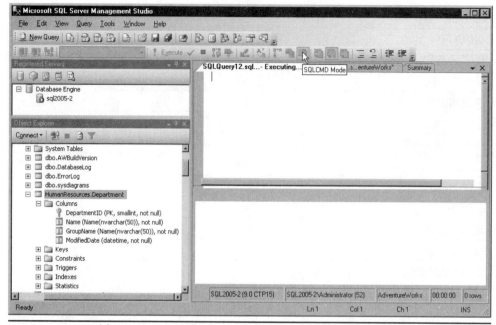

Figure 13-1   *Enabling sqlcmd mode in the Query Editor*

▶   Source control integration

▶   Showplan

Entering Query Editor's sqlcmd mode enables Query Editor to execute all of the commands that would normally only be accessible from the sqlcmd shell. For instance, special sqlcmd variables and commands can be executed, as can operating system commands such as dir and even del if they are prefaced with the !! symbol.

To get started using Query Editor to develop sqlcmd scripts, follow these steps:

1.   Open SQL Server Management Studio.

2.   Click the New Query button to start Query Editor.

3.   Click the sqlcmd button.

4.   Enter and execute the following script in Query Editor:

```
:setvar DirIn c:\temp
!! dir $(DirIn)
```

This script sets the contents of the variable DirIn to c:\temp and then executes the operating system command dir using the contents of the DirIn variable as a parameter. This type of sqlcmd script execution is possible in Query Editor only when the sqlcmd mode has been enabled. You can see the output of the sqlcmd script in Figure 13-2.

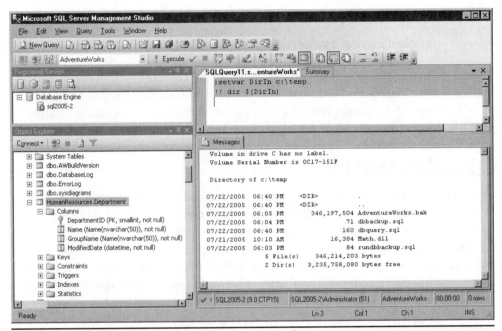

Figure 13-2   *Executing sqlcmd scripts with Query Editor*

Using sqlcmd Variables

One of the most powerful uses of the sqlcmd lies in its ability to execute scripts and substitute variable values at run time. The following listing shows a simple script named dbBackup.sql that can be used to back up the database that's specified in the DatabaseName variable:

```
BACKUP DATABASE $(DatabaseName) TO DISK = "c:\temp\$(DatabaseName).bak"
```

You can substitute the value of the variable either from the command line or by using the :setvar command from within the script. The following example illustrates how you can combine the sqlcmd command-line switches with variables used in scripts:

```
C:\temp>sqlcmd -S sql2005-2 -v DatabaseName="AdventureWorks" -i dbbackup.sql

Processed 21032 pages for database 'AdventureWorks', file 'AdventureWorks_Data'
on file 1.
Processed 2 pages for database 'AdventureWorks', file 'AdventureWorks_Log'
on file 1.
BACKUP DATABASE successfully processed 21034 pages in 16.091 seconds
(10.708 MB/sec).
```

NOTE

The sqlcmd utility uses a trusted connection by default.

This example uses the –S switch to specify the SQL Server system name. The –v switch is used to define a variable named DatabaseName and supply that variable with the value of AdventureWorks. The –i switch is used to tell the sqlcmd utility that the T-SQL command will come out of the file dbbackup.sql.

Using sqlcmd Script Nesting

Another powerful feature in sqlcmd that promotes code reuse is the ability to nest scripts. By using the built-in :r command, you can direct the sqlcmd utility to read in and execute the content of another sqlcmd script. To illustrate using script nesting, the following example executes the same backup script that was shown in the preceding example, except in this case, instead of executing the script from the command line, the rundbbackup.sql script uses the :r command to read and execute dbbackup.sql:

```
:connect sql2005-2
:setvar DatabaseName AdventureWorks
:r "c:\temp\dbbackup.sql"
```

In this example, the :connect command is used to connect to an instance of SQL Server 2005 named sql2005-2. Then the setvar command is used to set the contents of the DatabaseName variable to AdventureWorks. Next, the :r command is used to read and execute the dbbackup.sql script. Since the DatabaseName variable is already set within the runbackup.sql script, there's no need to pass the dbbackup.sql script any additional parameters.

Since rundbacklup.sql supplies the values for its variable internally, when using the setvar command, the only command-line parameter that's needed is the –I switch, which executes the contents of the rundbbackup.sql file.

```
C:\temp>sqlcmd -i rundbbackup.sql
sqlcmd: Successfully connected to server 'sql2005-2'.
Processed 21032 pages for database 'AdventureWorks', file 'AdventureWorks_Data'
on file 2.
Processed 2 pages for database 'AdventureWorks', file 'AdventureWorks_Log'
on file 2.
BACKUP DATABASE successfully processed 21034 pages in 16.018 seconds
(10.757 MB/sec).
```

Using sqlcmd Variables and T-SQL Statements

As you might expect, you can also use sqlcmd variables in conjunction with T-SQL to create flexible query scripts where the query variables can be substituted in at run time. The following listing gives you an idea of how to combine sqlcmd variables and T-SQL statements:

```
:setvar c1 DepartmentID
:setvar c2 name
:setvar c3 groupname
:setvar t1 humanresources.department
use adventureworks
select $(c1), $(c2) , $(c2) from $(t1)
```

The results of running this script from within Query Editor using the sqlcmd mode are shown in Figure 13-3.

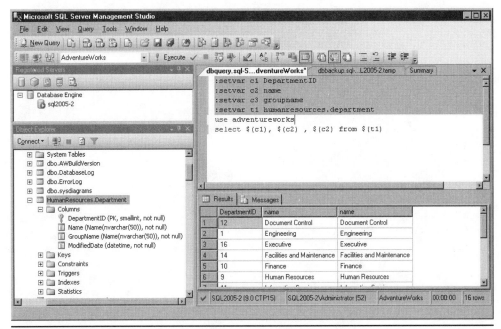

Figure 13-3   *Combining sqlcmd variables and T-SQL statements*

Summary

SqlCmd replaces the old isql nd osql utilities and at the same time brings with it several new features that enable you to create more powerful and flexible scripts. In this chapter you saw how to use the new SqlCmd utility both interactively and in batch. You also learned about its command line parameters, how to include scripts for added functionality, and how to use variables in your SqlCmd scripts.

APPENDIX

SQL Profiler

QL Profiler is a graphical user interface tool for the SQL Trace facility, which allows you to monitor an instance of SQL Server Database Engine or Analysis Services. Using SQL Profiler, you can interactively capture database activity and optionally save the data about the database events to a file or table. The saved data can then be replayed and analyzed at a later date. The SQL Server 2000 Profiler was limited to tracing only relational database calls. With SQL Server 2005 Profiler, you can save the trace file in XML format, as well as to the standard save formats of ANSI, Unicode, and OEM. Traced ShowPlan results can also be saved as XML and then loaded into SQL Server Management Studio for analysis.

You use SQL Profiler to monitor the events you are interested in watching. Once you identify the reasons you want to monitor the activity of the SQL Server instance, you can filter events so that only a pertinent subset of the event data is collected. These are some typical reasons for using the SQL Profiler:

▶ Monitor the performance of an instance of the Database Engine or Analysis Server.

▶ Analyze and streamline the performance of slowly executing queries.

▶ Perform query analysis by saving Showplan results.

▶ Identify the cause of a deadlock.

▶ Debug TSQL statements and stored procedures.

▶ Perform stress and benchmark testing by replaying traces.

▶ Replay traces of one or more users.

▶ Audit and review activity that occurred on an instance of SQL Server.

▶ Aggregate trace results to allow similar event classes to be grouped and analyzed.

Starting SQL Profiler

Unlike in previous versions of Profiler where you needed to be a System Administrator to run Profiler, SQL Server 2005 Profiler allows the same user permissions as the Transact-SQL stored procedures that are used to create traces. To run SQL Profiler, users need to have the ALTER TRACE permission granted to them.

You can start SQL Profiler in several ways. One way is from the Start | All Programs | Microsoft SQL Server 2005 | Performance Tools | SQL Server Profiler menu option. Another is from the SQL Server Management Studio menu, where you select Tools | SQL Server Profiler. You can also start SQL Profiler from the Database Engine Tuning Advisor's Tools | SQL Server Profiler menu option.

The first thing to do once SQL Profiler is started is to select File | New Trace from the main menu. A Connect To Server dialog will be displayed where you can specify the SQL Server instance you want to connect to. In the Server Type drop-down of the connection dialog, you can choose to connect to a Database Engine server or an Analysis Services server. Once the server type selection is made and the connection to the SQL Server instance is complete, a Trace properties dialog like the one shown in Figure A-1 will be displayed.

As you can see in Figure A-1, the trace properties dialog has two tabs: General and Events Selection. Options under the General tab allow you to

▶ Name your trace in the Trace name text box.

▶ Select a template to use. This drop-down is populated with the predefined templates and any user-defined templates created for the current trace provider type. The predefined templates are shown in Table A-1.

▶ Save your trace to a file. The trace data is captured to a .trc file.

▶ Save your trace to a table. The trace data is captured and saved to a database table.

▶ Enable a trace stop time. You can set the date and time for the trace to end and close itself.

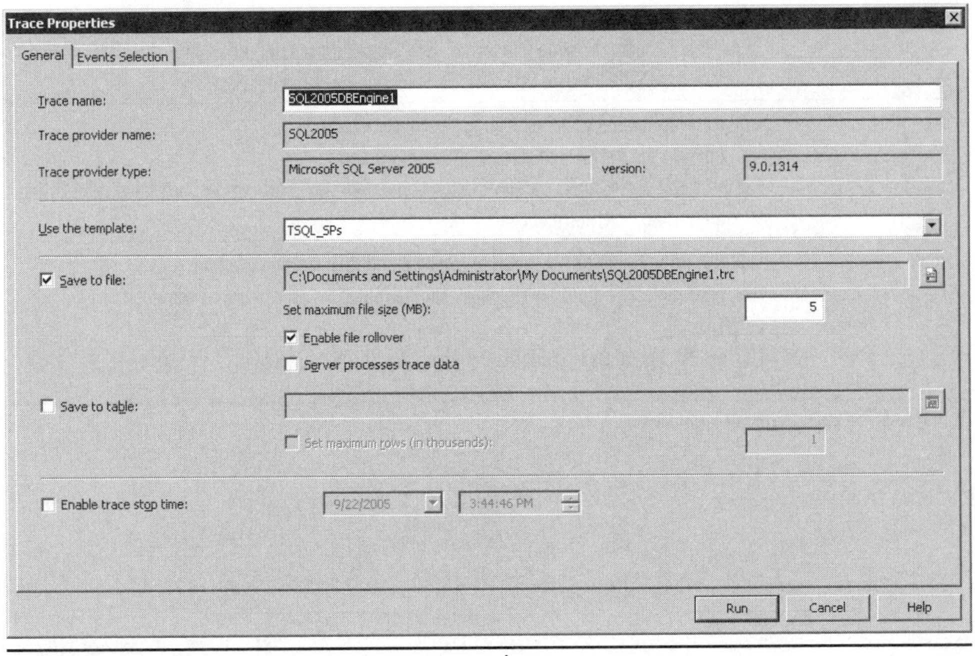

Figure A-1   *Profiler Trace Properties – General*

Template Name	Template Purpose and Event Classes
Standard (default)	Captures stored procedures and TSQL batches that are run. Use: Monitor general database server activity. Classes: Audit Login, Audit Logout, ExistingConnection, RPC:Completed, SQL:BatchCompleted, SQL:BatchStarting
SP_Counts	Captures stored procedure execution behavior over time. Classes: SP:Starting
TSQL	Captures TSQL statements submitted to SQL Server by clients and the time issued. Use: Debug client applications. Classes: Audit Login, Audit Logout, ExistingConnection, RPC:Starting, SQL:BatchStarting
TSQL_Duration	Captures TSQL statements submitted to SQL Server by clients and their execution time (in milliseconds). Groups them by duration. Use: Identify slow queries. Classes: RPC:Completed, SQL:BatchCompleted
TSQL_Grouped	Captures TSQL statements submitted to SQL Server and the time they were issued, grouped by the user or client that submitted the statement. Use: Investigate queries from a particular client or user. Classes: Audit Login, Audit Logout, ExistingConnection, RPC:Starting, SQL:BatchStarting
TSQL_Replay	Captures information about TSQL statements required if the trace is to be replayed. Use: Performance tuning, benchmark testing. Classes: CursorClose, CursorExecute, CursorOpen, CursorPrepare, CursorUnprepare, Audit Login, Audit Logout, Existing Connection, RPC Output Parameter, RPC:Completed, RPC:Starting, Exec Prepared SQL, Prepare SQL, SQL:BatchCompleted, SQL:BatchStarting
TSQL_SPs	Captures information about executing stored procedures. Use: Analyze the component steps of stored procedures. Classes: Audit Login, Audit Logout, ExistingConnection, RPC:Starting, SP:Completed, SP:Starting, SP:StmtStarting, SQL:BatchStarting
Tuning	Captures information about stored procedures and TSQL batch execution. Use: Produce trace output for Database Engine Tuning Advisor to use as workload to tune databases. Classes: RPC:Completed, SP:StmtCompleted, SQL:BatchCompleted

Table A-1 *Predefined Templates*

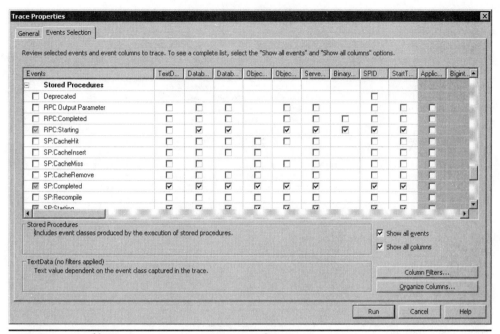

Figure A-2   *Profiler Trace Properties - Events Selection*

The second tab of the Trace Properties dialog, the Events Selection, is shown in Figure A-2. Here you can select or deselect any of the event classes to monitor during your trace. The Column Filters button starts an Edit dialog allowing you to set criteria for column filtering. The Organize Columns button displays a dialog that lets you change the order of the columns involved in the trace or group the columns, for example, by EventClass or StartTime.

Once the trace properties have been set, click the Run button to start the trace. Figure A-3 shows the SQL Profiler running a trace. As you can see in the figure, when a trace is started, a window is opened in the Profiler utility. The top portion of the window shows the EventClass that is being monitored and the TextData for the event, along with the columns related to the trace template set in the trace properties. In this example, the TSQL_SPs template was used for the trace, so the columns displayed in the window are: DatabaseName, DatabaseID, ObjectID, ObjectName, ServerName, BinaryData, SPID, and the Start Time of the event. The bottom portion of the window shows the TSQL that the event is executing. Clicking each line item listed in the top portion of the display will show its corresponding statement in the bottom portion of the display.

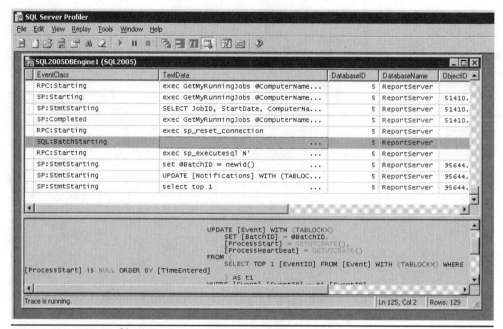

Figure A-3   *SQL Profiler trace*

Starting, Pausing, and Stopping a Trace

Once you have defined a trace by using SQL Server Profiler, you can start, pause, or stop capturing data by using the user interface menu options. The options are found under File | Run Trace, File | Pause Trace, and File | Stop Trace.

When you start a trace for the SQL Server Database Engine or Analysis Services, a queue is created and used as a temporary hold for captured events. Using SQL Profiler to access a trace opens a window in the interface, and the data is captured immediately. Only the name of the trace can be modified while the trace is running.

When you pause a trace, data is not captured until the trace is restarted. When the trace is restarted, data capture continues from that time on without the loss of previously captured data. You can change the name, events, columns, and filters of a trace while it is paused, but the destination of the trace and the server connection cannot be changed.

When you stop a trace, data ceases to be captured. After a trace is stopped, previously captured data will be lost when it is restarted, unless the data has been captured to a trace file or trace table. After stopping a trace, you can save the collected information to a table or file. The trace properties are saved when a trace is stopped, and you can change the name, events, columns, and filters.

Replaying a Trace

SQL Profiler contains the ability to save a trace and replay it at a later time. This replay ability allows you to reproduce activity captured in a trace. SQL Profiler features a multithreaded playback engine that can simulate user connections and SQL Server Authentication. Replay is especially helpful in troubleshooting an application or process. When a problem has been identified and corrected, you can run a trace against the corrected situation and also replay a trace from the problematic situation and compare the results.

The SQL Profiler Replay menu option allows trace debugging using the Toggle Breakpoint option and the Run To Cursor option. These options make it easier for you to break up the replay of a trace into shorter, more manageable segments for analysis.

Showplan Events

SQL Profiler allows you to gather and display query plan information in your trace. You can add Showplan event classes to your trace and even save these Showplan events to an XML file. You can extract Showplan events from a trace by selecting File | Export | Extract SQL Server Events | Extract Showplan Events from the main Profiler menu. This will display a Save File dialog box for you to save the extracted Showplan events to either a single .SQLPlan file or separate .SQLPlan files for each event. The file(s) can then be opened in SQL Server Management Studio for analysis.

You can also set your trace properties at configuration time to extract Showplan events. Click the Events Selection tab of the Trace Properties dialog and scroll to the Performance events as shown in Figure A-4. The Showplan events you can add to your trace are listed in Table A-2.

If you select the Showplan XML, Showplan XML For Query Compile, or Showplan XML Statistics Profile event, a third tab called Events Extraction Settings will be

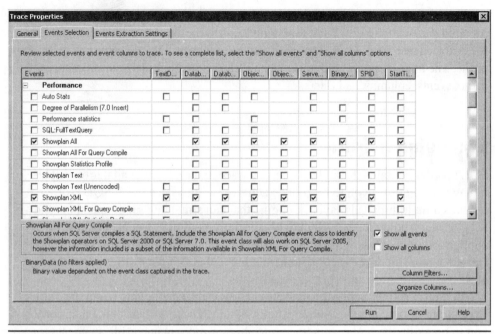

Figure A-4 *Trace Properties Performance Events*

Showplan Event	Description
Performance Statistics	Shows when a compiled Showplan is cached, recompiled, and dropped from the plan cache.
Showplan All	Shows the query plan with all compilation details of the executed TSQL statement.
Showplan All for Query Compile	Shows when SQL Server compiles a SQL statement. Returns a subset of the information available in Showplan XML for Query Compile.
Showplan Statistics Profile	Shows the query plan, including run-time details of executing SQL statements and the number of rows passed through the operations.
Showplan Text	Shows (as binary) the query plan for the executing TSQL statement.
Showplan Text (Unencoded)	Shows (as plain text) the query plan for the executing TSQL statement.
Showplan XML	Shows an optimized query plan, including data collected during query optimization.
Showplan XML For Query Compile	Shows the query plan when it is compiled.
Showplan XML Statistics Profile	Shows the query plan, including run-time details of executing SQL statements and the number of rows passed through the operations in XML format.

Table A-2 *Showplan Events*

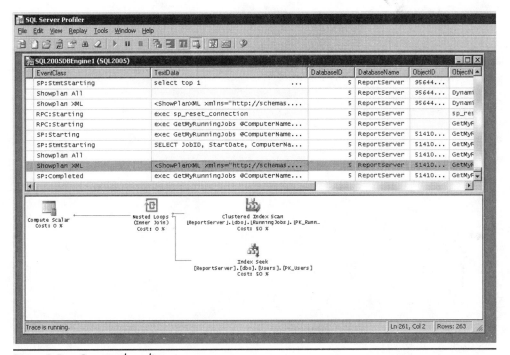

Figure A-5   *Query plan diagram*

displayed on the Trace Properties dialog. This tab will display an area for you to save the extracted Showplan events to either a single .SQLPlan file or separate .SQLPlan files for each event.

When the trace is run, you can select the Showplan items from the upper portion of the trace window to display the query plan diagram in the lower portion of the window. Figure A-5 shows a query plan diagram.

Index